Modern Data Architecture on AWS

A Practical Guide for Building Next-Gen Data Platforms on AWS

Behram Irani

BIRMINGHAM—MUMBAI

Modern Data Architecture on AWS

Group Product Manager: Niranjan Naikwadi
Publishing Product Manager: Tejashwini R
Book Project Manager: Kirti Pisat
Senior Editor: Sushma Reddy
Technical Editor: Sweety Pagaria
Copy Editor: Safis Editing
Proofreader: Safis Editing
Indexer: Tejal Soni
Production Designer: Ponraj Dhandapani
DevRel Marketing Coordinator: Vinishka Kalra

First published: August 2023

Production reference: 1290823

Published by Packt Publishing Ltd.
Grosvenor House
11 St Paul's Square
Birmingham
B3 1RB, UK.

ISBN 978-1-80181-339-6

www.packtpub.com

Contributors

About the author

Behram Irani is currently a technology leader with Amazon Web Services (AWS) specializing in data, analytics and AI/ML. He has spent over 18 years in the tech industry helping organizations, from start-ups to large-scale enterprises, modernize their data platforms. In the last 6 years working at AWS, Behram has been a thought leader in the data, analytics and AI/ML space; publishing multiple papers and leading the digital transformation efforts for many organizations across the globe.

Behram has completed his Bachelor of Engineering in Computer Science from the University of Pune and has an MBA degree from the University of Florida.

About the reviewers

Jongnam Lee is a Customer Engineer at Moloco, Inc., which provides ML-based retail media solutions to e-commerce businesses. As quality data is the core of machine learning, data analytics is the core of his job. Prior to Moloco, he was the Lead Solutions Architect of the AWS Well-Architected Analytics Lens program until March 2022. As a tenured Amazonian who joined the company in 2012, he served in various roles in AWS and Amazon.com, including Amazon.com's data lake operations and AWS cost optimization initiatives in 2018–2020. Before AWS, he was a senior software engineer at Samsung Electronics HQ in Korea for eight years.

Bo Thomas leads the AWS Analytics Specialist Solutions Architect organization for the US East, Latin America, and specialty business segments. In this role, he advises some of the largest companies in the world on how best to design and manage their analytics and AI/ML platforms. He has more than 10 years of experience leading analytics, data engineering, and research science teams across Amazon's businesses. Prior to his current role, he led Amazon.com's enterprise people data warehouse and data lake platforms.

Prior to working at Amazon, Bo was an officer in the US Army leading cavalry units, including a 15-month deployment to Iraq. He has a bachelor's degree in economics from West Point and an MBA from Duke University.

Gareth Eagar has worked in the IT industry for over 25 years, starting in South Africa, working in the United Kingdom for a few years, and is now based in the United States. In 2017, Gareth started working at Amazon Web Services (AWS), and has held roles as both a Solution Architect and a Data Architect.

Gareth has become a recognized subject matter expert for building data lakes on AWS, and in 2019 he launched the Data Lake Day educational event at the AWS Lofts in NYC and San Francisco. He has delivered a number of public talks and webinars on big data related topics, and in 2021 published a book called "Data Engineering with AWS"

Table of Contents

2

Scalable Data Lakes 27

Part 2: Purpose-Built Services And Unified Data Access

3

Batch Data Ingestion 53

4

Streaming Data Ingestion

5

Data Processing

9

Data Federation   167

10

Predictive Analytics   177

11

Generative AI   209

Part 3: Govern, Scale, Optimize And Operationalize

14

Data Governance   255

17

Preface

Many IT leaders and professionals know how to get data in a particular type of database and derive value from it. But when it comes to creating an enterprise-wide holistic data platform with purpose-built data services, all seamlessly working in tandem with the least amount of manual intervention, it is always challenging to design and implement such a platform.

This book covers end-to-end solutions of many of the common data, analytics and AI/ML use-cases that organizations want to solve using AWS services. The book systematically lays out all the building blocks of a modern data platform including data lake, data warehouse, data ingestion patterns, data consumption patterns, data governance and AI/ML patterns. Using real world use-cases, each chapter highlights the features and functionalities of many of the AWS services to create a scalable, flexible, performant and cost-effective modern data platform.

By the end of this book, readers will be equipped with all the necessary architecture patterns and would be able to apply this knowledge to build a modern data platform for their organization using AWS services.

Who this book is for

This book is specifically geared towards helping data architects, data engineers and those professionals involved with building data platforms. The use-case driven approach in this book helps them conceptualize possible solutions to specific use-cases and provides them with design patterns to build data platforms for any organization.

Technical leaders and decision makers would also benefit from this book as they will get a perspective of what the overall data architecture looks like for their organization and how each component of the platform helps with their business needs.

What this book covers

Prologue, Data and Analytics Journey so far, provides a historical context around what a data platform looks like in the on-prem world. In this prologue we will discuss the traditional platform components and talk about their benefits; then pivot towards their shortcomings in meetings new business objectives. This will provide context for the need to build a modern data architecture.

Chapter 1, Modern Data Architecture on AWS, describes what it means to create a modern data architecture. We will also look at how AWS services help materialize this concept and why it is important to create this foundation for current and future business needs.

Chapter 2, Scalable Data Lakes, lays down the foundation of the modern data architecture by establishing a data lake on AWS. We will also look at different layers of the data lake and how each layer has a specific purpose.

Chapter 3, Batch Data Ingestion, provides options to move data in batches from multiple source systems into AWS. We will explore different AWS services that assist in migrating data in bulk from variety of source systems.

Chapter 4, Streaming Data Ingestion, provides an overview of the need for a real-time streaming architecture pattern and how AWS services assist in solving use-cases that require streaming data ingested and consumed in the modern data platform.

Chapter 5, Data Processing, provides options to process and transform data, so that it can eventually be consumed for analytics. We will look at some AWS services that help provide scalable, performant and cost-effective big data processing; especially for running Apache Spark based workloads.

Chapter 6, Interactive Analytics, provides insights around ad-hoc analytics use-cases along with AWS services that help solve it.

Chapter 7, Data Warehousing, covers a wide range of use-cases that can be solved using a modern cloud data warehouse on AWS. We will look at multiple design patterns, including data ingestion, data transformation and data consumption using the data warehouse on AWS.

Chapter 8, Data Sharing, provides context around how data can be shared within a modern data platform, without creating complete ETL pipelines and without duplicating data at multiple places.

Chapter 9, Data Federation, provides mechanisms of data federation and the types of use-cases that can be solved using federated queries.

Chapter 10, Predictive Analytics, covers a whole range of use-cases along with services, features and tools provided by AWS to solve AI, ML and deep learning-based business problems; with the common goal of achieving predictive analytics.

Chapter 11, Generative AI, provides variety of use-cases across multiple industries that can be solved using GenAI and how AWS provides services and tools to help fast-track building GenAI based applications.

Chapter 12, Operational Analytics, introduces the need for operational analytics, especially log analytics and how AWS helps with this aspect of the data platform.

Chapter 13, Business Intelligence, provides context around the need for a modern business intelligent tool for creating business friendly reports and dashboards, that support rich visualizations. We will look at how AWS helps with such use-cases.

Chapter 14, Data Governance, lays ground work for the need for a unified data governance and covers many dimensions of data governance along with AWS services that assist in solving for those use-cases.

Chapter 15, *Data Mesh*, introduces the concept of a data mesh along with its importance in the modern data platform. We will look at the pillars of data mesh and provide AWS services that help solve use-cases that require a data mesh pattern.

Chapter 16, *Performant and Cost-Effective Data Platform*, covers a wide range of options to ensure the data platform built using AWS services is cost-effective as well as performant.

Chapter 17, *Automate, Operationalize and Monetize*, wraps up the book with concepts around automating the data platform using DevOps, DataOps and MLOps mechanisms. Finally, we will look at options to monetize the modern data platform built on AWS.

To get the most out of this book

The book is geared towards data professionals who are eager to build modern data platform using many of the AWS data and analytics services. A basic understanding of data & analytics architectures and systems is desirable along with beginner's level understanding of AWS Cloud.

Conventions used

There are a number of text conventions used throughout this book.

`Code in text`: Indicates code words in text, database table names, folder names, filenames, file extensions, pathnames, dummy URLs, user input, and Twitter handles. Here is an example: "Mount the downloaded `WebStorm-10*.dmg` disk image file as another disk in your system."

A block of code is set as follows:

```
INSERT INTO processed_cloudtrail_table
SELECT *
FROM raw_cloudtrail_table
WHERE conditions;
```

Bold: Indicates a new term, an important word, or words that you see onscreen. For instance, words in menus or dialog boxes appear in **bold**. Here is an example: "Select **System info** from the **Administration** panel."

Use-cases
Appear like this.

Get in touch

Feedback from our readers is always welcome.

General feedback: If you have questions about any aspect of this book, email us at `customercare@packtpub.com` and mention the book title in the subject of your message.

Errata: Although we have taken every care to ensure the accuracy of our content, mistakes do happen. If you have found a mistake in this book, we would be grateful if you would report this to us. Please visit `www.packtpub.com/support/errata` and fill in the form.

Piracy: If you come across any illegal copies of our works in any form on the internet, we would be grateful if you would provide us with the location address or website name. Please contact us at `copyright@packtpub.com` with a link to the material.

If you are interested in becoming an author: If there is a topic that you have expertise in and you are interested in either writing or contributing to a book, please visit `authors.packtpub.com`.

Share Your Thoughts

Once you've read *Modern Data Architecture on AWS*, we'd love to hear your thoughts! Scan the QR code below to go straight to the Amazon review page for this book and share your feedback.

`https://packt.link/r/1-801-81339-6`

Your review is important to us and the tech community and will help us make sure we're delivering excellent quality content.

Download a free PDF copy of this book

Thanks for purchasing this book!

Do you like to read on the go but are unable to carry your print books everywhere?

Is your eBook purchase not compatible with the device of your choice?

Don't worry, now with every Packt book you get a DRM-free PDF version of that book at no cost.

Read anywhere, any place, on any device. Search, copy, and paste code from your favorite technical books directly into your application.

The perks don't stop there, you can get exclusive access to discounts, newsletters, and great free content in your inbox daily

Follow these simple steps to get the benefits:

1. Scan the QR code or visit the link below

https://packt.link/free-ebook/9781801813396

2. Submit your proof of purchase
3. That's it! We'll send your free PDF and other benefits to your email directly

Part 1: Foundational Data Lake

In this part, we will explore what a modern data architecture entails and how AWS embraces this architecture pattern. We will then expand on how to setup a foundational data platform by building a data lake on AWS.

This part has the following chapters:

- *Chapter 1, Modern Data Architecture on AWS*
- *Chapter 2, Scalable Data Lakes*

Prologue

The Data and Analytics Journey So Far

"We are surrounded by data but starved for insights"

– Jay Baer

We have been surrounded by digital data for almost a century now and every decade has had its unique challenges regarding how to get the best value out of that data. But these challenges were narrow in scope and manageable since the data itself was manageable. Even though data was rapidly growing in the 20th century, its volume, velocity, and variety were still limited in nature. And then we hit the 21st century and the world of data drastically changed. Data started to exponentially grow due to multiple reasons:

- The adoption of the internet picked up speed and data grew into big data
- Smartphone devices became a common household entity and these devices all generated tons of data
- Social media took off and added to the deluge of information
- Robotics, smart edge devices, industrial devices, drones, gaming, VR, and other artificial intelligence-driven gadgets took the growth of data to a whole new level.

However, across all this, the common theme that exists even today is that data gets produced, processed, stored, and consumed.

Now, even though the history of data and analytics goes back many decades, I don't want to dig everything up. Since this book revolves around cloud computing technologies, it is important to understand how we got here, what systems were in place in the on-premises data center world, and why those same systems and the architectural patterns surrounding them struggle to cater to the business and technology needs of today.

In this prologue, we will cover the following main topics:

- Introduction to the data and analytics journey

- Traditional data platforms

- Challenges with on-premises data systems

- What this book is all about

If you are already well versed with the traditional data platforms and their challenges, you can skip this introduction and directly jump to *Chapter 1*.

Introduction to the data and analytics journey

The **online transaction processing** (OLTP) and **online analytical processing** (OLAP) systems worked great by themselves for a very long time when data producers were limited, the volume of data was under control, and data was mostly structured in tabular format. The last 20 years have seen a seismic shift in the way new businesses and technologies have come up.

As the volume, velocity, and variety of data started to pick steam, data grew into big data and the data processing techniques needed a major rehaul. This gave rise to the Apache Hadoop framework, which changed the way big data was processed and stored. With more data, businesses wanted to get more descriptive and diagnostic analytics out of their data. At the same time, another technology was gaining rapid traction, which gave organizations hope that they could look ahead to the future and predict what may happen in advance so that they could take immediate actions to steer their businesses in the right direction. This was made possible by the rise of artificial intelligence and machine learning and soon, large organizations started investing in predictive analytics projects.

And while we were thinking that we got the big data under control with new frameworks, the data floodgates opened up. The last 10 to 15 years have been revolutionary with the onset of smart devices, including smartphones. Connectivity among all these devices and systems made data grow exponentially. This was termed the **Internet of Things** (IoT). And to add to the complexity, these devices started to share data in near real time, which meant that data had to be streamed immediately for consumption. The following figure highlights many of the sources from where data gets generated. A lot of insights can be derived from all this data so that organizations can make faster and better decisions:

Figure 00.1 – Big data sources

This also meant that organizations started to carefully segregate their technical workforce to deal with data in personas. The people processing big data came to be known as data engineers, the people dealing with data for future predictions were the data scientists, and the people analyzing the data with various tools were the data analysts. Each type of persona had a well-defined task and there was a strong desire to create/purchase the best technological tool out there to make their day-to-day lives easier.

From a data and analytics point of view, systems started to grow bigger with extra hardware. Organizations started to expand their on-premises data centers with the latest and greatest servers out there to process all this data as fast as possible, to create value for their businesses. However, a lot of architecture patterns for data and analytics remained the same, which meant that many of the old use cases were still getting solved. However, with new demands from these businesses, pain areas started popping up more frequently.

Traditional data platforms

Before we get into architecting data platforms in a modern way, it is important to understand the traditional data platforms and know their strengths and limitations. Once we understand the challenges of traditional data platforms in solving new business use cases, we can design a modern data platform in a holistic matter.

Three-tier architecture

Throughout the 1980s and 1990s, the three-tier architecture became a popular way of producing, processing, and storing data. Almost every organization used this pattern as it met the business needs with ease. The three tiers of this architecture were the **presentation tier**, the **application tier**, and the **data tier**:

- The **presentation tier** was the front-facing module and was created either as a thick client – that is, software was installed on the client's local machine – or as a thin client – that is, a browser-based application.

- The **application tier** would receive the data from the presentation tier and process this data with business logic hosted on the application server.

- The **data tier** was the final resting place for the business data. The data tier was typically a relational database where data was stored in rows and columns of tables.

Figure 00.2 represents a typical three-tier architecture:

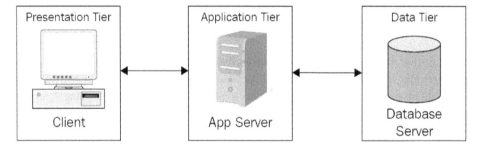

Figure 00.2 – A traditional three-tier architecture pattern

This three-tier architecture worked well to meet the transactional nature of businesses. To a certain extent, this system was able to help with creating a basic reporting mechanism to help organizations understand what was happening with their business. But the kind of technology used in this architecture fell short of going a step further – to identify and understand why certain things were happening with their business. So, a new architecture pattern was required that could decouple this transitional system from the analytics type of operations. This paved the way for the creation of an **enterprise data warehouse** (**EDW**).

Enterprise data warehouse (EDW)

The need for a data warehouse came from the realistic expectations of organizations to derive business intelligence out of the data they were collecting so that they could get better insights from this data and make the necessary adjustments to their business practices. For example, if a retailer is seeing a steady decline in sales from a particular region, they would want to understand what is contributing to this decline.

Now, let's capture the data flow. All the transactional data is captured by the presentation tier, processed by the application tier, and stored in the data tier of the three-tier architecture. The database behind the data tier is always online and optimized for processing a large number of transactions, which come in the form of INSERT, UPDATE, and DELETE statements. This database also emphasizes fast query processing while maintaining **atomicity**, **consistency**, **isolation**, and **durability** (**ACID**) compliance. For this reason, this type of data store is called OLTP.

To further analyze this data, a path needs to be created that will bring the relevant data over from the OLTP system into the data warehouse. This is where the **extract**, **transform**, and **load** (**ETL**) layer comes into the picture. And once the data has been brought over to the data warehouse, organizations can create the **business intelligence** (**BI**) they need via the reporting and dashboarding capabilities provided by the visualization tier. We will cover the ETL and BI layers in detail in later chapters, but the focus right now is walking through the process and the history behind them.

The data warehouse system is distinctly different from the transactional database system. Firstly, the data warehouse does not constantly get bombarded by transactional data from customer-facing applications. Secondly, the types of operations that are happening in the data warehouse system are specific to mining information insights from all the data, including historical data. Therefore, this system is constantly doing operations such as data aggregation, roll-ups (data consolidation), drill-downs, and slicing and dicing the data. For this reason, the data warehouse is called OLAP.

The following figure shows the OLTP and OLAP systems working together:

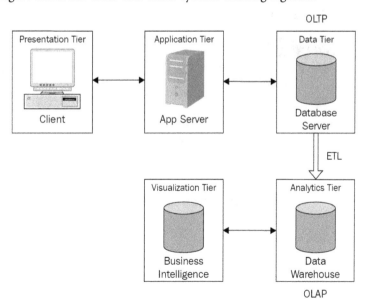

Figure 00.3 – The OLTP and OLAP systems working together

The preceding diagram shows all the pieces together. This architectural pattern is still relevant and works great in many cases. However, in the era of cloud computing, business use cases are also rapidly evolving. In the following sections, we will take a look at variations of this design pattern, as well as their advantages and shortcomings.

Bottom-up data warehouse approach

Ralph Kimball, one of the original architects of data warehousing, proposed the idea of designing the data warehouse with a bottom-up approach. This involved creating many smaller purpose-built data marts inside a data warehouse. A data mart is a subset of the larger data warehouse with a focus on catering to use cases for a specific **line of business** (**LOB**) or a specific team. All of these data marts can be combined to form an enterprise-wide data warehouse. The design of data marts is also kept simple by having the data model as a star schema to a large extent. A star schema keeps the data in sets of denormalized tables. There are known as fact tables, and they store all the transactional and event data. Since these tables store all the fast-moving granular data, they accumulate a large number of records over a short period. Then, there are the dimension tables, which typically store characteristics data such as details about people and organizations, product information, geographical information, and so forth. Since such information doesn't rapidly get produced or changed over a short period, compared to fact tables, dimension tables are relatively smaller in terms of the number of records stored. The following figure shows a bottom-up EDW design approach where individual data marts contribute toward a bigger data warehouse:

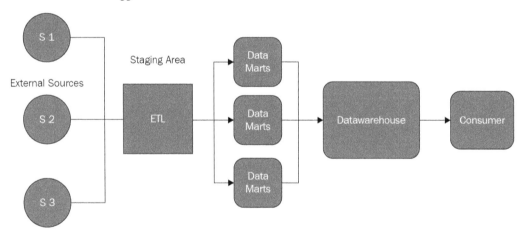

Figure 00.4 – Bottom-up EDW design

Benefits of the bottom-up approach

Let's look at a few benefits of the bottom-up approach:

- The EDW gets systemically built over a certain period with business-specific groupings of data marts.

- The data model's design is typically created via star schemas, which makes the model denormalized in nature. Some data becomes redundant in this approach but overall, it helps in making the data marts perform better.

- An EDW is easier to create since the time taken to set up individual business-specific data marts is shorter compared to setting up an enterprise-wide warehouse.

- An EDW that contains data marts also makes it better suited for setting up data lakes. We will cover everything about data lakes in subsequent chapters.

Shortcomings of the bottom-up approach

Now, let's look at the shortcomings of the bottom-up approach:

- It is challenging to achieve a fully harmonized integration layer because the EDW is purpose-built for each use case in the form of data marts. Data redundancy also makes it difficult to create a single source of truth.

- Normalized schemas create data redundancy, which makes the tables grow very large. This slows down the performance of ETL job pipelines.

- Since the data marts are tightly coupled to the specific business use cases, managing structural changes and their dependencies on the data warehouse becomes a cumbersome process.

Top-down data warehouse approach

Bill Inmon, widely recognized as the father of data warehouses, proposed the idea of designing the data warehouse with a top-down approach. In this approach, a single source of truth for the data in the form of an EDW is constructed first using a normalized data model to reduce data redundancy. Data from different sources is mapped to a single data model, which means that all the source elements are transformed and formatted to fit in this enterprise-wide structure that's created in the data warehouse. The following figure shows a top-down EDW design approach where the warehouse is built first before smaller data marts are created for consumers:

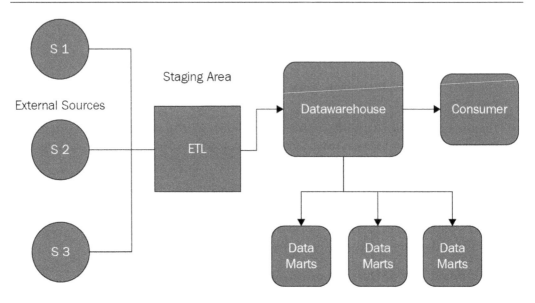

Figure 00.5 – Top-down EDW design

Benefits of the top-down approach

Let's look at a few benefits of the top-down approach:

- The data model is highly normalized, which reduces data redundancy
- Since it's not tied to a specific LOB or use case, the data warehouse can evolve independently at an enterprise level
- It provides flexibility for any business requirement changes or data structure updates
- ETL pipelines are simpler to create and maintain

Shortcomings of the top-down approach

Now, let's look at the shortcomings of the top-down approach:

- A normalized data model increases the complexity of schema design
- A large number of joins on the normalized tables can make the system compute-intensive and expensive over time
- Additional logic is required to create a business-specific data consumption layer, which means additional ETL processes are needed to create data marts from the unified EDW

Challenges with on-premises data systems

As data grew exponentially, so did the on-premises systems. However, visible cracks started to appear in the legacy way of architecting data and analytics use cases.

The hardware that was used to process, store, and consume data had to be procured up-front, and then installed and configured before it was ready for use. So, there was operational overhead and risks associated with procuring the hardware, provisioning it, installing software, and maintaining the system all the time. Also, to accommodate for future data growth, people had to estimate additional capacity way in advance. The concept of hardware elasticity didn't exist. The lack of elasticity in hardware meant that there were scalability risks associated with the systems in place, and these risks would surface whenever there was a sudden growth in the volume of data or when there was a market expansion for the business.

Buying all this extra hardware up-front also meant that a huge capital expenditure investment had to be made for the hardware, with all the extra capacity lying unused from time to time. Also, software licenses had to be paid for and those were expensive, adding to the overall IT costs. Even after buying all the hardware upfront, it was difficult to maintain the data platform's high performance all the time. As data volumes grew, latency started creeping in, which adversely affected the performance of certain critical systems.

As data grew into big data, the type of data produced was not just structured data; a lot of business use cases required semi-structured data, such as JSON files, and even unstructured data, such as images and PDF files. In subsequent chapters, we will go through some use cases that specify different types of data.

As the sources of data grew, so did the number of ETL pipelines. Managing these pipelines became cumbersome. And on top of that, with so much data movement, data started to duplicate at multiple places, which made it difficult to create a single source of truth for the data.

On the flip side, with so many data sources and data owners within an organization, data became siloed, which made it difficult to share across different LOBs in the organization.

Most of the enterprise data was either stored in an OLTP system such as an RDBMS or an OLAP system such as a data warehouse. What this meant was that organizations tried to solve most of their new use cases using the systems they had invested so heavily in. The challenge was that these systems were built and optimized for specific types of operations only. Soon, it became evident that to solve other types of data and analytics use cases, specific types of systems were needed to be in place, to meet the performance requirements.

Lastly, as businesses started to expand in other geographies, these systems needed to be expanded to other locations. And a lot of time, effort, and money was spent scaling the data platform and making it resilient in case of failures.

What this book is all about

Before we wrap up this prologue and dive into more details in subsequent chapters, I want to lay the foundation for what you should expect from this book and how the content is laid out.

When you think of a data platform in an organization, it contains a lot of systems that work in tandem to make the platform operational. A data platform contains different types of purpose-built data stores, different types of ETL tools and pipelines for data movement between the data stores, different types of systems that allow end users to consume the data, and different types of security and governance mechanisms in place to keep the platform protected and safe.

To allow the data platform to cater to different types of use cases, it needs to be designed and architected in the best possible manner. With exponential data growth and the need to solve new business use cases, these architectural patterns need to constantly evolve, not just for current needs but also for future ones. Every organization is looking to move to the public cloud as quickly as they can to make their data platforms scalable, agile, performant, cost-effective, and secure.

Amazon Web Services (**AWS**) provides the broadest and deepest set of data, analytics, and AI/ML services. Organizations can use AWS services to help them derive insights from their data. This book will walk you through how to architect and design your data platform, for specific business use cases, using different AWS services.

In *Chapter 1*, we will understand what a modern data architecture on AWS looks like, and we will also look at what the pillars of this architecture are. The remainder of this book is organized around those pillars. We will start with a typical data and analytics use case and build on top of it as new use cases come along. By doing this, you will see the progressive build-up of the data platform for a variety of use cases.

One thing to note is that this book won't have a lot of hands-on coding or other implementation exercises. The idea here is to provide architecture patterns and how multiple AWS services, along with their specific features, help solve a particular problem. However, at the end of each chapter, I will provide links to hands-on workshops, where you can follow step-by-step instructions to build the components of a modern data platform in your AWS account.

Finally, due to limited space in this book, not every use case for each of the components of the modern data platform can be covered. The idea here is to give you a simple but holistic view of what possible use cases might look like and how you can leverage some key features of many of the AWS services to get toward a working solution. A solution can be achieved in many possible ways, and every solution has pros and cons that are very specific to the implementation. Technology evolves fast and so do many of the AWS services; always do your due diligence and look out for better ways to solve problems.

Summary

With that, this short introduction has come to an end. The idea here was to provide a quick history of how data and analytics evolved. We went through the different types of data warehouse designs, along with their pros and cons. We also looked at how the recent exponential growth of data has made it difficult to use the same type of system architecture for all types of use cases.

This gives us a perfect launching pad to understand what modern data architecture is and how it can be architected using different AWS data and analytics services.

1
Modern Data Architecture on AWS

Before we dive deep into the actual data and analytics use cases and how to design and build them, let's address the elephant in the room—*what is a modern data architecture, and why build it on Amazon Web Services (AWS)?*

One of the fundamental tenets of a modern data architecture on AWS is to seamlessly integrate your data lake, data warehouse, and purpose-built data stores. In the previous prologue, we looked at what a data warehouse is and what it does. We also looked at the data tier in a three-tier architecture, typically referred to as a **relational database management system** (**RDBMS**) and considered a type of purpose-built store. The type of system we haven't really explored in much detail yet is the data lake. The next chapter is completely dedicated to data lakes, but before we go any further in this chapter, it is important to get some context around the need for data lakes in the first place.

In this chapter, we will cover the following main topics:

- Data lakes
- The role of a modern data architecture
- Modern data architecture on AWS
- Pillars of a modern data architecture

Data lakes

Simply put, a data lake is a centralized repository to store all kinds of data. Data can be structured (such as relational database data in tabular format), semi-structured (such as JSON), or unstructured (such as images, PDFs, and so on). Data from all the heterogenous source systems is collected and processed in this single repository and consumed from it. In its early days, Apache Hadoop became the go-to place for setting up data lakes. The Hadoop framework provided a storage layer called **Hadoop Distributed File System** (**HDFS**) and a data processing layer called **MapReduce**. Organizations started using this data lake as a central place for storing and processing all kinds of data. The data lake provided a great alternative to storing and processing data outside relational databases and data warehouses. But soon, the data lake setup on-premises infrastructure became a nightmare. We will look at those challenges as we build upon this chapter.

The following diagram shows at a high level a data lake being the central data repository for all kinds of data:

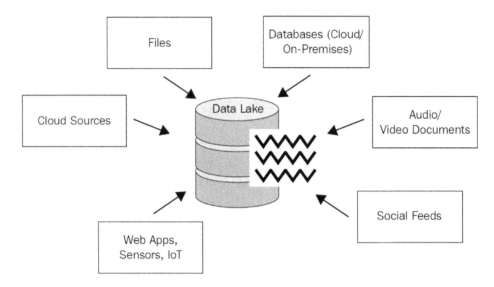

Figure 1.1 – A data lake conceptualization

Why the need for a data lake?

At a high level, we all now know what a data lake is. But we didn't really get to the core question — *Why do we need it in the first place?*

Let's look at some of the main reasons why data lakes play a key role:

- As data grew, so did the variety of data. Databases and data warehouses were designed to store and process structured data in rows and columns of tables. Deriving insights from semi-structured and unstructured data gained traction, which gave a push to build data lakes.

- In the prologue, we touched upon the data silo problem and how businesses struggle to get a complete view of data in a single place. Data lakes solve this problem by making all the enterprise-wide data available in a centralized location for analytics so that businesses can derive value from this data. This enables data democratization.

- For data to be stored in databases and data warehouses, a schema needs to be designed first. Table and column definitions need to be created before data can be loaded into these structures. But a lot of times, the data structures are defined by how the data eventually gets consumed. Data lakes allow a schema-on-read mechanism, which makes it easy to create schemas depending on data consumption patterns.

- As the data lake storage is in a centralized location, the data ingestion process becomes easier by simplifying the **extract, transform, and load** (**ETL**) pipelines. This allows for quicker ingestion of data into the data lake.

- Since databases and data warehouses are built for specific operations, they tend to perform better for specific use cases. However, the dedicated hardware/software makes these systems expensive and slow for all other types of analytics. A data lake decouples the storage from compute, which means that you don't have to keep the compute allocated to the process all the time. This helps lower setup and operating expenses.

The list of advantages could run into multiple pages, but it's obvious that data lakes are here to stay. Along the way, while data lakes looked promising for solving many use cases, their adoption hit some challenges, specifically in on-premises infrastructure.

Challenges with on-premises data lakes

The following are some of the challenges encountered so far with data lakes:

- Since data lakes are the central repository for all kinds of data from all types of systems in the entire organization, it becomes difficult to manage the security and governance of the data. Unless there are strong guardrails put around the data lake, there is always the fear of turning the data lake into a data swamp, which could lead to a security breach, with sensitive and confidential data being leaked out.

- With large amounts of data being collected, processed, and consumed, a lot of infrastructure and tools need to be put in place to make the data lake operational. So, the scalability, durability, and resiliency of this system are always a challenge, specifically in the on-premises world.

So, by now, we have understood some of the key data systems that make up a data platform—databases, data warehouses, and data lakes. We also now know how they help businesses to derive value from their data. While these systems come with a lot of promise and possibilities, the challenges we discussed around all of them are real. These challenges get amplified by the rigid constraints of on-premises infrastructure. Ultimately, it's the business that feels the pain from all the technological challenges.

We are now in the era of cloud computing, and just in the last decade, so much has changed and evolved. We are at a stage where we have the freedom to rearchitect entire systems to take advantage of the cloud. We no longer have to make all the compromises we made in the on-premises way of architecting data platforms.

This brings us to the focal point of this book, around what a modern data architecture looks like and why we need it.

The role of a modern data architecture

A modern data architecture removes the rigid boundaries between data systems and seamlessly integrates the data lake, data warehouse, and purpose-built data stores. A modern data architecture recognizes the fact that taking a one-size-fits-all approach leads to compromises in the data and analytics platform. And we are not just referring to seamless integration between data systems; it also has to encompass unified governance, along with ease of data movement.

A modern data architecture is a direct response to all the challenges we have seen so far, including exponential data growth, performance and scalability issues, security and data governance nightmares, data silo issues, and—of course—pinching high expenses.

The following diagram shows a modern data architecture at a high level:

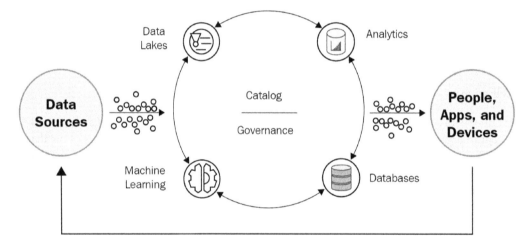

Figure 1.2 – Modern data architecture

All the data an organization collects plays a huge role in reinventing its business. The faster it can derive analytical insights from this data, the quicker it will make the right decisions to steer the business forward. However, as the data grows in volume and complexity, it sometimes slows down the business. To give an analogy, the bigger an object on Earth is, the more difficult it is to move it around. This is partly due to the role gravity plays in holding these objects down. In the same way, as data grows in organizations, either in data lakes or in purpose-built stores, the harder it becomes to move all this data around. So, in short, data also has its own gravity. So, in a modern data architecture, there should be mechanisms in place to allow for easy movement of data, with the eventual goal of deriving insights from it, using the right set of tools and services. The data movement can be inside-out, outside-in, around the perimeter, or shared across.

Inside-out

In this pattern, the data is first ingested and processed in the data lake, and then portions of this data, depending on the use case, are moved into a purpose-built store. For example, you have data from multiple **Software-as-a-Service** (**SaaS**)-based applications come to a data lake first, where it is ingested and processed using ETL tools, and a portion of this data is then moved into a data warehouse for daily reporting.

In the following diagram, the arrows show the outward movement of the data from the data lake into the purpose-built stores:

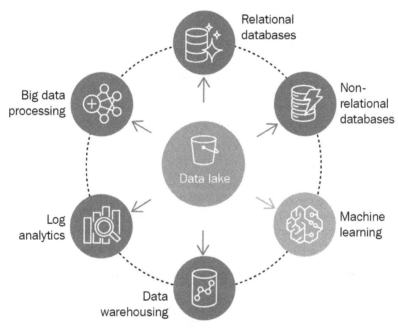

Figure 1.3 – Inside-out data movement

Outside-in

In this pattern, the data is ingested into a purpose-built store first, and then the data is moved over to a data lake to run analysis on this data. For example, in the three-tier architecture pattern we went through in the prologue, the application data is stored in a relational database. This data is then moved into the data lake for analytics purposes. There may be many such purpose-built systems from which the data can be brought into a centralized data lake.

In the following diagram, the arrows show the inward movement of the data from the purpose-built stores into the data lake:

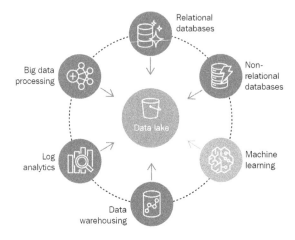

Figure 1.4 – Outside-in data movement

Around the perimeter

In certain situations, data needs to be passed along from one purpose-built store to another, for solving specific use cases. Since data is moving around, without the need to place it inside a data lake, this pattern is called data movement around the perimeter. For example, in our three-tier architecture, data can directly be loaded from a transactional database into a data warehouse for analytics.

In the following diagram, the arrows show the movement of data between the purpose-built stores:

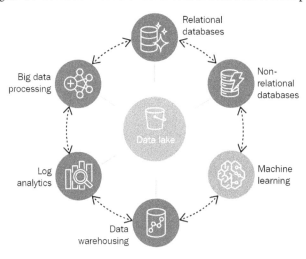

Figure 1.5 – Around the perimeter data movement

Sharing across

Finally, data holds little value if it cannot be shared where its value can be unlocked. A modern data architecture allows easy sharing of data, inside as well as outside the organization. For example, portions of data produced in one **line of business (LOB)** need to be shared with another LOB so that the whole organization can benefit from them.

Now that we have looked at the different patterns for data movement in a modern data platform, it leads us to the next section on how a modern data architecture looks like on AWS.

Modern data architecture on AWS

AWS has been a pioneer in cloud computing; it provides a broad and deep platform to help organizations build sophisticated, scalable, and secure applications and data platforms.

Here's a quick recap of why millions of customers choose AWS:

- **Agility**: Allows organizations to experiment and innovate quickly and frequently

- **Elasticity**: Takes away the guesswork around hardware capacity provisioning, allowing it to scale up and down with demand

- **Faster innovation**: This is possible because organizations can now focus on implementing things that matter to their businesses and not worry about IT infrastructure

- **Cost saving**: This is significant due to the economies of scale of cloud computing, coupled with pay-as-you-go models

- **Global reach**: This is now possible in minutes due to AWS' most extensive, reliable, and secure global cloud infrastructure

- **Service breadth and depth**: With over 200 fully featured services to support any cloud workload globally

There is a wealth of information on how AWS has transformed the whole technology space, and multiple books have been published capturing all this knowledge. However, we will zoom in on the data and analytics space and discuss how AWS helps to achieve a modern data architecture.

With a modern data architecture on AWS, customers have the option to leverage purpose-built tools and services to build their data platforms. Security and data governance can be applied in a unified manner. The modern data architecture on AWS also allows organizations to scale their systems at a low cost without impacting the overall system performance. Data can be easily shared data across organizational boundaries so that businesses can make decisions with speed and agility at scale.

To achieve all of this, AWS has provided five pillars for building a modern data architecture. Let's look at them in detail.

Pillars of a modern data architecture

A modern data architecture is required to break down data silos so that data analytics, descriptive as well as predictive using **artificial intelligence/machine learning (AI/ML)**, can be done with all the data aggregated into a central location. In order to meet all the business needs around deriving value out of the data in a fast and cost-effective manner, the architecture requires certain pillars to be in place, as follows:

- Scalable data lakes
- Purpose-built analytics services
- Unified data access, including seamless data movement
- Unified governance
- Performance and cost-effectiveness

The following diagram illustrates these pillars for you:

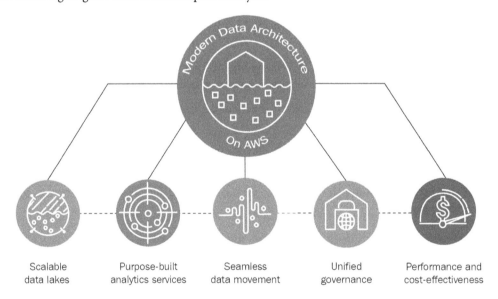

Figure 1.6 – Pillars of a modern data architecture on AWS

Let's explore each of the pillars in more detail.

Scalable data lakes

A data lake is the foundation of a strong modern data platform. Data lakes get pretty big in a short period of time since all the business data from multiple sources is brought to this central repository for analysis. Imagine if the IT team had to manage this infrastructure in terms of its scalability, reliability, durability, and **high availability** (**HA**), at the same time making sure it was performant and cost-effective.

This is where **Amazon Simple Storage Service** (**S3**) comes into the picture. S3 is an object storage service. It provides out-of-the-box features needed for managing a data lake, such as scalability, HA, and high-performance access to data operations. We have the entire next chapter dedicated to building scalable data lakes, and we will go through use cases and design patterns for building them on AWS.

The following diagram shows Amazon S3 as the central service for storing all the data in a data lake:

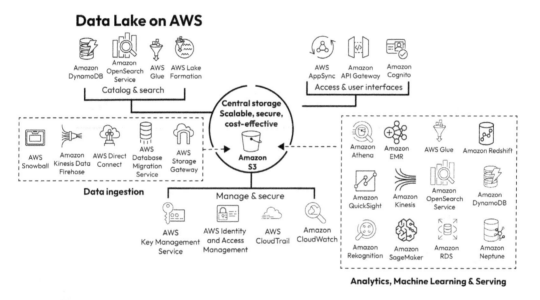

Figure 1.7 – Scalable data lakes on AWS

S3 is supported by other AWS analytics services that complement each other to create an end-to-end data platform. We will go through each of these components in the chapters to come.

Purpose-built analytics services

Leveraging the right tool for the right job is at the forefront of building a modern data architecture on AWS. And to achieve this pillar, AWS provides a wide range of data and analytics services, being able to cater to specific use cases so that the best price/performance is achieved.

The following diagram shows the purpose-built services that help to build a modern data platform:

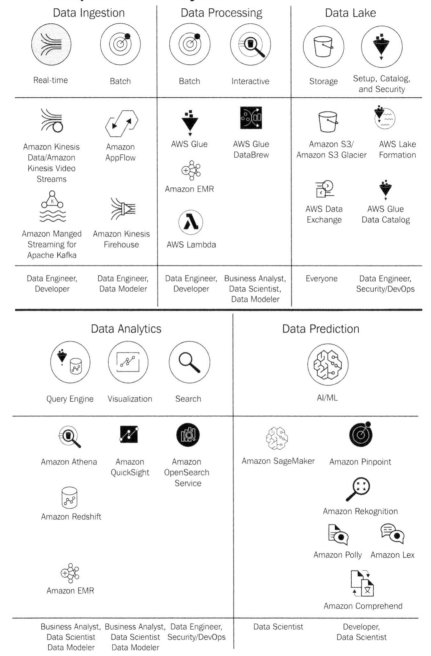

Figure 1.8 – Purpose-built analytics services on AWS

Specific AWS services are used at every stage of building the data platform. We have separate chapters to go into details of each section around data ingestion, data processing, data lakes, data analytics, and data prediction.

Unified data access

When you drive a luxury car, you can feel a difference in every aspect of the ride—plush interiors, a powerful engine, smooth handling, and so on. Similarly, a modern data platform is no good if only the consumers of the platform see its value. All the mechanisms by which you hydrate the platform with data have to be easy to build, operate, and maintain. The movement of data has to be made seamless and easy to operate. This topic has so many use cases and complexities that we have dedicated multiple chapters to it in this book.

Unified governance

If we all lived in a utopian society, what a waste of a topic security and data governance would be. Unfortunately, we live in a harsh reality where bad actors are everywhere, which makes the topic of unified governance and security the topmost priority focus area, always to be taken seriously.

Unified governance in a modern data architecture provides organizations with the simplicity and flexibility of managing access to datasets inside the data platform in one place. Equally important is the ability to conduct an audit of all access trails to ensure compliance. We have a dedicated chapter to understand which capabilities AWS provides to manage data governance across the platform.

Performant and cost-effective

And finally, what good is a data platform if it performs sluggishly or if you have to spend a fortune to keep it running? That's why it's important to understand and implement the right product feature in the right context, to make the platform operate in an optimal manner. Again, we have a chapter dedicated to this, where we go into detail on how AWS helps with this and which architectural best practices you should implement to keep the price/performance at a highly desirable level.

Before we conclude this chapter, as you may have noticed, most of our focus has been on technical topics so far, and the majority of the book is also geared toward technologists. However, a modern data strategy is successful only if it solves a business need, alleviates business pain points, and allows the business to use the data for maximizing its profits. By using a modern data architecture, you may be modernizing your data systems, creating a unified platform that breaks down data silos, or innovating for solving cutting edge use cases; just remember that it all ties back to the business and how the data platform helps it to stay ahead of the curve. So, in the following chapters, we will present use cases from a business point of view first and then get into the technical details of how to architect these using AWS services.

Summary

In this chapter, we looked at what data lakes are, why they are important, and what some of the challenges of on-premises data lakes are. We had enough context to pivot toward what a modern data architecture looks like and why it's important to build data platforms using this architecture pattern. And, as the climax was building up, AWS made a grand entry. We looked at the pillars of a modern data architecture on AWS. The stage is now set to get into details of each of these pillars. The flow of this book going forward is in line with these pillars.

With this chapter, our rollercoaster has just reached the top at cruising speed. Now, in the subsequent chapters, hang tight for all the thrills of the actual use cases and how the whole modern data platform slowly starts to take shape.

2
Scalable Data Lakes

In this chapter, we will look at how organizations can build a data platform foundation by creating data lakes on AWS.

We will cover the following main topics:

- Why choose Amazon S3 as a data lake store?
- Business scenario setup
- Data lake layers
- Data lake patterns
- Data catalogs
- Transactional data lakes
- Putting it all together

Why choose Amazon S3 as a data lake store?

Before we dive deep into the actual data and analytics use cases and explore how to design data lakes on AWS, it is first important to understand why **Amazon Simple Storage Service** (**Amazon S3**) is the preferred choice for building a data lake and why it is used as a storage layer to store all kinds of data in a centralized location.

If you recall from the discussions we had in *Chapter 1*, an ideal storage for building a data lake should inherently be scalable, durable, highly performant, easy to use, secure, cost-effective, and integrated with other building blocks of the data lake ecosystem. So, we ask a very important question: *why choose Amazon S3 as a data lake store?*

S3 checks all the boxes on what we look for in a store for building data lakes. Here are some of the features of S3:

- **Scalable**: S3 is a petabyte-scale object store with virtually unlimited storage
- **Durable**: S3 is designed for 99.999999999% (11 9s) of data durability
- **Available**: S3 standard storage is designed for 99.99% availability
- **Consistent**: Provides strong read-after-write consistency
- **High-performing**: Provides multiple upload and parallel requests
- **Easy to use**: Provides APIs, SDKs, event notifications, and lifecycle policies
- **Integrated**: Provides integration synergies with other AWS services
- **Security**: Security, compliance, and audit capabilities

In fact, there are a lot more features and advantages of using S3 as the storage layer for building data lakes, but our focus is on solving business use cases with data lakes, so we will not go into the weeds of how S3 works under the covers.

We are now at a stage where we can dive deep into designing and building data lakes as the foundation layer in a modern data platform.

Business scenario setup

The flow of this book is kept in such a way that it helps you get to the end state of building a modern data platform using AWS, with the ultimate goal of solving business use cases. To demonstrate all the building blocks of the data platform, it is important that I assume a fictitious entity and build a story around it. It's easier to understand concepts if there is steady progression and continuity in the storyline.

For this book, I will consider a financial organization and all its use cases. You can apply most of the design and architecture techniques to other sector use cases too. The bottom line is that organizations may have different business models, but the concepts that go into building a modern data platform on AWS, to a large extent, remain the same irrespective of the business domain. In other words, the same AWS services and functionalities will be leveraged in building any kind of data platform.

Let's consider a fictitious financial services company, GreatFin Corporation. It is a large enterprise organization having many **lines of business** (**LOBs**). Banking, mortgages, asset management, credit cards, and investment are some of the key areas in which it provides services to its customers. The following diagram shows some of the key segments served by GreatFin:

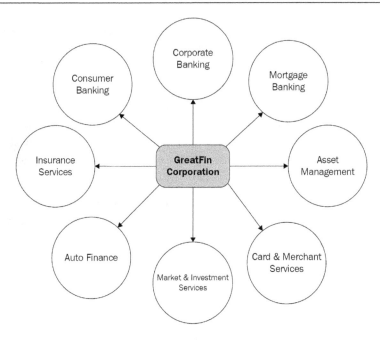

Figure 2.1 – Service areas of GreatFin, a fictitious financial company

We will slowly build a modern data platform by looking at specific use cases. So, let's dive straight into a business use case for GreatFin. The following use case is a broad and overarching one; we will eventually break it down into individual use cases, based on the specific functionalities desired from the data platform.

Use case for building a data lake

GreatFin has hundreds of source systems that collect, process, and serve data for its LOBs. Every system maintains its own data, and there is no effective mechanism in place to share all this data easily.

Due to the data silo problem, GreatFin, as an enterprise organization, struggles to accurately report information to its management. Due to fragmented data, the business also struggles to accurately identify a **single source of truth** (**SSOT**) for the data. Due to this, it is difficult for them to channel their efforts toward customer acquisition and retention, regularity compliance, fraud detection and prevention, monitoring for portfolio exposures to certain factors, uncovering market sentiments, minimizing exposure to companies with financial risks, and so forth.

The business desires to get faster insights from the data so that it can make quick decisions desires to get accurate data so that it can make better decisions; desires a self-service mechanism to discover, consume, and publish data so that it can be more independent and Agile; and, most importantly, desires the ability to handle customer data with care and integrity. The end goal of the business is to improve customer experiences, stay ahead of the competition by innovating, and always be prepared for future unknowns.

The business goals are quite broad but clear from the preceding use case. Business requests often drive technology decisions. From an IT point of view, these goals can be achieved in multiple ways; platform architectures can be designed in so many ways.

In the traditional pattern, you could solve this use case by building a data warehouse. In fact, you can still solve it that way even today, but we get reminded of the principles of building modern data architecture on AWS. The foundational principle is that a one-size-fits-all approach should be avoided. So, even though a data warehouse can solve many components of this use case, it will not provide an optimal solution for all aspects of the current use case, and it will add to the rigidity as newer use cases come up in the future.

So, from an IT point of view, to deal with the data silo problem, we first want to build a centralized data platform that can serve as the foundation for many other use cases to follow. And we also want to build it keeping scalability, durability, resiliency, performance, cost, and flexibility in mind. This leads us to design our data lake on AWS as the foundation. Let's look at the different layers that we may have to design and build in our data lake on S3.

Data lake layers

Now that we have a broader business use case for setting up a data lake, let's look at a use case that will help us define what the different layers of a typical data lake are and why they are required.

> **Use case for creating data lake layers**
>
> GreatFin has different LOBs, and within each of these LOBs, multiple personas have different tasks to perform on the data. Each persona may need specific access to different sets of data. They will all need the data to be formatted and stored in a certain way for them to do their day-to-day operations easily. For example, data engineers may need access to the raw source data so that they can profile the data and understand the quality of the data. Data scientists may need access to a standardized form of datasets so that they can do feature engineering for creating **machine learning** (**ML**) models. Data analysts may need access to business-friendly datasets so that they can derive insights from the data.

Before we get into the details of designing different layers in a data lake, let's understand what these layers are and why we need them. A layer of a data lake is just a logical separation of data, stored in multiple S3 buckets and prefixes. Before we design a data lake in AWS, it is important to understand why these layers are needed and what role each layer plays in the data lake.

Each layer has a well-defined purpose, and the data flows from one layer to the other in an organized manner. You can design as many layers as you want; the idea is that by clearly assigning a purpose behind each layer, it allows for clear segregation for the type of data each layer should hold, and also allows for the implementation of persona-based access patterns to the data in these layers. If you remember from our previous chapter, if a data lake is not well thought out and designed, it quickly becomes an unmanageable data swamp, and we want to avoid that.

The following diagram shows the key layers of a data lake on S3. The number of such layers along with their nomenclature may vary by implementation, but the core concepts behind them hold true for all types of design:

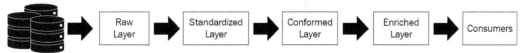

Figure 2.2 – Layers of a data lake on S3

We will go through each of these layers, one by one.

Raw layer

All the data that resides in the source systems first needs to be brought over into S3, using a suitable data ingestion mechanism. We have multiple chapters coming up on different ways to ingest data into a data lake, but for now, our focus is on setting up the storage layer in S3. As the name suggests, the raw layer acts as a common location where data from all the source systems is brought over without any changes.

How you organize data in the raw layer will be defined by your data governance strategy, but here are some possibilities:

- You could create just one bucket in S3 for all the raw data and then create a hierarchy of prefixes for each source system, database, schema, table, and so forth

- You could create separate buckets to store raw data from each of the source systems

- You could also create separate buckets/prefixes even within the raw layer, one to land the source data and another to archive the raw data after it's processed

Keeping data in the raw layer helps in many ways, as set out here:

- Firstly, there is the data traceability aspect, where at any stage in the data flow, if there is a need to find out the original source data value/type, you don't have to trace it all the way back to the original source systems. It's a lot easier to locate and find the lineage of the data if all the raw data resides in a centralized data lake.

- Secondly, since there is no fixed schema in the raw layer, it's easier and faster to build data pipelines to meet the consumption pattern.

- Thirdly, it gives data engineers, data analysts, and data scientists the ability to analyze, profile, and leverage the source datasets from a single location.

The data in the raw layer is source-centric, which also means that all data issues found in the source will also be present in the raw layer. The data in the S3 bucket, designated for the raw layer, may just be in the form of large files inside a single S3 prefix in unoptimized formats such as text, CSV, or JSON. And, at this point, the raw data is just in the form of files without a clear mechanism to query the data inside them. This is where the standardized layer comes to the rescue.

Standardized layer

There is a whole chapter on data processing ahead in the book, but in essence, when we create a data transformation pipeline, the data is read from the raw layer, transformed, and put in the standardized layer. The standardized layer, again, may be a single S3 bucket or multiple ones, depending on the governance strategy adopted.

When data is put in the standardized layer of the data lake, it undergoes certain validations and data quality checks along the way. The data in the standardized layer is put in optimized files such as Parquet files, and these files are partitioned in multiple S3 prefixes.

The files in the standardized layer then get their own schema. This is done by extracting the metadata of the data stored in files and storing it in a central data catalog. The raw layer, along with the standardized layer, is also referred to as the staging zone since these two layers together are used to iron out all data issues pertaining to the source systems, and it also shields the final consumers from these issues. The following diagram depicts the staging zone:

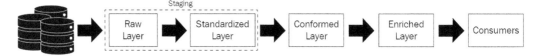

Figure 2.3 – Staging zone

Since the metadata of the data in the standardized layer is added to a data catalog, it becomes easy to access the data by writing SQL queries. At this point, you don't have to deal with files in S3 buckets, even though certain personas may want access to this data directly. The standardized layer serves as a self-service interface for data exploration and **business intelligence** (**BI**). As and when the data pipeline refreshes the data from the raw to the standardized layer, this data is available for making any kind of business decision.

There is one more thing the standardized layer helps with—the issue of schema evolution. The source system may introduce schema changes at any time—a new column gets added to a table, an existing column type gets changed, and so forth. Schema changes create issues in a data lake setup since data lakes are created with a schema-on-read setup. If we don't adapt to source schema changes, the data pipelines will break down or the consumers will have issues with data.

The standardized layer shields the consumers from schema drift by introducing schema validation logic and by adding schema evolution controls. You can create a process to automatically fix the schemas in the standardized layer or have it flagged so that an administrator can take appropriate actions. Optionally, you can also have a separate bucket/prefix to store invalid data that fails the data quality checks, and a separate bucket/prefix to archive standardized datasets if they are no longer relevant.

The following diagram shows the key responsibilities that happen between the raw layer and the standardized layer. The landing zone inside the raw layer can be used as a placeholder for all the initial and incremental files from the source system. You can then copy it to the raw zone partitioned by dates, for easy search and archival:

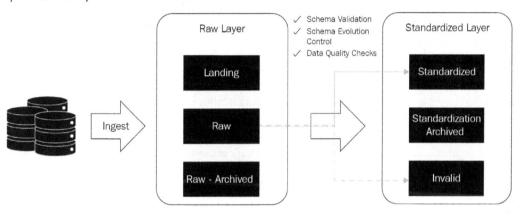

Figure 2.4 – Activities in a standardized layer

Once the data is cleansed, optimized, partitioned, and cataloged in the standardized layer, it is ready to take the shape of what the business wants to see. A conformed layer is another logical separation in the data lake, using separate S3 buckets and new prefixes.

Conformed layer

The conformed layer stores common entities that the business understands and is interested in.

The data from the conformed layer can be used for self-service reports and BI. For example, you may have a person entity with name, age, address, profession, income, status, and so forth. Basic information about this person, such as name and age, can be a straight pull from the standardized layer; however, status may be a derived field based on some business rules. For example, it may be based on someone's past and present business dealings with the organization.

Enriched layer

In any organization, data is used to either monetize the business or to make the business operationally better. In either case, businesses want to leverage data as a product. The enriched layer can be used to create final datasets that are directly used by the business, either internally or externally, to drive toward monetization or gain insights for operational excellence. An example could be a dashboard that is used by the LOB owners to make daily operational decisions.

So, we've been through the logical layers for setting up a data lake. In reality, these are just ways of organizing data in Amazon S3. There is no hard and fast rule that all these four layers must exist as is. Sometimes, three layers are created, and you may also name them bronze, silver, and gold layers. As long as each layer has a clear and well-defined purpose, along with governance strategy, the number of layers and their nomenclature doesn't really matter.

All four layers we created have a clear purpose, and all four layers are created for specific personas in the organization who would use the data in those layers for their day-to-day job. The raw and standardized layers are more source-system-centric and mainly used by data analytics, data engineers, and data scientists, whereas the conformed and enriched layers are business-centric. Organizations may want a single view of the data in the business layers across the whole enterprise. But sometimes when the organization is very large with lots of LOBs, it's easier to divide and conquer the business data. This brings us to data lake patterns.

Data lake patterns

There are two types of data lake patterns, as follows:

- Centralized pattern
- Distributed pattern

Let's discuss each of them. Note that you can use a hybrid pattern too, depending on your use case.

Centralized pattern

In a centralized pattern, the business data is stored and accessed from a central location, to be used throughout the enterprise. For example, it may be easy to manage entity information in a centralized location; entity information such as name, address, gender, age, and profession of a person. It's easier to manage such datasets in a centralized way, from a governance point of view as well as to avoid data duplication.

Certain LOBs may have additional properties of the data that are relevant only to their use cases. For example, the marketing department may also want to see **customer lifetime value (CLV)**, **net promoter score (NPS)**, marketing preferences, and so on for a person. These additional attributes can then be derived inside the enriched layer of the marketing domain. The following diagram shows a centralized pattern for the conformed layer:

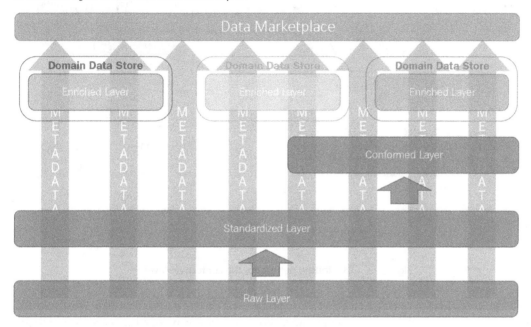

Figure 2.5 – Centralized pattern for the conformed layer

A centralized pattern can become a bottleneck for large organizations with lots of independently operated LOBs. Centrally managing and deriving specific datasets relevant to each LOB may become cumbersome.

Distributed pattern

A distributed pattern allows each LOB to operate its own conformed and enriched layers. This way, they can build and curate the datasets relevant to their business, independent of the centralized datasets.

The following diagram shows an example of a distributed pattern where the conformed layer and the enriched layer are both decentralized and put in the hands of individual LOBs:

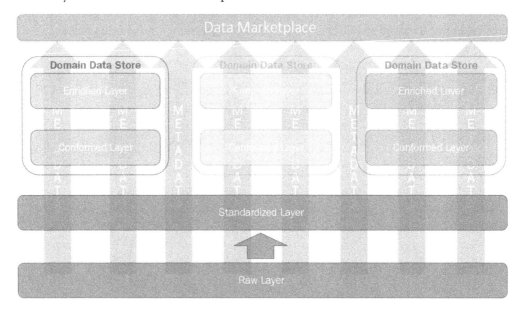

Figure 2.6 – Distributed pattern for the conformed layer

What we have discussed so far is all about the logical separation of data in a data lake. We discussed how each layer plays a distinct role in the data platform and how you can either have a centralized pattern or a distributed pattern for segregating the data. It's all theoretical up to this point. The actual implementation of it in AWS is where all the fun is. And in the next few sections, we will dive deep into the details.

Another thing to clarify here is that the concept of centralized versus distributed data lakes takes many different forms when it comes to actual implementation on AWS. Depending on the use cases, some of the data layers may be hybrid during actual implementation, meaning both raw and standardized layers in an S3-based data lake and both conformed and enriched layers in a purpose-built store such as a data warehouse.

An AWS account is a logical boundary that all AWS customers use to constrain the activities they want to do inside that boundary. Many customers use multiple AWS accounts to logically separate how each LOB operates. All resources created inside that account belong to that account owner, and eventually, all accounts come under a root account for billing and an overall governance point of view. Setting up infrastructure the right way on AWS is a broad topic, but for the purposes of setting up data lakes, a centralized pattern may have all the data and metadata managed inside a single AWS account, whereas a distributed pattern may entail setting up data lake resources in multiple such AWS accounts. We have a chapter on *data mesh* architecture later in the book, which talks about creating distributed data platforms using multiple AWS accounts.

All the data in the data lake is stored in S3 as files, but to easily access the data inside them, we need to create some kind of metadata that will allow us to easily query the data inside the files, without having to understand the underlying format of the files. This brings us to the topic of data catalogs.

Data catalogs

We talked about a data lake in AWS being a combination of the data in S3 buckets and the metadata of this data stored in a catalog. We will solve the mystery of creating a technical catalog in AWS by introducing another critical service for building a modern data platform, **AWS Glue**—a serverless data integration service. Now, Glue is actually an umbrella service consisting of multiple parts. It has the Glue ETL part, which is used for building data integration work, and we have multiple chapters on data ingestion and integration. The component of Glue that is relevant to our data catalog discussion is **Glue Data Catalog**. Let's unfold more about the catalog in Glue and how it helps with our data lake in S3.

Glue Data Catalog

As the data passes through layers of the data lake in S3, the metadata of the data is captured and stored in Glue Data Catalog. It creates and stores the technical metadata in the form of **data definition language (DDL)** statements. Glue Data Catalog becomes a central repository that stores all the metadata of the data lake so that different personas do not have to deal with file operations to get the required data from S3; instead, they would just query the data via SQL statements.

There are multiple ways to populate the data catalog in Glue. The most common way, in the context of a data lake in S3, is to scan the data inside a given S3 bucket or prefix and automatically populate the metadata in Glue Data Catalog. This is achieved by running a **Glue crawler**. A crawler is a heuristics-based mechanism by which Glue is able to infer the schema of the underlying datasets. It uses classifiers to determine the format, schema, and its associated data properties. Glue provides some in-built classifiers for common file formats such as JSON, CSV, Parquet, and so forth. If there are file formats that are different from what the built-in classifier can recognize, then you can build a custom classifier to specify the rules of the file format.

The following diagram shows the sequence of Glue using a crawler to populate Glue Data Catalog with the metadata of the underlying data in S3:

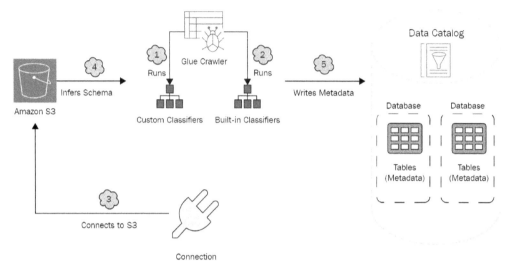

Figure 2.7 – Sequence of populating Glue Data Catalog

The sequence is as follows:

1. When the Glue crawler is triggered, it first looks for any custom classifiers that can infer the data format in the data source you provided—in our case, the data is in the S3 data lake.

2. If no custom classifiers are provided, then it uses the built-in classifiers.

3. It then connects to the data store—in our case, it's the S3 data lake.

4. It infers the schema.

5. And finally, it populates Glue Data Catalog with the schema information.

At the end of this whole process, you will see one or multiple tables being created in the database you select in Glue Data Catalog.

The following screenshot shows a sample glue crawler. It requires a name, source type, source location, role, and schedule to run:

Figure 2.8 – Glue crawler in action

The crawler is run either on demand, scheduled to run at a specific time, or created as a trigger step in a data workflow. Once it completes its run, it either creates a new table in the catalog if the table didn't exist before, or it updates the existing table if the schema has evolved. You can also control what to do when the crawler discovers a new schema in the datasets.

Once the crawler run is complete, you can check the metadata of the table created in the Glue console. The following screenshot shows different components of the table captured from the underlying data in S3. Some of the key fields are the type of classification, input/output format, table properties, and the actual data types identified from the S3 data files:

Figure 2.9 – Glue table created after the crawler has run

When we talk about building data lakes, it's usually all the components of the platform, including data ingestion, data transformation, data consumption, and data governance. However, the core foundation of a data lake is the storage layer in S3 and the metadata layer in Glue Data Catalog; therefore, this chapter just focuses on these two aspects. As we get into other chapters, we will unfold specific areas of data lakes and other purpose-built data stores, and continue our use-case-driven journey toward solving business problems.

In recent times, as use cases have changed, data lakes also have evolved. **Online transaction processing (OLTP)** systems such as relational databases and **online analytical processing (OLAP)** systems such as data warehouses both have the ability to maintain transactions, which means that both systems are ACID-compliant systems. However, as data started to grow inside data lakes, organizations were looking for a simplified, single type of system that could provide the best of both worlds—OLTP and OLAP type of support from the data lake itself. This need gave rise to frameworks on the data lake to support transactional use cases. Let's dive into this in a bit more detail.

Transactional data lakes

Let's introduce this topic with a use case from GreatFin.

> **Use case for a transactional data lake**
>
> GreatFin wants to comply with the *right to be forgotten* **General Data Protection Regulation (GDPR)** compliance in Europe. It wants to have the ability in all its systems, including its analytics environments, to easily locate, update, or delete records as and when required.

The need to create transactional data lakes came about due to many business use cases and the challenges associated with them, such as the following:

Use Case	Challenge
Compliance requirements	Compliance and privacy laws—for example, the GDPR requires the deletion of certain data within a specific timeframe and/or across all datasets
Change data capture (CDC)	CDC from the source databases and incremental data processing into the target data lakes—that is, support for insert, create, update, and delete operations on the data lake
ACID transactions	ACID-compliant transactions to support multiple concurrent read and write operations on the same data lake table
Streaming data ingestion	Support for streaming data ingestion, which includes late event handling and small file compaction
Data quality	Data quality support, data versioning, time travel, and so forth

To change the content of any file, the file has to be first opened, specific content needs to be located and updated with a new value, and finally, the whole file needs to be saved again. Since all the data in an S3 data lake is stored in files, achieving all these new requirements meant that new frameworks were required, and this gave rise to prominent open source table formats such as **Apache Hudi**, **Apache Iceberg**, and **Delta Lake**.

In this section, we will focus on the use cases for using these frameworks and not get into a philosophical debate about which is better than the other. All of them have their own strengths and are widely used by many organizations. And we rather not get into the weaknesses of any, simply because these frameworks are constantly evolving, to plug in gaps that are discovered during various implementations.

We will also not get into the technical details of how each framework works under the covers since our focus is on when to use them and how they help in building a modern data platform on AWS using data lakes on S3.

Since in this chapter, we are just unfolding the storage and metadata aspects of the data lake, we will focus on how these transactional data lake table formats store the data on S3 and how the metadata gets created in Glue Data Catalog. In subsequent chapters, as we unfold the data processing layers, we will again visit this topic.

Transactional data lakes using Apache Hudi

Hudi table format was first built by Uber as an incremental processing framework that can perform low-latency data operations on data stored in data lakes. It was open sourced to the **Apache Software Foundation (ASF)** in 2017 and ever since has gained popularity with many organizations, including AWS. Some of the key features of Apache Hudi are presented here:

- Provides upsert and delete data operations with fast and pluggable indexing
- Incremental queries support
- Transaction support along with rollbacks and concurrency control
- Built-in CDC and data streaming
- Auto file sizing and compactions
- Built-in metadata tracking
- Schema evolution support
- Support for multiple execution engines such as Spark, Trino, and Hive

The best thing about using Hudi for transactional data lakes on S3 is that it works seamlessly with open file formats such as Parquet. So, when you are processing the data from the raw to the standardized layer in S3, the raw files are converted into Parquet by the Hudi framework. Hudi logic can also create a table in Glue Data Catalog.

Datasets on S3 created by any Hudi-supported execution engine are called Hudi datasets. Hudi creates three types of files on S3, as follows:

- Data files in open file formats such as Parquet
- An index to efficiently locate rows in the file
- The timeline metadata to support time travel and incremental read/write

Also, to assist in different types of use cases, Hudi offers two types of tables, as follows:

- Copy-on-Write
- Merge-on-Read

The following screenshot (which is also available on the Hudi portal) provides a quick summary of the trade-offs between the two types of tables. You can use either of them to meet specific requirements for the use case:

Trade-off	Copy-on-Write	Merge-on-Read
Data latency	Higher	Lower
Update cost (I/O)	Higher	Lower
Parquet file size	Smaller	Larger
Write amplification	Higher	Lower

Figure 2.10 – Trade-off between the two types of Hudi tables

There is a lot to Apache Hudi, but in this chapter, I just wanted to introduce it and help understand its features. We will visit it again during our next chapter when we talk about how to explore the data that we stored in the S3 data lake. Before I wrap up on Hudi, I want to highlight some cases where leveraging Hudi with AWS might be the best table format option:

- Requiring flexibility in managing mutating datasets—that is, upserts and deletes
- Needing low latency for streaming data ingestion at scale
- Native integration with AWS services

Transactional data lakes using Apache Iceberg

Iceberg table format was developed at Netflix to address its challenges with huge petabyte-scale tables. It was open sourced to ASF in 2018, and ever since, its adoption has grown many folds. Some of the key features of Apache Iceberg are presented here:

- Schema and partition layout evolution
- Time travel for change tracking
- Support for multiple execution engines such as Spark, Trino, and Hive

Iceberg table format has also found its support in multiple AWS services, and we will explore them in our following chapters. When you store Iceberg datasets in Parquet file format in S3, you can use Glue Data Catalog to create a tabular structure that then can be used by other AWS services for data operations. Iceberg also stores some metadata/manifests files in S3 to manage transactional and other operations support.

From a use case point of view, Apache Iceberg table format is a good fit when tables on the data lake are very large in size, and also when the partition strategy or schema may evolve constantly.

Transactional data lakes using Delta Lake

Delta Lake table format was developed by Databricks and eventually got open sourced. Delta Lake table format also supports most of the key features such as ACID transactions, time travel, and schema evolution and enforcement. It also supports unified batch as well as streaming data processing, along with support for major execution engines, and works well with Parquet file format.

The following diagram shows a typical data lake setup in S3 using Delta Lake data layers and mechanisms:

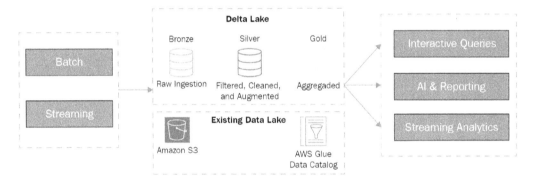

Figure 2.11 – Delta Lake representation of a data lake on S3

Delta Lake uses a transactional log-based approach, also called a DeltaLog, to track and maintain the operations of the table. Delta Lake support has also made it into multiple AWS services, which we will explore as we get to the specifics of it in the following chapters.

Putting it all together

So far, we have discussed the different storage layers in a typical data lake in S3 and defined the purpose of each of the layers. We also introduced the concept of creating metadata using a Glue crawler and storing it in Glue Data Catalog. Finally, we looked at use cases for building transactional data lakes. This is a good time to pivot back to the GreatFin business requirements we introduced earlier and apply these data lake foundational concepts to our use case.

> **Marketing use case**
>
> Suppose the marketing department at GreatFin wants to find certain top leads for offering a new type of **certificate of deposit** (**CD**) with a higher interest rate to select a few high-net-worth customers only. In this case, the customer data will be stored in multiple systems, from different LOBs.

Let's walk through what each layer in the data lake might look like.

Raw layer example

The following diagram is a depiction of data stored in a raw layer bucket in S3. Since we keep the data in the raw layer as close to the source data, we would simply ingest the relevant datasets from the source database into their respective database prefixes in S3, followed by the S3 prefix representing the schema, followed by the prefix representing the table, and finally, the data files inside it:

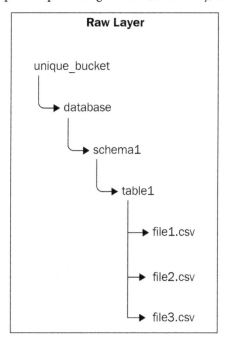

Figure 2.12 – Data stored in the raw layer of S3

Once we ingest and organize all the source data in the raw layer, we can then proceed to check for schema validation and evolution, data quality, and CDC and also apply any other technical transformation to the raw datasets before they are moved into the standardized layer—that is, another S3 bucket structure.

Standardized layer example

The standardized layer structure may resemble that of the raw layer since the data structures in the standardized layer are still geared toward source database structures. The major difference in this layer is that the data files are stored in an optimized Parquet file format and possibly compressed using a Snappy algorithm.

And, of course, the metadata from this layer is cataloged and stored in Glue Data Catalog in the form of tables. The following diagram shows a sample hierarchy of how data can be organized in the standardized layer of S3:

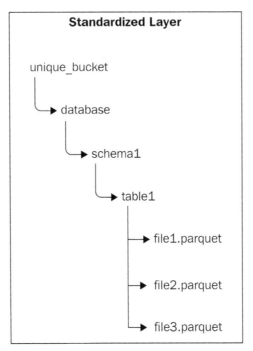

Figure 2.13 – Data stored in the standardized layer of S3

There is another very important concept I will introduce here, but we will go into details of it in the next chapter. When we store the data in the standardized layer, often this dataset is ready for consumption by multiple personas in the organization. For them to efficiently locate the data files and/or efficiently query the data via the catalog, the data in S3 may need to be partitioned into specific prefixes, depending on the usage patterns for the data. This separating of datasets into S3 prefixes based on certain values from the datasets is called **data partitioning**. For the catalog to be aware that the data is partitioned in S3, the DDL in the Glue Data Catalog will also have partitioning information. We will look at the table metadata details in our next chapter.

The following diagram shows a sample hierarchy of how data can be organized in the standardized layer of S3 when it's partitioned by a customer identifier value from that dataset. In this case, all data files related to *customer ID 1* will be stored in that prefix:

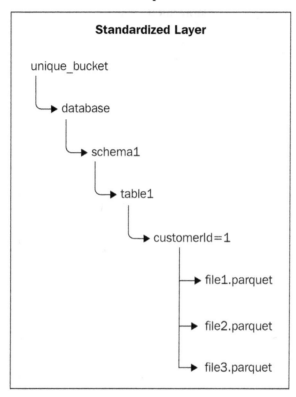

Figure 2.14 – Data stored in the standardized layer of S3 using partitions

The next layer is the conformed layer, which takes the data from the standardized layer and gives it some business meaning.

Conformed layer example

In this use case, the marketing team wants to get top leads by offering them a new CD option. Now, in our conformed layer on S3, we may want to organize datasets for the marketing department, followed by a leads table, followed by data partitioned by region and year, followed by the data files having those datasets. These datasets will have a corresponding table in Glue Data Catalog. In essence, we have applied certain business rules to the data and created a brand new dataset that provides direct value to the business—in this case, the marketing department.

The following diagram shows a sample hierarchy of how data can be organized in the conformed layer of S3, structured for consumption by the marketing department:

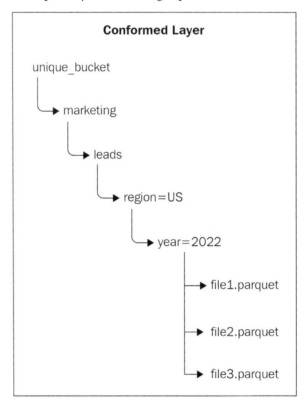

Figure 2.15 – Data stored in the conformed layer of S3

Finally, the business may want to augment the leads dataset with some external data attributes so that the final results provide it with all the necessary information to complete the use case it intended to solve.

Enriched layer example

This resultant dataset is stored in the enriched layer, and it becomes a data product. The following diagram shows a sample hierarchy of how data can be organized in the enriched layer of S3:

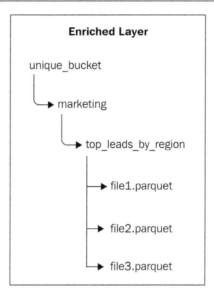

Figure 2.16 – Data stored in the enriched layer of S3

Before we wrap up this chapter, one thing to note is that we could have very well derived the final outcome on the fly from the standardized layer itself. However, we chose to store the derived datasets in conformed and enriched layers because on-the-fly computation/transformation for large datasets would degrade the performance of such operations. Also, doing it that way makes the whole security and governance of the platform a laborious process. That is why each layer of the data lake is actually geared toward different personas and how they interact with the data on a day-to-day basis.

Summary

In this chapter, we went through why so many organizations prefer to build their data lakes on Amazon S3. We then went through different layers of data lakes in S3 and the purpose of each of them. Along with the layers of data, we also looked at how Glue Data Catalog helps to capture the metadata about the data in the form of tables. We also touched upon a new trend around having to build a transactional data lake, which involves selecting a table format that aligns closely with the specific use case being solved. Finally, we put it all together to solve a specific use case and saw it all come together, at least from the data storage and catalog side of things.

We have the data in S3 and we have the catalog of this data in Glue Data Catalog in the form of tables. The real value of this setup is that businesses can easily consume this data to derive insights from it. This leads us to the next section of this book around different purpose-built services and how each of them plays a role in building a modern data platform on AWS.

Part 2: Purpose-Built Services And Unified Data Access

In this part, we will explore the eco-system of purpose-built AWS analytics services that help build a modern data platform. We will have a use-case driven discussion around each of these services and how all these services work in tandem to create a holistic data platform. We will also look at how certain AWS services help in achieve seamless data movement across the data platform.

This part has the following chapters:

- *Chapter 3, Batch Data Ingestion*
- *Chapter 4, Streaming Data Ingestion*
- *Chapter 5, Data Processing*
- *Chapter 6, Interactive Analytics*
- *Chapter 7, Data Warehousing*
- *Chapter 8, Data Sharing*
- *Chapter 9, Data Federation*
- *Chapter 10, Predictive Analytics*
- *Chapter 11, Generative AI*
- *Chapter 12, Operational Analytics*
- *Chapter 13, Business Intelligence*

3

Batch Data Ingestion

In this chapter, we will look at the following key topics:

- Database migration using AWS DMS
- SaaS data ingestion using Amazon AppFlow
- Data ingestion using AWS Glue
- File and storage migration

So far, we have looked at creating scalable data lakes using Amazon S3 as the storage layer and AWS Glue Data Catalog as the metadata repository. We looked at how you can create layers of a data lake in S3 so that data can be systematically managed for specific personas in your organization. The very first layer we created in S3 was the raw layer, which is meant to store the source system data without any major changes. This also means that we need to first identify all the source systems that we need data from so that we can create a centralized data lake.

The mechanism by which we bring the data over into the raw layer of the data lake in S3 is also termed **data ingestion**. Data ingestion can either be in batches, where we bring the data over in bulk at regular intervals, or in near real time, where we bring the data over as soon as an event occurs. In this chapter, we will dive deep into the batch mechanisms of ingesting data into our data platform, which includes the data lake built on S3 and other purpose-built data stores on AWS.

If you recall the pillars of modern data architecture from *Chapter 1*, one of the pillars was *Seamless data movement*. Ingesting data from external systems into AWS, typically the raw layer of the data lake in S3, is the first step of this data movement. In any data platform, the movement of large amounts of data from one system to another is always a complex undertaking that involves building and orchestrating multiple data pipelines.

When you build a modern data architecture on AWS, the data movement mechanism should be as seamless as possible. To achieve this, AWS provides a variety of data ingestion and data migration services. In this chapter, we will look at some of these services and their use cases for batch data ingestion.

Database migration using AWS DMS

In the prologue, we saw how in recent times, types and volumes of data have exponentially grown. However, a vast amount of data still resides in relational data stores, such as databases and data warehouses. So, let's get going with relational data stores as the low-hanging fruit for data migration, and tie it back to our GreatFin corporation's use cases.

> **Use case for database migration and replication**
>
> All **lines of business** (**LOBs**) at GreatFin have their transactional data sitting in on-prem databases such as Oracle and SQL Server, and they want the data all centralized in a data lake for them to have self-service analytics and derive insights from the data across all these systems.
>
> Some reports need to get the latest data for analytics as soon as the source databases commit the transaction. This will allow the business to see near-real-time dashboards in order for them to make quick decisions.
>
> At the same time, some LOBs want their existing on-prem databases to be migrated to cost-effective open source databases in AWS.
>
> Finally, some legacy data warehouses are not able to adapt to the rapid changes in business requirements, and the LOBs want to modernize those data warehouses.

The reason I clubbed all three use cases together is simply that the solution to all of them revolves around data movement into a different data store, and all three can easily be solved by using AWS Database Migration Service (AWS DMS). Let's look at this further:

- The first use case is basically asking for data stored in one set of data stores to be migrated to an S3-based data lake, and then have an ongoing data replication so that any ongoing data in the source gets synced up in the data lake

- The second use case requires a source database to be migrated to a new target database, preferably a lower-cost, open source one

- The third use case revolves around modernizing an existing data warehouse by migrating the existing data warehouse to a modern one in AWS

Before we get into the architecture for leveraging DMS for all of the use cases, let's quickly do an overview of the service and why it's so popular for database migration.

AWS DMS overview

AWS DMS is a service that allows easy migration and replication of databases and data warehouses to AWS. One of the primary reasons for its popularity is that it's a **no-code/low-code service** that allows for easy setup and operations. Some typical use cases for using DMS are presented here:

- Migrating databases and data warehouses

- Upgrading major versions of a database

- Ingesting data in an S3 data lake

- Creating cross-region read replicas, and so forth

DMS is a managed service, which means there are no clusters to create or software to install. You can choose a replication instance yourself if the workload state is known and steady or just pick the serverless replication option if the workload state is unknown and uneven. So, in essence, all you have to do is this:

1. Create source and target endpoints.

2. Select a replication instance or pick a serverless replication.

3. Create a task that will do the mapping between the source and the target.

The rest is all configuration-based.

One cool feature of DMS is its ability to process **change data capture** (**CDC**). When you set up a task, you can select an option that allows the DMS task to turn into CDC mode, after it has completed the initial data migration. The following screenshot shows the migration types that DMS supports, which includes the CDC mode:

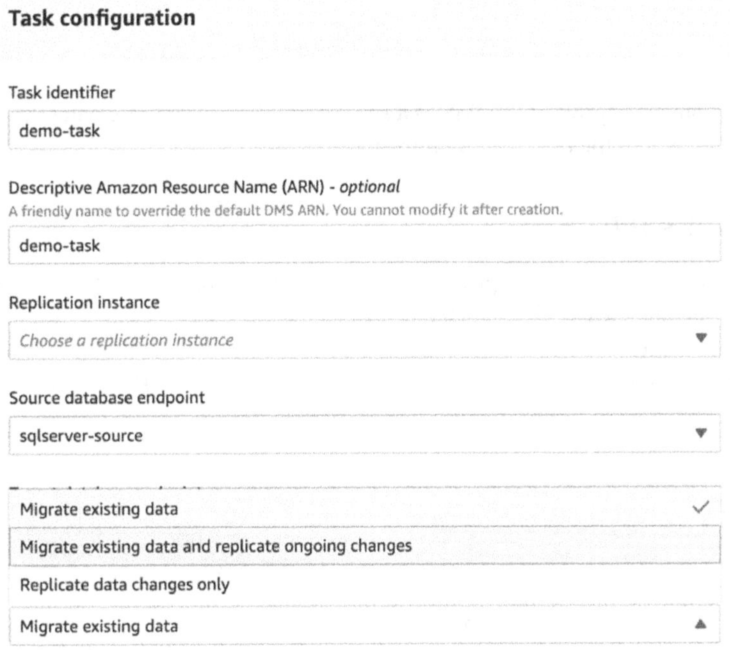

Figure 3.1 – DMS migration types

DMS pulls the initial data from the source tables into the target destination, and after the initial data is loaded, it then looks for any data commits in the log system of the underlying database. This makes DMS a perfect fit for continuous data replication to the target without any user intervention. The following diagram shows a typical deployment of a DMS service, where the replication instance has an implicit backup, for **high-availability (HA)** purposes:

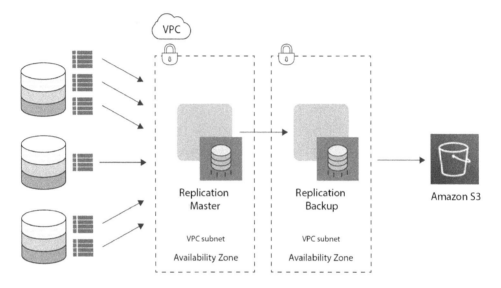

Figure 3.2 – DMS deployment

Now that we have some background in DMS as a service to migrate/replicate datasets, let's see how we could use it to apply it to the use cases we introduced earlier.

AWS DMS usage patterns

We now know that DMS assists in migrating/replicating data from many source data stores to many target ones. A complete list of supported lists of sources and targets can be found in the AWS documentation. The source and target can be the same, which makes such migrations homogeneous, whereas in many cases they may be different, which makes such migrations heterogeneous. The following diagram shows an example of both types of migrations:

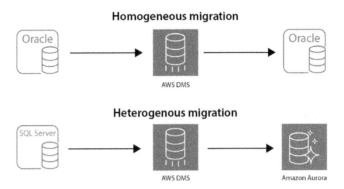

Figure 3.3 – Types of migrations

The reason I bring this up is that for heterogeneous migrations, before we can migrate the data, we have to deal with the complexity of making sure all the schemas and other source-specific structures are mapped to the target data store. Some of it might be an easy conversion, but some other changes may need manual intervention. In this case, another standalone tool comes in handy, which is **AWS Schema Conversion Tool (AWS SCT)**.

SCT helps to convert the schema from source into target structures by automatically converting the structures it can correlate. For other things, it will provide suggestions on what needs to be manually changed. SCT also has the ability to copy the data over after schema conversion, but we will use SCT just for schema conversion and prefer DMS to copy the data over.

The following diagram shows the two-step process for heterogeneous migrations, where SCT and DMS are both used in tandem:

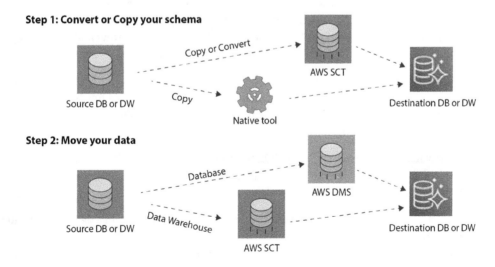

Figure 3.4 – Data migration process

A new serverless schema conversion solution has also been added inside the DMS service itself. Depending on the supported source and target systems, you can choose the standalone SCT tool or the **DMS Schema Conversion (DMS SC)** workflow.

This legwork on DMS now sets the stage for the three use cases we introduced earlier in this chapter. The following architecture diagram depicts a fan-out approach, where a single DMS instance may be used to migrate multiple sources to multiple targets:

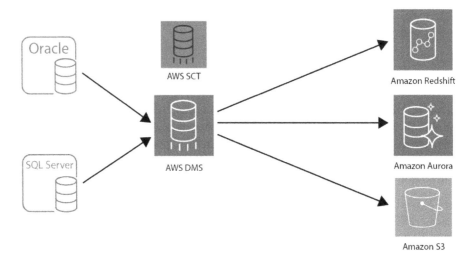

Figure 3.5 – Fan-out migration/replication

For the use case where data from Oracle and SQL Server, as the source systems, needs to be migrated/replicated to open source databases such as PostgreSQL and MySQL in AWS, the target will be **Amazon Aurora**, which is a fully managed database service from AWS supporting both PostgreSQL and MySQL databases.

For the use case where the existing source Oracle data warehouse needs to be migrated to an AWS-managed data warehouse, the target will be **Amazon Redshift**, which is a fully managed data warehouse service from AWS. We have a chapter dedicated to building a data warehouse on AWS and will revisit data ingestion in that chapter.

For the use case where the source Oracle and SQL Server database data needs to be brought into a data lake in S3, the target will be set as S3. DMS will put files in S3 when the tasks run. Let's explore a bit more how the data lake gets hydrated with data using DMS.

A DMS task when run will first pull the relevant data from the tables of the source database and put it into the S3 bucket/prefix assigned. After the initial tables are copied into S3 as files, it will switch into CDC mode where any new commits that happen on the source database are directly pulled in from the log system and put into S3 again as individual files. The following screenshot shows how the structure of the files will look on S3:

```
Bulk dump File                                    Ongoing CDC Files

s3://uniquebucket/schemaName/tableName            s3://uniquebucket/schemaName/tableName
s3://uniquebucket/hr/employee
                                                  <time-stamp>.csv
/schemaName/tableName/LOAD001.csv                 <time-stamp>.csv
/schemaName/tableName/LOAD002.csv                 <time-stamp>.csv
/schemaName/tableName/LOAD003.csv                 . . .

. . .

101,Smith,John,7-Jun-15,New York              I,101,Smith,John,7-Jun-15,New York
102,Smith,John,9-Oct-16,Los Angeles           U,101,Smith,John,9-Oct-16,Los Angeles
103,Smith,John,12-Mar-19,Tampa                U,101,Smith,John,12-Mar-19,Tampa
104,Smith,John,16-Mar-19,Tampa                D,101,Smith,John,16-Mar-19,Tampa
```

Figure 3.6 – S3 file structures with DMS

The preceding examples show files in CSV format but you can use Parquet format too. The initial data from the tables that get loaded in the raw layer of S3 have larger file sizes, but as soon as it gets into CDC mode, you will get plenty of small files containing CDC data. Inside the files, you will find a flag that will indicate whether the record was an insert, an update, or a delete in the source. Based on these flags, you can perform the relevant operations while moving the data from the raw layer into the standardized layer of the data lake. In the data processing chapter, we will dig into details of how the data is transformed and consolidated in the data lake.

In this section, we went through the use case for using DMS to ingest data into the data lake as well as any of the supported purpose-built stores. DMS is well suited for ingesting data from a variety of relational and NoSQL data stores. But what if the data resides in a SaaS-based application? This leads us to our next section.

SaaS data ingestion using Amazon AppFlow

We are in an era where a lot of applications are SaaS based. Every SaaS-based application is different and has its own mechanism for capturing and storing data. Many SaaS applications also allow for reporting inside them, but many times, organizations want a holistic view across the whole data platform, which means they may want to join different datasets from multiple such applications, to derive the right level of insights from the data.

Let's try to correlate this with a use case from GreatFin. If you recall from *Chapter 2*, the marketing department wanted to find top leads for offering a new type of **certificate of deposit** (**CD**) account to select a few high-net-worth customers. Let's use that example to build our SaaS data ingestion use case.

> **Use case for data migration from a SaaS application**
>
> The marketing department ran a campaign to identify top leads who would be a great fit for offering a new CD account. The lead information is stored in `salesforce.com`, which is a ubiquitous **customer relationship management** (**CRM**) SaaS application. The consumer banking org now wants to join this dataset with datasets it has in its internal systems to identify and send offers to the relevant individuals.

In our data migration using AWS DMS section, we already ingested transactional data into the data lake from Oracle and SQL Server. This dataset includes information about customers and how they interact with the bank. Now, the missing piece of the puzzle is the leads data that was collected in the Salesforce CRM system. Once we ingest this leads data into the data lake, we can join different tables to figure out an exact list of individuals who should get an invitation for the new CD account.

This is a perfect time to introduce **Amazon AppFlow**, which is a fully managed, low-code, and serverless service for ingesting SaaS data into AWS data stores, including S3 data lakes. Let's get into the details of AppFlow.

AppFlow overview

AppFlow is specifically designed to migrate data from SaaS applications into AWS data stores. The best thing about AppFlow is that it does not require a lot of technical heavy lifting to make it work. Because of its low-code/no-code approach, it is the go-to service for technical as well as non-technical personas, for ease of data movement from SaaS applications. AppFlow comes with out-of-the-box connectors for many SaaS-based applications, and it also has a connector SDK that allows the creation of custom connectors. Now, let's get into the details of our use case.

AppFlow usage patterns

Our use case required the data from `salesforce.com` to be extracted and migrated to the S3 raw layer first, and it will flow through the remaining layers before being finally joined with other datasets and consumed using a reporting tool. The following diagram shows the flow, with AppFlow extracting the Salesforce data using its built-in connector and pushing this data into the target S3 raw bucket:

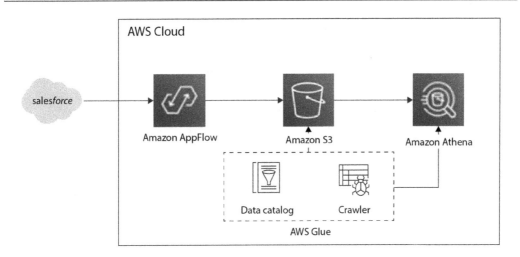

Figure 3.7 – AppFlow data ingestion into S3 data lake

Once the data is standardized, conformed, and enriched with other datasets, it's ready for reporting using any of the reporting tools. In our case, we are using **Amazon Athena**, which is a serverless service for ad hoc interactive analytics. We have a full chapter dedicated to Athena later in the book.

There are many such use cases where AppFlow comes in really handy, as follows:

- Zendesk is a SaaS application that helps with support tickets and case management. You can use AppFlow to migrate this data to the S3 data lake for reporting and analytics.

- SAP ERP data can easily be ingested into the S3 data lake using AppFlow.

- Datadog is well known for its log-/metric-gathering capabilities. AppFlow also helps here to get the data over to the S3 data lake for analytics.

- Marketo is a popular SaaS application for new leads/email responses. AppFlow comes in handy here too.

Likewise, there are many other SaaS applications that are supported out of the box, and many more keep getting added. You can always check the list from the AppFlow documentation on AWS. The following diagram shows a typical topology for using AppFlow:

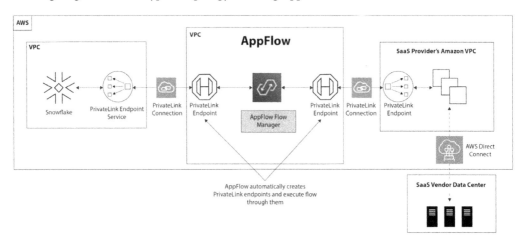

Figure 3.8 – AppFlow topology with PrivateLink enabled

With PrivateLink enabled, the data does not traverse over the public internet, thus creating a more secure networking route for the data flow from the SaaS application into the target data store; in our case, it is the S3 data lake.

So far, we looked at DMS and AppFlow for batch ingestion of data into the data lake. Both tools cater to an admin type of persona in the organization who is not required to be very technical. Both these AWS services are low-code types of services that allow for quick ingestion of data into the data lake without a lot of coding. However, data ingestion is sometimes a lot more complex and requires some sort of ETL pipelines to be built, hence the data engineers come into the picture. This is a perfect time to introduce another component of Glue that helps perform data ingestion operations.

Data ingestion using AWS Glue

In our data lake in *Chapter 2*, we introduced Glue Data Catalog, which is one of the key components of data lake design. Glue is also a popular ETL tool for data engineers, who want to ingest data from the source systems and transform the data as it flows between the different layers of the data lake. Glue provides complete flexibility to deal with any kind of data engineering complexity. In essence, Glue ETL can help extract data from any source system, transform it, and load it into any target system.

Since this chapter is all about batch data ingestion and we want to keep most of our focus on ingesting data into the data lake in S3, we will focus on those use cases. We have a dedicated chapter for data processing later, where we will revisit Glue ETL.

> **Use case for data ingestion using modern ETL techniques**
>
> The business at GreatFin wants to derive value from all the data available in its existing data stores; some are stored in older-generation data stores, some in niche data stores, and some data schemas in the data stores are not modeled in the best way to take advantage of the data stored inside those structures.
>
> The IT team at different LOBs has a challenge at hand to create a data ingestion mechanism that can periodically bring all this data into a data lake, for data analytics.

From a use-case point of view, it's not very different from the other use cases we've seen in this chapter. The business wants to get access to all the data; however, the devil lies in the details. DMS and AppFlow solved a specific type of low-hanging fruit, which is migrating/replicating data from a certain set of databases and SaaS applications respectively. But Glue ETL comes into the picture in the following scenarios: when some of the data sources are not supported out of the box by other services; if there is a lot of customization in the source data store; if there are certain types of data structures that are not supported; if there is some level of data processing that needs to be done to even bring the data into the raw layer of the data lake.

The one important aspect of using Glue ETL as the mechanism for data ingestion is that it's a versatile service that allows for a high degree of custom work, which means that data engineers can build complex data pipelines and make them part of the end-to-end data flow across all layers of the data lake. So, in essence, Glue ETL can be a one-stop shop for all things data engineering, including data ingestion. Let's get started with an overview of Glue ETL.

Glue ETL overview

Glue ETL is a fully managed serverless service that makes it easy for data engineers to author and execute ETL jobs. Data engineers can script their own jobs and schedule them to run at a specific time or after a particular event. The jobs can either be written in PySpark, Scala Spark, or just as pure Python code. Glue now also supports Ray (`Ray.io`), a new open source framework that helps scale Python workloads. Spark jobs in Glue can also be authored to leverage streaming ETL, which we will cover in our next chapter.

Batch data ingestion requires a connection to the source data store. For the purpose of ingesting data into the S3 data lake, the target will be an S3 bucket that will be set up in the raw layer of the data lake. Since the data in the raw layer of the lake is close to the source data, it does not undergo any major data processing.

To make the life of data engineers easy, Glue ETL has a few key components—Glue Studio, Glue connectors, and Glue workflows.

Glue Studio is a drag-and-drop UI that makes ETL jobs easier to create and less time-consuming, as it takes away the level of effort required to write scripts from scratch. The best thing about it is that you can use it to generate boilerplate code just by using the drag/drop features, and then you can even customize jobs by adding your own code.

Glue connectors make it easy to connect to external systems so that source and target mapping can be done inside the Glue Studio without having to write all the code from scratch for connectivity.

Glue workflows make it easy to orchestrate all jobs and their dependencies in a single location. The Glue workflow UI allows you to design workflows using drag-and-drop features.

Glue Studio

The whole purpose of Glue Studio is to make data engineers' life easier, so when you get into the studio console, you will see three sections, as shown in the following screenshot:

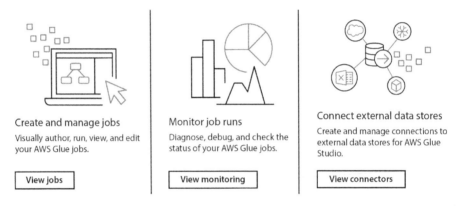

Create and manage jobs
Visually author, run, view, and edit your AWS Glue jobs.

View jobs

Monitor job runs
Diagnose, debug, and check the status of your AWS Glue jobs.

View monitoring

Connect external data stores
Create and manage connections to external data stores for AWS Glue Studio.

View connectors

Figure 3.9 – Glue Studio options

Using Glue Studio, you can create and manage your jobs along with connectors to external systems, and you can also monitor those jobs for success/failure. As a data engineer, the first job you would create will always be that of data ingestion into the target store. When the target store is an S3 data lake, the immediate task is to put the data in the raw layer without much processing.

There will be a series of Glue ETL jobs in a data pipeline that will move the data between the different layers of the data lake, doing specific operations along the way. Since the focus of this chapter is batch data ingestion, let's keep our usage patterns limited to getting the data from the source systems into the data lake.

The following screenshot shows the different ways in which you can author a job using Glue Studio:

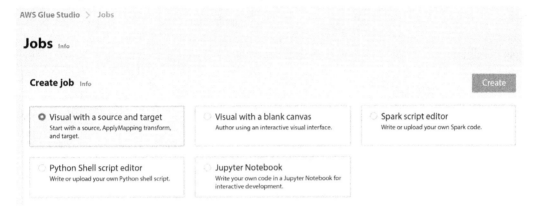

Figure 3.10 – Glue Studio job authoring options

Data engineers get many options to create their jobs, either through visual drag-and-drop features, by writing their own scripts, or via Jupyter notebooks.

Glue connectors

Connectors in Glue play a big part in allowing easy connectivity to different systems. This is especially true for data ingestion jobs where we want to connect to source systems and get the data into the target systems. Connectors will make this operation easier to implement as all the boilerplate connection logic is hidden inside the connectors.

Another cool thing about connectors in Glue is that it's integrated with AWS Marketplace, so any vendor can publish its connector for users to discover and implement. The following screenshot shows a few of the connectors in the marketplace; you can search for other connectors too:

Figure 3.11 – Glue Studio connectors via AWS Marketplace

Glue workflows

Workflows in Glue make it easy to bring all individual data pipeline components into a **single pane of glass** (**SPOG**). You can have multiple Glue components such as Glue ETL jobs, Glue crawlers, and trigger conditions in a single workflow, each with dependencies baked in so that when the workflow executes, all the individual components execute one by one on their own and the whole data pipeline, along with error handling, gets processed without manual intervention.

Now that we understand all the critical parts needed for Glue ETL, let's get into the usage patterns for using Glue ETL for data ingestion.

Glue ETL usage patterns

At the heart of Glue ETL is Apache Spark, which allows for large-scale distributed data processing. Spark also has APIs that allow the source connectors to work easily so that the job can fetch data from the source and sink into the target. The following diagram summarizes typical usage patterns for AWS Glue:

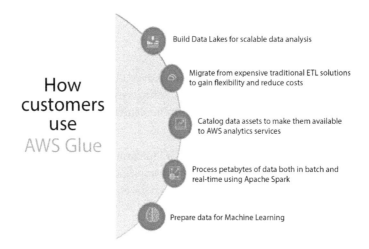

Figure 3.12 – Typical usage patterns for AWS Glue

AWS Glue is a multi-purpose service, and Glue ETL is just one component of it. Even with Glue ETL, you can do many functions such as data migration/ingestion using source and target connectors, data processing, data streaming, data exploration, and so forth. Since this chapter is about data ingestion into the raw layer of the data lake in S3, let's look at Glue ETL usage patterns to ingest data from various data sources into the data, so as to satisfy the use case for GreatFin we introduced earlier in the *Glue ETL overview* section.

The following diagram shows a high-level architecture of how you can use Glue ETL to connect to the required source system and migrate data in the raw layer of the data lake in S3:

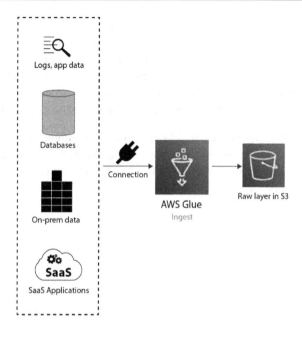

Figure 3.13 – Typical Glue ETL data ingestion architecture

Glue connectors make it easy to connect to many of the source systems so that it's easy to pull the data from those systems into the data lake. Many connectors are available in AWS Marketplace, and you can even bring your own connector too. The following diagram highlights Glue ETL versatility by connecting to many applications:

Figure 3.14 – Glue ETL connector ecosystem example

Now, let's touch base on Glue workflows again. You can have multiple jobs that you can orchestrate in a workflow that will pull data from multiple data sources/schemas/tables. However, if there are many such databases or tables in a source, it becomes tedious to create workflows for individual tables. Of course, you can use Glue crawlers to crawl and discover the source database structures. But the complexity of incremental data pulls also needs to be baked in. To make this whole experience seamless, **AWS Lake Formation** provides a concept called **blueprints**.

Blueprints take care of the boilerplate logic of data ingestion by providing templates that you can use to fast-track the data ingestion task. The following diagram highlights how the blueprint sits at the top of all Glue activities to create a wrapper around all the individual tasks you would otherwise create manually for a data ingestion workflow:

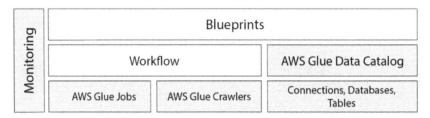

Figure 3.15 – Lake Formation blueprint for Glue workflows

Depending on the type of ingestion you want to execute, you can select that type from the Lake Formation console, and it will further guide you through a series of steps including source and target connections, database/schema/table, and so forth. Here is a screenshot of the Lake Formation **Blueprints** console where you can pick the type of blueprint you want for your data ingestion:

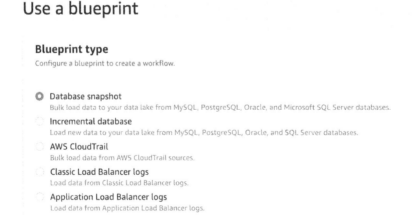

Figure 3.16 – Lake Formation blueprint types

If anything is not available in the blueprint, you can always do your own Glue job setup with a connector from the marketplace and orchestrate those jobs on your own. Once the blueprint is executed, under the covers it just creates and executes a Glue workflow. The following screenshot shows an executed Glue workflow that was auto-created by a Lake Formation blueprint:

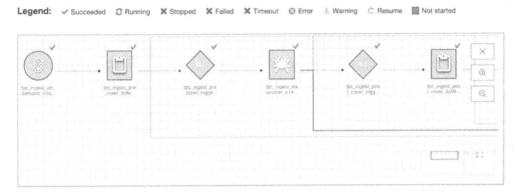

Figure 3.17 – Glue workflow created by a Lake Formation blueprint

We will get into Glue ETL again in our data processing chapter later in the book, but so far, we have seen mechanisms by which you can connect to source systems and quickly ingest data using some of the AWS purpose-built data ingestion services.

But what if the data on your on-prem system is stored in files or in storage devices? Files are everywhere and are generated by multiple mechanisms. So, we need to discuss ways by which we can ingest files into our data lake in S3. Let's dig into that in the following section.

File and storage migration

A lot of data still resides in files for many reasons. When the data resides in files, we just need an easy transfer mechanism to bring it over into the raw layer of the data lake in S3. In this section, we will explore some of the AWS services that make it easy to transfer files into the AWS ecosystem.

AWS DataSync

AWS DataSync makes it easy to continuously migrate on-prem data into many AWS storages, including Amazon S3. DataSync has an agent that needs to be deployed that will help do all the heavy lifting for the data migration. Before we look at the usage patterns, let's look at a use case at GreatFin that makes DataSync very appealing.

Use case for data migration using AWS DataSync

Multiple LOBs at GreatFin want to save costs by retiring multi-terabyte data stored on their on-prem storage systems. They want to continuously replicate new data as it arrives on their on-prem storage. Also, because of regulatory requirements, they have to retain this data and make it available for reporting purposes.

The use case is straightforward, and it needs a mechanism to seamlessly migrate data stored in on-prem storage as files into S3 so that it's part of the data lake for retention as well as for reporting. Let's look at the usage patterns for DataSync.

DataSync usage patterns

Typical usage patterns for DataSync involve migration of application data into AWS, archival of on-prem storage, and replication for data protection and recovery. The following diagram represents a typical migration pattern for data from on-prem storage systems into S3, where it can then be processed for data lake operations such as reporting. This way, we can also keep costs lower and meet the regulatory requirements:

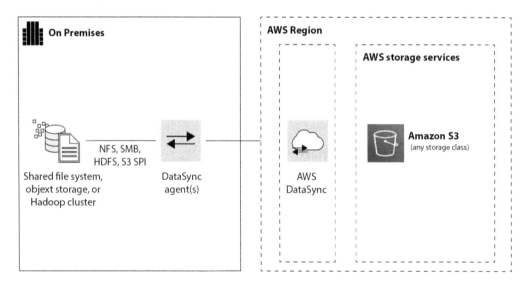

Figure 3.18 – DataSync architecture pattern

Now, let's look at another file transfer mechanism that AWS provides.

AWS Transfer Family

AWS Transfer Family makes the tedious task of secure file transfers easy. If you use FTP, SFTP, or FTPS protocols for transferring data, then this AWS service will make it easier to manage those transfer workloads in S3. Let's add some more color by bringing up a use case from GreatFin.

> **Use case for file transfer using AWS Transfer Family**
>
> GreatFin wants to simplify its file transfer workflows by reducing the complexity of setting up its own infrastructure. The current solution is error-prone with inconsistent alerting and doesn't always meet the **service-level agreements (SLAs)**.

Sometimes IT problems bleed into the business, and that's what this use case suggests. GreatFin, at an enterprise level, needs a managed file transfer service that can be automated with low code.

AWS Transfer Family usage patterns

Typical usage patterns involve transferring files for data lake operations, digital media content aggregation and distribution, subscription-based data products, and any other use case that would use the FTP, SFTP, or FTPS protocols. The following diagram shows an architecture setup for using SFTP using the AWS Transfer Family service:

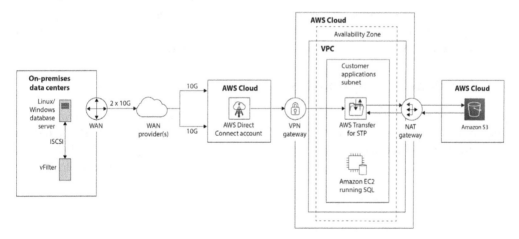

Figure 3.19 – AWS Transfer Family architecture pattern

Finally, let's look at another file transfer mechanism that AWS provides that comes to your doorstep as a hardware device.

AWS Snow Family

When you have petabytes of data that needs to be moved one time in the fastest possible time and without using a lot of network bandwidth, that's where AWS Snow Family comes in handy. It's a service that provides different types of storage hardware that gets shipped to your address. You can plug those devices into your data source, transfer the data into the devices and even ship it back to AWS. AWS will then load this data into the final AWS storage of your choice.

The Snow devices come in two major types based on configuration and use case, as follows:

- **AWS Snowcone** is a small and rugged device that is ideal for secure portable computing
- **AWS Snowball Edge** has bigger hardware capacity and also comes with its own built-in compute

Let's look at the usage of Snow devices in a use case from GreatFin.

> **Use case for one-time large data migration using AWS Snow Family**
>
> GreatFin wants to migrate its multi-petabyte data store from on-prem to AWS. It has limited network bandwidth, and based on calculations from IT teams, this migration would take many months to complete over the wire. GreatFin wants to do the initial data migration in a faster, cheaper, and more efficient manner.

The key words in the use case are *multi-petabytes of data* and *one-time migration*. This makes a great use case for getting the data into a snowball and shipping it back to AWS for transferring the data into the target data store in AWS. Let's get into the details of solving this use case.

AWS Snow Family usage patterns

One of the most common patterns for solving the extremely large data stores from on-prem to AWS is using a combination of AWS DMS and AWS SCT along with AWS Snowball Edge. SCT and DMS work in tandem to copy the data over to the Snow device and later help to get this data loaded into the target store in AWS. The following architecture diagram shows this whole process in detail:

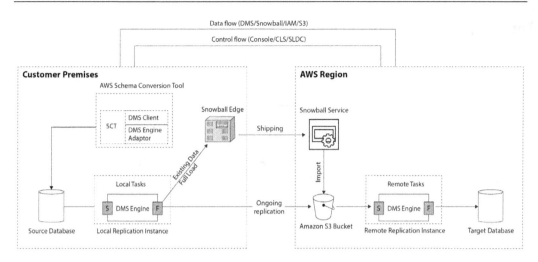

Figure 3.20 – Large data store migration using AWS Snow Family

I've provided a link to the step-by-step procedure for this migration in the *References* section at the end of this chapter.

Summary

In this chapter, we looked at how you can migrate data in batches into different AWS storage systems, especially a data lake in S3. Data ingestion is mostly the first step in data migration, and it can get really complicated if the correct set of tools is not leveraged for appropriate source and target data stores.

We also looked at how you can use DMS and SCT to migrate/replicate on-prem databases into AWS data stores and how you can bring over data into the data lake built on S3. We then looked at how you can use AppFlow to migrate data from SaaS-based applications into the data lake. We also looked at how the versatility of Glue ETL helps during the initial data ingestion stage. And finally, we looked at all the other storage and file transfer services, including DataSync, Transfer Family, and Snow Family.

This brings us to the end of an important chapter where we were able to hydrate data stores in AWS with purpose-built modern data ingestion services. Since this book is around design and architecture, I'm providing some reference links next for anyone who wants to try out some hands-on exercises in their AWS accounts.

References

- DMS workshop: `https://catalog.us-east-1.prod.workshops.aws/workshops/976050cc-0606-4b23-b49f-ca7b8ac4b153/en-US/400`

- AppFlow workshop: `https://catalog.us-east-1.prod.workshops.aws/workshops/9787ec94-1ace-44cc-91e5-976ad7ddc0b1/en-US/salesforce/salesforce2s3`

- Glue ETL data ingestion blog: `https://aws.amazon.com/blogs/big-data/ingest-data-from-snowflake-to-amazon-s3-using-aws-glue-marketplace-connectors/`

- Data migrations using Snowball Edge: `https://docs.aws.amazon.com/dms/latest/userguide/CHAP_LargeDBs.SBS.html`

4

Streaming Data Ingestion

In this chapter, we will look at the following key topics:

- The need for streaming architectures and its challenges
- Streaming data ingestion using Amazon Kinesis
- Streaming data ingestion using Amazon MSK
- Streaming services usage patterns

Chapter 3, Batch Data Ingestion, was all about batch data ingestion, where we saw multiple ways of ingesting data in batches. Batch data ingestion is still the bedrock of many data pipelines since it helps to serve so many business use cases. For many such use cases, data analytics can be performed with data that's not fresh – that is, data is not available for consumption in the analytics environment as soon as it's produced in the source system. For a very long time, deriving reactive insights from data was fine as OLAP systems were meant to perform analytics on data that was typically a day old.

However, data in these modern times gets generated in large volumes and moves fast from one system to another. With the onset of cloud computing, the use cases have evolved too, where the faster businesses can analyze the data and take action, the better outcomes they can achieve.

The need for streaming architectures and its challenges

Many times, as time passes by, the value of insights from data diminishes. *Figure 4.1* represents the value of data to the decision-making process where, as time passes by, its value decreases:

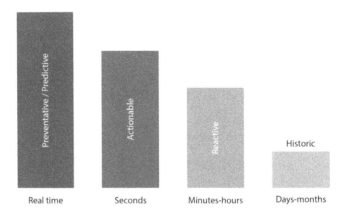

Figure 4.1 – Time value of data toward decision making

For organizations to do real-time analytics, data needs to be ingested from the source, processed immediately, and stored in the destination as soon as the event occurs. This allows organizations to derive insights from the data in real time. The need to get data in real time has many advantages:

- Getting data in real time for analytics helps businesses make faster decisions and stay ahead of the competition

- Analyzing real-time data allows early detection of security threats and anomalies in the data

- IoT systems continuously send data in the form of events, and all this data needs to be captured and stored for analytics

- Log data needs to be proactively monitored to detect any failures that may affect critical applications

There are many more reasons why organizations want real-time data for analytics and that's where streaming ingestion data has become a critical part of the overall modern data architecture.

Before we discuss the challenges of setting up a streaming platform, let us discuss the critical components of a real-time streaming architecture. *Figure 4.2* shows the key components of real-time analytics:

Figure 4.2 – The key components of real-time analytics

Let's briefly understand, with the help of the following table (*Figure 4.3*), what these components do in the streaming process:

Stage	Description
Data source	Sources can be any device or application that produces real-time data.
Stream ingestion	Stream ingestion is where the real-time data is onboarded in a streaming platform in real time as the events occur.
Stream storage	The streaming platform needs to have the ability to store real-time data in the order it receives it. The duration can be set so that consumers can replay any of the real-time data whenever they want within that period.
Stream process	The streaming data also can undergo transformations so that it can be consumed in the format the consumer wants.
Data sink	Finally, the data gets stored in a target store, most commonly in a data lake or a data warehouse, so that it can be used by the consumers to derive real-time insights from the data.

Figure 4.3 – Real-time streaming component details

Based on these components, it may seem straightforward to create streaming data pipelines, but in reality, building such pipelines comes with its own set of challenges, specifically in on-premises systems. Some of the challenges of data streaming are as follows:

- The streaming platform is difficult to set up and maintain
- It's not easy to scale since the data in the stream have different velocities
- It's difficult to build a fault-tolerant and highly available system
- It's complex to manage the platform and expensive to maintain its operations
- Integration with other tools and services requires additional development work

This brings us to the central theme of this chapter: how do we ingest data into our data platform without going through all these challenges? This is where real-time data streaming using AWS services comes into the picture, and in this chapter, we will look at those AWS services that make it easy for organizations to build streaming data pipelines.

Our focus is on how to solve streaming use cases, so we will focus on architectural patterns instead of going into the weeds of how these services work. Let's get started with a very popular AWS service for streaming.

Streaming data ingestion using Amazon Kinesis

Amazon Kinesis was created specifically to alleviate all the pain points associated with setting up and operating a streaming platform. Organizations want to build real-time streaming data pipelines that make it easy to collect, process, and analyze data in real time. That's what Kinesis brings to the table. It's a serverless, fully managed, and scalable service for handling real-time streaming use cases. It seamlessly integrates with other AWS services and you only pay for what you use.

There are a lot of use cases that do different things with streaming data. Some use cases require the data to be processed and analyzed with the lowest latency possible; some use cases can withstand some delays in getting the data but expect the data to be compacted and aggregated for query efficiency; and some use cases require the data to be analyzed as it's passing through the stream itself.

As you may recall, one of the tenants of modern data architecture on AWS is to leverage purpose-built services for specific types of use cases. Amazon Kinesis also has multiple services that cater to specific types of streaming use cases.

Figure 4.4 lists the four Kinesis services that cater to specific types of streaming use cases. All of them can be chained together in a particular architectural pattern to solve the problem at hand:

Figure 4.4 – Different Kinesis services

Let's discuss the first three since they are the main ones that are used for structured and semi-structured data analytics. We will introduce them by covering a use case from GreatFin to better understand their purpose.

Amazon Kinesis Data Streams

Amazon **Kinesis Data Streams** (**KDS**) is a streaming service that allows you to ingest, process, and store streaming data at any scale. It's a serverless service, which means there is no software or hardware to provision or manage. We will briefly touch on how it works but more importantly, our focus is when to use it and what use cases it solves. So, let's kick things off with a use case from GreatFin.

> **Use case for Amazon KDS**
>
> Being a financial organization, GreatFin has customer-facing web applications that provide critical services. These applications are designed to be highly available and fault tolerant. However, even with the best of systems, sometimes, things go wrong. Businesses want to make sure that in the event of issues with the application, the IT team proactively monitors issues and tracks such errors in real time so that widespread issues can be detected early; this early intervention would avoid complete system breakdown. This will help keep customer satisfaction high, which, in turn, helps the business grow.

In IT terms, what the business is saying is to monitor all the critical application logs in real time and catch issues with the service. These errors need to be monitored proactively and notifications need to be sent to the admin team for action.

Before we solve this problem, let's quickly go over some basic concepts of how KDS works. This will give you a better context as we solve the given use case and other similar ones.

KDS overview

KDS makes it easy to ingest, store, and consume streaming data. The following diagram summarizes the components of KDS and its ecosystem:

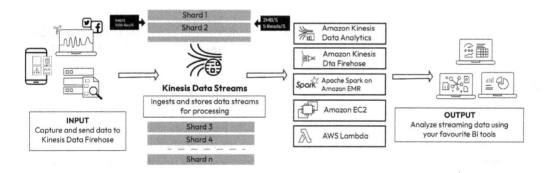

Figure 4.5 – KDS components

KDS provides the mechanisms to capture streaming input data, ingest it into the stream, store it, and finally allow output-consuming systems to read from the stream. KDS consists of one or more shards, where each shard provides a fixed capacity to the stream. Depending on the expected volume of data that's produced and consumed, you can allocate appropriate units of shards. With KDS's on-demand mode, you don't need to worry about allocating a specific number of shards; the system will scale on its own.

KDS also has many other functional aspects, such as partition keys, sequence numbers, data records, and so forth. I won't go into the functionality details of KDS here as this book is about when to use KDS and what design patterns to use for particular use cases.

The best thing about KDS is its ability to integrate with different kinds of producer and consumer services. The following figure shows some of the predominantly used tools and services that integrate with KDS:

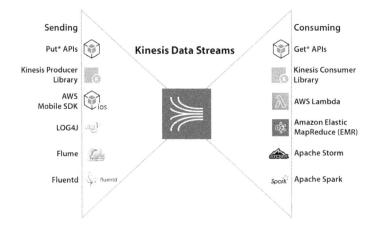

Figure 4.6 – KDS integration tools/services

If you are curious about how the service works and wish to understand all its features and functionalities, the best place to go would be the AWS documentation portal for KDS. We would rather spend our time-solving use cases, so let's get back to the use case we introduced earlier in this section around proactively monitoring critical applications of GreatFin.

The challenge with the use case we introduced – which is also true for most enterprise applications – is that some of these applications provide low-latency high-volume services to the customers. The infrastructure is usually a farm of scalable servers that serve the web traffic and return the response to the customers. With such a setup, the volume of logs that gets generated is huge, and combing through such high-volume rolling logs for errors in real time is even more challenging.

Even though this problem can be solved in multiple ways, one of the easier ways would be to stream the logs in Amazon KDS, filter the data using a Lambda function, and send all the HTTP 500 error details in a Slack channel that's being monitored by a team of system admins. The following figure shows a simple architecture pattern for this data flow:

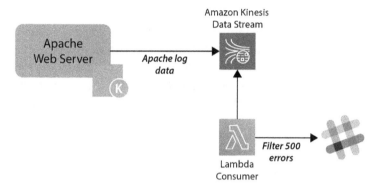

Figure 4.7 – Web application real-time log monitoring using KDS

In this use case, the Kinesis agent can be used to send the logs into the stream and the Lambda function can be the mechanism that processes this data and funnels the appropriate error codes into the Slack channel. We will look into a few other use cases in our streaming usage patterns section later in this chapter, but for now, let's move on to the next Kinesis service.

Amazon Kinesis Data Firehose

The main purpose of Amazon Kinesis Data Firehose is similar to KDS – that is, to provide a platform for streaming data. However, the key differentiation is that Firehose provides a white-glove service when it comes to specific destinations. What this means is that for certain destinations such as Amazon S3, Amazon Redshift, Amazon OpenSearch Service, Splunk, and some other HTTP endpoints, Firehose will do all the heavy lifting to ensure that the data, when delivered to these target destinations, is directly ready for consumption by the users.

Let's look at a use case so that the purpose of Firehose is clearer.

> **Use case for Amazon Kinesis Data Firehose**
>
> GreatFin wants to store and analyze all financial applications' log data promptly. The purpose should be to extract, format, and store critical elements from the logs so that this data can easily be queried and the necessary reports can be generated. As the data volume will be huge, the business wants the final solution to be very cost-effective but near real-time at the same time; a delay of up to 3 minutes is tolerable.

The key terms in this use case are ingesting a large volume of log data, cost-effective storage, and near real-time consumption. Let's quickly understand the basics of Firehose before we provide the solution for this use case.

Kinesis Data Firehose overview

Firehose provides a zero-administration streaming platform that allows direct-to-datastore integration. The streaming data in Firehose can be buffered, partitioned, transformed, and even reformatted before it goes to its destination. This makes Firehose a perfect choice for streaming near real-time data for analytics operations, where sub-second latency is not required but the process needs to be efficient. The following diagram summarizes Firehose's components and its ecosystem:

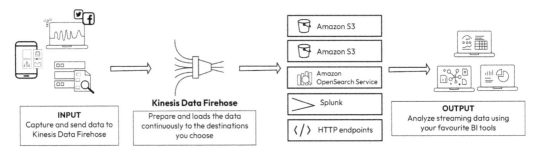

Figure 4.8 – Firehose components

As you can see from *Figure 4.8*, Firehose is a natural choice of streaming platform if the destination is one of the five displayed. Buffering in Firehose can be configured either as a time-based buffer, which is between 1 and 15 minutes, or it can be configured as a volume-based buffer, which is between 1 and 128 MB. The buffer gets flushed to the destination upon whichever threshold is hit first.

Firehose also lets you transform/normalize the streaming data by letting you configure a Lambda function. It can easily convert the final output in Parquet/ORC format for optimized operations. There are many other features of Firehose that you can easily read about in the official AWS documentation. For now, I'll move on to how/when to use Firehose.

So, the use case we introduced earlier in this section was to collect, format, convert, and store the logs data for easy consumption in reports. The reports need to get the data in near real time and the storage needs to be cost-effective.

If we parse this into IT terms, the data lake in S3 happens to be one of the most cost-effective forms of storage you can have. So, now, we just need a mechanism to capture and ingest logs data into S3 in a near real-time manner, basically under 3 minutes. We also need a way to normalize the logs data – that is, a way to extract critical elements from it and store it in a structured manner. Finally, for efficiency, we need to convert the final data into Parquet format and store it in an S3 bucket, partitioned by date, so that it's easy to query the data based on date ranges.

With this context about the use case, all roads lead to Firehose, and *Figure 4.9* shows an easy way to solve this use case:

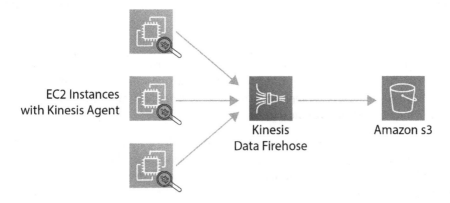

Figure 4.9 – Processing application logs using Firehose

One thing I will keep emphasizing multiple times in this book is that a particular use case can be solved using any combination of AWS/external services. There will always be pros and cons of each such design pattern. It's important to identify what matters to the business most as it eventually leads to them favoring a particular architectural pattern over the other. In this use case, the storage cost was emphasized, so we went with an S3-based pattern.

We will revisit the logs use case in other chapters and change the scenario to drive home the point that other services need to be weighed in too, keeping in mind the important aspects of the final solution. Now, let's move on to the next Kinesis family member.

Amazon Kinesis Data Analytics

So far, we have differentiated KDS from Kinesis Data Firehose, and with the help of use cases, we have demonstrated when to use them. But what if you want to perform some analytics on the data that's still passing through the stream? Let's dig into this by introducing a use case.

> **Use case for Kinesis Data Analytics**
>
> Being a financial company, GreatFin wants to make sure that all application logs are also proactively monitored and that any deviation from the norm is immediately notified. Some examples of deviation from the norm are if the network traffic is noticed from an IP address that's outside the usual ones that are expected, continuous failed attempts to authenticate to an account in rapid succession, and patterns typically associated with DDoS attacks. All these abnormalities observed in the application logs can be a sign of bad actors trying to breach security. The business wants to monitor and catch all these anomalies in the data in real time and immediately notify admins so that they can take action.

So, we must stream the application logs and do analytics on this streaming data to catch and process anomalies in the data. Note that there are many possible services and tools to solve this use case. We will look into how **Kinesis Data Analytics** (**KDA**) will solve this. But first, let's get an overview of KDA.

KDA overview

KDA assists in interacting with streaming data in real time. You can use SQL, Python, Scala, or Java as your preferred choice of programming language for interacting with the streaming data; you can also use an integrated **Apache Flink** application for more advanced use cases. KDA Studio notebooks make it easy to interactively analyze the data in the stream.

KDA supports many built-in functions that make the task of data filtering, aggregation, and transformation easy to build. Since it's a fully managed and highly scalable service, this allows for sub-second latency for analyzing the data that's passing through the stream. You can also use many types of window functions to tap into the data for your use case. The following diagram summarizes KDA's components and its ecosystem:

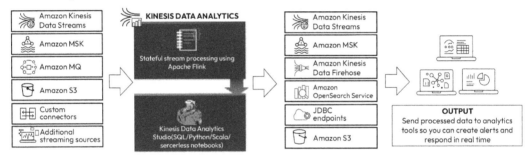

Figure 4.10 – KDA components

The support for Apache Flink makes KDA a one-stop shop for creating sophisticated streaming applications that also support stateful processing, strong data integrity, and in-memory fast processing. As always, refer to the AWS documentation to learn everything about KDA. Let's pivot toward the use case we introduced to see how KDA helps in anomaly detection.

To detect anomalies in data, KDA provides a built-in function, called a random cut forest, that leverages a machine learning algorithm to identify outliers in the data. One cool thing about Amazon Kinesis is that all its services can seamlessly chain up with each other to create the final solution.

So, for this use case, we will use KDS as the streaming ingestion platform, from which KDA can easily read the data, identify the anomaly in the data using the random cut forest function, and output the results back into a different KDS stream. You can then use a Lambda function to further process the data before it's sent out to a notification service. In our case, we will send it to a Slack channel that is being actively monitored:

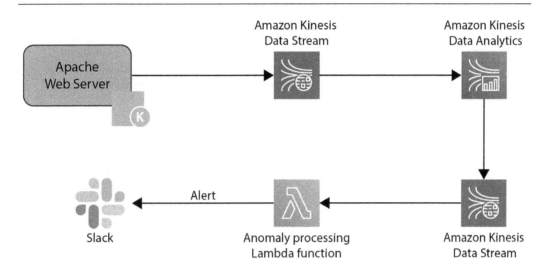

Figure 4.11 – Streaming data anomaly detection using KDA

We will cover some more usage patterns for Kinesis and how it works with other AWS services later in this book. But first, let's get into another important streaming service that revolves around the popular open source framework Apache Kafka.

Streaming data ingestion using Amazon MSK

Apache Kafka is a very popular open source distributed event streaming platform. For years now, organizations of all kinds have been using Kafka to power their event-driven systems. Kafka provides low sub-second latency and is a highly scalable framework.

One downside of using this open source framework is that you have to set up, manage, and operationalize production-grade infrastructure. This means making sure the system is highly resilient and scalable, is always patched with software updates, has all the bells and whistles, such as logging, monitoring, and notification setup, and, of course, is performant and cost-effective. Doing all this is sometimes error-prone and complex to manage.

In the era of cloud computing, organizations want all the advantages of Kafka but don't want to deal with managing all the infrastructure behind the scenes. This is where Amazon **Managed Streaming** (**MSK**) for Apache Kafka comes to the rescue. MSK takes away all the overhead of managing the infrastructure and provides a fully managed, highly available Apache Kafka service. Let's get going by introducing a use case for MSK.

> **Use case for Amazon MSK**
>
> Some **lines of business** (**LOBs**) at GreatFin want to have a real-time transactional analytics data lake that gets continuous data feed from the operational systems. This will allow them to interactively query live data, enabling real-time analytics to make quick business decisions.

From this use case, it looks like we already have multiple pieces of the data platform in place from *Chapter 2*, where we looked at creating a transactional data lake in S3 using one of the many table formats. The additional ask here is that the business wants to analyze the data as soon as it's created, updated, or deleted in the source RDBMS system. As always, there are many ways to solve this problem, but since we are on the topic of Amazon MSK, we will use a design pattern that leverages it. But first, let's get an overview of MSK itself.

Amazon MSK overview

Amazon MSK still uses the same open source Kafka releases. The big differentiation is that all the infrastructure heavy lifting is done under the hood with MSK. The topology of the Kafka cluster also remains the same, with each server instance making up the Kafka broker. The following figure shows a typical Kafka cluster setup, where producers send the events to the Kafka topics and the consumers read from it:

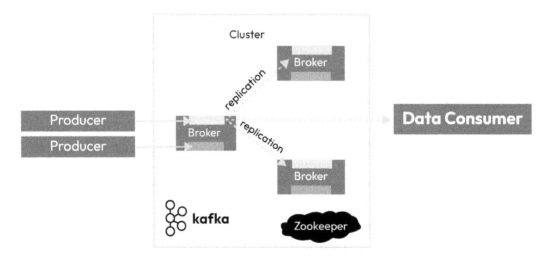

Figure 4.12 – Apache Kafka anatomy

Amazon MSK provides two types of setups; one is the provisioned setup, where you get to choose the type and count of EC2 instances you want in your cluster setup. There is a calculator utility that allows you to right-size the cluster. The provisioned model is more suitable for use when you have a steady and continuous workload; this allows you to right-size it and make it cost-optimized.

For workloads that are variable, spiky, or non-continuous, Amazon MSK also provides a serverless option, where you don't need to worry about rightsizing the infrastructure. The service will internally manage the scaling part and you get charged for the data volume you stream and retain.

In essence, MSK allows developers to focus more on developing their applications and less on managing the infrastructure. It makes Apache Kafka more secure, highly available, and accessible throughout your organization for all streaming use cases.

Now, the other puzzle we need to solve is: what are the best ways for the producers and consumers to connect to the Kafka cluster so that the streaming data pipeline is easy to set up? That's where Kafka Connect comes to help. It's a module in the Kafka ecosystem that allows developers to easily connect to many of the data producers and consumers without writing a lot of boilerplate code. Amazon MSK also extends that same module to have its own MSK Connect module. For our use case, we will also use MSK Connect to connect to the producer and the consumer.

Now, let's get back to the use case we introduced earlier, where the business wants data in real time for analytics. Let's consider one of the source systems as Amazon Aurora, a relational database service that supports PostgreSQL as well as MySQL databases. To get real-time data flowing into our transactional data lake, we need to capture the change data from the source and use any one of the transactional table formats used in the S3 data lake.

Figure 4.13 shows the architecture for solving our use case. MSK Connect helps connect the producer to the cluster, which in our case is Amazon Aurora. It also helps connect to the consumer, which in our case is the Apache Hudi process in the data lake. You can use other table formats too, depending on the specifics of your use case. Once the data has been processed by Hudi and placed in the conformed layer of the S3 data lake, the data is ready for real-time analytics through the use of interactive SQL analytics reports or the creation of BI visualizations:

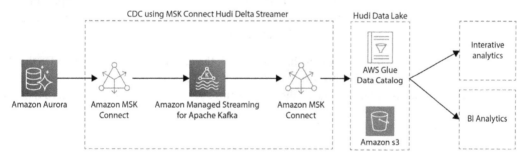

Figure 4.13 – Event streaming architecture using Amazon MSK

Now that we have covered all our streaming services, let's look at how we can create hybrid architecture patterns to solve other types of streaming use cases.

Streaming services usage patterns

Any architecture pattern you come up with for your organization's use case has many dimensions to it. Some of the factors that influence these decisions are overall costs, the specifics of functional and non-functional requirements, people skillsets, future use cases, preference for a specific service, and so forth. Let's get into some other use cases that can be solved using a combination of the AWS streaming services we covered in this chapter.

> **Use case for streaming change data in S3 data lakes**
>
> The IT team likes using AWS DMS to capture change data from relational databases into the raw zone of the data lake. However, DMS creates tons of tiny files that then need to be consolidated into the conformed layer of the data lake in S3. For many data sources, this setup works well and the data pipeline is performant and cost-effective. However, for certain extremely large ERP systems, the volume of CDC data generates millions of tiny files, all dumped into a single S3 bucket prefix. This makes the data pipeline cumbersome to manage and difficult to debug and reprocess when there are failures. The team is looking to optimize this solution for such ERP sources.

If you recall from *Chapter 3*, we used DMS to ingest batch data into the S3 data lake. We also used its CDC capability to get all the changes that happen in the source database. Once we have all this data coming in the raw layer of S3, we can run another batch job to read all these tiny CDC files and finally consolidate them into the conformed layer of S3 in optimized Parquet files. Now, in this case, since the ERP system generates tons of changes to the data at any given period, the raw layer gets inundated with all these small files.

What if we somehow figure out a way to create bigger-sized files, typically around 100 MB, partition in time-based prefixes in S3, and store the raw data in Parquet format? This would make the final consolidation process smoother and the data pipeline can be simplified too.

Figure 4.14 describes this architecture where, instead of S3 as the target for DMS, we make KDS the target, which can then be chained with Kinesis Data Firehose. Finally, Firehose will put the final data files in S3. This way, you can leverage all the great features of Firehose to get an optimized data structure in the data lake:

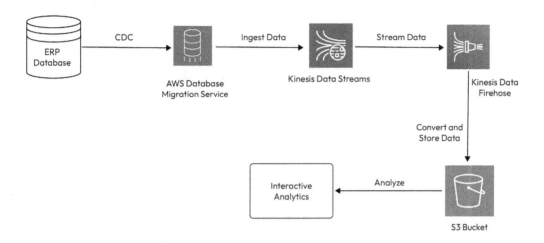

Figure 4.14 – CDC data pipeline using DMS and Kinesis

Let's look at one more use case from GreatFin.

> **Use case for click stream conversions**
>
> The consumer finance LOB uses data analytics to understand which products their consumers are browsing for on the web. Based on the click stream data, the business will check the conversation rate, identify any anomalies in the conversion, and analyze all the data from the click streams to provide a better marketing campaign.

As the web consumers of GreatFin click on various products and services, valuable information is generated about the consumers' behavior, including what products were looked at versus what products were purchased. All this data can be funneled into the data platform as events data.

First, this data is captured and stored by KDS. From there, the pipeline gets forked into two paths – the first one uses Kinesis Data Firehose to collect all the raw data into the S3 data lake, whereas the other path goes via KDA, where conversion rates are calculated over a window of time and any anomalies detected in the conversion are sent out as notifications via an SNS message. The Lambda function is used to process the final anomaly message before it is sent out. There is another Firehose database that stores all the conversion data in the S3 data lake.

The reason I have brought this use case up is to show you the synergies of the AWS services and how they all chain up together to create a seamless data pipeline. There might be multiple more paths that your use case will take you through but always try to use a purpose-built service to get the job done instead of forcing a single service to be the jack of all trades. *Figure 4.15* shows the entire streaming data pipeline we just discussed for our click stream use case:

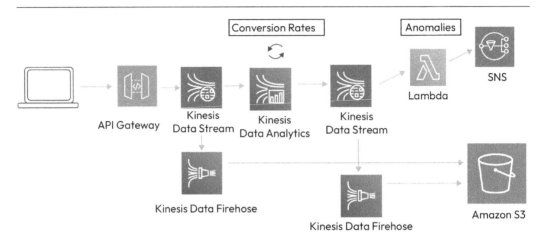

Figure 4.15 – Multiple Kinesis services working together

There are many more streaming use cases, some of which we will introduce as and when we discover those topics in the upcoming chapters of this book. Meanwhile, if you are curious to try some hands-on labs for Kinesis and MSK, don't forget to try the workshops I've put in the *References* section at the end.

Before I close this chapter, one more key component for streaming is Spark structured streaming. Apache Spark also has a streaming component, mainly for processing the data it receives continuously. However, Spark Streaming is typically used during the data processing stage. In the next chapter, as we embark on the topic of data processing and data transformations, we will look at a use case for Spark Streaming.

Summary

In this chapter, we looked at how businesses benefit by leveraging real-time data for analytics. We introduced Amazon Kinesis Streams, Amazon Data Firehose, and Kinesis Data Analytics as the streaming services we would use in modern data architecture and how customers leverage these services in their data platform. We also looked at Apache Kafka as an open source framework for supporting streaming use cases and how Amazon MSK provides a scalable, secure, easy-to-manage, and cost-effective platform for using Kafka as the data streaming engine. We also looked at some other use cases that leverage a combination of streaming services put together to create a seamless data pipeline using purpose-built AWS services. Streaming use cases always come up in everything we do, so look out for some more design patterns later in this book. Enjoy doing the hands-on workshops in the next chapter!

References

- Amazon Kinesis workshop: `https://catalog.us-east-1.prod.workshops.aws/workshops/2300137e-f2ac-4eb9-a4ac-3d25026b235f/en-US`

- Amazon MSK workshop: `https://catalog.us-east-1.prod.workshops.aws/workshops/c2b72b6f-666b-4596-b8bc-bafa5dcca741/en-US`

5
Data Processing

In this chapter, we will look at the following key topics:

- Challenges with data processing platforms
- Data processing using Amazon EMR
- Data processing using AWS Glue
- Data processing using AWS Glue DataBrew

Let's quickly recap what we have covered so far in this book. We set the foundation by creating the layers of a data lake on Amazon S3. The layers represent distinct storage areas where all the data can exist in a centralized location. The next piece of the puzzle we solved was to get data from disparate sources into the raw layer of the data lake in S3. Then, we spent the whole of *Chapter 3* looking at batch data ingestion mechanisms, followed by *Chapter 4*, where we discussed streaming data ingestion mechanisms.

So, till this point, all the data is in the raw layer of S3; of course, it can also go directly to the conformed layer, if you have processed and optimized the data on the fly during the ingestion process. If you recall from *Chapter 2*, we discussed how data flows between each layer of the data lake, and at every layer, the data is processed/transformed. The data transformations can be technical in nature—for example, the data flow from the raw to the standardized layer undergoes data quality checks, or the transformations can also be based on business rules, specifically when the data flows from the standardized to the conformed layer and from the conformed to the enriched layer.

This quick recap brings us to the central theme of this chapter: how do we transform all this data, and which tools/services should we use to further build our data processing pipeline? This is where we look at a few more AWS services that can help there. But before we get into the details, let's look at some challenges with data processing platforms in general.

Challenges with data processing platforms

Data processing or data transformation is an essential part of any data pipeline, and data engineers play a big role in making sure that the data reaches its final destination, where it's ready for consumption. In the recent decade, the volume, velocity, and variety of data have made data processing challenging. Data turned into big data, and processing all this data in a sequential manner using powerful monolithic systems turned out to be inefficient. Data processing techniques took a positive direction when a horizontal scaling framework using **Apache Hadoop** was created. Hadoop was able to process big data much more efficiently using many commodities' hardware.

Even though Hadoop was promising, *the MapReduce way* of processing big data was not fast enough for many organizations. The creation of **Apache Spark** changed the way we process data, and even today, many modern data processing systems and platforms primarily use Spark as the go-to in-memory-distributed data processing framework of choice.

This chapter gets into the details of how AWS supports the Spark framework, but first, it's important to understand the challenges of any big data processing system; in order to drive home the point as to why we should use AWS data processing services when building a modern data architecture platform.

Let us walk through many of these challenges around data processing. These challenges can be with data processing systems deployed on-premises, in the cloud, or even hybrid.

Challenge 1 – Fixed costs for an on-premises data processing platform

This is a big challenge, especially when setting up a big data processing platform in the on-premises infrastructure. Since Hadoop and Spark need a large number of compute instances, it's really difficult to right-size the infrastructure. This forces organizations to enter into multi-year commitments for hardware, software, and their associated support fees. So, even though data processing is fast, the fixed capital cost is difficult to sustain year over year as workloads grow bigger.

Challenge 2 – Compute is always on, even when not required

In the on-premises world, since organizations procure hardware upfront for peak workload demands, the infrastructure is frequently underutilized and sometimes not utilized at all. This results in compounded inefficiencies in the data processing platform.

Challenge 3 – Tight coupling between the storage and compute layers

This is a big challenge for many reasons. With Hadoop and Spark, the **Hadoop Distributed File System (HDFS)** is the default filesystem for storage in on-premises infrastructure. This means that compute and storage are tightly coupled together. To make the data available all the time, even during failures, a lot of redundancy needs to be baked in, which again balloons up the costs of maintaining this system.

Challenge 4 – Scalability issues

Even though extra hardware is provisioned initially, many times workloads may vary significantly; this requires additional infrastructure to be set up, leading to slower data processing and even job failures due to inadequate scalable infrastructure. Scalability issues eventually affect business outcomes.

Challenge 5 – Operational issues

This challenge is not just with on-premises infrastructure but also relates to self-managed big data platforms created in the cloud. A self-managed Spark cluster constantly needs patching, upgrades, maintenance, fine-tuning, and so forth. These operational overheads often force organizations to spend a lot more on managing the data processing platform itself, which creates an imbalance in the **return on investment (ROI)**.

Challenge 6 – Limited capabilities

Even after spending so much effort, resources, and money, the data processing platform still has limited capabilities. This is due to the fact that a data processing platform can have many features and functionalities, and incorporating all of them in a single platform is difficult and time-consuming. On top of this, the data processing platform requires a lot of IT intervention, which creates a bottleneck with semi-technical business personas, who demand more and more self-service data analytics capabilities.

Challenge 7 – Third-party vendor lock-in

There are many independent software providers in the data processing space. Also referred to as **extract, transform, load (ETL)** vendors, they help organizations to focus on their business outcomes versus managing the data processing platform. However, there is always the fear of vendor lock-in, as the data pipelines created on the vendor's platform only work with their products, which makes it difficult for organizations to migrate away from it, if the need arises in the future.

We could go on and on with the challenges of creating and maintaining data processing platforms. However, by describing some of the aforementioned challenges, we now have a good understanding as to why there is a need to have better data processing services that can help different personas in the organization manage and operate the data processing platform. This is a great time for us to pivot toward how AWS helps in making data processing easy. Let's first start with a very popular data processing platform in AWS.

Data processing using Amazon EMR

Amazon EMR is a platform that enables big data processing at a scale. It's a managed service that contains over 20 open source frameworks, including popular data processing engines such as Hadoop, Spark, Hive, Presto, and Trino. It was specifically created keeping in mind all the challenges we went through with a data processing platform.

There is so much information about EMR that a separate book exists that describes in detail each and every aspect of EMR. However, the purpose of this book is not to explain all of these aspects in detail but to understand when EMR can be used and which use cases it helps to solve. But let's first get an overview of EMR.

Amazon EMR overview

EMR provides all the necessary tools that are required to process data at scale. EMR manages the underlying software and hardware needed to provide a cost-effective, scalable, and easy-to-manage data platform. The best way to get an overview of a service is to understand what it brings to the table, so let's quickly look at all the benefits of using EMR:

- **Separation of compute from storage** allows the EMR clusters to be turned off when there are no workloads to be processed. This separation is achieved due to the fact that data is stored in Amazon S3 and EMR is able to read from S3 and write to S3, instead of HDFS. This transparent way of dealing with S3 using the **EMR File System** (**EMRFS**) connector allows all existing Hadoop ecosystem frameworks to work seamlessly with S3 as the storage layer.

- **Built-in disaster recovery** (**DR**) allows the EMR cluster to keep operating even if certain nodes go down. And since the data is highly durable and available in S3, even in the event of compute issues, the data is still safe for reprocessing.

- EMR provides **multiple versions of open source projects to choose from**, and the latest version is updated in EMR within 30 days of getting released in the community version. This allows organizations to leverage the latest features from these projects.

- **An EMR cluster can auto-scale depending on the workloads**. This not only ensures that jobs get completed within the desired timeframe but also ensures that idle compute is scaled down so that unnecessary cost is not incurred.

- With **four modes of setup**—EMR on **Amazon Elastic Compute Cloud** (**Amazon EC2**), EMR on **Amazon Elastic Kubernetes Service** (**Amazon EKS**), EMR Serverless, and EMR on AWS Outposts, organizations can pick and choose the best kind of deployment based on specific jobs or applications. More details on types of EMR setups can be found in the AWS documentation portal (`https://docs.aws.amazon.com`).

- **EMR can also leverage spot instances** to bring costs substantially down, sometimes providing savings of up to 90% of the on-demand pricing.

- **Performance improvements in the EMR runtime**, for Apache Spark and other projects, make running Spark on EMR faster than the open source version of Spark. Also, with custom Graviton instances on AWS, Spark performance is improved even more.

- **Integrated with EMR Studio**, which makes collaborative work using Jupyter Notebook easier for data engineers and data scientists.

- **Provides extensive security options**, including authentication, authorization, encryption, infrastructure protection, logging, monitoring, and notifications.

- Finally, all the integration synergies with other AWS services make the analytics ecosystem even more **powerful, cost-effective, and easy to leverage**.

The following diagram shows a high-level architecture of an EMR cluster. It consists of a leader node(s) that manages the cluster; the core nodes provide compute, memory, and storage; and the task nodes only provide additional compute and memory, making it a perfect choice for assigning spot instances to it:

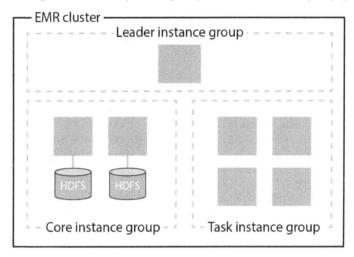

Figure 5.1 – EMR cluster architecture

An EMR cluster also provides the flexibility to assign different types of compute instances depending on the type of workload. The following diagram highlights the types of instances and the scenarios where they are beneficial:

General Purpose	Compute Intensive	Memory Intensive	Storage Intensive
M5 Family	C5 Family	R5 Family	D3 Family
M6g Family	C6g Family	R6g Family	I4 Family
M7g Family	C7g Family	R7g Family	
Batch Process	**Machine Learning**	**Interactive Analysis Apache Spark**	**Large HDFS**

Figure 5.2 – EMR compute flexibility

Typically, EMR is used for the migration of large self-managed Hadoop clusters or processing extremely large datasets that can benefit from the price performance of the EMR platform. The data processing projects that are in EMR are geared toward data engineers who can create Spark jobs in EMR and build their ETL pipelines.

Let's understand the usefulness of EMR by highlighting some use cases from GreatFin.

Use-case scenario 1 – Big data platform migration

Use case for Amazon EMR

Many years ago, GreatFin embarked on a journey to create a centralized big data processing platform by leveraging open source frameworks such as Hadoop, Spark, and Hive. The platform was created on-premises, and the team was able to customize and operationalize this platform so that data engineers could build data pipelines for their respective **lines of business** (**LOBs**).

Due to recent exponential growth in data, many visible cracks have started to appear in the home-grown big data platform—scalability issues, reliability issues, multiple outages, constant upgrades and maintenance, performance issues, and, of course, growing costs. All these challenges have led GreatFin to lose focus on business outcomes. The leadership team now wants to remove all barriers from its data processing platform so that everyone spends more time on business outcomes and less time on managing the data processing platform.

This use case clearly highlights the challenges of self-managing a big data processing platform. We will look at how Amazon EMR can alleviate the pain points around this use case.

If you recall from *Chapter 2*, we discussed different table formats for setting up a transactional data lake in S3. EMR supports these table formats to provide the perfect execution engine for processing all data between the layers of the data lake. Also, EMR can read the metadata of the data from the Glue Data Catalog. This whole setup makes EMR a perfect service to process and transform the data that goes into the data lake in S3. The following diagram highlights this aspect of EMR:

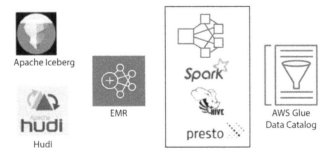

Figure 5.3 – EMR projects and their seamless support for transactional data lakes

This use case requires the migration of the data processing platform from a self-managed to an AWS-managed EMR platform. This will allow the data engineers to focus more on business-specific tasks and less on managing and maintaining the infrastructure behind them. Also, by moving to EMR, GreatFin will not only get all the benefits of EMR but will also be able to substantially bring down the **total cost of ownership (TCO)** of its data processing platform.

The following diagram highlights the flow of how EMR sits in between the data layers in the S3 data lake so that it can seamlessly process and transform data as it passes through the different layers:

Figure 5.4 – EMR as the data progressing platform in the S3 data lake

Let's look at another typical use case where EMR comes in really handy.

Use-case scenario 2 – Collaborative data engineering

Use case for Amazon EMR Studio

Data engineers at GreatFin have been building data pipelines for many years now; however, that whole process is isolated per team and is cumbersome to prototype, test, and debug. Overall, it's not easy to collaborate and build new data processing applications, and the whole process is far from being agile.

For data engineers, Jupyter notebooks are central to their line of work as it allows developers to test code before they can deploy it. However, managing these notebooks is not trivial. Data engineers or even data scientists need to focus less on the notebook infrastructure and more on the business logic they need to create. They need an easy way to build applications by collaborating with others in the team. They need all the bells and whistles that would make it easy for them to test, debug, and deploy code in production. That's where EMR Studio comes into the picture.

EMR Studio is a fully managed IDE within the EMR service that allows for interactive data analytics. It has fully managed Jupyter notebooks, integration with GitHub repositories, a simplified UI for debugging code, an easy way to create and delete EMR clusters, integration with workflow orchestration services, and so forth.

The following diagram is a typical flow for data engineers to make it easy for them to bring their work from the prototype phase all the way into production, with the least amount of time and effort:

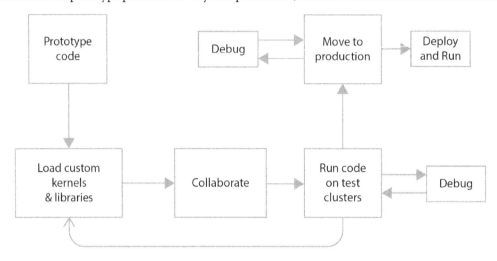

Figure 5.5 – Typical data engineering workflow

EMR has over 20 open source projects that cater to different aspects of data; we will not get into use cases for each of them in this book. However, we will come back to EMR in our future chapters to discuss certain frameworks that would come in handy to solve those particular use cases. For now, let's move on to our beloved service that has come up in most chapters so far—AWS Glue for data processing.

Data processing using AWS Glue

If you recall our conversations from the last few chapters, we kept bringing up AWS Glue for multiple use cases, including for data catalogs, crawlers, classifiers, and batch ingestion using connectors. Now, we come to **Glue ETL**, which is the most distinct feature of Glue. Since Glue is a fully managed and serverless service, it excels in data transformation types of tasks, usually undertaken by data engineering personas in an organization. You can create Glue ETL jobs using Spark, Python, or Ray. Spark is a common platform for creating distributed computing-based ETL jobs. Since EMR also provides Spark and Glue also has Spark, in the following table, let's try to simplify certain scenarios where you would prefer to use one over the other:

EMR typical usage	Glue ETL typical usage
Since EMR alleviates all the infrastructure and operational heavy lifting of Hadoop-based platforms, self-managed Hadoop clusters are often migrated to EMR	Quick data processing jobs using low-code/no-code data transformation with the help of drag-and-drop UI features
Process large amounts of data on a daily basis where the business is sensitive to the price performance of the platform	Wide range of source and target connectors that make it easy to create ETL jobs, without having to write boilerplate code
Customized data warehouse using Hive and customized analytics cluster using PrestoDB/Trino	Serverless environment for execution of Python and Ray jobs
Complex custom data processing pipelines	Workflow environment for scheduling and orchestration of jobs
Collaborative data processing environment using Jupyter and Zeppelin notebooks	Quick creation of blueprint-based data migration jobs

Even EMR has a serverless offering, but Glue specializes in the creation and execution of Spark-based data transformations, whereas EMR helps with a wide variety of use cases by leveraging other types of open source projects.

Since we have already covered the basics of Glue, let's dive straight into some data processing use cases for Glue ETL.

Use-case scenario 1 – ETL pipelines using Spark

Use-case for AWS Glue ETL

GreatFin is modernizing its enterprise data warehouse and has identified all the source systems that will feed into the data warehouse on a nightly basis. LOBs are looking to provide their data engineers with an ETL tool that will allow them to embrace Apache Spark and also let them focus on the data processing aspect instead of managing the Spark environment, including hardware and software.

Key words in this use case are *Spark*, *ease of use*, and *no provisioning of hardware and software*. Just to reiterate, you can solve this with so many different services, but AWS Glue stands out due to its cost-effective and scalable platform. As I mentioned in the previous chapters, Glue has a lot of features and provides an umbrella of services. One of the most popular features of Glue is its ETL service, which is used by data engineers to perform data processing. As the data in the S3 data lake flows between different layers from raw all the way to enriched, a lot of ETL jobs need to be created. At every step, data transformation occurs by applying technical or business rules.

The following diagram demonstrates the use of Glue ETL to perform data processing for the use case we introduced earlier in this session. In this case, the source is Amazon S3 and the target is an enterprise data warehouse. All the data processing in the middle is done by Glue ETL:

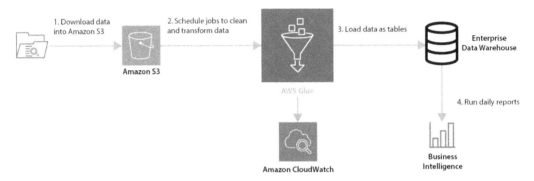

Figure 5.6 – Typical data engineering workflow

The preceding use case is a typical pattern for data processing for batches of data. Setting this data processing job using Glue Studio is straightforward. All you have to do is use the drag-and-drop features in the visual editor of Glue Studio, then add the source, any transformations, and the target. The following screenshot shows a sample visual job in Glue Studio for loading data from S3 into Amazon Redshift, which is a data warehouse. We will cover Redshift in a separate chapter, but this simple drag-and-drop feature in Glue creates the job we want for our use case. You can create complete multi-step jobs using many of the transformations available in Glue Studio:

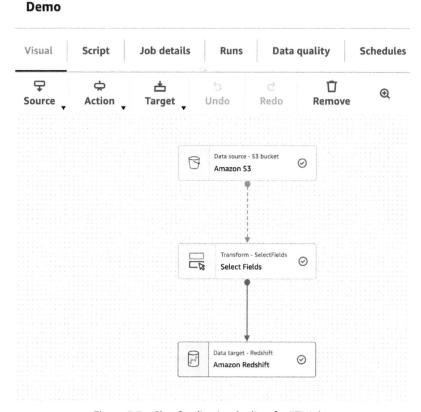

Figure 5.7 – Glue Studio visual editor for ETL jobs

The best thing about Glue Studio is that it generates the necessary code from the visual transformations, and it still gives data engineers the ability to modify and refine the code. Here is the sample code Glue Studio generated for the preceding ETL job, in the **Script** tab:

```
import sys
from awsglue.transforms import *
from awsglue.utils import getResolvedOptions
from pyspark.context import SparkContext
from awsglue.context import GlueContext
from awsglue.job import Job

args = getResolvedOptions(sys.argv, ["JOB_NAME"])
sc = SparkContext()
glueContext = GlueContext(sc)
spark = glueContext.spark_session
job = Job(glueContext)
job.init(args["JOB_NAME"], args)
```

```
# Script generated for node Amazon S3
AmazonS3_node1674520548705 = glueContext.create_dynamic_frame.from_
options(
    format_options={},
    connection_type="s3",
    format="parquet",
    connection_options={"paths": ["s3://aws-glue-bgi-data"],
        "recurse": True},
    transformation_ctx="AmazonS3_node1674520548705",
)


# Script generated for node Select Fields
SelectFields_node1674520595819 = SelectFields.apply(
    frame=AmazonS3_node1674520548705,
    paths=[],
    transformation_ctx="SelectFields_node1674520595819",
)


# Script generated for node Amazon Redshift
AmazonRedshift_node1674520619102 = glueContext.write_dynamic_frame.
from_catalog(
    frame=SelectFields_node1674520595819,
    database="glue-demo",
    table_name="s3_nyctaxi",
    redshift_tmp_dir=args["TempDir"],
    transformation_ctx="AmazonRedshift_node1674520619102",
)


job.commit()
```

As you can see from the preceding snippet, Glue Studio generated all the code, which can be modified by the data engineers. Data engineers save a lot of time by not having to manually write all the Spark code. This allows for faster rollout of ETL jobs in the production environment.

When streaming data gets ingested in real time, the processing of this data also needs to be done in real time. This is where Glue streaming comes into the picture. In *Chapter 4*, we introduced multiple AWS services to onboard and process streaming data. Glue streaming is particularly helpful for complex data processing in near real time. Let's introduce a use case to drive home the point.

Use-case scenario 2 – ETL for streaming data

Use case for AWS Glue streaming ETL

Some LOBs at GreatFin want to access transitional data from some critical applications in near real time for analytical purposes so that they can make instant decisions based on the data. They don't want to build reports on the **relational database management system (RDBMS)** database as it will impact the application's performance. The business wants to get the change data transformed and synced up from the source system into the data lake in near real time so that business analysts can create ad hoc reports on this data.

The bottom line is the business wants the latest copy of the data, as it changes in the source system, to be made available in the target data lake as soon as possible. The key point here is **change data capture (CDC)** in the data lake is desired. This brings us back to one of the many transactional table formats we discussed—Hudi, Iceberg, and Delta Lake. The other requirement is that the source data needs to be transformed. To summarize the architecture, we first need to build a transactional data lake in S3. The CDC data from the source database is captured as events, and this data is then transformed and the changes consolidated in the data lake before it can be consumed by the data analyst.

To process streaming data, Glue streaming is a perfect service to perform complex transformations on streaming data, which means data transformations—including a lot of table joins and aggregations—are handled with ease with Spark Streaming. Glue streaming handles all the Spark Streaming infrastructure behind the scenes in a scalable manner.

You might have heard me say this many times, but I'll repeat it again. A particular use case can be architected in many ways using many services. A lot of services have overlapping features and functionalities. So, even though we could just use Amazon Kinesis itself to process the data, we chose Glue streaming in this case as the data processing and data consolidation requirements were complex.

The following diagram highlights the architectural pattern. **Database Migration Service (DMS)** would capture the changes from the source database and send the changes to **Kinesis Data Streams (KDS)**. KDS is the streaming platform for capturing and storing streaming data. The complex data processing is done inside the Glue streaming platform, and finally, Hudi tables are created so that the final consolidated data is available for ad hoc queries, using a query processing engine such as Amazon Athena:

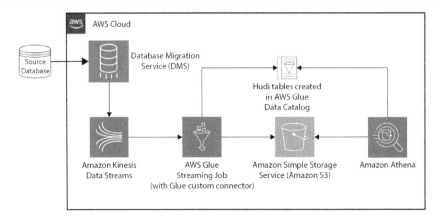

Figure 5.8 – Glue streaming architectural pattern

Glue is a versatile service, and data engineers love the serverless Spark engine in Glue for creating complex data processing pipelines. But not everyone is a data engineer in the organization, and sometimes you need business analysts and other less technical personas to also understand patterns in data and create data processing rules, without having to write code. This brings us to another data processing service at AWS, built specifically in mind for business analysts who want to use a more visual and intuitive service for discovering data patterns and applying data processing rules to them.

Data processing using AWS Glue DataBrew

In the quest to build an end-to-end data platform, IT teams in organizations spend a significant amount of time creating data processing ETL pipelines. Typically, data processing is the responsibility of data engineers, who have to understand the rules of data transformations and then implement them. This means that other personas in the organization, such as data scientists or data analysts, have to rely on data engineers to help them with the structure of data they are looking for in their day-to-day tasks. The change cycles involve ETL, normalizing, cleaning the data, and finally, orchestrating and deploying in automated data pipelines. The whole process takes weeks and sometimes months. This creates a bottleneck and delays the final business outcomes.

AWS Glue DataBrew solves this exact problem by providing a serverless, no-code data preparation service, specifically targeted at data scientists and data analysts. With DataBrew, end users can visually explore any amount of data easily from the data lake, data warehouse, or database. Without writing any code, users can do data processing by leveraging 250+ built-in functions to combine, transpose, or pivot data using the DataBrew UI. DataBrew provides transformations for data cleaning, normalization, and aggregation, along with transformations for correcting invalid, misclassified, or duplicated data.

Users can also save all these data transformation steps in the form of recipes, which can then be automatically applied to any new incoming data. Overall, it provides a very intuitive and visual way of understanding data patterns and applying data processing logic without writing any code. This makes the overall ETL process faster to implement for data scientists and data analysts.

The following screenshots show how the whole UI of DataBrew makes data profiling and data processing easy without any coding:

Figure 5.9 – Glue DataBrew UI

The following diagram illustrates where DataBrew fits in among different personas in the organization:

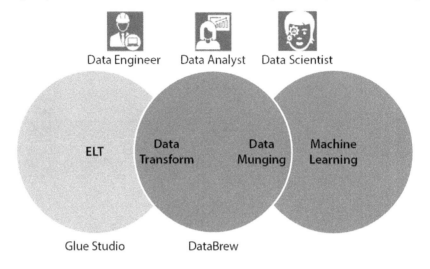

Figure 5.10 – AWS Glue DataBrew positioning

Let's introduce one of the use cases for DataBrew to highlight the usage pattern in the overall data platform.

Use-case scenario – Low-code/no-code visual data processing

Use case for AWS Glue DataBrew

GreatFin has a managed file transfer mechanism for some LOBs, where different format data files arrive in an ad hoc manner from external vendors. The end outcome is to parse these files, apply some technical and business rules to the data, and make it available for dashboard reporting. As this mechanism is an ad hoc and one-time activity every month, the IT team is looking to provide a no-code solution that can be used by a data analyst to profile the data in the files and apply data processing rules before it can be made available for **business intelligence (BI)** reports.

The use case is straightforward and typical for using DataBrew as a solution. The following diagram establishes the architectural pattern to solve this use case. The file transfer mechanism would place the files in Amazon S3, and the data analysts can get the file from S3 using DataBrew, profile the data, apply any of the built-in transformation functions available within the service, and output the data in another S3 location for the BI reporting tool to visualize the data for the business. This is a typical use case for using DataBrew effectively, without having to spend time on a lot of development cycles:

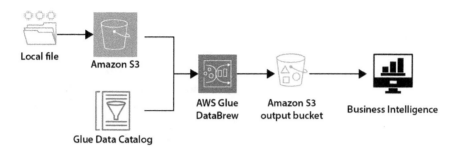

Figure 5.11 – DataBrew for no-code, ad hoc data processing

Before we wrap up this chapter, I want to bring together all the components of AWS Glue to highlight how AWS Glue helps solve so many use cases for data and analytics and assists multiple personas in the organization to make their day-to-day tasks easier. The following diagram summarizes all the different features and components of AWS Glue and how each of them works in tandem in the data platform ecosystem:

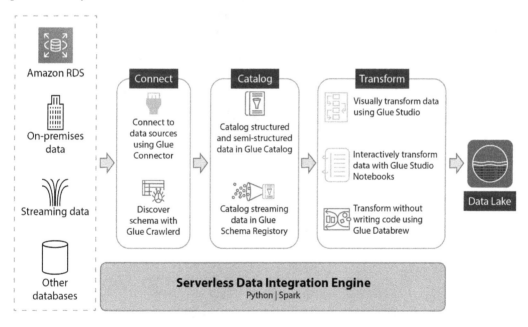

Figure 5.12 – AWS Glue components in the overall data platform

Summary

In this chapter, we covered a major topic around data processing in the modern data architecture journey. We looked at how you can use Amazon EMR to solve many big-data processing use cases. EMR provides a fully managed platform for many open source projects, including the most popular ones—Spark, Hive, and Presto. We also revisited AWS Glue and looked at how Glue Studio assists data engineers in creating complex ETL jobs for data processing. We also covered a Glue streaming use case and how it complements the other streaming services that AWS provides. Finally, we looked at AWS Glue DataBrew and how it assists data scientists and data analysts to quickly profile data and apply data processing rules in an intuitive manner.

There are many more use cases that can be solved using some of these services, but at least what we covered in this chapter gives a basic understanding of solving typical use cases for these services. As always, the best way to learn is to be hands-on and implement solutions in the AWS account. I've provided some workshop links next so that you can practice what we learned in this chapter.

So far, we have looked at setting up data lakes in AWS, along with data ingestion and data processing. Now, the data is ready for consumption. Data can be consumed in so many different ways with so many different services. We will cover data consumption patterns in detail in the next few chapters. Let's start with interactive analytics first.

References

- Amazon EMR workshop: `https://catalog.us-east-1.prod.workshops.aws/workshops/c86bd131-f6bf-4e8f-b798-58fd450d3c44/en-US`

- AWS Glue workshop: `https://catalog.us-east-1.prod.workshops.aws/workshops/ee59d21b-4cb8-4b3d-a629-24537cf37bb5/en-US`

- AWS Glue DataBrew workshop: `https://catalog.us-east-1.prod.workshops.aws/workshops/6532bf37-3ad2-4844-bd26-d775a31ce1fa/en-US`

6
Interactive Analytics

In this chapter, we will look at the following key topics:

- Analytics using Amazon Athena
- Analytics using Presto, Trino, and Hive on Amazon EMR

One of the fundamental principles of building a modern data architecture on AWS is hinged around using purpose-built tools for solving specific use cases. An enterprise data platform once fully built has many components, each with a specific purpose for solving a particular business use case.

In *Chapter 2, Scalable Data Lakes*, we went through the fundamentals of building a data lake on AWS using Amazon S3 as the storage layer and the AWS Glue Data Catalog as the technical metadata layer. Each layer of the data lake has data that may be of use to different personas in an organization. The most basic ask from each of these personas will be to provide them the ability to query datasets in the data lake using the SQL syntax so that they can derive insights from the data. Interactive analytics, using specific tools and services, allow these personas to query the data from the data lake so that they can use the results to derive insights for their organization.

Interactively querying the data in the S3 data lake is one of the very basic use cases that are expected out of any modern data platform. Many personas in the organization, including data engineers, data analytics, and data scientists, leverage the interactive analytics option to do their day-to-day job. Every persona has a specific task to do, and they just want the ability to write and execute SQL queries to get data from multiple datasets in the data lake, in a tabular output format. In other words, they don't want to spend any time managing the infrastructure behind the interactive query engine.

This brings another AWS service to the forefront, **Amazon Athena**. Let's dig into the details of Athena and look at the kinds of use cases it helps to solve.

Analytics using Amazon Athena

Amazon Athena is a serverless service that allows anyone to interactively query data in an S3 data lake using **American National Standards Institute** (**ANSI**) SQL. Athena is integrated with the Glue Data Catalog, which means that as soon as the metadata about the data is captured in the catalog, Athena is able to view and query those tables without any additional setup.

With no infrastructure to manage, along with direct out-of-the-box integration with Glue Data Catalog, this makes Athena a very popular service for multiple personas in the organization for interactive and ad hoc analytics. And being a serverless service, the pricing model of the service, 5 dollars per terabyte of data scanned, is also very appealing to organizations. With the correct optimization techniques, you can effectively roll out Athena as the service of choice throughout your organization for all types of interactive analytics use cases, for querying the data stored in the S3 data lake.

From a business point of view, Athena has a broader impact. Let's look at some of the areas where it performs well:

- **Speed**: As a fully managed and serverless service, Athena helps business applications with faster **time to market** (**TTM**).

- **Agility**: Creating reports from data using Athena is a quick and iterative approach. This makes the development of **business intelligence** (**BI**) reports more agile.

- **Operational efficiency**: Athena takes away all the infrastructure heavy lifting from the users, making it operationally easy to manage.

- **Cost optimization**: The pay-as-you-query model with Athena helps reduce costs.

Since this book is about applying AWS service features to solve specific business problems, we will have a quick glance at the basics of Athena and then dive straight into the use cases.

Amazon Athena basics

Under the covers, Athena uses Trino (`https://trino.io`), which is an open source SQL query engine. The engine is specifically designed for interactive analytics at low latencies. You can get started by writing a SQL query in the Athena console itself. When you run the query, the query gets executed behind the scenes using the optimal number of resources, to maintain a fast performance for each query.

Athena supports many types of files and table formats in the data lake. File formats such as CSV, JSON, Parquet, and **Optimized Row Columnar** (**ORC**) are supported out of the box, and table formats such as Apache Iceberg-, Apache Hudi-, and AWS Lake Formation-governed tables are also supported. The following is a screenshot from the Athena console, showing different aspects of an interactive query:

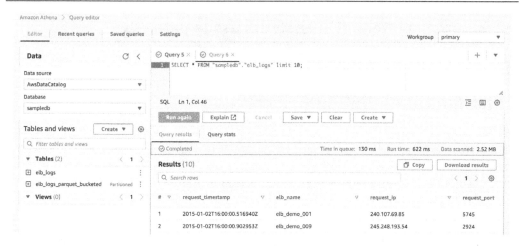

Figure 6.1 – Amazon Athena query editor

Athena is a multitenant architecture. Resources are isolated across different AWS accounts, and isolation is also supported within the same AWS account using workgroups. Using Athena workgroups inside an account allows different users, teams, or applications to isolate their workloads. Account admins can set usage controls or thresholds either at the workgroup level or even at the query level. Workgroups also make it easy to log, monitor, and debug queries.

The following diagram highlights this multitenancy architecture of Athena using workgroups:

Figure 6.2 – Amazon Athena workgroups

Athena also has a lot of other features; let's cover some of them in terms of how they can help solve business use cases.

Amazon Athena interactive analytics usage patterns

Using our financial company, GreatFin, let's look at some use cases where Athena will fit well.

> **Use case for serverless interactive analytics reports**
>
> Data analysts across all **lines of business (LOBs)** at GreatFin want the ability to create self-service reports and also leverage these reports for building BI dashboards. Some datasets, especially in the securities LOB, are hundreds of terabytes in size. They want the agility to derive insights from their data without having to deal with infrastructure complexity and IT support. Also, high performance, tight security, and low operational costs are of prime importance to these LOBs.

What the business is asking for is precisely the reason why Amazon Athena was created — a fast, secure, performant, and serverless SQL query execution engine. Let's look at how Athena plugs into our architecture.

The following diagram shows how easily Athena can fit into the modern data architecture pattern, without any heavy infrastructure setup:

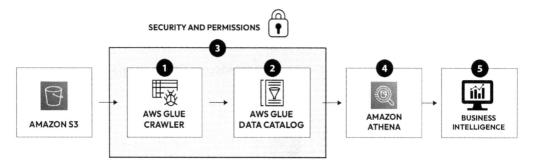

Figure 6.3 – Interactive analytics on the S3 data lake using Amazon Athena

Here are the steps for getting the data ready for consumption via Athena:

1. Glue crawlers scan the datasets in the S3 data lake and populate the Glue Data Catalog.

2. The Glue Data Catalog serves as a central metadata repository.

3. Security settings, along with permissions, are applied so that only authorized personas get access to the data. We will dive deep into this topic in our data governance chapter later in the book.

4. Once the metadata is cataloged, the business can use Athena to query the data and create analytics reports.

5. Athena allows most **Java Database Connectivity (JDBC)**-compliant tools, including BI services, to connect and create visualizations. We will cover this topic in detail in our BI chapter later in the book.

The use case we introduced for GreatFin requires the data in the S3 data lake, the metadata in the Glue Data Catalog, and finally requires a query execution engine such as Athena to create reports. The data lake may also be transactional in nature, which requires the use of any of the transactional table formats—Hudi, Iceberg, or Delta Lake. Data gets ingested from many of the source systems; we looked at batch ingestion using AWS DMS and streaming data ingestion using Amazon Kinesis in the earlier chapters. The ingested data is then processed using Amazon EMR or AWS Glue and made available in different layers of the S3 data lake, for consumption by various personas in the organization.

Amazon Athena can query this processed data from the data lake, and it also supports various transactional table formats, so let's take a look at the architecture setup of Athena with each of the table formats.

Amazon Athena with Apache Hudi

Athena supports the Hudi table format (`https://hudi.apache.org`) for querying. Once Hudi datasets are created in S3 and cataloged in Glue, Athena can then query those tables and use the many features of Hudi tables.

The following diagram highlights the overall architecture pattern for using Athena as an ad hoc analytics query engine. Data ingestion can be either batch or streaming; this data is then processed and stored as Hudi datasets, and finally, ad hoc reports can be generated by using the Athena query execution engine:

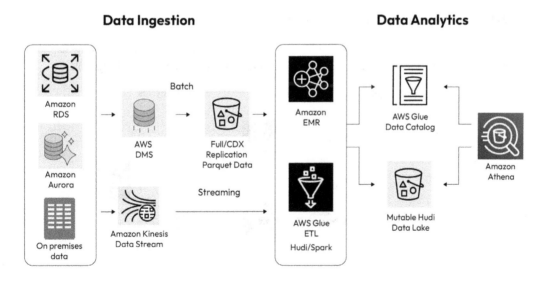

Figure 6.4 – Amazon Athena with Apache Hudi

The following code snippet is a sample DDL for the Hudi table that will be created in the Glue Data Catalog when the data processing is complete. Athena can understand this metadata and fetch the underlying Hudi datasets when a user submits a query in Athena. Note that the S3 bucket name has to be globally unique:

```
CREATE EXTERNAL TABLE demo_hudi_table(
    `_hoodie_commit_time` string,
    `_hoodie_commit_seqno` string,
    `_hoodie_record_key` string,
    `_hoodie_partition_path` string,
    `_hoodie_file_name` string,
    `id` string,
    `timestamp` string,
    `name` string,)
PARTITIONED BY (
    `date` string)
ROW FORMAT SERDE
'org.apache.hadoop.hive.ql.io.parquet.serde.ParquetHiveSerDe'
STORED AS INPUTFORMAT
'org.apache.hudi.hadoop.HoodieParquetInputFormat'
OUTPUTFORMAT
'org.apache.hadoop.hive.ql.io.parquet.MapredParquetOutputFormat'
LOCATION
's3://athena-hudi—demo-bucket/hudi_prefix'
```

Amazon Athena with Apache Iceberg

Athena can also query Iceberg tables (`https://iceberg.apache.org`). The following diagram demonstrates the architecture pattern for using Athena for ad hoc analytics for Iceberg tables:

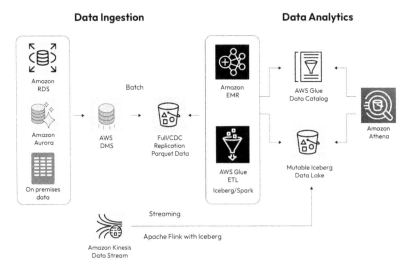

Figure 6.5 – Amazon Athena with Apache Iceberg

The following code snippet is a sample DDL for the Iceberg table that will be created in the Glue Data Catalog when the data processing is complete. Athena can understand this metadata and fetch the underlying Iceberg datasets when a user submits a query in Athena. Note that the S3 bucket name has to be globally unique. AWS Glue crawlers also support Iceberg tables:

```
CREATE TABLE demo_iceberg_table (
    id int,
    name string)
PARTITIONED BY (name, bucket(16,id))
LOCATION 's3://athena-iceberg—demo-bucket/iceberg-prefix'
TBLPROPERTIES (
    'table_type'='ICEBERG',
    'format'='PARQUET')
```

Amazon Athena with Delta Lake

Athena can also query Delta Lake format tables (https://delta.io/). The following code snippet is DDL for the Delta Lake table that will be created in the Glue Data Catalog when the data processing is complete. Athena can understand this metadata and fetch the underlying Iceberg datasets when a user submits a query in Athena. Note that the S3 bucket name has to be globally unique:

```
CREATE EXTERNAL TABLE demo_delta_table
LOCATION 's3://athena-delta—demo-bucket/delta-prefix'
TBLPROPERTIES (
    'table_type'='DELTA')
```

ETL with Amazon Athena

Athena is typically used for consuming the data from the data lake using SQL queries, so typical personas using Athena would be data analysts and data scientists. However, Athena can also assist these personas by allowing them to do quick and easy ETL operations using SQL in Athena so that they don't have to rely on data engineers to build the data pipelines for ETL. Let's discuss this with a use case from GreatFin.

> **Use case for using Amazon Athena for ETL operations**
>
> All LOBs at GreatFin have a team of data analysts who analyze the data as per the business needs and produce reports. LOBs already use many AWS services, and all the AWS service API trails get collected in AWS CloudTrail. From time to time, IT teams need to analyze the CloudTrail events to find specific data elements. They need a quick, easy, and ad hoc way to generate reports from these logs

This is the kind of use case that doesn't require a lot of data engineering. Data analysts need the ability to do quick ETL on this log data. CloudTrail provides the ability to put raw log trails in the S3 data lake and catalog the data using the Glue Data Catalog. The trail data is in raw format, meaning CloudTrail provides the events in a specific JSON format. In reality, some transformation may be needed on this data to derive specific kinds of ad hoc insights.

For the CloudTrail data in a raw layer, we need to apply some transformation before we can consume the data. Transformations can be applied on the fly in the query itself; however, many times it's more optimal to process the data first and then store the transformed results in the standardized layer of S3 so that it can be directly queried using SQL statements and reports generated from this data. Optimal file size and format are of the essence when it comes to Athena, hence the need to perform some ETL on this data before it can be queried. We will cover Athena's optimization techniques later in the book.

To achieve this kind of easy ETL using SQL, Athena provides CREATE TABLE AS (CTAS) and INSERT INTO statements that allow data analysts to create a table with the selected data transformations inside SQL itself. The CTAS statement will create a new table in the data lake and can store the transformed data in a new S3 location.

The following diagram highlights the architecture for this ETL pattern using Athena:

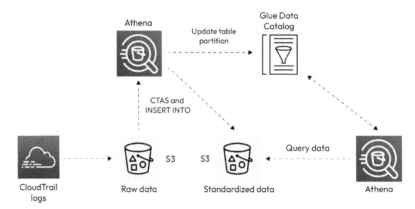

Figure 6.6 – ETL with Amazon Athena

The following sample DDL statement is what CTAS would look like. Just by using a single SQL query, users can transform raw data and store it in an optimized file format such as Parquet so that Athena can query the final standardized datasets optimally. All the data transformation logic will come in the SELECT clause of the SQL query:

```
CREATE TABLE processed_cloudtrail_table
WITH (
    external_location = 's3://unique_bucket_name/ cloudtrail_tables/',
    format = 'PARQUET')
AS SELECT *
```

```
FROM raw_cloudtrail_table
WHERE conditions;
```

Once the standardized table is created with CTAS using the initial dataset from the raw table, you can then use `INSERT INTO` statements to add new data as and when it comes into the raw table. The following sample DDL statement shows what an `INSERT INTO` statement would look like. Typically, the `conditions` clause will also have some date range so that subsequent sets of raw data can be processed and inserted into the existing standardized table that was created with the CTAS statement:

```
INSERT INTO processed_cloudtrail_table
SELECT *
FROM raw_cloudtrail_table
WHERE conditions;
```

Before we wind down the use case of doing ETL using Athena, Athena also recently came out with a functionality that allows usage of Apache Spark within the Athena console itself to explore datasets and do data engineering using Spark. This gives data analysts an integrated environment to quickly do data profiling and ETL work. This saves time since the data analysts don't have to rely on data engineers to prepare datasets for them. The fact that Apache Spark-based notebooks have made it into many data and analytics services highlights the importance of its versatility, to prepare data and draw insights from it.

The following screenshot shows an Athena notebook that is used to run Spark-based ETL code and analyze the data stored in the S3 data lake using the Glue Data Catalog:

Figure 6.7 – Amazon Athena notebook editor

So far in this chapter, we have looked at how Amazon Athena provides a serverless platform to execute interactive queries, to consume the data stored in the S3 data lake. However, organizations may sometimes prefer to build their own analytics query execution platform. Let's look at another AWS service that assists in such a use case.

Analytics using Presto, Trino, and Hive on Amazon EMR

If you recall from *Chapter 5*, we introduced Amazon EMR as one of the services for processing big data. EMR has over 25 open source projects, and we went through a use case where Apache Spark in EMR was leveraged to solve a data processing problem. EMR also has a few projects that assist in ad hoc query execution and allow users to interactively executive SQL queries to get the data stored in the S3 data lake. Let's shed some light on these projects.

Presto/Trino

Presto is an open source project that provides a fast analytics query execution engine for data stored in many types of storage, most commonly used with data stored in data lakes. Presto, also known as PrestoDB, was first created on Facebook. In 2019, Presto development eventually forked into two, with PrestoDB and PrestoSQL. To keep the name confusion at a minimum, PrestoSQL was renamed Trino in 2020.

Amazon EMR supports both PrestoDB and Trino. Organizations can pick and choose either of the two projects for building their interactive analytics platform. Let's bring up a use case for using Presto/Trino.

> **Use case for Presto/Trino on Amazon EMR**
>
> The securities LOB at GreatFin gets billions of trade transactions every day. For regulatory compliance and fraud detection, the LOB has to ingest, process, and analyze petabytes of data. It uses Amazon EMR to process the data on a daily basis and wants to create hundreds of reports that will be analyzed by hundreds of data analysts daily. The business is sensitive to the cost and performance of the reporting system. Due to the large volume of data that needs to be analyzed daily, they want to keep tight control over the costs; at the same time, they want to make sure the performance is fast and that most queries finish under tight SLAs.

For most use cases, it is preferable to use Amazon Athena as a query execution engine for performing interactive data analytics, using the data in the S3 data lake. However, the preceding use case is something that may benefit from leveraging a customized Presto/Trino cluster on EMR. Hundreds of analysts would be submitting thousands of queries every day. Since this usage pattern will scan large volumes of data on a daily basis, using auto-scaling with the Spot instance feature on EMR, they can keep the EMR cluster costs under control. At the same time, using Presto/Trino, the IT team can customize and fine-tune the cluster performance to meet the query SLAs. Also, in this case, the team can control which version of Presto/Trino it prefers and can control software upgrade cycles on its own, depending on the specific feature sets they desire from a specific release of the project.

The following diagram depicts the architecture pattern for setting up Presto on EMR. The data analyst can submit queries via the Hue interface in EMR, via the JDBC/**Open Database Connectivity** (**ODBC**) client, or via APIs; this gives flexibility and tooling options for submitting queries:

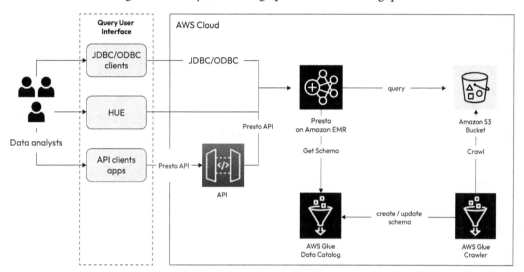

Figure 6.8 – Interactive analytics with Presto on Amazon EMR

Apache Hive

Another popular engine for analytics is Apache Hive. Hive also allows interactive analytics by providing SQL capabilities on the S3 data lake using HiveQL. Hive also has a metadata layer, but most customers building data platforms in AWS leverage the Glue Data Catalog for metadata management since it's serverless and fully managed by AWS, whereas using Hive as a metadata layer adds extra infrastructure setup and management.

Hive is evaluated as a possible query execution engine for interactive analytics on S3 data lakes for very large datasets. In today's world, there are so many service options for interactive analytics, but it's always good to evaluate Hive to see if any of its specific features would help solve the use case more optimally.

I will not go into the details of Hive in this chapter, but you can find information on Hive in much of the documentation available online (`https://hive.apache.org`). In case you decide to choose Hive for any reasons required by your use case, just keep in mind that EMR supports Hive out of the box.

There are many more paid third-party interactive analytics query engines out there, but I've covered the key ones that most customers would use when building a modern data architecture using AWS services.

Summary

In this chapter, we looked at how Amazon Athena and Presto, Trino, and Hive on EMR help organizations perform ad hoc interactive data analytics on the data stored in the S3 data lake. Athena is a serverless platform that integrates with the Glue Data Catalog and provides data analysts with the ability to write and execute SQL queries without having to manage the platform itself. Using Athena, organizations can focus on the business logic needed for reports versus spending time on creating and managing the infrastructure that's required by the platform.

We also looked at cases when creating a Presto/Trino cluster on Amazon EMR may be more beneficial for interactive analytics. This is particularly helpful when there are very large volumes of datasets that need to be scanned by thousands of queries on a daily basis and where performance SLAs are strict. Using Presto/Trino on EMR, customers can control cost and at the same time improve query performance by custom tuning the underlying cluster.

This is not the last time we will visit Athena. Over the years, Athena has grown into a service that has the ability to solve many other use cases. We will revisit Athena in the upcoming chapters and highlight its versatility.

For now, enjoy doing some hands-on interactive analytics activities with Athena by following the instructions from the workshop link provided in the *References* section.

In our next chapter, we will cover a very important component of a modern data platform —data warehousing using Amazon Redshift.

References

- Amazon Athena workshop: `https://catalog.us-east-1.prod.workshops.aws/workshops/9981f1a1-abdc-49b5-8387-cb01d238bb78/en-US`

7
Data Warehousing

In this chapter, we will look at the following key topics:

- The need for a data warehouse
- Data warehousing using Amazon Redshift
- Data warehouse modernization with Redshift
- Data ingestion patterns
- Data transformation using ELT patterns
- Data security and governance patterns
- Data consumption patterns

The concept of data warehouses has existed for a long time and organizations have been able to use data warehouse systems to do **online analytics processing** (**OLAP**). Deriving analytical insights from the data from these systems is the main goal of every organization. However, as we discussed in *Chapter 1*, the traditional data warehouse setup became challenging in the age of cloud computing. With the ever-growing volume, velocity, and variety of data in recent times, traditional on-premises data warehouses are not able to handle all the new use cases businesses users wish to solve.

The need for a data warehouse

Before we dive deeper into the topics of data warehouses, once again, let's distinguish between using a data lake versus a data warehouse. Both systems help solve a lot of overlapping use cases and can be used interchangeably for most common use cases. However, there are major differences between them. Essentially, a data lake is a schema-on-read centralized repository that's flexible enough to store all kinds of structured, semi-structured, and unstructured data at any scale and allows all personas in an organization to derive value from this data easily and cost-effectively. A data warehouse, on the other hand, is a schema-on-write structured repository that stores structured and semi-structured data that's used for analytics and **business intelligence** (**BI**). It excels in data aggregations, slice and dice data operations, roll-up and roll-down data operations, data cubes, and all other OLAP kinds of use cases. Both systems co-exist and complement each other and help organizations build a holistic modern data platform.

Since the inception of data warehouses, there has been a steady increase in the kind of use cases that an enterprise data warehouse needs to support. Not only have these use cases expanded but the different personas that use data platforms, to support their day-to-day tasks, have expanded too. Executives, business leaders, data analysts, data scientists, data engineers, managers, support agents, and so many other personas want to access fresh data in real time to make accurate decisions.

The following figure describes a flywheel effect of data. Data enables business outcomes when it's used by different personas in the organization:

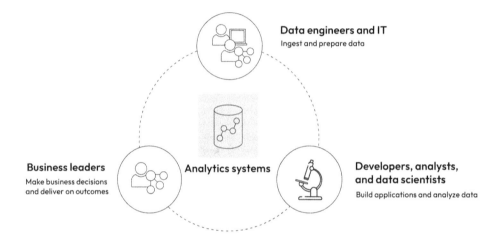

Figure 7.1 – Data analytics flywheel with different personas

A data warehouse is a foundational element of modern data architectures, so what does a modern data warehouse look like? The following figure highlights some key aspects of what organizations look for in a modern data warehouse:

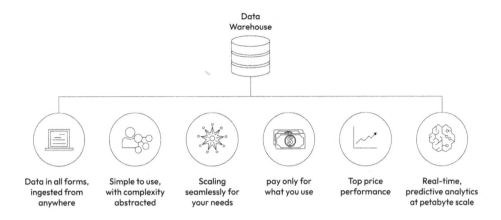

Figure 7.2 – Key aspects of a modern data warehouse

As part of the modern data architecture, organizations are looking to build their data platforms with tools that not only meet all their use cases but also give them the best price performance at scale. We will dive straight into one of the most important components of a data platform: a modern data warehouse that uses Amazon Redshift.

Data warehousing using Amazon Redshift

Amazon Redshift is a fully managed, petabyte-scale cloud data warehouse service. It is designed on the principles of **massively parallel processing** (**MPP**) architecture, which allows users to analyze large volumes of data efficiently. Redshift addresses a whole range of analytical use cases, but more importantly, it addresses the top three areas of what businesses are looking for:

1. Analyzing data by breaking down data silos.
2. Providing the best price performance at scale.
3. Providing easy, secure, and reliable insights from the data.

Before we look at some use cases, let's quickly understand the basics of Redshift.

Amazon Redshift basics

Redshift uses a massively parallel, shared-nothing architecture. It uses columnar storage, which means data is stored in columns instead of rows.

This columnar storage approach has several advantages in terms of data compression, query performance, and analytics:

- **Compression**: Columnar storage allows for better compression rates compared to row-based storage because similar data types and values are stored together, enabling more efficient compression algorithms to be applied. This results in reduced storage costs and improved query performance as less disk space is required to store the data.

- **Query performance**: Since columnar storage stores all the values for a single column together, it allows the query engine to read only the columns needed to satisfy a specific query. This capability, known as **predicate pushdown**, can significantly speed up query execution as it minimizes the amount of data that needs to be read from disk.

- **Analytical workloads**: Columnar storage is well suited for analytical workloads where queries often involve aggregations, filtering, and calculations on subsets of columns rather than entire rows. Redshift's columnar storage format allows it to perform exceptionally well for these types of workloads.

- **Minimizing I/O**: With columnar storage, only the columns required for a query are read from disk, reducing **input/output (I/O)** operations and improving overall query performance.

By utilizing columnar storage and various other optimization techniques, Amazon Redshift provides a scalable, fast, and cost-effective solution for data warehousing and analytics needs.

Also, Redshift automates a lot of operational activities, such as failover, recovery, maintenance, backups, analysis, vacuum, and so forth. Users have the option to create Redshift in two types of deployment modes – provisioned and serverless. Let's take a look.

Provisioned deployment

In provisioned mode, the user can pick and choose the type and number of Redshift compute instances they want for their workload. By default, a leader node is assigned to the cluster. The leader node acts as a SQL endpoint for the submitted queries. It compiles the queries, generates efficient execution plans, and stores the metadata. It also coordinates parallel processing by pushing the execution down to all the compute nodes. Finally, it gathers all the returned data before sending it back to the user. The compute nodes all have their own local storage, compute, and memory. They execute the queries in parallel and return the results to the leader node. Some operations such as copy, unload, backup, and restore are directly executed by the compute nodes themselves.

Redshift also has a mechanism where it can directly query data that's stored in the S3 data lake. This is possible due to another layer called Redshift Spectrum. All the tables in the S3 data lake are cataloged in the Glue Data Catalog, and Redshift can connect to these external tables and query them via the Spectrum layer. This ability of Redshift to transparently and seamlessly get data from the S3 data lake makes the enterprise data platform unified and frictionless. The following figure shows the Redshift cluster architecture:

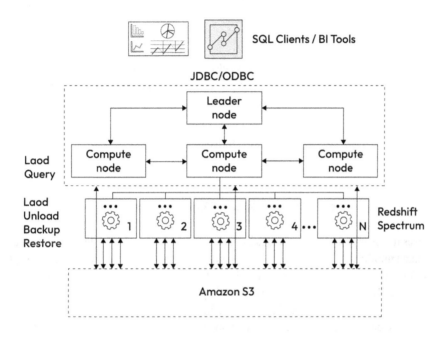

Figure 7.3 – Amazon Redshift cluster architecture

While creating the cluster, you can pick the node type. **Dense compute** (**DC2**) comes with a fixed amount of memory, CPU, and storage. DC2 nodes are a good option for smaller workloads under 1 TB of data. However, as data grows over 1 TB and beyond, it makes sense to go with a newer type of node, called **RA3**, in which the storage is detached from the compute, so you do not have to pay for extra compute when only the storage is growing rapidly. In RA3 types of nodes, the data is stored on **Redshift Managed Storage** (**RMS**), which is essentially S3 under the hood for cold data. So, the RMS costs are comparable to S3 costs. Other than cost, RA3 nodes also help in certain use cases such as data sharing across multiple Redshift clusters. We will cover data sharing in the next chapter. But for now, just keep in mind that there are two types of nodes you can select when provisioning a Redshift cluster. For further details on the types and sizes of each of the nodes, refer to the AWS documentation.

The following figure highlights the separation of storage and compute in the RA3 node type in a Redshift cluster:

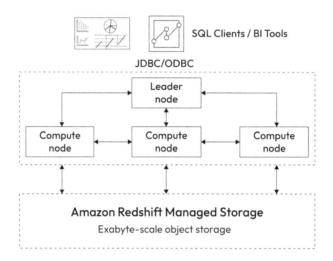

Figure 7.4 – Amazon Redshift RA3 node architecture

Redshift achieves massively parallel operations by further partitioning each node into slices. Each type of node has a fixed number of slices and each slice has dedicated CPUs, memory, and storage. All slices store data and operate in parallel, independent of each other. The leader node distributes the data to be stored on each slice depending on the data distribution pattern selected. Redshift provides key-based data distribution along with all, even, and auto. It also has sort keys as a concept. The performance of Redshift is largely dependent on an optimal data distribution and sorting pattern. Since this book is about use cases and how to solve them, I won't go into the architectural weeds of Redshift.

In fact, over the last few years, a lot of the operational overhead of using Redshift has been simplified. Many of the manual features have been automated using machine learning. In recent years, there has been significant improvement in the price performance of Redshift; at the same time, ease of use and operational aspects have been simplified.

Without going into too much detail, let's quickly go over some other key features in the provisioned deployment:

- **Concurrency scaling**: This allows Redshift to add transient capacity to your cluster so that you can handle concurrent read and write requests when a burst of user activity occurs. This feature allows the queries to be executed without them having to wait in the queue.

- **Resizing**: The cluster can be resized at any time after its initial creation. Classic or elastic resize options allow nodes to be added or removed depending on the new capacity required by the cluster so that they can efficiently operate on a day-to-day basis.

- **Pause and resume**: This feature allows the cluster to be stopped and restarted at any time. This allows for cost savings during periods when the cluster is not being used.

- **Workload management** (**WLM**): This helps you manage different types of workloads by prioritizing different queues and allocating a certain number of resources to each such type of queue, depending on the priorities.

- **Advanced query accelerator** (**AQUA**): This feature makes certain analytics operations such as compression, encryption, filtering, and aggregation faster. This is achieved through AWS-designed custom hardware.

There are a lot more features in Redshift that cover broader areas, such as security, ease of use, performance, reliability, automation, data modeling, data storage, data ingestion, and so forth. In our use case discussions, we will cover some of these features in action.

Serverless deployment

Redshift's provisioned mode of deployment is great if your workload is steady and you know your capacity usage upfront. This allows you to purchase **reserved instances** (**RIs**), which can substantially bring down the cost of the cluster. However, some workloads don't need the cluster running all the time, such as in dev/test environments. Also, some workloads are periodic, variable, or spiky. In such scenarios, provisioned clusters may sit idle for long periods or may need extra ad hoc hardware.

Redshift Serverless is a perfect choice for such kinds of workloads as you only pay for the compute resources that are used during the execution of the queries. **Redshift processing units** (**RPUs**) get allocated during query execution and you pay for those RPUs metered on a per-second basis. When you instantiate Redshift Serverless, it creates an endpoint to which any client can connect. Redshift internally manages scaling and many other operational aspects of the cluster.

Data warehousing is a vast topic and Redshift also has many features that help solve a variety of use cases. We will not be able to cover all of them in this chapter, but we will cover the key ones, so let's get started.

Data warehouse modernization using Redshift

We will start with the most obvious high-level use case: organizations that want to modernize their data warehouses. The primary reason to modernize is that traditional data warehouses are unable to keep up with the new emerging use cases. Due to their architectural limitations, traditional data warehouses are not able to handle the exponential growth in data volume along with the new variety of data that's being produced. Long story short, traditional data warehouses have become slow, complex, and expensive. Let's bring up the use case from GreatFin again.

> **Use case for data warehouse modernization**
>
> GreatFin has an on-premises data warehouse that is nearing its end of life. The continuous requests from businesses to support newer types of data analytics use cases have made this platform difficult to operate and expand. Its performance is becoming slow and the infrastructure and operating expenses are growing steadily. They want to migrate all the data from their traditional data warehouse into a fully managed, scalable, and modern cloud-based data warehouse.

Data warehouse modernization is the most common request that organizations make, for obvious reasons – to meet new business use cases and to improve the cost and performance of the system. The biggest step in data warehouse modernization is migrating data from existing systems into the new platform. Data may reside in traditional data warehouses, alongside other relational databases. Migrating to Redshift needs to be planned and executed well. The following figure highlights the necessary steps during the migration journey:

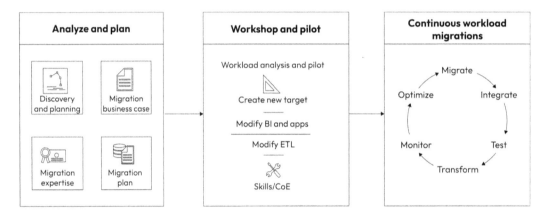

Figure 7.5 – Customer journey for migration to Amazon Redshift

The migration journey has many steps and typically, the start of the journey is the most challenging. Organizations can either take a big bang approach and migrate everything as part of a large project or they can choose to break it down into multiple iterations. Not all data from all systems needs to be migrated at the same time. A plan would typically cover short, medium, and long-term migration strategies, where the most important but simpler datasets are covered in the short/medium term, and the most complex and large ones in the long term.

A pilot phase is created to try out a **proof of concept** (**PoC**) first, followed by an implementation phase, which is labeled as the **minimum viable product** (**MVP**). An MVP is a functioning production system, but only with important functionality, so that it can be used for making business decisions. Multiple iterations of MVPs are how the final target state platform gets built over a certain period. The same approach applies to data warehouse modernization on Redshift. Let's look at the different steps involved in the whole process.

Data ingestion patterns

One of the most complex and time-consuming parts of data warehouse modernization is data onboarding. Data can be onboarded in many different ways, using many different services. It all boils down to the requirement and the need for onboarding data in a particular manner. Let's explore some typical data onboarding patterns for Amazon Redshift.

Data ingestion using AWS DMS

Let's start with a use case first, so that the importance of DMS can be better understood when it comes to loading data into Redshift.

> **Use case for batch loading data into Amazon Redshift**
>
> GreatFin uses multiple databases and traditional data warehouses for their enterprise analytics reporting needs. They want to modernize their data warehouse using Amazon Redshift and would like to bulk load all the historic data from these existing systems into Redshift. They are looking for a fast, easy, and cost-effective way to do this in Redshift.

As you may recall from our batch data ingestion chapter, we discussed **Schema Conversion Tool** (**SCT**) as a tool that can help convert the source schema into target equivalent structures. We also covered, **Database Migration Service** (**DMS**), which can help migrate data from multiple data sources over to the target. SCT and DMS both support Amazon Redshift as a target system and help with the schema and data migration processes, respectively, cutting down the time required for such batch data migrations.

The cool thing about DMS is that once the batch data is migrated over, you can also configure it in incremental mode, where it continuously replicates ongoing data changes from the source system into Redshift, thus keeping both systems in sync. The following figure highlights the importance of

AWS DMS as an ally during the migration process. Data from multiple sources can be ingested into Redshift in a fast and cost-effective manner:

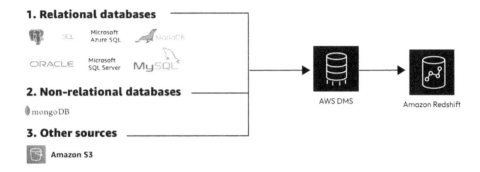

Figure 7.6 – AWS DMS service for migrating data from data sources into Redshift

DMS and SCT are popular choices, but many organizations rely on ETL services such as AWS Glue, Amazon EMR, or other third-party tools to extract data from sources, transform it, and load it into the target Redshift tables.

Data ingestion using auto-copy

Irrespective of the choice of ETL tool for loading data into Redshift, the secret sauce for all of them is that Redshift uses the COPY command under the hood to load bulk data into the cluster. Since the COPY command gets executed on all the slices of the compute nodes in parallel, it is by far the most optimal way of loading bulk data into a Redshift cluster. The COPY command leverages S3 as a temporary storage area so that it can read the files and load them concurrently into Redshift tables. The following is some sample code of using the COPY command to load data into the customer table from the given S3 location using an IAM role that has the necessary permissions:

```
COPY CUSTOMER
FROM 's3://demobucket/customer'
iam_role 'arn:aws:iam::0123456789:role/DemoRedshiftRole';
```

The COPY command needs to be executed explicitly, either by some tool or by some script. But there are scenarios where data files continuously get loaded into the S3 bucket. So, we need some functionality to automatically detect when a file is placed in S3 and subsequently load the data into a Redshift table. This is where Redshift's copy job comes in handy. The copy job continuously monitors an S3 location and when new files are detected, it automatically executes the COPY command to load the data into the Redshift table. This eliminates the need to manually schedule scripts to load data into Redshift. The following figure highlights the data flow of a copy job in Redshift:

Figure 7.7 – Amazon Redshift auto-copy job for loading tables

ETL operations to load the data in Redshift still require time and effort to set up the data pipelines, either via DMS, Glue, other ETL vendor tools, or just via COPY command scripts.

Data ingestion using zero-ETL

Many times, this is overhead for the data engineering team as they just need to get the data from their transactional database into Redshift. AWS recently introduced a first step in simplifying database storage replication without setting up any ETL tools or services. Amazon Aurora is a relational database service built for the cloud with full MySQL and PostgreSQL compatibility. New functionality now allows data to be automatically replicated from the Amazon Aurora database into Amazon Redshift at the storage level. This eliminates the need to create an ETL pipeline. Redshift continuously gets the transactional data in near real time.

The following diagram shows the Amazon Aurora zero-ETL integration mechanism with Amazon Redshift. This pattern also emphasizes one of the pillars of modern data architecture on AWS – seamless data movement:

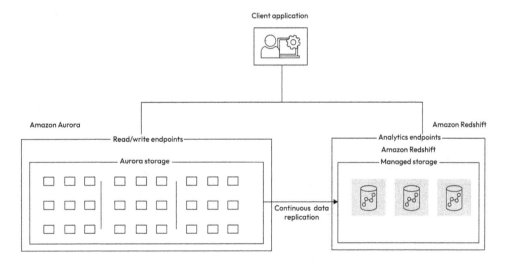

Figure 7.8 – Amazon Aurora zero-ETL integration with Amazon Redshift

Lets disucss real-time streaming data ingestion into Redshift next.

Data ingestion for real-time streaming data

Previously, we looked at a batch (bulk) data loading use case for Redshift. However, data analytics is rapidly moving toward deriving insights in near real time, which means that there are many use cases where the data produced in a streaming manner also needs to be ingested into Redshift in near real time. We discussed how the COPY command in Redshift optimizes the bulk data loading process. Redshift's architecture is not optimized for a high frequency of individual insert, update, or delete queries as they all have to pass through the leader node. So, a new way of ingesting streaming data into Redshift had to be architected. Let's discuss **Redshift streaming ingestion (RSI)** by introducing a use case.

> **Use case for streaming data into Amazon Redshift**
>
> GreatFin stores large volumes of consumer click stream data in their Redshift data warehouse so that they can analyze the data and send targeted offers based on the types of financial products they are interested in. Currently, this data is loaded into Redshift on a nightly basis from their transactional database. Due to the nature of their competition, where speed is critical, consumer-facing orgs at GreatFin want to make the offers appear as early as possible. One suggestion is to load the streaming data, in parallel, into Redshift so that they get the same data for real-time analytics inside their data warehouse.

This is a classic use case where the business wants to derive insights as fast as possible to retain a competitive edge. This is a trend across all industries these days. Before we solve this use case using RSI, recall that a use case can be solved in many ways and you can use **Kinesis Data Analytics (KDA)** or any other streaming architecture analytics pattern. We've pivoted toward RSI because the architecture, design, and, most importantly, data related to this use case are already inside Redshift. So, the team is well versed in data engineering and operational aspects of using Redshift as the service of choice. The following figure shows the design pattern for solving real-time streaming analytics by leveraging RSI:

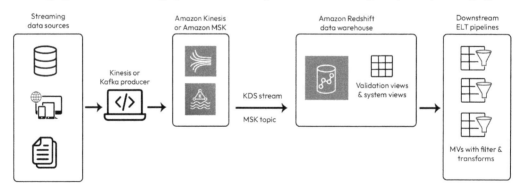

Figure 7.9 – Amazon streaming ingestion architecture

RSI can leverage Amazon Kinesis Data Streams or Amazon MSK as the platform to get the streaming data ingested. Redshift uses **materialized views** (**MVs**) to land the stream data; this MV can be automatically or manually refreshed so that Redshift gets access to the latest data from the stream. The data from these MVs can then be used to perform transformations or be used directly in reporting.

Let's go through the steps to get this solution working:

1. First, we need to create a role that has access to the KDS stream or MSK topic; whichever streaming service you have set up to get the click stream data.

2. Create an external schema for the stream data:

   ```
   CREATE EXTERNAL SCHEMA customer_data FROM KINESIS
   IAM_ROLE 'arn:aws:iam::0123456789:role/redshift-streaming-role';
   ```

3. Create a streaming materialized view for this data to land:

   ```
   CREATE MATERIALIZED VIEW customer_mv sortkey(1) AUTO REFRESH YES
   AS
       SELECT
       refresh_time,
       approximate_arrival_timestamp,
       partition_key,
       shard_id,
       sequence_number,
       json_parse(kinesis_data) as payload
       FROM customer_data."customer_stream_data"
       WHERE CAN_JSON_PARSE(kinesis_data);
   ```

   In this case, `customer_stream_data` is the name of the KDS stream that you have created as a place to store the click stream data. Some handy columns in the MV can be used during any transformation logic. The MV is put in auto-refresh mode so that it keeps getting refreshed as the data arrives in the stream.

   Getting this latest data for analytics is as simple as querying the MV itself. You can write complex logic to join this with other tables to transform and use the data for reporting purposes:

   ```
   SELECT * FROM customer_mv;
   ```

Based on this near real-time analytics, customized offers can be presented to customers who are browsing for financial products of interests online.

We just went through how to onboard batch as well as streaming data inside Redshift. The data may be transformed and loaded directly into the final tables in Redshift for consumption. This pattern is called **extract, transform, and load** (**ETL**). However, often, data needs to be made available in the data warehouse before it can be transformed and consumed. This pattern is known as **extract, load, and transform** (**ELT**). Let's look at a use case on how Redshift can be used to perform ELT.

Data transformation using ELT patterns

There are several reasons why ELT patterns may be more appealing for certain data projects. Sometimes, you need the data available in raw format as soon as possible, sometimes, it's the comfort level of personas using a particular programming language or tool, and other times, it's just about cost efficiency. Amazon Redshift also provides a platform where data engineering teams can create their ELT pipelines. Let's introduce a use case to understand this pattern.

Use case for ELT inside Amazon Redshift

GreatFin uses DMS to create a continuous data ingestion pipeline from many source data stores in Redshift. Once the data has landed in Redshift, a bunch of technical and business rules need to be applied to this data before it's ready for consumption. Different teams are well versed in the SQL programming language and prefer to write ANSI-SQL logic to transform the data. The teams also want to save costs by not introducing another ETL service.

Stored procedures

Redshift eases data transformations by leveraging SQL-based data processing. As an architecture best practice, first, the raw data is loaded into staging tables in Redshift. Staging tables are temporary tables that can be used to get the initial raw data inside Redshift, after which certain ELT jobs can be run to process the data before it's loaded into the final tables. Staging tables are also used to perform merge (upsert) operations daily.

Once the data is in the staging tables, you can use stored procedures in Redshift to process the data and load it into the final tables. The following figure demonstrates the implementation of this architecture:

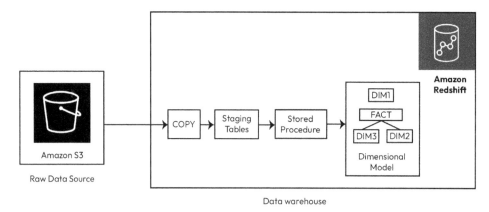

Figure 7.10 – Amazon ELT architecture using stored procs

Stored procs in Redshift can be coded in SQL syntax, which makes it a popular choice for many database engineers. Also, implementing and executing the ELT logic within Redshift can help save costs as organizations can pay upfront for **reserved instances (RIs)** for the Redshift provisioned cluster and leverage the same infrastructure for ELT logic during non-peak hours; essentially, they get the transformations done without having to pay extra for any other tools.

Let's take a look at a sample stored proc in Redshift:

```
CREATE OR REPLACE PROCEDURE customer_evaluation()
LANGUAGE plpgsql
AS $$
BEGIN
    INSERT INTO customer (name, age, address, score)
    SELECT
cus_stg.name,
cus_stg.age,
addr_stg.address,
CASE
    WHEN cus_stg.score < 0 THEN 'negative'
              ELSE 'positive'
          END AS value_creation
    FROM customer_stg cus_stg
    JOIN address_stg addr_stg
    ON cus_stg.id = addr_stg.cus_id;
END;
$$;
```

This is a very simple stored proc that joins data from two staging tables and performs derived business transformation logic before the data is inserted into the base table for consumption. You can write complex logic to perform all kinds of data transformations in the stored procedure, to populate all the final set of facts and dimension tables in Redshift.

Materialized views (MVs)

The stored proc logic can also be pre-computed and stored in an MV. An MV is a database object that contains the results of a precomputed query. It is essentially a table that is built and stored based on the definition of a query. MVs in Redshift are also leveraged a lot for ELT work as they can pre-compute the results and keep it handy for queries to return faster responses. So, stored procs can be used for extensive work that spans multiple tables with complex transformation logic, whereas MVs help execute queries faster by keeping the consumer's logic pre-computed for faster results.

The following code shows the same logic we created in the stored proc, inside an MV:

```
CREATE MATERIALIZED VIEW customer_mv AS
SELECT
cus_stg.name,
cus_stg.age,
addr_stg.address,
CASE
            WHEN cus_stg.score < 0 THEN 'negative'
                ELSE 'positive'
        END AS value_creation
    FROM customer_stg cus_stg
    JOIN address_stg addr_stg
    ON cus_stg.id = addr_stg.cus_id;
```

Redshift recently introduced integration with Apache Spark, which makes it easy to build and run Spark applications on Redshift. This integration allows native Redshift connectors for Spark-based services such as EMR and Glue to connect to Redshift.

With that, we have done all the hard work of getting the data ingested and transformed inside Redshift. However, before this data can be consumed, certain security measures need to be in place so that only the right set of people and personas can get access to certain portions of the data.

Data security and governance patterns

Redshift has a very broad and robust set of security and governance mechanisms that allow tight control of the data and the infrastructure around it. We may not be able to cover all use cases around security and access control patterns regarding Redshift but let's list some key aspects so that you understand how robust these features are and how they can cover a wide range of governance patterns:

- **Encryption**: Redshift supports encryption of data both at rest and in transit

- **Auditing and compliance**: Redshift provides detailed logs and audit trails for security and compliance purposes

- **Data masking**: Redshift provides masking capabilities to protect sensitive information

- **User management**: Redshift provides a comprehensive user management system that allows administrators to control who has access to which data, and at what level

- **Access Control Lists (ACLs)**: Redshift allows you to assign specific access rights to users and groups, ensuring that the right people have access to the right data

- **Resource-level permissions**: Redshift supports resource-level permissions, which allow administrators to grant and revoke access to specific resources (such as tables, schemas, or databases) based on user roles

- **Multi-factor authentication (MFA)**: Redshift supports MFA for added security

- **Role-based access control (RBAC)**: Redshift supports RBAC, which allows administrators to assign roles and permissions to users based on the tasks they perform

- **Network isolation**: Redshift allows you to create isolated networks to ensure that sensitive data is only accessible from within the network

- **Continuous data auditing**: Redshift allows you to continuously audit data access and usage patterns, making it easier to detect and respond to potential security threats

We won't be able to go through all the use cases around security mechanisms in Redshift, so let's pick an important one around data governance.

Fine-grained access control

Let's pick one of the use cases around fine-grained access control in Redshift.

> **Use case for fine-grained access control for data inside Amazon Redshift**
>
> GreatFin's consumer org has a lot of PII data in their Amazon Redshift data warehouse and all aspects of data security are paramount. They want to make sure that only the right set of people get access to datasets that are relevant to their day-to-day operations. They would like to enable role-based security along with table-level, column-level, and row-level access patterns. They also want to enable data masking for certain PII information.

Security is the most important aspect of any data platform, especially data security. The aforementioned requirements revolve around data security and the business wants to clamp down on who gets what kind of access to the data. The best aspect of data security inside Redshift is that it's a one-stop shop for enabling restrictions. Just by leveraging Redshift commands, data admins can grant and restrict fine-grained access control patterns to users, groups, or roles. Let's see some sample SQL commands that will help solve this use case:

```
-- create a new read only role for customer data
CREATE ROLE customer_ro;

-- create an analyst user for customer data
CREATE USER customeranalyst password 'Test@123';

-- grant the customer schema usage along with select access to all
tables of this schema to the customer read only role we had created in
the previous step
```

```
GRANT USAGE ON SCHEMA customer TO ROLE customer_ro;
GRANT SELECT ON ALL TABLES IN SCHEMA customer TO ROLE customer_ro;

-- assign the analyst user we had created earlier to the read only
customer role
GRANT ROLE customer_ro TO customeranalyst;
```

As soon as the customer analyst user logs into the query editor, they can now get read-only access to the objects that were assigned to their role. This is a simple example of how easy it is to create and assign RBAC in Redshift.

But many times, data access needs to be restricted further inside a particular table. Now, let's see some sample code regarding column-level and row-level access controls.

If we want to restrict access to only a few columns of the table, we can achieve this inside Redshift by executing a simple command:

```
-- grant access to certain columns of customer details table to the
read only analyst role
GRANT SELECT (name, gender, ssn, net_worth) ON customer_details TO
customer_ro;
```

After a while, the business decided that this analyst role should not see any rows of the table where the net worth of the customer is over $1 million. This can also be easily achieved by executing row-level policy statements:

```
-- create a row level policy for access to rows with net worth less
than $1M
CREATE RLS POLICY policy_customer_analyst
WITH (net_worth INTEGER)
USING (
    net_worth IN (SELECT net_worth FROM customer.customer_details
WHERE net_worth < 1000000)
);

-- attach the row level policy for the customer details table to the
read only analyst role
ATTACH RLS POLICY policy_customer_analyst ON customer.customer_details
TO ROLE customer_ro;
```

```
-- enable RLS for the customer details table
ALTER TABLE customer.customer_details ROW LEVEL SECURITY ON;
```

To take this a step further, let's say the business doesn't want this analyst role to see the full **social security number (SSN)**. Just the last four digits should be shown while the remaining digits should be obfuscated. Redshift also supports data masking using simple commands. Let's see how we can achieve this in code:

```
--create a user-defined masking policy function that partially
obfuscates the SSN
CREATE OR REPLACE FUNCTION REDACT_SSN(ssn VARCHAR(11))
RETURNS VARCHAR(11) AS $$
BEGIN
   RETURN 'XXX-XX-' || substring(ssn, 7, 4);
END;
$$ LANGUAGE plpgsql;

--create a masking policy that applies the redact_ssn function
CREATE MASKING POLICY mask_ssn_partial
WITH (ssn VARCHAR(11))
USING (REDACT_SSN(ssn));

--attach mask_ssn_partial to the read only analytics role
ATTACH MASKING POLICY mask_ssn_partial
ON customer.customer_details(ssn)
TO ROLE customer_ro;
```

As these examples show, just using simple SQL commands, fine-grained access control can be set inside Redshift. These self-contained security measures make data governance easy to operationalize inside Redshift.

Now that we have secured the data, let's look at some of the data consumption patterns Redshift provides.

Data consumption patterns

All the effort of ingesting, curating, and securing data in Redshift is so that it can be consumed by different personas inside the organization, as well as outside by the customers of the company. The following figure highlights some of the main ways in which data is consumed from Redshift:

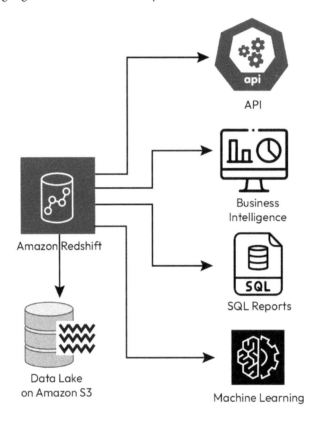

Figure 7.11 – Amazon Redshift consumption patterns

Let's dive into the details of some of the consumption patterns with Redshift and also understand the use cases better.

Redshift Spectrum

Before we look at use cases that consume data stored in Redshift, we have to address the elephant in the room first – Redshift Spectrum. Redshift Spectrum provides a unique ability inside Redshift to transparently query the data stored in the S3 data lake. The data lake tables that are stored in the Glue Data Catalog can be queried and joined with regular Redshift tables. This is truly what a modern data warehouse looks like and its plays a pivotal role in creating a modern data architecture on AWS.

Let's elaborate more by using a use case from GreatFin.

> **Use case for Redshift Spectrum**
>
> GreatFin is a financial conglomerate with many divisions and multiple data warehouses and data lakes. Multiple orgs have created their own central data lakes on S3 while modernizing their data warehouse on Redshift. Different personas and applications use data from both these systems. To avoid redundant copies of data, the business is looking for a simplified and single pane of glass to query all the data from within Redshift itself. This way, there will be no data duplication, no extra application logic, or multiple query engines.

This style of architecture is also referred to as a data lakehouse design pattern. The data lake is the central location for storing all kinds of data and the data warehouse is dedicated to structured and semi-structured data that's specifically used for analytical reporting. When you design and build a modern data architecture on AWS, the data lake is the central force and the data warehouse is one of the many purpose-built stores, so in that sense, the AWS philosophy of creating a well-rounded data platform goes far beyond just a data warehouse surrounding the data lake.

This architectural pattern has many more important usages. Think about an archival strategy that you can design, where vast amounts of historical data is pushed out of Redshift into the S3 data lake, and you still retain the ability to query this data as and when any reports would need it. In essence, you have designed an exabyte scale platform where you don't need to worry about future scalability issues.

The following figure highlights the importance of Redshift Spectrum and its ability to seamlessly join forces with other AWS services to create this transparent layer of data access across the board. Redshift users get the unique ability to query the data stored in the S3 data lake without knowing where the actual results are coming from. The spectrum layer in Redshift transparently fetches the data from the S3 data lake by executing queries against the tables stored in the Glue Data Catalog:

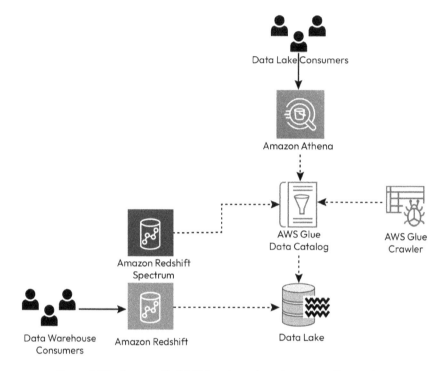

Figure 7.12 – Amazon Redshift Spectrum-based consumption pattern

Let's look at some sample code to see how easy it is to query external S3 data inside Redshift using the Spectrum layer:

```
--create external schema in Redshift and register the Glue Data
Catalog database
CREATE EXTERNAL SCHEMA customer_history_schema FROM DATA CATALOG
DATABASE 'customer_db'
iam_role 'arn:aws:iam::0123456789:role/DemoSpectrumRole'
CREATE EXTERNAL DATABASE IF NOT EXISTS;
-- Create an external table in this external schema
CREATE EXTERNAL TABLE customer_history_schema.customer (
    name varchar(255),
    gender char(2),
    age integer
)
STORED AS PARQUET
LOCATION 's3://my-bucket/data/';
```

```
-- join data for customer table inside Redshift with the historical
customer data stored in S3
SELECT name, gender, age
FROM customer_schema.customer
UNION
SELECT name, gender, age
FROM customer_history_schema.customer
```

The final query doesn't even know if the data is inside Redshift or external to it. This makes creating consumer patterns so much easier as you can leverage the same set of logic to get data from both of these systems.

Amazon Redshift recently introduced a seamless enhancement that simplifies the process of querying AWS data lakes. It can now automatically mount the AWS Glue Data Catalog, eliminating the need to manually set up an external schema in Redshift for accessing data lake tables. With this improvement, you can effortlessly browse the Glue Data Catalog and directly query data lake tables within Amazon Redshift Query Editor v2 or your preferred SQL editors using your IAM credentials or IAM role.

Now that we have sorted out the concept of Redshift Spectrum first, all the other consumption patterns can leverage this design pattern to get the data from the data platform as a whole. Let's move on to the next consumption pattern for Redshift and see how external web portals can get data from Redshift.

Redshift Data APIs

Let's introduce the concept of sharing Redshift data using APIs by bringing up a use case from GreatFin.

> **Use case for consuming Redshift data using APIs**
>
> GreatFin's consumer business provides its customers with a portal on the public internet where they can log in to see custom dashboards of their weekly, monthly, and yearly activities regarding their credit card transactions. Customers can view aggregated categories of purchases, their top 10 highest purchases, the sum of total savings on deals, and so forth. They can also drill down to specific reports. GreatFin uses Amazon Redshift for analytical purposes and would like to have a fast, secure, and interactive way of incorporating request/response-driven architecture from its web portal.

As soon as you see a request/response pattern with an external website, it typically entails an event-driven architecture. Redshift Data APIs simplify the way you interact with Redshift data by calling functions that return responses to the request made. You can programmatically create a request/response type of architecture by having a Lambda function call Redshift via the data APIs and return the RESTful response to the external consuming portal using Amazon API Gateway. This is a typical architecture pattern for creating complex event-driven architectures. You can leverage other AWS services to orchestrate schedule-based events too.

The following figure demonstrates a simple event-driven architecture pattern for solving our use case:

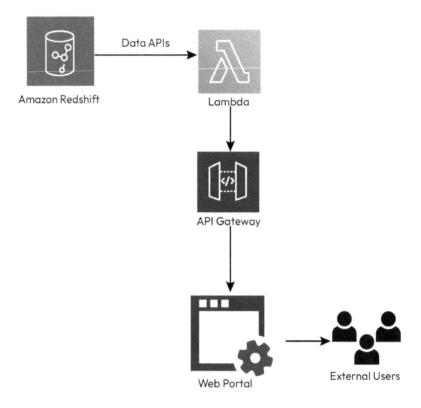

Figure 7.13 – Event-driven architecture using Redshift Data APIs

Here is some sample code that shows how to call the Redshift Data APIs within a Lambda function. You can put complex logic inside the Lambda to get the request from API Gateway and send the final response back:

```
--sample python code that will go inside a lambda function which uses
Redshift Data APIs to fetch data from Redshift
boto3.client("redshift-data").execute_statement(
    ClusterIdentifier = 'test-redshift-cluster',
    Database = 'test',
    DbUser = 'testuser',
    Sql = 'select * from customer_schema.customer')
```

Now let's move on to a use case for data consumption for our internal persona – data analysts who want to create ad hoc reports using SQL Editor.

SQL reports

Let's introduce SQL reports consumption patterns by bringing up a use case from GreatFin.

> **Use case for consuming Redshift data using SQL Editor**
>
> GreatFin has a lot of data that constantly gets ingested in their Redshift cluster. The business wants to understand patterns in the data, see changes over time, and understand deviations and special signals from the data. They have hired many data analysts who would perform data exploration and make discoveries from the data. They want the ability to write ad hoc SQL queries to analyze, collaborate, and share their findings while also being able to instantly visualize data so that they can understand the trends and patterns in them.

This is a typical use case for all personas, not just data analysts, who use SQL workbench types of tools to make JDBC/ODBC connections to Redshift and write SQL queries to get insights into the data. To help simplify this use case, Redshift provides query editor v2, which is a serverless, free-to-use web-based interface to simplify all the needs in this use case. The query editor provides many functionalities, such as browser-style data exploration, wizards to simplify data operations, and options to collaborate and share SQL notebooks. It also helps visualize the data in many charts, making it easy to understand trends and patterns from the data.

The following screenshot just shows some of the capabilities of query editor v2 inside Redshift:

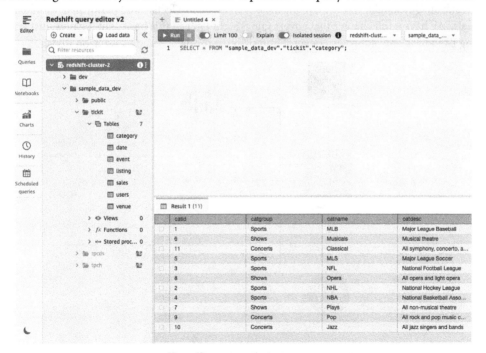

Figure 7.14 – Redshift query editor v2

Query editor notebooks are also used by data scientist personas to understand correlation in the data as they prepare the data for ML modeling inside Redshift. More on this topic will be provided later in this book.

Before we wrap up this chapter, let's look at another common data consumption pattern for Redshift that is implemented via BI tools.

Business intelligence (BI) dashboards

We'll introduce the BI consumption pattern by bringing up a use case from GreatFin.

> **Use case for consuming Redshift data using BI tools**
>
> GreatFin managers and LOB executives would like to understand sales by region, by date, and by market segments. They would also like to understand trends in customer data and the reasons behind them. A lot of other business **key performance indicators** (**KPIs**) need to be tracked and displayed in a visual dashboard so that it's easy to analyze the data and track business health.

BI tools that show the KPIs of the business visually have been around for a very long time. A lot of such tools can connect to Redshift via JDBC/ODBC connections and help create a visual dashboard.

The following figure highlights some of the visualization tools that can connect to Redshift. One of them is Amazon QuickSight, which helps businesses create cost-effective and performant dashboards and visuals. We have a full chapter that covers QuickSight later in this book, but for now, just know that using BI tools is one of the key consumption patterns for data stored in Amazon Redshift:

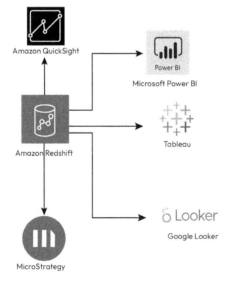

Figure 7.15 – BI tools with Amazon Redshift

We covered a lot in this chapter, but there are so many other things you can do in Redshift that a separate book is needed to go through every aspect. Some other key pieces of the puzzle are still pending, including data sharing patterns, data federation patterns, and machine learning in Redshift. We will cover each of these topics in the next few chapters as they encompass other services above and beyond just Redshift.

The following figure highlights the ecosystem of use cases, some of which we covered in this chapter and some of which we will cover in our chapters ahead:

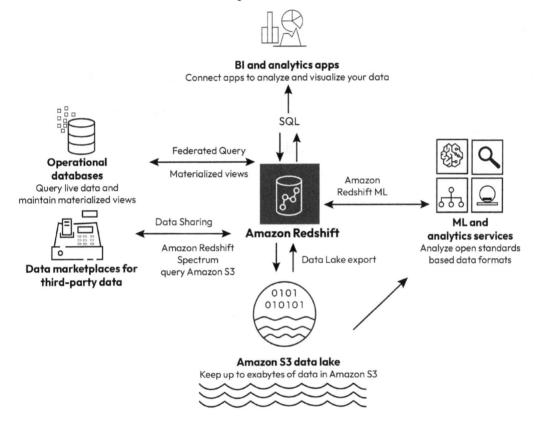

Figure 7.16 – Amazon Redshift's ecosystem of use cases

With this, we have concluded data warehousing on Redshift. As always, it's good to practice with some hands-on labs; links to those workshops can be found in the *References* section.

Summary

In this chapter, we looked at how Amazon Redshift helps modernize data warehouses. We covered the basics of what Amazon Redshift looks like and how some of its features help meet next-gen business use cases. We went through each type of use case, starting from an overarching use case around modernizing legacy on-premises data warehouses by migrating the data to Amazon Redshift. We then looked at some of the data ingestion use cases that most organizations use to get the data inside Redshift. Once the data was ingested, we looked at how to leverage the compute power of Redshift to transform data using the ELT pattern. Stored procs, MVs, and Apache Spark connectors are all supported by Redshift to help process the data so that it can be ready for consumption.

Before the data can be consumed, we had to learn how to control and set security measures for the data that resides in Redshift. We applied some fine-grained access control patterns such as RBAC, row-level and column-level security, and data masking. Finally, we looked at some of the data consumption patterns with Redshift. We covered a key use case for transparently consuming data from an S3 data lake using Redshift Spectrum. Data can also be consumed using APIs with Redshift Data APIs, using SQL using Redshift query editor v2, and using BI tools such as Amazon QuickSight.

In the next chapter, we will look at how to share data, not just internally from Redshift and S3 data lakes, but also to and from external marketplaces.

References

- Amazon Redshift workshops:
  `https://catalog.us-east-1.prod.workshops.aws/workshops/9f29cdba-66c0-445e-8cbb-28a092cb5ba7/en-US`

- `https://catalog.us-east-1.prod.workshops.aws/workshops/380e0b8a-5d4c-46e3-95a8-82d68cf5789a/en-US`

- Modernization workshops: `https://awsworkshop.io/tags/redshift/`

8

Data Sharing

In the previous chapter, we looked at how the data stored in Amazon Redshift can be consumed. But imagine that, in a large company such as our GreatFin example, every **line of business** (**LOB**) produces and consumes its own data gathered from multiple channels. For a company to be truly data-driven, the data silos need to be broken and there needs to be an easy way to share data across all LOBs, without the need to physically move the data around as duplicate copies.

First, we will look at how you can share data inside your organization, from a data lake on S3 as well as from the data warehouse we built on Redshift.

In this chapter, we will look at the following key topics:

- Internal data sharing
- External data sharing

Internal data sharing

Organizations have many internal LOBs and each LOB has many personas that interact with the data produced by their department. Different LOBs often want access to portions of data from other departments for many reasons, including cross-sell, up-sell, fraud detection, and other critical insights about their customers. First, let's look at a use case on how each LOB can share data that they have curated inside their S3 data lake.

Data sharing using Amazon Athena

Previously, we covered how you can create a data lake on Amazon S3 and then interactively query it using Amazon Athena. In a simple scenario, the data produced by one LOB is only consumed by the personas inside the same LOB. But to unlock the true value of data, organizations prefer that each LOB shares relevant sets of data with other LOBs. When organizations prefer to create a centralized enterprise data lake, the question becomes, how can each LOB access the datasets that belong to them? And if each LOB has its own data lake in its own AWS account, how can they share curated datasets from their S3 data lake with other LOB accounts?

Sometimes, files need to be shared directly from the S3 bucket itself, and for such purposes, simply putting in an S3 bucket policy allows cross-AWS account sharing of data. However, most times, structured data needs to be shared at the database and table level. This leads us to the topic of sharing datasets across AWS accounts via Glue Data Catalog so that different personas across LOBs can query the tables using Amazon Athena. Let's explore this concept using a use case from GreatFin.

Use case for sharing an S3 data lake across multiple AWS accounts

GreatFin has multiple LOBs, each with its own S3 data lakes. The S3 data and Glue Data Catalog reside in a producer AWS account that is tightly governed by a LOB account. The producer account has cataloged this data using Glue Data Catalog. Other LOBs are interested in getting access to some portions of the data so that they can query it from their own AWS account. A simple and seamless way to query datasets across AWS accounts is being requested.

The key here is a simple and seamless way to access data from the S3 data lake across different LOBs in different AWS accounts. The following figure depicts what this use case entails and how we can leverage Athena to access Glue Data Catalog in another AWS account:

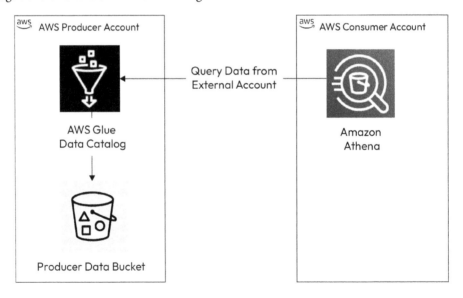

Figure 8.1 – AWS cross-account data sharing from an S3 data lake

Let's look at an example to see how this architecture pattern of data sharing would work. Let's assume that the producer AWS account has data about customers and the customer table is created in Glue Data Catalog. This customer table can be queried via Athena from the same producer account but the catalog is not visible to other AWS accounts. So, in essence, we need to enable certain things in the producer account so that the customer table can be queried via Athena from a different consumer AWS account.

Before we provide cross-account access to the table in Glue Data Catalog, let's provide access to the underlying S3 bucket itself so that the consumer account has access to the underlying datasets in S3. The following example code shows an S3 bucket policy that grants bucket access to the consumer account:

```
{
    "Version": "2012-10-17",
    "Statement": [
        {
            "Effect": "Allow",
            "Principal": {
                "AWS": "arn:aws:iam::<consumer-account-id>:role/Dev"
            },
            "Action": [
                "s3:GetObject",
                "s3:ListBucket"
            ],
            "Resource": [
                "arn:aws:s3:::<producer-bucket>",
                "arn:aws:s3:::<producer-bucket>/customer/*"
            ]
        }
    ]
}
```

The bucket policy grants read access to the producer bucket, where the customer table data is stored, to the consumer AWS account.

Once S3 cross-account access has been sorted out, the consumer account needs access to the customer table stored in Glue Data Catalog. To achieve this, we need to put in a Glue resource policy. The following code shows a sample Glue resource policy in the producer account, which allows Athena, in the consumer account, to query the customer table from the producer's catalog:

```
{
    "Version": "2012-10-17",
    "Statement": [
        {
            "Effect": "Allow",
            "Principal": {
                "AWS": "arn:aws:iam::<consumer-account-id>:role/Dev"
            },
            "Action": [
                "glue:*"
            ],
            "Resource": [
```

```
            "arn:aws:glue:<Region>:<producer-account-
             id>:catalog",
            "arn:aws:glue:<Region>:<producer-account-
             id>:database/producer_db",
            "arn:aws:glue:<Region>:<producer-account-
             id>:table/producer_db/customer"
        ]
     }
   ]
}
```

Once the policies have been set in the producer account, the consumer account needs to create a new data source that points to Glue Data Catalog that was shared by the producer account. To do this, the consumer need to go into the Athena console in AWS and create a new data source and select **S3 - AWS Glue Data Catalog**.

The following screenshot highlights this option in Athena:

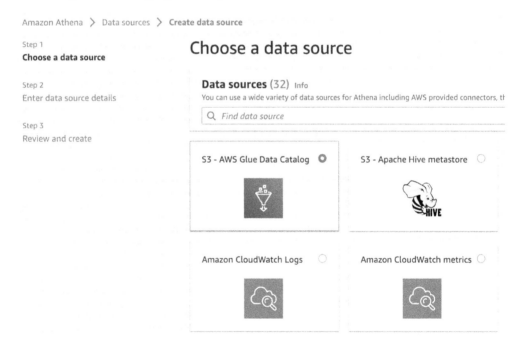

Figure 8.2 – Creating a new data source in Athena

Once you've selected **S3 - AWS Glue Data Catalog**, you need to register the catalog of the producer account by providing the producer account's ID. The following screenshot shows this configuration setup. Once the registration is complete, you will see the shared producer catalog objects in the consumer Athena console:

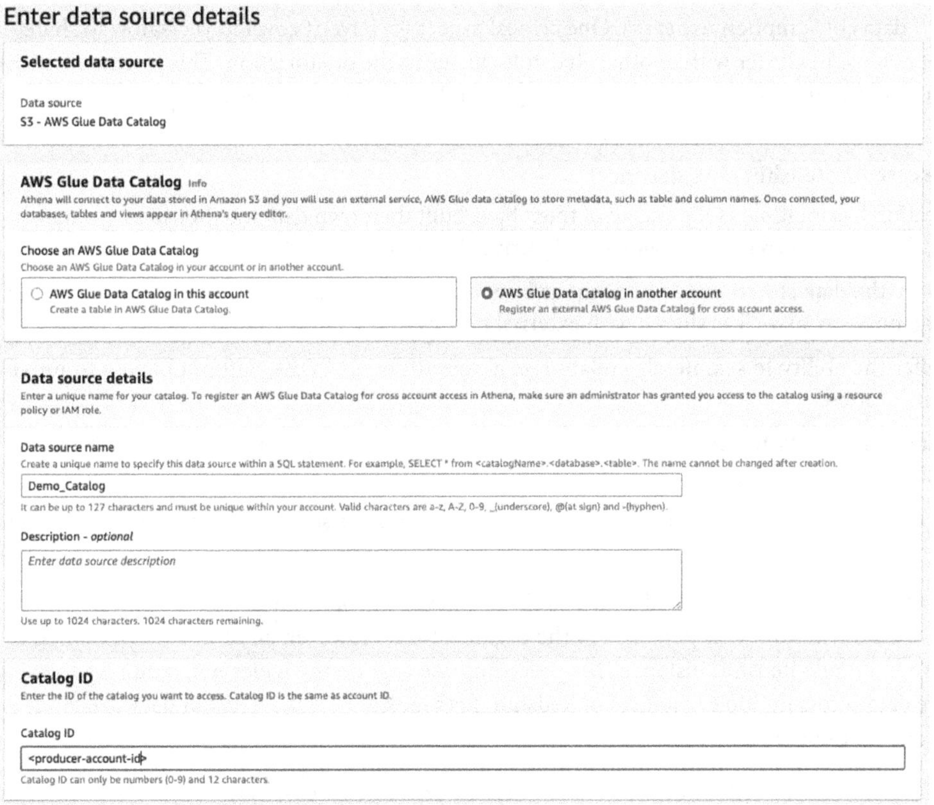

Enter data source details

Selected data source

Data source
S3 - AWS Glue Data Catalog

AWS Glue Data Catalog Info
Athena will connect to your data stored in Amazon S3 and you will use an external service, AWS Glue data catalog to store metadata, such as table and column names. Once connected, your databases, tables and views appear in Athena's query editor.

Choose an AWS Glue Data Catalog
Choose an AWS Glue Data Catalog in your account or in another account.

○ AWS Glue Data Catalog in this account
Create a table in AWS Glue Data Catalog.

◉ AWS Glue Data Catalog in another account
Register an external AWS Glue Data Catalog for cross account access.

Data source details
Enter a unique name for your catalog. To register an AWS Glue Data Catalog for cross account access in Athena, make sure an administrator has granted you access to the catalog using a resource policy or IAM role.

Data source name
Create a unique name to specify this data source within a SQL statement. For example, SELECT * from <catalogName>.<database>.<table>. The name cannot be changed after creation.

Demo_Catalog

It can be up to 127 characters and must be unique within your account. Valid characters are a-z, A-Z, 0-9, _(underscore), @(at sign) and -(hyphen).

Description - optional

Enter data source description

Use up to 1024 characters. 1024 characters remaining.

Catalog ID
Enter the ID of the catalog you want to access. Catalog ID is the same as account ID.

Catalog ID

<producer-account-id>

Catalog ID can only be numbers (0-9) and 12 characters.

Figure 8.3 – Cross-account sharing of Glue Data Catalog

To query the producer account database, all you have to do is use the following query structure:

```
SELECT * FROM "Demo_Catalog"."producer_db"."customer" limit 10;
```

This is an easy way of sharing the contents of an S3 data lake across multiple LOBs that use their own AWS accounts.

Sharing data via cross-sharing Glue Data Catalog is suitable for small and quick implementations. For large-scale implementations with lots of databases, schemas, and tables in the data lake, governance becomes difficult with IAM and resource policy changes. Also, fine-grained access control at the row, column, and cell levels is not possible with this mechanism. We will look into data sharing again in our data governance chapter to learn about other ways to share data in a more governed manner. Let's move on to another data sharing topic, but this time, for the data that's stored in the data warehouse inside Amazon Redshift.

Data sharing using Amazon Redshift

We covered a lot of use cases for Redshift in the previous chapter and we concluded with a bunch of Redshift data consumption use cases. One critical aspect we haven't covered yet is how to share data from one Redshift cluster with another Redshift cluster in the organization. This is where Redshift's data sharing feature comes in handy. Let's look into it by bringing up a use case.

Use case for Redshift data sharing

GreatFin has multiple LOBs and all of them have built their own data warehouse with Amazon Redshift. Each LOB has the following objectives in mind:

- Offer the data stored inside Redshift as a service so that it can be used by LOBs inside the organization, as well as shared with external parties

- Offer the ability to seamlessly collaborate across different LOBs, without having to move data around

- Have the ability to separate the write-heavy ETL workloads from read-heavy business intelligence workloads

- Have the ability to share data between different environments such as dev, test, and production

---

In the previous chapter, we looked at fine-grained access control mechanisms to share only relevant pieces of data with different personas in the organization. However, all of this was assumed to be done from a single Redshift instance. The preceding use case casts a wider net, requiring the ability to share data across multiple instances of Redshift. Let's look at how the Redshift data sharing feature helps solve all these specific use cases.

Redshift data sharing, only with RA3 instance types, provides an easy way to share live data across multiple Redshift clusters without the need to move the data around. Just by using SQL commands, one Redshift cluster can share any part of its dataset with other Redshift clusters in any AWS account. The following figure highlights the data sharing mechanism of Redshift:

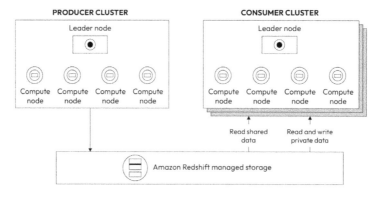

Figure 8.4 – Redshift data sharing

The producer Redshift cluster can provide read-only access to its data to any number of consumer Redshift clusters. The consumer clusters can also be producers of datasets and, at the same time, get access to query datasets that have been shared with them by other clusters.

Let's go over the architecture details for each of the four use cases that GreatFin wants to achieve. The first one was around having the ability to provide the data inside Redshift as a service to any other consumers, either inside or outside the organization. This means that a producer Redshift cluster provides data sharing access to another consumer Redshift cluster; as new consumers are onboarded, the same mechanism becomes a scalable and repeatable process. The following figure depicts the architecture for Redshift data sharing as a service:

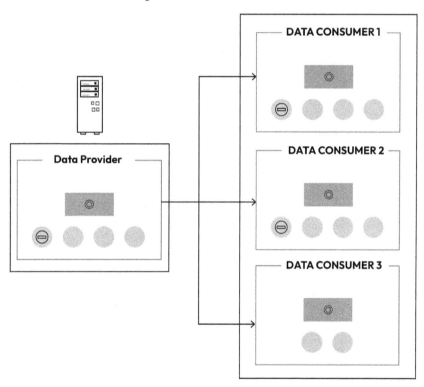

Figure 8.5 – Redshift data sharing to enable data as a service

The second part of the use case is to give different LOBs the ability to seamlessly share data, without the need to move this data to the other LOB. The following figure highlights this architecture pattern using Redshift data sharing:

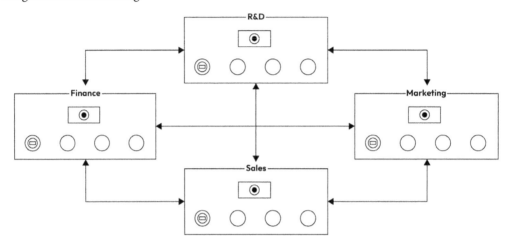

Figure 8.6 – Redshift data sharing to enable cross-LOB collaboration

The third request from the use case was to give the LOBs the ability to separate the data warehouse workloads based on usage patterns. This means we want to have a dedicated Redshift cluster for write-heavy operations such as data loading and data transformations inside Redshift while separating the read-heavy workloads into their own Redshift clusters.

The following figure highlights this architecture pattern, where the ETL cluster is separated and data is then shared with the consumer clusters. The thing to note is that data sharing is agnostic to the type of Redshift deployment. The ad hoc query cluster may not always need the cluster up and running, so it's better to have it run in serverless mode. You can mix and match any number of clusters in either of the configuration choices, be it provisioned or serverless, based on usage patterns:

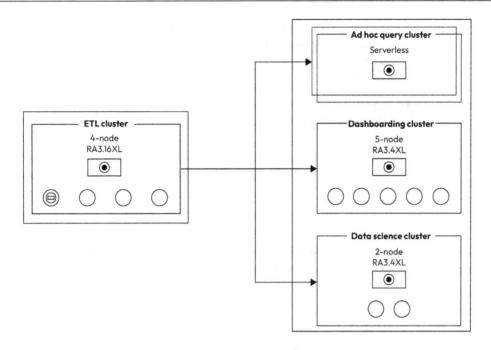

Figure 8.7 – Redshift data sharing to enable segregation of workload types

Finally, the last part of the use case asks for the ability to share data with different environments. Organizations typically keep different environments – dev, test, and prod – for different purposes. Instead of loading all the data in all the environments, it's sometimes beneficial to have the ability to just share data from one Redshift environment to another. Redshift data sharing can help with this use case too.

The following figure highlights the data sharing aspect of Redshift to assist with different environments:

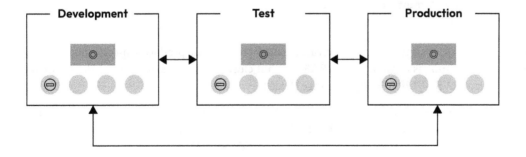

Figure 8.8 – Redshift data sharing to improve agility with multiple environments

Now that we have gone through all the use cases for using Redshift data sharing, let's quickly look at how easy it is to enable data sharing in Redshift. On the producer cluster, the following sample commands would enable a data share and give access to the schema/objects from the producer cluster in one AWS account to a consumer cluster in another account:

```
-- Create a datashare container for sharing objects
CREATE DATASHARE CustomerShare ON cust_db;

-- Add desired schemas, tables for sharing
ALTER DATASHARE CustomerShare ADD ALL TABLES IN SCHEMA cust;

-- Share with separate AWS accounts
GRANT USAGE ON DATASHARE CustomerShare TO ACCOUNT '0123456789';
```

On the consumer Redshift cluster, the following sample commands will enable the cluster to get read-only access to the objects that are being shared by the producer cluster:

```
-- List the data shares available and review contents for each
DESC DATASHARE CustomerShare;

-- Create a local database and schema reference to the shared objects
CREATE DATABASE cust_db FROM DATASHARE CustomerShare OF ACCOUNT
'0123456789' NAMESPACE 'ee8672e3-d691-4fc6-986b-1971578ecc0a';
CREATE EXTERNAL SCHEMA cust_schema FROM REDSHIFT DATABASE cust_db
SCHEMA cust;

-- Grant permissions on shared databases and schemas to user and
groups in the cluster
GRANT USAGE ON DATABASE cust_db TO John;
GRANT USAGE ON SCHEMA cust_schema TO GROUP analyst_group;

-- start querying the table as if its local
SELECT * FROM cust_db.cust.customer;
```

Just by using SQL commands, you can create a data share from the producer-to-consumer Redshift cluster. Data sharing is possible on the RA3 Redshift cluster type as the underlying data store is a common layer of **Redshift Managed Storage** (**RMS**).

So far, we have looked at sharing data internal to the organization. However, a lot of companies have data that can be monetized and would like to share data as a product with external companies via a marketplace. Let's get into the details of how this can be done in AWS.

External data sharing

Every organization produces and collects a lot of data. Often, data that's produced is consumed for internal operations, but there are many cases where some data that's collected can be monetized by offering it to other companies that can use this data to enrich their analytical insights. As you may recall from our data lake chapter, we created an enriched layer for data that could use a combination of internal data and external data to produce datasets that help derive precision insights.

Creating a vision for sharing data externally to make money is easy; however, the real challenge is around setting up all the mechanisms to do this in a scalable, secure, and cost-effective manner. Creating a secure and optimal technical handshake between the data providers and data consumers is not easy. Producers and subscribers both want a secure and easy-to-use cloud-native platform that can seamlessly enable data sharing by providing self-service options.

To solve this problem, AWS created a service called AWS Data Exchange. Let's get into the details of this service.

Data sharing using AWS Data Exchange

Data Exchange enables customers to easily find and subscribe to third-party data. It also allows data producers to provide their data assets on the AWS Marketplace for subscribers to find them. Let's understand this better by looking at a use case from GreatFin.

> **Use case for AWS Data Exchange**
>
> GreatFin, as a financial organization, produces a lot of important data about its customers. They want to sell packaged data products to other companies; at the same time, they want to seek data from other third-party vendors to enrich their customer data. GreatFin's LOBs have data in files, an S3 data lake, and also inside Amazon Redshift. They also want the ability to sell data via API requests.
>
> Even though selling data is the primary goal, they want to ensure correct fine-grained access controls are in place to secure the data. Finally, they don't want to build any infrastructure to do the undifferentiated heavy lifting, including billing functionality for the data assets they sell and subscribe to.

AWS Data Exchange offers five ways you can share and subscribe to data. It covers all the aspects of the use case that we just laid out. The following figure highlights those five ways; we will go over them one by one:

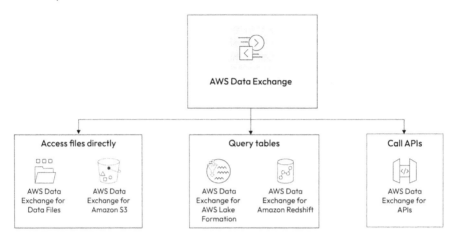

Figure 8.9 – AWS Data Exchange data sharing modes

File-based data sharing is useful for datasets such as images, PDFs, CSV files, and other kinds of files that need to be exchanged between the producer and the subscriber. In a typical architecture pattern, subscribers can set up auto exports of data once the publisher provides new files. New files and existing revisions can be tracked by Amazon EventBridge, which gets notified by Data Exchange when new datasets are added to the product that's being subscribed to. Files are also scanned for any security threats before being made available to consumers.

The following figure highlights this architecture pattern for publishing and consuming file-based data sharing using AWS Data Exchange:

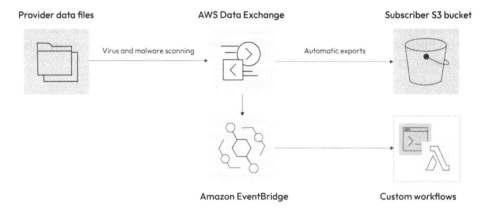

Figure 8.10 – AWS Data Exchange for data files

The next pattern for Data Exchange is sharing data via S3 buckets. Here, the publishers and subscribers also deal with files but having them land in S3 saves the effort of setting up a file transfer mechanism. Subscribers can directly get access to the data stored in S3 buckets created by the provider, eliminating the need to transfer data and create duplicates. With S3 being a highly scalable and durable object store, this mode becomes a key part of the data exchange architecture pattern for large amounts of data cost-effectively.

The following figure highlights this architecture pattern for publishing and consuming data in S3 using AWS Data Exchange:

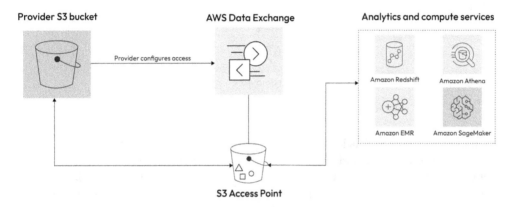

Figure 8.11 – AWS Data Exchange for Amazon S3

A lot of data is also stored in Redshift clusters, which serve as the foundational data warehouses for many organizations, including in our example of GreatFin. Data Exchange makes it easy to publish and subscribe to objects inside Redshift. As data goes into the publisher's Redshift tables and views, it becomes immediately available to the subscribers. This makes it a seamless way to exchange the data stored in Redshift without having to create any data pipelines. With Redshift's elastic architecture, publishers and subscribers can set up either a provisioned cluster or a serverless one and get the best price performance for monetizing the data.

The following figure highlights this architecture pattern for publishing and consuming data in Amazon Redshift using AWS Data Exchange:

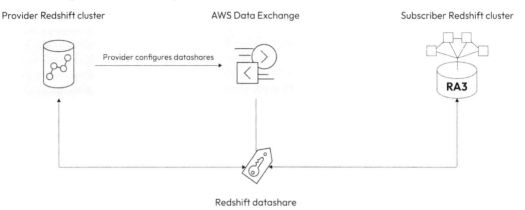

Figure 8.12 – AWS Data Exchange for Amazon Redshift

For data that resides in the S3 data lake and the metadata that resides in Glue Data Catalog, we can easily grant access to databases and tables using AWS IAM policies. However, what we have not looked at so far is fine-grained access control, at the row and column level, in the S3 data lake. We have a chapter on data governance in which we will go into the details of how you can use AWS Lake Formation to control detailed access to the data that's in the S3 data lake. But for now, let's just keep in mind that for data exchange patterns that need fine-grained access control, we can leverage Data Exchange with Lake Formation.

The following figure highlights this architecture pattern for publishing and consuming data with AWS Data Exchange using fine-grained access controls when leveraging AWS Lake Formation:

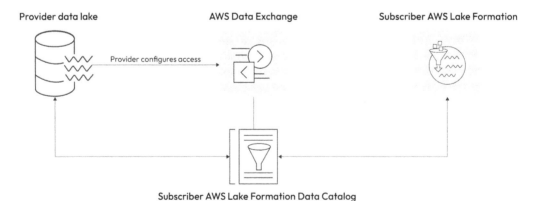

Figure 8.13 – AWS Data Exchange with AWS Lake Formation

The final architecture pattern for exchanging data is using APIs. A lot of SaaS-based companies offer their data products in the form of APIs, where any subscriber can request specific datasets using the APIs provided by the publisher. Data Exchange can help facilitate this mode too by allowing easy exchange of data using APIs.

The following figure highlights this architecture pattern for publishing and consuming data with APIs using AWS Data Exchange:

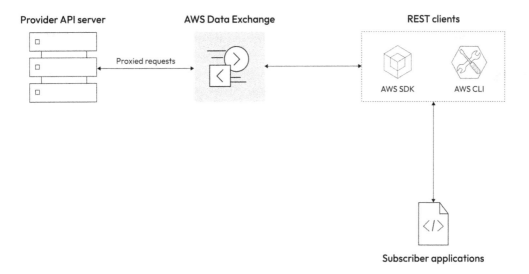

Figure 8.14 – AWS Data Exchange with APIs

There is a lot more to sharing data in a governed fashion. AWS recently announced two new services, Amazon DataZone and AWS Clean Rooms, which also facilitate data sharing in a governed manner. We will cover these two services in our data governance chapter as many of the other features and functions of these services fit well when designing data governance for a data platform.

Summary

In this chapter, we looked at how organizations can share data that's internal to the organization as well as externally for monetization. Internal data sharing can be as easy as sharing the data in the S3 data lake by providing cross-account access to Amazon Athena. Athena can read data from a shared Glue Data Catalog, making it easy to share different objects from the catalog. We also looked at how Redshift's data sharing feature helps in sharing data that's stored in one Redshift cluster with many other clusters in the organization. By creating a producer cluster and providing grants, the consumer cluster can easily access the objects shared with it.

Finally, we looked at patterns for sharing data external to the organization by leveraging AWS Data Exchange. Data Exchange helps us share datasets via various modes, such as files, S3, Redshift, Lake Formation, and APIs. Without data sharing features, complex ETL pipelines would have to be built to move data around and duplicate copies of data would exist. Seamless data sharing is a key part of the modern data architecture on AWS.

In the next chapter, we will look at a completely different way to access and query data without needing to move it around – data federation. It's an interesting topic with specific use cases that benefit from it. As always, if you are interested in doing some hands-on workshops, don't hesitate to try out some of the exercises provided next.

References

- Amazon Redshift data sharing workshop: `https://catalog.workshops.aws/seamless-data-sharing-using-amazon-redshift/en-US`

- AWS Data Exchange workshop: `https://catalog.us-east-1.prod.workshops.aws/workshops/e5548031-3004-49ad-89be-a13e8cd616f6/en-US`

9
Data Federation

In the previous chapter, we explored different use cases for sharing data, both internally and externally with the organization. Data sharing is a very critical aspect of any data platform, where data stored in an Amazon S3-based data lake and in an Amazon Redshift data warehouse is seamlessly shared, without the need to create duplicate copies. Every data platform has distinct components for data storage, as well as for data computations. In the data sharing model, we focused on sharing data between similar systems – for example, using Amazon Athena to share data stored in an S3 data lake and using Amazon Redshift to share data with other Redshift clusters.

Data doesn't always get stored, processed, and shared within homogeneous systems. A lot of times, data is captured in heterogeneous systems and those systems may not even reside inside the AWS ecosystem. This brings us to the question, how do we seamlessly and transparently query datasets from a simple pane of glass, without moving data around? This is where the concept of data federation kicks in. Let's get into the details of how we can federate data from other systems using Amazon Athena and Amazon Redshift.

In this chapter, we will look at the following key topics:

- Data federation using Amazon Athena
- Data federation using Amazon Redshift

Data federation using Amazon Athena

Amazon Athena is primarily used to query data from S3 data lakes. However, to query data across heterogeneous sources, Athena provides a feature called Federated Query. This feature enables different personas, such as data analysts, data engineers, and data scientists, to execute queries across disparate data sources from Athena itself. The single biggest differentiator for Federated Query is that the execution of such queries happens inside the systems that store the data.

Athena executes these federated queries using connectors. Athena provides many connectors to a variety of source systems. Using these connectors, Athena can pass portions of the query that need to be executed in the source system. This execution is assisted by AWS Lambda functions, which optimize the query's execution and gather the data received from the underlying systems. Since Lambda functions are serverless and scalable, this allows Athena to query larger datasets in the originating system by submitting queries in parallel. Let's quickly look at how federated queries work in Athena before we jump into the use cases.

Amazon Athena Federated Query overview

Athena Federated Query allows Athena to be a single pane of glass for querying data from data lakes, data warehouses, transactional systems, on-premises systems, SaaS-based applications, and other kinds of frameworks. Athena can connect to all these systems using connectors that leverage Lambda functions. The following figure highlights the architecture pattern for Athena Federated Query:

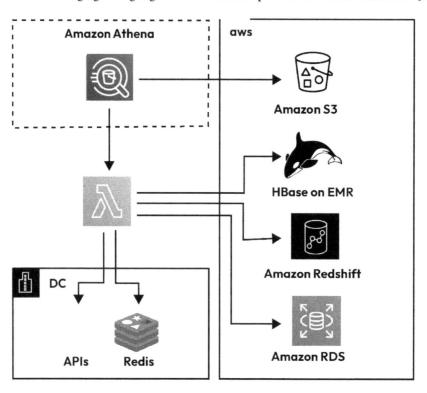

Figure 9.1 – Athena Federated Query architecture overview

Athena provides many connectors that allow you to connect to many heterogeneous systems. The following figure highlights many of the systems Athena can run federated queries from:

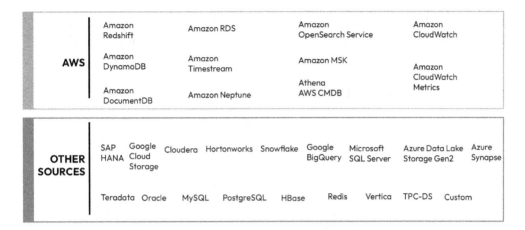

Figure 9.2 – Supported sources for Athena Federated Query

The way Federated Query in Athena works is as follows:

1. First, Athena calls the connector logic to list the schemas and tables from the source system.

2. When Athena is doing the query planning, it calls the connector logic again to fetch the partitions and splits them to create parallel processing logic.

3. When the query is executed, Athena calls the connector logic to retrieve records from all the splits of the partition.

4. If the returned data is more than what each Lambda function can handle, Athena uses an S3 bucket to temporarily spill the data over.

As you can see, the bulk of the work for federated queries in Athena is done by the connector function. Athena also pushes some predicates down to the connector so that they can be executed at the source system.

The following figure highlights how federated queries work in Athena:

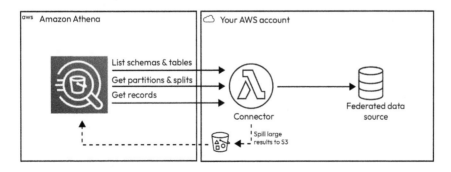

Figure 9.3 – Athena Federated Query in action

The good thing about this mechanism is that all the complexity is hidden under the covers inside the connector logic. This makes it very easy to set up federated queries in Athena, so that the focus remains on solving business use cases, instead of setting up all the building blocks.

Amazon Athena Federated Query use case

Let's dive straight into a use case for Athena Federated Query.

> **Use case for Athena Federated Query**
>
> GreatFin has data stored in many heterogeneous systems. For example, they use Amazon RDS to store all customer transaction data, Amazon DynamoDB to store all the metadata for the customers, Amazon Redshift to store all the historical data, and some API-based systems running on-premises. They want to find relevant customer insights from the data without having to move the data into a central location first. They are looking for a mechanism that will allow them to write a single query from a single interface, that will transparently join all the relevant datasets from all these different systems and give them the report in real time.

This is the kind of use case for which Athena Federated Query was created: the ability to tap into live data from many heterogeneous sources. The following figure highlights the architecture pattern to query live data from the sources described in the use case using Athena Federated Query:

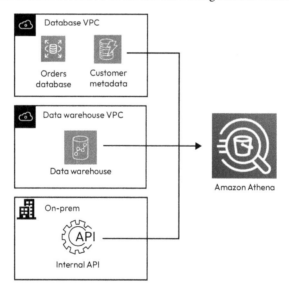

Figure 9.4 – Athena Federated Query design pattern

From our use case, let's say GreatFin wants to find all customers who have spent over a certain amount but have had delays with their shipping. The orders data is stored in RDS, the customer metadata is stored in DynamoDB, the historical data is stored in Redshift, and the APIs running on-premises capture the shipping status. Once we have created connections to all these sources in Athena, we can write the following sample query to quickly get this report from Athena itself without having to move data around or manually find data from all systems separately:

```
SELECT cm.email, cm.full_name
FROM active_orders ao
    LEFT JOIN customer_metadata cm
    ON ao.customer_id = cm._id
    LEFT JOIN order_history oh
    ON ao.customer_id = oh.customer_id
    LEFT JOIN shipping_status ss
    ON ss.shipment_id = ao.shipment_id
WHERE ss.shipment_delayed = 'Y'
    AND SUM(oh.order_total) > 5000
GROUP BY cm.email, cm.full_name
```

Creating a data source connection is fairly straightforward. Most of the connector information is provided in the Lambda function that is created as part of the Athena connection.

The following screenshot highlights the **Create data source** screen in Athena for creating a Redshift connection. To create a Lambda function that does all the connection work for you, just click on the **Create Lambda function** button:

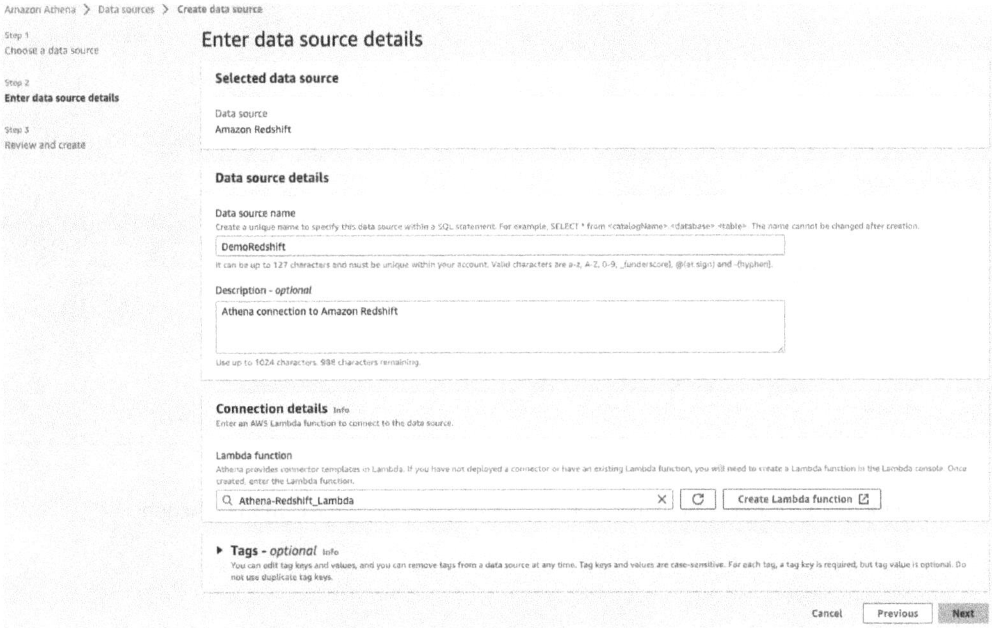

Figure 9.5 – Athena Federated Query – Create data source

The following screenshot highlights the Lambda function creation page, where you need to provide connection configurations such as a connection string, data source credential secrets, a bucket name for data spill, a subnet, a security group, and so forth. Once the Lambda function has been created, the data source connection will be ready for use in Athena:

Application settings

Application name
The stack name of this application created via AWS CloudFormation

```
AthenaRedshiftConnector
```

SecretNamePrefix
Used to create resource-based authorization policy for "secretsmanager:GetSecretValue" action. E.g. All Athena Redshift Federation secret names can be prefixed with 'AthenaRedshiftFederation' and authorization policy will allow "arn:${AWS::Partition}:secretsmanager:${AWS::Region}:${AWS::AccountId}:secret:AthenaRedshiftFederation*". Parameter value in this case should be 'AthenaRedshiftFederation'. If you do not have a prefix, you can manually update the IAM policy to add allow any secret names.

```
MyRedshiftSecret/redshiftsecret
```

SpillBucket
The name of the bucket where this function can spill data.

```
SpillBucket_XXX
```

▼ JdbcConnectorConfig

DefaultConnectionString
The default connection string is used when catalog is "lambda:${LambdaFunctionName}". Catalog specific Connection Strings can be added later. Format: ${DatabaseType}://${NativeJdbcConnectionString}

```
redshift://jdbc:redshift://redshift1.host:3306/default?...&${MyRedshiftSecret&...
```

DisableSpillEncryption
If set to 'false' data spilled to S3 is encrypted with AES GCM

```
false
```

LambdaFunctionName
This is the name of the lambda function that will be created. This name must satisfy the pattern ^[a-z0-9-_]{1,64}$

```
myRedshiftAthenaConnectorFunction
```

LambdaMemory
Lambda memory in MB (min 128 - 3008 max)

```
3008
```

LambdaTimeout
Maximum Lambda invocation runtime in seconds. (min 1 - 900 max)

```
900
```

PermissionsBoundaryARN
(Optional) An IAM policy ARN to use as the PermissionsBoundary for the created Lambda function's execution role

```
```

SecurityGroupIds
One or more SecurityGroup IDs corresponding to the SecurityGroup that should be applied to the Lambda function. (e.g. sg1,sg2,sg3)

```
sg123
```

SpillPrefix
The prefix within SpillBucket where this function can spill data

```
athena-spill
```

SubnetIds
One or more Subnet IDs corresponding to the Subnet that the Lambda function can use to access you data source. (e.g. subnet1,subnet2)

```
subnet1
```

Figure 9.6 – Athena Federated Query – creating a data source Lambda function

As you saw based on this use case, Athena Federated Query simplifies the data platform even further and makes it easy to query all these data sources seamlessly from within Athena. Some other use cases that can benefit from this architecture pattern are as follows:

- Joining orders data from relational databases with log activity data from AWS CloudWatch

- Combining data from different sources in file formats such as JSON, CSV, and Parquet

- Accessing historical data stored in legacy systems without needing to relocate it

- Joining datasets from SaaS, NoSQL, APIs, and other heterogeneous systems to make it easy to write queries just by using the ANSI SQL language

In this section, we looked at how Athena can federate data and join datasets from other systems. But what if the bulk of the enterprise data is already loaded in a data warehouse such as Amazon Redshift and certain datasets need to join with other datasets from systems outside Redshift to create a complete report? This is where Amazon Redshift federated queries come in handy. We'll look at this next.

Data federation using Amazon Redshift

Federated queries can be executed even from inside Redshift, allowing Redshift data to be joined with data from relational data sources such as PostgreSQL and MySQL, either on Amazon RDS or on Amazon Aurora. For certain use cases, it does not make sense to spend time creating an ETL pipeline to load data inside Redshift. Redshift can connect to these sources and distribute the execution of such queries down to the data source itself to improve performance.

The following figure highlights the current data sources that Redshift federated queries can work with. With the federated architecture in place inside Redshift, more source connectors may get added in the future, to expand the ecosystem and broaden the use cases that can be solved with this architecture pattern:

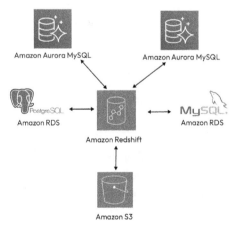

Figure 9.7 – Redshift federated queries

Amazon Redshift federated queries use case

To understand this better, let's consider a use case where federated queries from Amazon Redshift would be useful.

> **Use case for Redshift federated queries**
>
> GreatFin uses Amazon Redshift across multiple LOBs for reporting purposes and Amazon Aurora PostgreSQL is used as a transactional database. The relational database stores live operational data gathered from customer-facing applications. Instead of moving this live data for certain smaller tables into Redshift for reporting purposes, the business is seeking a mechanism from Redshift itself to query these operational tables stored in PostgreSQL and join them with other datasets within Redshift. This will eliminate continuous data movement and also get the most accurate reporting results.

Querying live data from **operational data stores** (**ODSs**) is an important use case for leveraging Redshift federated queries. In our data warehousing chapter, we emphasized that moving data around creates operational complexity and it is also time-consuming to build and maintain ETL pipelines. Not every table from an ODS may need to be copied over into Redshift for reporting. Sometimes, it makes sense to just query such ODS tables in place and fetch the datasets required to join it with other larger datasets stored inside Redshift. This is where Redshift federated queries solve this use case. To enable federated queries, all you need to do is execute some SQL statements inside Redshift.

The following sample code creates a new external schema that points to an Aurora PostgreSQL database:

```
CREATE EXTERNAL SCHEMA pgschema
FROM POSTGRES
DATABASE 'database-123' SCHEMA 'mypgschema'
URI 'database-123.cluster-democluster.us-east-1.rds.amazonaws.com'
IAM_ROLE 'arn:aws:iam::0123456789:role/Redshift-SecretsManager'
SECRET_ARN 'arn:aws:secretsmanager:us-west-
2:0123456789:secret:demo123';
```

Once this is done, to execute a query against the PostgreSQL database from Redshift, you just need to reference the externally created schema, along with the table you need data from. The following sample code fetches the most recent count of customers from the ODS:

```
SELECT count(*) FROM pgschema.customer;
```

Another use case for federated queries from Redshift would be to apply quick data transformations and load the source tables into target tables without building complex ETL pipelines. With the possibility of new source connectors being added in the future, the ecosystem will grow further and a lot more use cases will be solved with federated queries.

Before we close this chapter, it is important to keep in mind that data federation should not be used in all scenarios, specifically if the target tables have huge volumes of data, or if the target stores do not support fast and parallel execution of all such pushed down queries from Athena and Redshift. Use this feature judiciously, especially in scenarios where you don't have to build ETL pipelines for certain key tables, from where you need to pick up real-time data values, to complete your reports.

As always, feel free to do the workshops listed in the *References* section of this chapter.

Summary

In this chapter, we looked at how data federation helps organizations quickly fetch data using a single pane of glass from multiple heterogeneous source systems.

We looked at how different connectors in Amazon Athena allow for a quick and easy way to join datasets from other sources. Athena's connectors make it a seamless and transparent user experience where reports can be created just by writing SQL statements inside Athena, to join datasets from the underlying data stores.

We also looked at how Amazon Redshift can assist in federated queries, by fetching data stored in ODS systems such as MySQL and PostgreSQL. A use case that typically gets solved by this mechanism is querying live operational data that's constantly getting updated in the ODS.

The next chapter is critical in our modern data platform journey as we will discuss everything about predictive analytics and how it helps organizations think big with their data.

References

Here are some references for you to enhance your knowledge:

- Amazon Athena Federated Query workshop: `https://catalog.us-east-1.prod.workshops.aws/workshops/9981f1a1-abdc-49b5-8387-cb01d238bb78/en-US/40-federatedquery`

- Amazon Redshift federated query blog: `https://aws.amazon.com/blogs/big-data/accelerate-amazon-redshift-federated-query-adoption-with-aws-cloudformation/`

10
Predictive Analytics

A few years back, any discussion on **artificial intelligence/machine learning** (**AI/ML**) used to be a niche topic, relegated to the end chapters of most data platform books. The primary reason for this lack of urgency was due to the fact that AI/ML projects didn't give a positive **return on investment** (**ROI**) for most businesses, due to the high **total cost of ownership** (**TCO**), for making AI/ML-based predictions a reality. However, with the onset of cloud technologies and the benefits it brings to businesses, AI/ML has become one of the primary topics of discussion and implementation for almost all businesses. We are now at a stage where any organization not doing any kind of predictive analytics is at risk of losing out to its competitors, who are constantly striving to look into the future and make business decisions based on it.

The topic of AI/ML is dense, and often, you will see a series of books catering to specific areas of it. Since we only have a chapter for it in this book, keeping in sync with the same theme of this book, we will keep our discussions to how **Amazon Web Services** (**AWS**) services can help organizations solve their predictive analytics use cases. For this predictive analytics chapter, we will mostly leverage use cases around structured/semi-structured data and highlight how AWS services can derive value from this data by predicting outcomes that help organizations take proactive decisions across all facets of their business.

Before we dive into AWS services used for AI/ML-based predictive analytics, let's quickly look at what role these technologies play in helping organizations look into the future, based on what has already occurred in the past.

In this chapter, we will look at the following key topics:

- Role of AI/ML in predictive analytics
- Barriers to AI/ML adoption
- AWS AI/ML services overview
- AWS AI services, along with use cases
- ML using Amazon SageMaker, along with use cases
- ML using Amazon Redshift and Amazon Athena

Role of AI/ML in predictive analytics

Before we get into the role of AI/ML, let's quickly understand how AI, ML, and **deep learning (DL)** are co-related.

AI refers to a field of computer science that focuses on creating intelligent machines or systems that can perform tasks that typically require human intelligence. AI aims to simulate human cognitive processes such as learning, reasoning, problem-solving, perception, and language understanding. Out of the many possibilities, some examples of AI are speech recognition, **computer vision (CV)**, **natural language processing (NLP)**, learning, and problem-solving.

ML is a subfield of AI that focuses on the development of algorithms and models that allow computers to learn and make predictions or decisions without being explicitly programmed. ML also gets referred to as predictive analytics since it's able to predict outcomes. Examples of ML usage in business terms would be sales forecasting, fraud detection, sentiment analysis, and image and speech recognition.

ML provides three approaches to learning—**supervised learning (SL)**, **unsupervised learning (UL)**, and **reinforcement learning (RL)**. In SL, input and output labels are present in the data and the algorithm maps the inputs with the output. In UL, there are no labels in the data, and the algorithm discovers patterns from the data. RL uses a continuous feedback loop to create an optimal output based on rewards and penalty mechanisms. A perfect example of RL is playing board games with a computer.

ML also has a branch where the human brain is mimicked by using **neural networks (NNs)**. This branch is referred to as DL. DL is particularly useful in areas around speech and image recognition.

The following diagram encapsulates the relationship between AI, ML, and DL:

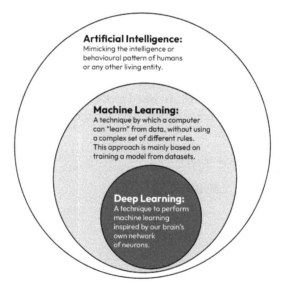

Figure 10.1 – Relationship between AI, ML, and DL

Now that we have the definitions and differences sorted out, let's understand what role AI/ML plays in predictive analytics. To understand this better, the following diagram represents some of the questions each department in an organization would want to ask:

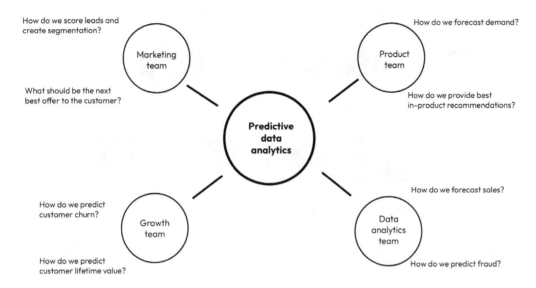

Figure 10.2 – Typical questions asked by organizations

Organizations that can most accurately predict possible future outcomes will have a definite edge over their competitors. Predictive analytics refers to when organizations apply ML algorithms to train a model based on data they have collected. The trained model then can predict future possibilities when similar new datasets are provided as input. The end goal of organizations is to infer outcomes and make key decisions based on the predictions. Accurate predictions lead to better proactive decisions.

However, to get to the end outcome of predicting results, a lot of steps need to be followed. Even though ML algorithms play a critical role in building models that can infer future results, some steps need to occur before and after the models are created. The following diagram highlights the steps that lead toward creating a predictive analytics platform:

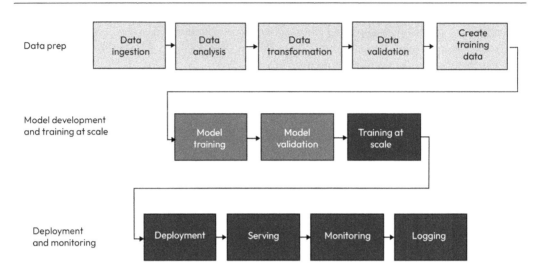

Figure 10.3 – Typical ML steps for predictive analytics

We will go into a use-case-driven discussion of many of these ML steps and how AWS services and features help simplify the whole process. For now, just remember that ML technologies help organizations build data platforms that can perform predictive analytics. These predictions can then be incorporated into ML-driven applications that can be deployed internally to help different personas make business decisions or be deployed to external customers to make their interactions very personalized.

Different ML algorithms perform different kinds of predictions. For example, a linear regression algorithm is used for risk analysis, along with sales and demand forecasting. A logistics regression algorithm can be used to predict if someone will default on a bank loan. A random forest algorithm can be used to create a risk profile for a loan applicant. A K-means clustering algorithm is frequently used to identify groupings and patterns in data. Likewise, many such algorithms allow businesses to build ML-driven applications and products. In this chapter, we will focus on data-driven predictive analytics.

Before we look at how AWS services can help in AI/ML, it is critical to understand the traditional barriers that have made it difficult for the widespread adoption of AI/ML technologies in general.

Barriers to AI/ML adoption

For many years, AI/ML technology adoption was challenging for many organizations for many reasons. Let me quickly summarize some of them here:

Challenge	Reasons
Expensive infrastructure	Training ML models on large datasets required a lot of compute, memory, and storage. Multiple iterations of tuning made this whole process very expensive on traditional on-prem infrastructure as all this hardware had to be procured upfront.
Not enough data scientists and ML builders	Building ML systems required niche skill sets with an understanding of complex ML algorithms. This made it difficult for organizations to easily acquire resources that had all the necessary skill sets to help them build an ML platform.
Tedious and time-consuming processes	Accessing, processing, and labeling large volumes of data is a laborious process, and a lot of data preparation is needed even before the ML models can be trained.
Too many platforms, tools, and algorithms to choose and manage	For every kind of problem, there are specific tools and algorithms to understand and manage. This complicates the adoption of any AI/ML platform.
Tedious operational processes	Even after the platform is up and running, the operational overhead is high as multiple ML pipelines need to be built, which again requires different tools and expertise.
Tough to implement ML governance	It's tough to master the art of implementing governance in ML processes. It is difficult to simplify access control across the full ML life cycle.

These are just some of the reasons AI/ML traditionally has lagged in adoption. It was different to get an ROI on such projects.

However, with cloud technologies, a lot of these barriers got broken down, and organizations could clearly see the huge potential of a successful AI/ML project. Without further delay, let's jump straight into how AWS services can help with such projects and how predictive analytics is again at the forefront of every modern data platform being built.

AWS AI/ML services overview

AWS provides a very broad set of AI/ML services, right from specialized infrastructure and ML frameworks that allow ML engineers to custom train their ML models and deploy them on custom hardware. This includes ML frameworks such as PyTorch, TensorFlow, and Apache MXNet. ML infrastructure often requires plenty of CPU and GPU power. AWS provides many types of **Amazon Elastic Compute Cloud** (**Amazon EC2**) instances such as the P3 and Trn1 instances that are suitable for ML training. AWS also provides ML accelerators such as AWS Trainium for DL training and AWS Inferentia for high-performance ML inferences.

The next layer of services revolves around ML. AWS ML services are created specifically keeping in mind many of the barriers to ML adoption. In order to democratize ML, it is essential to have different services geared toward different personas in the organization. For the same reason, AWS has created ML services that can help multiple personas, even those that do not understand ML technologies. Amazon SageMaker is a service that helps build, train, and deploy ML models with a broad set of tools and fully managed infrastructure capabilities. Business analysts who have limited knowledge of ML can easily use SageMaker Canvas as a no-code platform to quickly generate ML predictions. SageMaker Studio Lab allows anyone to experiment with ML without any hassles of setting up the environment. We will dig deeper into SageMaker and its use cases later in this chapter.

The topmost layer of the stack is the collection of AI services that AWS offers. AI services cater to common use cases in each domain where the models are prebuilt. AI services can either be for core purposes such as Amazon Polly for text-to-speech, Amazon Transcribe for speech-to-text, and Amazon Rekognition for image processing or can be for specialized purposes, such as Amazon Fraud Detector for fraud detection and Amazon Monitron for predicting industrial equipment failures. The following diagram summarizes the high-level areas where AWS is able to assist with AI/ML services:

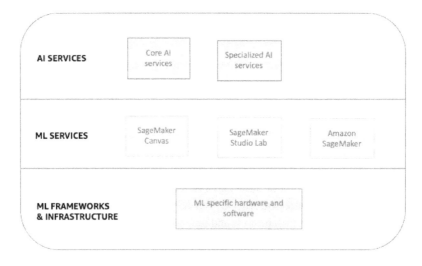

Figure 10.4 – AWS AI/ML stack

Let's begin our use-case-driven journey by looking at which AI services AWS has to offer.

AWS AI services, along with use cases

AWS offers over 20 AI services providing different capabilities in core as well as specialized categories. Core areas include vision, speech, text, and chatbots, whereas specialized areas include business processes, search, healthcare, industrial, DevOps, and generative AI. For the purpose of this chapter, we will not be able to cover each and every AWS AI service along with its use cases, but we will quickly summarize them here so that you are aware of when to use them for your specific use cases:

AWS AI service	Description	Common use cases
Amazon Rekognition	Makes it easy to perform image as well as video analysis. You can build apps that leverage Rekognition to identify people, text, objects, and other activities from pictures and videos.	• Identity verification • Workplace safety • Inventory management • Damage detection • Content moderation
Amazon Translate	Provides language translation in batch as well as in real time.	• Media subtitles • Social media and game chats • **Voice of Customer (VoC)** analysis
Amazon Comprehend	Discovers insights from text and provides analysis of the content along with context.	• Customer sentiment analysis • Automated document processing • Call center and support ticket automation
Amazon Textract	Helps extract printed text, handwriting, or any other data from documents in an automated manner.	• Compliance and control • Automatic indexing and searching material from documents • Business process automation

Amazon Transcribe	Automatic speech recognition in batch as well as in real time.	• Medical transcription • Video captions • Voice messaging
Amazon Polly	Helps convert text to speech.	• Content creation • E-learning • Accessibility
Amazon Lex	Helps build conversational interfaces inside any application using text and voice.	• Chatbots
Amazon Personalize	Helps build a recommendation system and create personalized user experiences.	• Customer personalization • Similar items
Amazon Forecast	Helps deliver highly accurate forecasts.	• Resource planning • Demand forecasting • Financial planning
Amazon Fraud Detector	Helps quickly detect online fraud.	• Real-time payments • New account sign-ups • Online checkouts
Amazon Lookout for Metrics	Helps detect anomalies in metrics and also identify their root causes in an automated manner.	• Manufacturing quality control • Supply chain monitoring • **Key performance indicator (KPI) monitoring of IT infrastructure**

Amazon Kendra	Intelligent search services that can find contextual answers across documents, websites, and databases.	• Internal and external search applications • Content management
Amazon HealthLake	Enables automated extraction, indexing, and querying of health data at scale.	• Hospital optimization • Clinical decision support • Improving healthcare services
AWS Panorama	Monitors and improves industrial production processes using CV.	• Factory safety monitoring • Quality control in industrial equipment
Amazon Monitron	Monitors and predicts equipment maintenance.	• Predictive equipment maintenance
Amazon Lookout for Equipment	Anomaly detection in industrial machinery.	• Anomaly detection in machinery
Amazon Lookout for Vision	Visually spots defects and anomalies.	• Surface defects • Product defects

For other specific purposes, some other AWS AI services also exist, such as Amazon Omics, Amazon Comprehend Medical, Amazon CodeGuru, Amazon DevOps Guru, and so on. Generative AI is the latest trend, and services such as Amazon Bedrock and Amazon CodeWhisperer help in that field. We will look at generative AI services in our next chapter. New AI-based services will keep coming out, but I summarized most of them in the preceding table, along with the use cases they help to solve. If you have use cases that easily fall under the sweet spot of any of these AWS AI services, feel free to dig deeper into them and try them out. I will include some workshop links at the end of the chapter, in the *References* section.

Since our book is all about building modern data architecture using AWS services, let's introduce a use case that can help us augment and enhance the capabilities of the data platform. Since you have already understood how to create a data warehouse using Amazon Redshift, let's build upon that and see how some of these AWS AI services can help expand the capabilities of the platform.

> **Use case for using AWS AI services in a modern data platform**
>
> The GreatFin consumer-facing **line of business** (**LOB**) collects all data in its Redshift data warehouse for analytics purposes. Consumers frequently review products and services and provide valuable feedback. GreatFin analyzes this feedback so that it can better serve its customers' requests. The feedback contains valuable insights, such as product/service satisfaction or grievances, customer sentiment, feature improvements, and so forth. Also, much of the feedback is in different languages. GreatFin needs to design a process that can convert all feedback into English and then perform an analysis of the feedback to provide a better service. The eventual business goal is better customer satisfaction and improved **customer lifetime value** (**CLV**).

This use case is tricky to solve using traditional data technologies as understanding different languages and correctly converting them to a standard language is never easy. The other part of the use case is where the sentiments of the feedback need to be extracted so that appropriate actions can be taken. It would be extremely tedious to do this manually or write logic to go through all possible sentiments and to understand the context behind those sentiments. In a modern data architecture, technologies should work without friction to achieve a positive result in all use cases.

Now, it's pretty evident that this language translation and comprehension of sentiments in text is part of the ML process. So, the obvious choice would be to extract the feedback from the data warehouse and feed it to an ML algorithm that could train and build an ML model. This task would require setting up a new project that would take months and would also require a team of data scientists and ML engineers to get to the end outcome.

To avoid this exact pain of extra time and budget to get to the end result, we would instead prefer to use AWS AI services to quickly get the desired outcomes without spending time on endless cycles of ML model training. If you look back at the table of AWS AI services, we listed previously, Amazon Translate would help convert the feedback from all other languages into English, and Amazon Comprehend would help with sentiment analysis. The following diagram shows the high-level architecture for solving this use case:

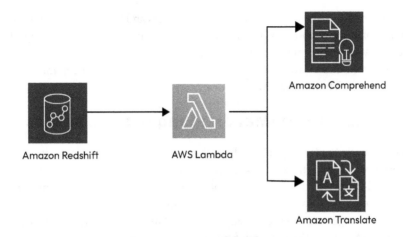

Figure 10.5 – AWS AI services to augment analytics use cases

However, the bigger question is this: How do we invoke these two AI services from Amazon Redshift so that data in the feedback column is used as input and we get back the output we desire from these services? The answer lies in Redshift **user-defined functions** (**UDFs**). Redshift allows you to register and use Lambda functions as external functions. Inside this lambda function, you would put your logic to pass the input to any of the AWS AI services that you want to leverage for your use case and get back the outcome from them. In a way, UDFs shield all the complexity and make it transparent for Redshift SQL engineers to just call this function from Redshift itself and get back the output required from other AWS services.

The following is a sample UDF in Redshift that you can call to get the sentiment behind the feedback field. The output of this function will return a positive result because the input feedback depicts a happy sentiment:

```
SELECT f_sentiment_analysis('I am extremely satisfied by this
product', 'en') AS sentiment
```

Similarly, you can create a UDF for language translation. The lambda function behind this SQL function will do all the heavy lifting of calling the Amazon Translate service and getting back the desired response.

You can either store the output back into the same Redshift table or push it into a **Simple Storage Service** (**S3**) data lake using the Redshift Spectrum layer. The possibilities are endless. This is just a sample use case; you can enrich your data platform by calling any of the 20+ AI services that AWS offers to fast-track the process of achieving business outcomes.

By now, you'll have got the gist of which AI services AWS offers and how they can be used to quickly augment your data platform without the need to spend a lot of time and effort building ML models. However, there are a vast number of use-cases where there is a need to analyze the data, create features, and train and deploy models in order to derive final inferences. Let's dive deep into some services AWS provides to fast-track building an ML platform.

ML using Amazon SageMaker, along with use cases

One of the biggest barriers to ML adoption has been that not everyone in the organization understands how the ML process works or has the skill sets to build an end-to-end ML platform. Amazon SageMaker is a comprehensive ML service that helps different personas easily use the platform to build, train, and deploy ML models for any use case. Data scientists want to quickly prepare the data to train and build ML models. ML engineers want to quickly deploy and manage these models at scale. Business analysts want to make ML predictions without having to learn ML technologies. This is where Amazon SageMaker as an ML platform helps. It's a collection of tools that make every step of the ML process easier, faster, and cheaper to implement for different personas in the organization. The following diagram depicts this aspect of SageMaker:

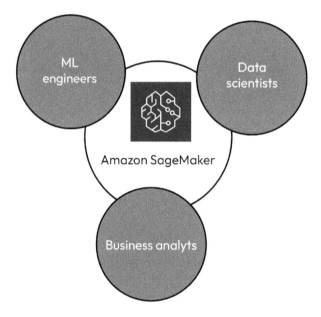

Figure 10.6 – Amazon SageMaker user personas

Let's get started with Amazon SageMaker and look at all its components. We will also look at specific use cases solved by each of the SageMaker tools.

Amazon SageMaker Canvas

One of the biggest challenges with ML platforms is the lack of resources, along with time and budget constraints. Adoption and use of ML-based outcomes exponentially grow if business analysts can leverage ML platforms without having to spend a lot of time learning how to build ML models. A common ask from business analysts has been to provide them with low-code/no-code-based tools so that they can also analyze data and build ML models quickly, without knowing the underlying ML algorithms.

This is where Amazon SageMaker Canvas helps. It's a low-code/no-code and very intuitive UI-based tool that can help quickly build and deploy ML models. Canvas has built-in **automated ML** (**AutoML**) that can quickly build models and generate accurate predictions. These models can be shared with other teams, thus making it a collaborative approach to building. The usage-based costs make Canvas a very appealing tool for businesses as they don't have to spend significant costs upfront. Overall, SageMaker Canvas makes it possible to democratize ML.

Let's understand Canvas better with a use case from GreatFin.

> **Use case for using Amazon SageMaker Canvas**
>
> The GreatFin mortgage LOB wants to decrease the number of loan defaulters by proactively understanding if a person would repay the loan or not before approval is given. The bank has years of loan data that it wants to analyze to quickly decide the risk profile. However, the team does not have expertise in building predictive ML processes. There are many business analysts who understand the data, and GreatFin would like to provide them with the right set of tools to quickly analyze the data, build ML models, and provide batch as well single-value predictions for loan status as the outcome.

The key here in this use case is the persona responsible for creating a predictive analytics process—the business analyst. Ideally, they would want to use a no-code solution where they can provide the input dataset, click a few buttons, and get the ML model trained and deployed for inferencing.

Let's walk through this process by showing how easy it is to solve this use case using Amazon SageMaker Canvas. Canvas provides an intuitive UI where the analyst can easily import datasets either from files or from Amazon S3, Amazon Redshift, and Snowflake. The following screenshot shows the Canvas console for importing datasets:

Figure 10.7 – Amazon SageMaker Canvas: data import

Not only you can import datasets, but you can also join different datasets to create a unified view of the data. Once data is imported/joined in Canvas, you can view the data inside the UI itself.

The following screenshot shows a sample dataset imported inside Canvas:

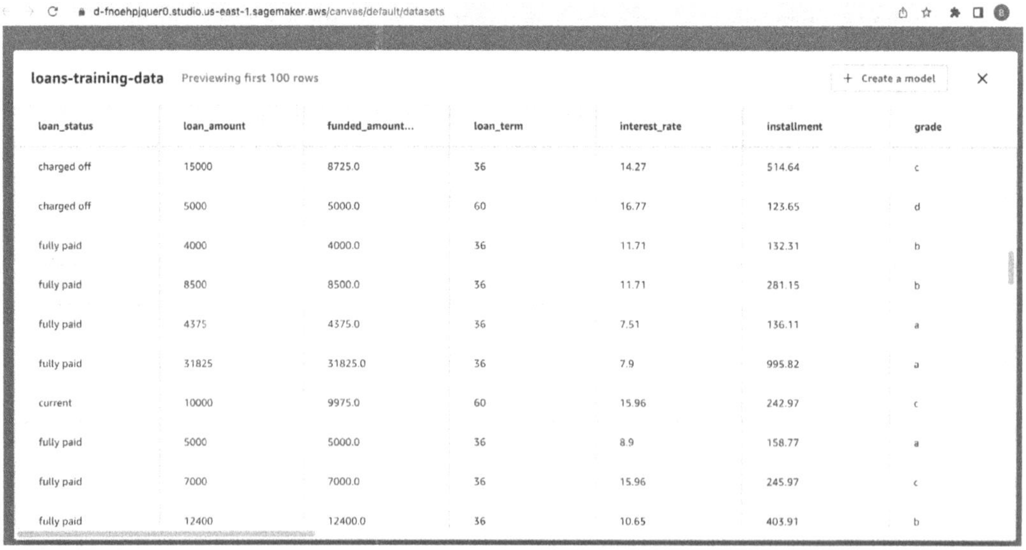

loan_status	loan_amount	funded_amount...	loan_term	interest_rate	installment	grade
charged off	15000	8725.0	36	14.27	514.64	c
charged off	5000	5000.0	60	16.77	123.65	d
fully paid	4000	4000.0	36	11.71	132.31	b
fully paid	8500	8500.0	36	11.71	281.15	b
fully paid	4375	4375.0	36	7.51	136.11	a
fully paid	31825	31825.0	36	7.9	995.82	a
current	10000	9975.0	60	15.96	242.97	c
fully paid	5000	5000.0	36	8.9	158.77	a
fully paid	7000	7000.0	36	15.96	245.97	c
fully paid	12400	12400.0	36	10.65	403.91	b

Figure 10.8 – Amazon SageMaker Canvas: data exploration

Once the data is verified and the analyst ensures all the feature columns are present for model training, just with the click of a few buttons, the training process can begin automatically. The following screenshot shows the model-building screen:

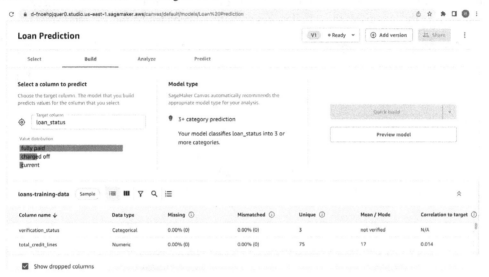

Figure 10.9 – Amazon SageMaker Canvas: ML model building

In the model-building screen, the analyst just has to pick the target column to predict and build the model. Canvas uses AutoML to build and tune the model. The analyst can also look at details of which columns in the dataset had the most impact on the model. The accuracy details of the model can also be viewed. The following screenshot shows a detailed analysis of the ML model built in Canvas:

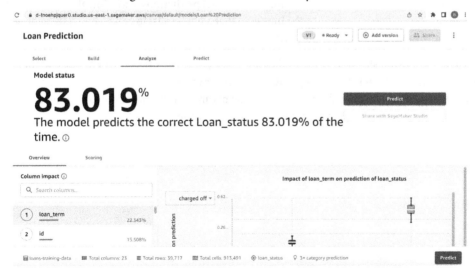

Figure 10.10 – Amazon SageMaker Canvas: ML model analysis

Canvas also provides advanced metrics around the ML model so that it's easy to understand what went into the model build and in what ways the model will affect the accuracy of the predictions.

The following screenshot shows the advanced metrics for the model build. The matrix seen is a confusion matrix that compares the actual values with those predicted by the ML model:

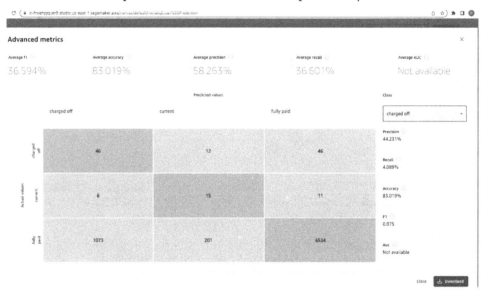

Figure 10.11 – Amazon SageMaker Canvas: ML advanced metrics

Finally, when the model is ready, the analyst can start the prediction by either introducing a batch of new data to predict or do individual predictions. Individual predictions also allow the analyst to run what-if scenarios on different aspects of the inputs so that a final decision can be taken in favor of the loan applicant with modified loan conditions.

The following screenshot shows a single prediction section in the Canvas UI where a change in input values will provide the final loan status predictions. This gives the analyst a quick and easy way not just to predict the loan status but also to change the terms and conditions of the loan if the change in some parameters can bring about a more favorable result for the applicant:

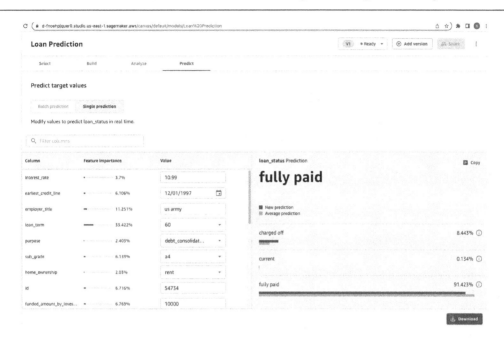

Figure 10.12 – Amazon SageMaker Canvas: ML predictions

We saw from this use case how easy it is for a business analyst without much knowledge of ML to quickly import datasets, build ML models, and get predictions. Many more use cases, such as sales conversion, churn prediction, sales and demand forecasting, credit risk scoring, and fraud detection can easily be achieved just by using SageMaker Canvas.

Canvas provides a low-code/no-code approach to ML that can be quick and easy to use but provides limited customization. ML-oriented personas such as data scientists and ML engineers need more sophisticated but integrated tools that can make their day-to-day job easy. With that context in mind, let's get going with SageMaker Studio and all that it brings to the table.

Amazon SageMaker Studio

Amazon SageMaker Studio provides a unified interface where all the stages of the ML life cycle can be performed by different ML personas. The ML life cycle often has many steps to it, and each step requires a different set of tools. Many tools can bring complexity and also increase the cost. This is why SageMaker Studio brings all these different tools under a single umbrella so that there is a seamless way to build the end-to-end ML pipeline. In a typical ML pipeline, data first needs to be prepared and features from the data need to be processed and stored. Bias needs to be detected from the features first before the model can be trained from these features. Data scientists would require a notebook environment to do some of these steps. These models need to be tuned before they can be deployed in production. Inference endpoints need to be set up and configured, and the final predictions need to be managed and monitored for drift.

Just the sheer number of steps and the different tools for each of these steps can be an overwhelming experience for an ML persona. SageMaker Studio unifies all these steps and provides tools to make the entire project seamless and fast-track the process of deriving business value out of the ML platform.

The following screenshot shows all the ML steps that can be performed inside SageMaker Studio itself:

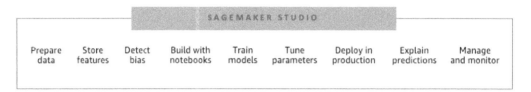

Figure 10.13 – Amazon SageMaker Studio: ML steps

Let's go into each such stage of the ML pipeline and see which tools SageMaker Studio provides to simplify the task.

Amazon SageMaker Data Wrangler

The phrase *garbage in, garbage out* is often used to highlight the fact that if the data quality of the underlying input data is bad, then the end output will also be bad. This is particularly true for the ML process. ML predictions are sensitive to which data they are trained on. The very first step in the ML pipeline is to make sure the data is prepared appropriately for the problem being solved. Raw source data may not yield the correct ML outcomes as ML algorithms may not be able to build the best model based on the raw data.

The process of transforming raw data into something that can be used to feed the ML algorithm to generate the most accurate model is called **feature engineering**, and the data elements derived from this process are called **features**. Uncovering features from raw data needs a lot of data wrangling—exploring, cleaning, and transforming raw data. The goal of data scientists is simple: take the raw data and create features out of it so that ML models are as accurate as possible. This process needs a tool that can help wrangle the data. This is where Amazon SageMaker Data Wrangler comes to the rescue.

SageMaker Data Wrangler makes it easy to import data from multiple sources—AWS-based sources as well as other third-party data sources. The following screenshot shows the SageMaker Data Wrangler import screen. The Data Wrangler tool is baked inside SageMaker Studio:

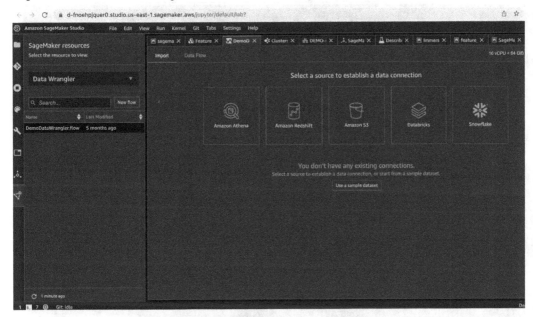

Figure 10.14 – Amazon SageMaker Data Wrangler: data import

It then makes it easy to get insights from the data and view its quality. The data exploratory features allow you to understand the data better so that you can prepare it according to the end goal.

The following screenshot shows some of the data insight capabilities of Data Wrangler inside SageMaker Studio:

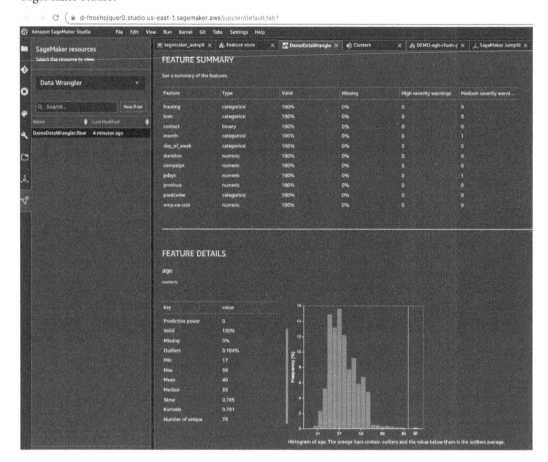

Figure 10.15 – Amazon SageMaker Data Wrangler: data insights

After the data is analyzed, data scientists can quickly add data transformations in a visual manner to make the whole experience of data wrangling very intuitive, without writing boilerplate code.

The following screenshot shows the visual data flow created using the SageMaker Data Wrangler tool:

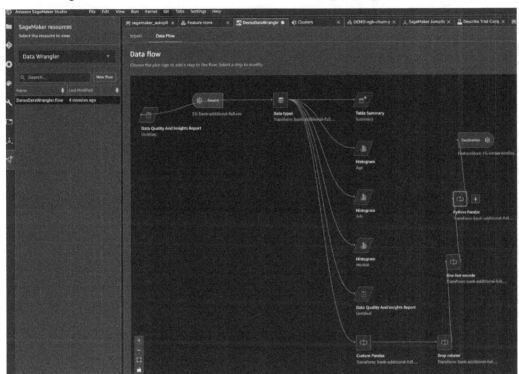

Figure 10.16 – Amazon SageMaker Data Wrangler: data flow

Once the data is imported and explored, the final prepared data needs to be stored as features so that the ML model-building process can take it as input for its training. An ideal feature store should be able to store and retrieve the features with low latency and should support both mechanisms—online and offline. Keeping the features consistent over a period of time, along with sharing them with other teams, is also a challenge. To solve this problem, SageMaker also provides a feature store—Amazon SageMaker Feature Store. Let's get into the details.

Amazon SageMaker Feature Store

Finding a data store to store all the ML features is the easy part. The real challenge is to ensure there is no drift in features over a period of time and make sure there are no feature duplications. Also challenging is to have a feature store that supports easy sharing and collaboration of features across multiple teams, to ensure there is a **single source of truth** (**SSOT**) for all features. Amazon SageMaker Feature Store solves all these challenges, plus more.

SageMaker Feature Store makes it easy to store features in an online store for low-latency predictions as well as in an offline store for batch inferences. The following screenshot shows the process of creating a feature store inside SageMaker Studio:

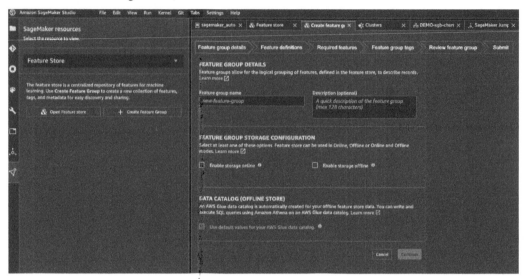

Figure 10.17 – Amazon SageMaker Feature Store: creation process

Once the feature store is created, you can have the final step in the data-wrangling process point to the feature store so that all features are mapped and stored. You can then visually search and discover features inside the studio, and all team members can also share the features and visualize them in a collaborative manner.

The following screenshot shows features that were created and stored in the offline feature store. The offline feature store can also be queried through Amazon Athena as these features are stored in an S3 data lake and cataloged in Glue Data Catalog:

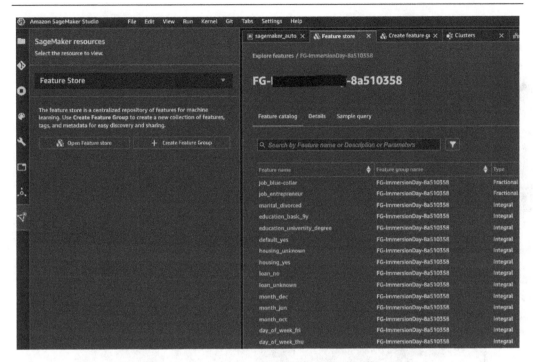

Figure 10.18 – Amazon SageMaker Feature Store: offline store

Once the features are ready, it's time to use ML algorithms and build models. This task requires specific tools such as notebooks, built-in algorithms, prebuilt solutions, and AutoML processes, and provides support for most of the major frameworks such as Hugging Face, PyTorch, TensorFlow, and MXNet. All this is baked inside SageMaker Studio. Let's quickly go over some of the tools available that help train and build an ML model.

Amazon SageMaker Studio notebooks

These are fully managed Jupyter notebooks that are preconfigured with different ML environments. The notebooks help ML personas to build and easily debug their logic, and also make it easy to convert the code into production-ready jobs. These notebooks take away the heavy-lifting aspects of building and deploying models as every activity that is part of the ML pipeline is closely integrated with the notebook itself. Another advantage of using SageMaker notebooks is that these notebooks can run in a preconfigured compute instance for jobs that can be easily finished on time within that instance itself, or for large jobs, the notebook environment can be configured to run on an auto-scaling **Amazon Elastic MapReduce (Amazon EMR)** cluster so that appropriate resources are added as needed to complete the job and terminated when not being used. This way, the ML engineer can leverage the full power of distributed computing, using Apache Spark on the EMR cluster. In short, the infrastructure management burden is taken away from the ML persona, who can focus on building the most accurate ML model.

The following is a screenshot of a SageMaker Studio notebook, which is a tool of choice for many ML practitioners:

Figure 10.19 – Amazon SageMaker notebook

Even though a notebook is the primary tool to help build models, there are other tools and features that assist in the overall build process. I will quickly summarize them here:

- **Studio Lab**: A free ML development environment that helps to get familiar with ML and allows you to experiment with it, without any infrastructure setup.

- **Autopilot**: Helps automatically create ML models and provides visibility into the process.

- **JumpStart**: UI-based program that allows anyone to quickly discover and deploy prebuilt models and algorithms for the most common use cases. This vast library of resources fast-tracks the whole process of model building.

- **Bring Your Own Model/Container**: Allows anyone to bring their own custom ML algorithm and containers to build and deploy using the SageMaker platform.

Training ML models takes time; however, most of that time is spent tuning the model to provide accurate predictions. This requires hyperparameter tuning and running the model multiple times to get the best outcome. The whole process of training and tuning is laborious. SageMaker helps to reduce this time significantly by providing built-in tools inside the studio.

When it comes to training and tuning, SageMaker Studio provides a few tools to help accelerate this process. I will summarize them here, but feel free to explore each of them in detail as SageMaker is a vast area to understand in depth:

- **Training Compiler**: Allows you to train DL models faster
- **Automatic Model Tuning**: Helps optimize hyperparameter tuning
- **Managed Spot Training**: Helps reduce training job costs
- **Debugger**: Helps to debug and profile training jobs faster
- **Experiments**: Helps to track, visualize, and share model artifacts across teams

The final steps in the ML pipeline are to deploy and manage the models. SageMaker provides a bunch of tools to help with this process too. To prevent this chapter from getting too bloated, I'll keep it to a summary here:

- **Real-time inference**: Useful for steady traffic patterns
- **Serverless inference**: Useful for intermittent traffic patterns
- **Multi-model and multi-container endpoints**: Helps reduce costs
- **Inference Recommender**: Helps to select the best compute instances and configurations in an automated manner
- **Model Monitor**: Helps to maintain the accuracy of the deployed models
- **Kubernetes and Kubeflow integration**: Helps to simplify Kubernetes-based ML

We went through the process of ML and the tools SageMaker provides to assist in all of these processes. Across all these processes, there is this constant fear of bias creeping in, which can degrade the accuracy of the ML predictions. **SageMaker Clarify** helps with this problem and allows you to identify imbalances in data during the preparation phase as well as checks for bias during the model-training process. It detects drift in bias and models over time and explains individual predictions. Clarify is also baked into the SageMaker Studio experience.

Before we move on to a SageMaker use case, we need to shed some light on one of the most complex topics about managing an ML project. How do we manage, standardize, and streamline all the operational aspects of managing an ML project? Managing all the operational aspects of ML is also called MLOps, and SageMaker provides a tool called SageMaker Pipelines to help automate and orchestrate different steps in the ML workflow. It helps ML builders to create **continuous integration and continuous deployment (CI/CD)** pipelines for ML. It also helps to track lineage for troubleshooting. We will come back to this topic in the last chapter of the book, where we discuss how to make the entire modern data platform operate autonomously.

Let's get to a use case for SageMaker by bringing up a scenario from GreatFin.

Use case for Amazon SageMaker

GreatFin would like to build a real-time predictive analytics application that can immediately provide the result of a new credit card application with either an approved or a denied decision. All consumer-related data is stored in the S3 data lake. The team is looking for an end-to-end ML platform that can help its data scientists and ML engineers build this application. The goal of the team is to make the whole ML process easy, cost-effective, and performant.

Most organizations need an end-to-end platform that can help with all the steps in a typical ML pipeline. At every step of the ML journey, specific tools of SageMaker can help simplify the process, to help build an accurate predictive analytics application.

To achieve this use case, the data scientists start by preparing the training datasets that are stored in the S3 data lake. To create features required to achieve the final outcome, SageMaker Data Wrangler is used. The features are stored in an online SageMaker Feature Store for real-time predictions. SageMaker Studio notebooks help the data scientists train the ML model, which is then hosted on a SageMaker Elastic Inference accelerated endpoint for faster predictions.

When the end application submits a customer profile for an approval decision, the request is routed via an AWS API Gateway instance, which then passes it to a lambda function for submission to the inference endpoint. The final inference decision is routed back to the end application. The inferences can be made in batch mode too with some modifications to the flow. As seen from this use case, different tools in SageMaker work in tandem to make ML projects fast, easy, and cost-effective.

The following diagram demonstrates the full architecture flow for solving this use case:

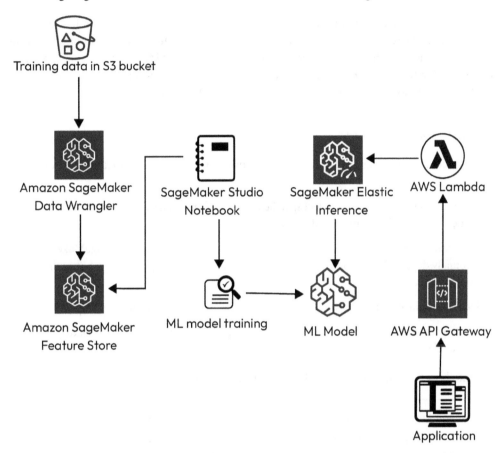

Figure 10.20 – Real-time predictions using Amazon SageMaker

The training data for this use case is in an S3 data lake, but it could very well be stored in a data warehouse inside Amazon Redshift. The same architecture will work for sourcing the training data from Redshift. But what if there aren't any data scientists in the team to help with this project? One of the key aspects of a modern ML platform is that it should democratize the use of ML technologies across different personas. Data engineers who are proficient in writing SQL-based code is in abundance in many organizations. To help them create ML models, AWS has integrated ML capabilities inside Amazon Redshift and Amazon Athena so that data engineers can create ML models just by writing SQL. Let's get into the details of this in our next section.

ML using Amazon Redshift and Amazon Athena

Many times, all the data is already processed, stored, and consumed out of Amazon Redshift using SQL-based queries. Database engineers can easily create complex SQL-based consumption patterns, but they lack the understanding to stitch together all the components of ML pipelines using SageMaker. To make their day-to-day-job lives easy, they can now build ML models inside Amazon Redshift using SQL syntax. Redshift ML handles all interactions with Amazon SageMaker, transparent to the data developer.

Some of the benefits of using Redshift ML are set out here:

- **Simplicity**: Makes it easy to create ML models using SQL. Even the predictions are done using SQL statements.

- **Flexibility**: Allows the user to select specific ML algorithms such as XGBoost. Under the covers, the best ML model is automatically trained and tuned.

- **Performant**: Even though under the covers the models are trained with SageMaker, they are eventually deployed in Redshift, and after that, all predictions happen on Redshift itself, making it performant.

- **Secure**: All the data stays inside your VPC, making the process secure.

- **Cost-optimized**: You only pay for model training, whereas predictions are made at no extra cost inside Redshift.

Let's dig into how Redshift ML works by bringing up a use case.

> **Use case for Amazon Redshift ML**
>
> GreatFin wants to predict customer churn based on customer activities so that it can proactively provide support and help before the customer decides to discontinue their relationship with the bank. The activity data is stored in Amazon Redshift for reporting purposes. The GreatFin consumer analytics team only has data developers who are experts in creating reports using SQL queries. GreatFin is looking for options to create an analytics solution for predicting customer churn in a performant, secure, and cost-effective manner.

This use case has all the buzzwords for implementing a solution using Redshift ML. To train the model inside Redshift, a SQL statement is all that's required to get back a trained model. The following diagram shows a sample training query and how that query gets passed to SageMaker behind the scenes to train the ML model:

TRAIN

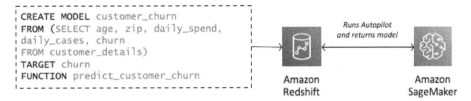

Figure 10.21 – Training model using Amazon Redshift ML

Once the model is trained, it's ready for prediction. The following diagram shows the sample SQL statement that gets executed on Redshift to get churn predictions from Redshift:

PREDICT

Figure 10.22 – Predictions using Amazon Redshift ML

You saw in this simple example how easy it was to create an ML model and predict results just by using SQL statements inside Redshift. There are many more use cases that Redshift ML can help solve when the data is in the data warehouse. Some of them are listed in the table here:

Use case	Problem type
Customer churn prediction	Classification
Demand and sales forecasting	Multiclass classification
Fraud detection	Classification
Price and revenue prediction	Linear regression
CLV prediction	Linear regression
Loan approval	Logistic regression
Advertisement optimization	Multiclass classification

Just to round up this section, Amazon Athena also allows you to make ML predictions by using SQL functions. In Athena, you can use the `USING EXTERNAL FUNCTION` clause to point to the SageMaker endpoint for getting inference results inside Athena.

The whole field of AI/ML and the use of Amazon SageMaker is a very vast topic, and we touched up many of the key components and highlighted the usage with some use cases. We have now come to the end of this chapter, but there is a lot more still to learn and unpack; we will bring up AI-/ML-based functionalities in other services too as we uncover them in the chapters ahead. Don't forget to try out many of the SageMaker-related workshops from the *References* section.

Summary

In this chapter, we looked at how AI/ML technologies play a big role in predictive analytics so that organizations can stay ahead of the curve and proactively make decisions before things happen. But at the same time, we also looked at many of the barriers related to the adoption of AI/ML and how AWS is able to overcome all these barriers.

We introduced the different stacks of how AWS provides services specific to each of these layers. For the AI layer, AWS provides a long list of 20+ services that help with specific types of AI problems such as speech, image, text, and so forth. These services help fast-track solutions that can be solved by pre-trained ML models.

We then looked at Amazon SageMaker as an ML service that has many components to it. SageMaker Canvas helps business analysts with low-code/no-code types of tools so that they can quickly create ML models and predict business outcomes. We looked at how SageMaker Studio has various tools inside it to help with each phase of the ML pipeline. SageMaker Data Wrangler helps to prepare data so that data scientists can perform feature engineering. These features then get stored in SageMaker Feature Store for batch and well as online predictions. SageMaker notebooks allow ML engineers to train and create ML models. SageMaker also provides tools such as Autopilot and Debugger and monitoring tools to help during the train, build, and deploy process. SageMaker Clarify helps detect bias and drift across all stages of ML.

We then looked at how personas proficient in SQL can leverage Amazon Redshift and Amazon Athena to create predictive analytical solutions inside these tools themselves. Just by using SQL syntax, developers can quickly create ML models and use these models to predict outcomes. A lot of use cases can be solved inside the data lake in S3 and inside the data warehouse in Redshift.

In our next chapter, we will look into the latest trend around generative AI and how AWS helps solve industry use cases with some of its offerings.

References

- Amazon SageMaker Canvas workshop: `https://catalog.us-east-1.prod.workshops.aws/workshops/80ba0ea5-7cf9-4b8c-9d3f-1cd988b6c071/en-US`

- Amazon SageMaker workshop: `https://catalog.us-east-1.prod.workshops.aws/workshops/63069e26-921c-4ce1-9cc7-dd882ff62575/en-US`

- Amazon SageMaker Data Wrangler workshop: `https://catalog.us-east-1.prod.workshops.aws/workshops/327375b8-425b-49d4-b0da-241da0595ecf/en-US`

- Amazon Redshift ML workshop: `https://catalog.us-east-1.prod.workshops.aws/workshops/4efa7f96-66a8-4b39-b7ea-c34595b2352b/en-US`

- Content moderation workshop using AWS AI services: `https://catalog.us-east-1.prod.workshops.aws/workshops/1ece9ffd-4c24-4e66-b42a-0c0e13b0f668/en-US`

11
Generative AI

Generative AI (**GenAI**) suddenly got a lot of attention after Chat-GPT was made available to the public. It was mesmerizing to see it generate human-like outputs across various domains without explicitly providing detailed instructions to the system. GenAI creates new content and ideas such as images, text, videos, music, stories, and so forth, all of which are powered by large models that are pre-trained on vast amounts of data. These pre-trained models are called **foundational models** (**FMs**).

GenAI's capabilities and possibilities have excited businesses too in terms of how they can use this technology to help their customers and make their experiences even better.

Some of the use cases that GeAI can solve are as follows:

- **Text**: Content writing, chat, taking notes, and sales and support
- **Code**: Code generation and documentation, text to SQL
- **Image and video**: Image/video generation, media and ads, social media, and design
- **Speech**: Voice synthesis and translation
- **Others**: Gaming, music, and chemistry

In this chapter, we will look at the following key topics:

- How does generative AI help different industries?
- Fundamentals of generative AI
- Generative AI on AWS
- Analytics use case with GenAI

How does generative AI help different industries?

Since we will not be able to dive deep into every use case across many industries, the least we can do is highlight how GenAI can disrupt the conventional ways of solving use cases across many sectors. Every organization wants to ensure that it can transform its business outcomes by incorporating GenAI into its operations. Every industry has many low-hanging use cases where GenAI can accelerate its business outcomes.

Financial services

Since our book revolves around GreatFin, a financial conglomerate, let's start with how GenAI helps solve several important but tedious use cases within the financial services industry. Here are some examples:

- **Fraud detection**: GenAI can play a crucial role in identifying and preventing fraudulent activities in financial transactions. By analyzing extensive datasets, generative models can detect patterns and anomalies, enabling the identification of suspicious transactions and the implementation of early warning systems for potential fraud.

- **Risk assessment and modeling**: Financial institutions can utilize GenAI to enhance risk assessment and modeling. These models generate synthetic data that simulates real-world scenarios, allowing institutions to simulate various risk factors, market conditions, and economic scenarios. This assists in better understanding and managing potential risks associated with investments and financial decisions.

- **Portfolio optimization**: GenAI can aid in optimizing investment portfolios. By analyzing historical data, generative models can generate synthetic scenarios and simulate the performance of different investment strategies. This helps financial advisors and portfolio managers make informed decisions regarding asset allocation and risk management.

- **Fraudulent document detection**: The application of GenAI can help detect fraudulent documents, such as counterfeit IDs, forged signatures, or fake invoices. By training models on large datasets containing both authentic and fraudulent documents, GenAI can identify patterns and discrepancies that indicate potentially fraudulent activities.

- **Algorithmic trading**: GenAI models are valuable in algorithmic trading by generating predictive models and signals for making trading decisions. By analyzing historical market data and identifying patterns, generative models can assist in identifying potential market trends, price movements, and trading opportunities.

- **Chatbots and virtual assistants**: GenAI can be utilized to develop intelligent chatbots and virtual assistants for customer service and support in the financial sector. These chatbots can understand customer queries, provide personalized recommendations, assist with account management, and offer financial advice.

It is important to note that the responsible and ethical use of GenAI in financial services is crucial. Financial data should be handled with proper data governance, privacy protection, and adherence to regulatory compliance standards to ensure the trust and security of customer information.

Healthcare

GenAI holds significant potential for a wide range of applications in the healthcare industry. Here are several notable use cases:

- **Medical imaging analysis**: GenAI can aid in the analysis of medical images, including X-rays, MRIs, and CT scans. By training on extensive datasets of labeled images, generative models can assist in detecting anomalies, identifying diseases, and automating image segmentation.

- **Disease diagnosis and prognosis**: GenAI models can contribute to disease diagnosis and prognosis. By analyzing diverse patient data, such as medical records, genetic information, and symptoms, generative models can offer insights for accurate disease diagnosis, risk assessment, and personalized treatment planning.

- **Medical data generation and augmentation**: GenAI allows you to generate synthetic medical data, which can augment existing datasets. This synthetic data can address limitations in real patient data availability and privacy concerns, enhancing the training of AI models and improving their performance and generalization capabilities.

- **Virtual patient simulation**: GenAI can create virtual patient models that simulate realistic physiological responses and medical conditions. These simulations are valuable for medical education, training healthcare professionals, and testing treatment strategies within controlled and safe environments.

- **Personalized medicine**: GenAI plays a role in personalized medicine by leveraging individual patient data to generate tailored treatment recommendations. By considering factors such as genetic information, medical history, and lifestyle, generative models help optimize treatment plans and improve patient outcomes.

However, compliance with regulatory guidelines, protecting patient privacy and confidentiality, and addressing potential biases are paramount to ensuring the safe and ethical use of these technologies in healthcare settings.

Life sciences

GenAI has a wide range of valuable use cases within the life sciences field. Here are some notable examples:

- **Drug discovery and design**: GenAI can expedite the process of drug discovery by generating novel molecular structures with desired properties. By analyzing extensive chemical databases, generative models can suggest potential drug candidates and aid in designing new molecules that target specific diseases or biological pathways.

- **Synthetic biology**: GenAI has applications in synthetic biology by designing and generating novel genetic sequences. These sequences can be utilized to engineer organisms with desired traits, produce specific proteins or enzymes, or develop biofuels.

- **Biomarker discovery**: GenAI contributes to biomarker discovery, which involves identifying biological indicators of diseases or physiological states. By analyzing large datasets of genomics, proteomics, or metabolomics data, generative models can discover new biomarkers that aid in disease diagnosis, prognosis, and personalized treatment strategies.

- **Protein structure prediction**: GenAI plays a crucial role in predicting the three-dimensional structure of proteins. By training on known protein structures and their corresponding sequences, generative models can generate potential structural conformations, assisting in understanding protein functions, interactions, and drug-binding sites.

- **Data augmentation and simulation**: GenAI assists in augmenting life sciences datasets by generating synthetic data. This synthetic data helps address limitations in real data availability, supports the training of AI models, and enables scenarios to be simulated to test hypotheses or optimize experimental protocols.

- **Genomic sequence generation**: GenAI models can generate synthetic genomic sequences, facilitating the study of genetic variation, gene regulation, and evolutionary processes. Synthetic sequences allow you to explore genomic landscapes, simulate mutations, and investigate genetic diseases.

- **Drug repurposing**: GenAI aids in identifying new applications for existing drugs. By analyzing drug characteristics, known disease mechanisms, and molecular interactions, generative models can suggest potential drug repurposing opportunities, accelerating the discovery of new therapeutic uses.

GenAI's ability to generate innovative solutions, simulate scenarios, and expedite data analysis holds great promise for advancing research, discovery, and innovation in the life sciences field. However, it is essential to adhere to ethical guidelines, ensure data privacy, and comply with regulatory requirements to ensure responsible and effective utilization of GenAI in these domains.

Manufacturing

GenAI holds tremendous potential for transforming the manufacturing industry with several impactful use cases. Here are some notable examples:

- **Product design and optimization**: GenAI can revolutionize product design by generating and optimizing designs based on predefined parameters and constraints. By leveraging generative models, manufacturers can explore a wide range of design possibilities, improve product performance, and accelerate the product development process.

- **Process optimization**: GenAI can optimize manufacturing processes by analyzing data from sensors, equipment, and production systems. By identifying patterns, anomalies, and optimization opportunities, generative models enable manufacturers to enhance efficiency, minimize waste, and achieve better quality control.

- **Quality control and defect detection**: GenAI can significantly improve quality control in manufacturing. By analyzing sensor data, images, or other relevant data sources, generative models can detect defects, anomalies, and variations in real time, allowing for timely corrective actions and ensuring higher product quality.

- **Supply chain optimization**: GenAI plays a vital role in optimizing supply chain operations. By analyzing data related to inventory, demand, transportation, and logistics, generative models can generate insights and simulations that assist in optimizing inventory levels, improving distribution efficiency, and ultimately enhancing the overall performance of the supply chain.

- **Predictive maintenance**: GenAI facilitates predictive maintenance by analyzing sensor data from machinery and equipment. By detecting patterns and anomalies, generative models can predict maintenance needs, optimize maintenance schedules, and minimize unplanned downtime, leading to improved operational efficiency and cost savings.

- **Resource and energy optimization**: GenAI models contribute to resource allocation and energy optimization in manufacturing. By analyzing historical data and generating predictive models, GenAI helps optimize resource utilization, minimize waste, and improve energy efficiency, resulting in reduced costs and environmental benefits.

- **Production planning and scheduling**: GenAI assists in production planning and scheduling by generating optimized plans while considering various constraints and objectives. By incorporating factors such as demand, capacity, and constraints, generative models enable manufacturers to optimize production schedules, reduce lead times, and enhance overall operational efficiency.

GenAI's potential in design optimization, process improvement, quality control, and predictive analytics holds great promise for advancing manufacturing operations. By harnessing the power of GenAI, manufacturers can unlock new efficiencies, improve product quality, and drive innovation in the industry.

Media and entertainment

GenAI holds immense potential for transforming the media and entertainment industry with a plethora of captivating use cases. Here are some notable examples:

- **Content generation:** GenAI empowers the creation of diverse forms of content, spanning text, images, music, and videos. By leveraging vast datasets, generative models can generate fresh and unique content, automating content creation for various platforms and expanding creative possibilities.

- **Personalized recommendations**: GenAI enhances recommendation systems by generating personalized suggestions for users. By analyzing user preferences, viewing habits, and historical data, generative models can generate tailored recommendations for movies, TV shows, music, and other media, elevating the user experience.

- **Virtual characters and avatars**: GenAI brings virtual characters and avatars to life for applications in video games, virtual reality experiences, and animated films. By harnessing generative models, developers can create customizable and realistic characters, heightening user immersion and interactivity.

- **Visual effects and animation**: GenAI revolutionizes visual effects and animation production. By leveraging generative models, artists and animators can automate or enhance the creation of stunning visual effects, character animations, and realistic simulations, unlocking new levels of visual storytelling.

- **Storytelling and narrative generation**: GenAI supports the creation of compelling stories and narratives. By analyzing story structures, character arcs, and plot elements from existing narratives, generative models can generate new storylines, plot twists, and dialogues, fueling the creative process for content creators and writers.

- **Image and video editing**: GenAI automates and enhances image and video editing tasks. Generative models can improve image quality, remove noise, apply stylistic filters, and even generate fresh visual content based on specific artistic styles or preferences, streamlining the editing workflow.

- **Music composition**: GenAI sparks creativity in music composition across various genres and styles. By training on extensive musical data, generative models can compose melodies, harmonies, and rhythms, offering composers and musicians a wellspring of inspiration and novel musical expressions.

GenAI's capacity to generate captivating content, deliver personalized recommendations, bring virtual characters to life, enhance visual effects, assist in storytelling, revolutionize editing, and inspire musical compositions revolutionizes the media and entertainment industry. Leveraging GenAI technologies empowers content creators, artists, and entertainment companies to push boundaries, captivate audiences, and pioneer new frontiers of creativity and entertainment.

Other industries such as energy, automotive, and telecom can all benefit from the power of GenAI to automate and simplify how they all run their operations. By highlighting all these use cases, I wanted to just give a glimpse of what the future would look like with GenAI. However, understanding the power of GenAI is one thing, but getting to a state where all these industries can easily and cost-effectively build GenAI-based systems is a completely different story.

To assist with many of the industry-specific use cases we went through in this section, it's just a matter of time until specific GenAI services are launched by AWS. This space is evolving far too rapidly to catch up in a single book. Always keep an eye on all the new announcements in the near term that align with the use case you intend to solve. For example, AWS HealthScribe was recently announced, which helps automatically generate clinical notes from patient-clinician conversations.

To assist in building GenAI-based applications, AWS provides many core services and features that help in this journey. Before we get into how AWS can help with GenAI, let's look at some fundamentals behind the magic we see from GenAI.

Fundamentals of generative AI

The fundamental of GenAI always revolves around FMs. These FMs are pre-trained on vast amounts of unstructured data and contain a large number of parameters, sometimes in the billions, which makes the FMs capable of learning new complex concepts. FMs that are used for natural language processing, such as the ones from OpenAI's GPT-3 and GPT-4, which are used in Chat-GPT, are pre-trained on a diverse range of internet text, enabling them to learn patterns, grammar, and general knowledge from vast amounts. These FMs are also called **large language models (LLMs)**.

FMs differ from other ML models in several ways:

- **Scale**: FMs are trained on massive amounts of data, often involving billions of parameters. This large scale allows them to capture complex patterns and relationships in the data.

- **Pre-training and fine-tuning**: FMs undergo a two-step training process. First, they are pre-trained on a large corpus of publicly available text from the internet, which helps them learn language patterns and general knowledge. Then, they are fine-tuned on specific tasks using task-specific datasets to make them more applicable to real-world problems.

- **General-purpose**: FMs are designed to be general-purpose, meaning they can be applied to a wide range of tasks and domains. They can perform tasks such as text classification, language translation, question-answering, sentiment analysis, and more, without requiring extensive task-specific training.

- **Transfer learning**: FMs leverage transfer learning, which means they can transfer the knowledge they've learned during pre-training to new tasks with relatively minimal fine-tuning. This enables them to adapt to specific tasks more efficiently as they already possess a strong understanding of language and context.

- **Contextual understanding**: FMs excel at capturing contextual information in text. They can understand the meaning of words and phrases concerning the broader context of the sentence, paragraph, or document. This contextual understanding allows them to generate coherent and contextually relevant responses.

- **Generation capabilities**: FMs can not only understand and classify text but also generate new text based on the input or prompt they receive. This makes them suitable for tasks such as text completion, story generation, and dialogue systems.

While foundational models have demonstrated remarkable capabilities, they also come with challenges and considerations, including ethical concerns, data biases, and potential misuse. It's important to use and develop these models responsibly, taking into account the potential implications and biases they may carry.

The following figure highlights, at a high level, how FMs differ from other ML models we are used to building:

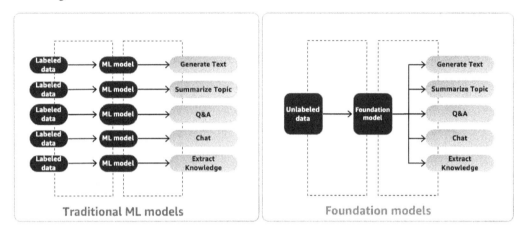

Figure 11.1 – Differences in FMs versus other ML models

Most popular FMs currently help with text generation, but multimodal FMs are quickly catching up. This is where the model is trained with text and images to get a broad category of tasks accomplished.

At this point, we understand GenAI and its business potential, and how FMs and LLMs help in this process. However, something we haven't covered yet is how we can customize the FMs so that they can be used to solve domain-specific use cases across many industries.

Customizing FMs for domain-specific GenAI involves a series of steps to adapt the models to the particular requirements and characteristics of the target domain. Here's an overview of the process:

1. **Define the domain**: Clearly define the specific domain or industry for which you want to develop the GenAI model. Understand the unique challenges, data characteristics, and desired outputs within that domain.

2. **Gather domain-specific data**: Collect a comprehensive and representative dataset specific to the domain. This dataset should include relevant examples, annotations, or labels that align with the GenAI task you aim to accomplish.

3. **Preprocess and prepare the data**: Clean and preprocess the collected data to ensure its quality and consistency. This may involve data cleaning, normalization, feature extraction, or other necessary steps specific to the domain.

4. **Fine-tune the model**: Utilize transfer learning techniques to fine-tune the pre-trained foundational model on the domain-specific dataset. This process involves retraining the model with the collected data while preserving the knowledge learned from the foundational model.

5. **Make model architecture modifications**: Consider modifying the architecture of the foundational model to better suit the specific domain. This may involve adjusting the model's layers, adding domain-specific modules, or incorporating domain-specific knowledge into the model design.

6. **Hyperparameter tuning**: Optimize the hyperparameters of the model for the target domain. Fine-tune parameters such as the learning rate, batch size, regularization techniques, or activation functions to achieve the best performance and convergence for your specific task.

7. **Evaluation and iteration**: Evaluate the customized GenAI model using appropriate evaluation metrics specific to the domain. Assess the model's performance, generate samples, and iterate on the customization process if necessary to improve the model's effectiveness.

8. **Domain-specific constraints and rules**: Incorporate any specific constraints, rules, or regulations relevant to the target domain into the GenAI model. Ensure that the generated outputs align with the domain-specific requirements and adhere to any legal or ethical guidelines.

9. **Continuous learning and adaptation**: Keep the GenAI model up to date by continuously monitoring and incorporating new data and domain-specific knowledge. Adapt the model as the domain evolves or when new data becomes available to maintain its relevance and effectiveness.

By following these steps, you can customize foundational models to develop powerful domain-specific GenAI models that address the unique challenges and requirements of your target industry or domain. Still, there are so many ML steps to build, test, and deploy before you can get to the end outcomes. However, fine-tuning an existing model, as defined in *step 4* previously is not the only technique for customizing a LLM. Many other techniques can also be levevared for specific use cases such as the following:

- **Prompt Engineering**: Craft prompts carefully to steer the model toward the desired behavior during inference

- **Dataset Augmentation**: Expand training data with techniques such as backtranslation, synonym replacement, and so on to generalize model

- **Architecture Modification**: Add/remove components such as encoder layers, attention heads based on experiments and model analysis

- **Conditioning**: Provide conditional context to model such as the speaker identity, previous dialog, external knowledge, and so on to influence its predictions

- **Chain of Thought Prompting**: Provide explicit line-by-line reasoning prompts to induce certain logic

- **Active Learning**: Iteratively select the most informative samples to fine-tune on, to maximize performance with minimal data

- **Model Training Objectives**: Train model to optimize different losses such as instruction following, summarization, consistency, and so on based on your end goals

- **Knowledge Injection**: Incorporate external knowledge source such as domain-specific ontologies to influence model behavior

- **Model Compression**: Use distillation, pruning, and quantization to customize model for specific hardware constraints

We won't be able to get into details of all these techniques but the key is to leverage the model foundations and adapt it for your specific use case through training techniques, architecture tuning, probing, and injecting custom knowledge.

This is where AWS services assist in the process. Amazon SageMaker is still at the forefront of building and deploying FMs, but some other AI services pitch in too, to make it easy to fast-track the GenAI process cost-effectively.

Now, let's pivot to how AWS can help with GenAI.

Generative AI on AWS

Ever since the art of the possibility, using GenAI has become obvious, and almost all cloud service providers and software vendors have shown a sense of urgency in providing new services/tools to help organizations build GenAI-based applications for their use cases. AWS also provides a few services that directly assist with this. Keep in mind that new services, along with new features in existing services, will continue to roll out going forward, so keep an eye on new ways of solving business use cases in the future.

To unlock the potential of GenAI, AWS focuses on a few considerations that organizations care for. Let's look at them and introduce AWS services that support these considerations.

Firstly, building ML models is never trivial; in our predictive analytics chapter, we discussed the many stages that need to be addressed before and after training an ML model. Building and using FMs at scale needs a lot of work. AWS recently announced a new service called Amazon Bedrock, which makes it easy to build and scale GenAI-based applications using FMs.

Amazon Bedrock

Amazon Bedrock makes it easy to build and scale generative AI applications with FMs from AI21 Labs, Anthropic, Stability AI, and Amazon. Bedrock manages the infrastructure and security for integrating and deploying the FMs into applications. This allows customers to focus on building GenAI-based applications instead of managing the underlying infrastructure. Bedrock supports Amazon FMs such as Titan Text and Titan Embeddings. It also supports other FMs such as Jurassic-2 from AI21 Labs, Claude from Anthropic, and Stable Diffusion from Stability AI.

With Bedrock, customers can easily fine-tune the model for specific tasks by simply selecting a few labeled examples from Amazon S3. This eliminates the need for extensive data annotation.

Let's consider a scenario involving a marketing manager at GreatFin, the financial company we have used in this book, who is responsible for developing persuasive and targeted advertising and campaign content for a new financial service offering. Utilizing Bedrock, the manager can provide a concise collection of labeled examples, comprising successful taglines and relevant descriptions from previous campaigns, to fine-tune a dedicated version of the foundational model exclusively tailored to their requirements.

By leveraging Bedrock's capabilities, the marketing manager's labeled examples enable the model to grasp the company's unique value proposition and the messaging that resonates with its target audience in the financial sector. This empowers the manager to effortlessly generate compelling content for diverse marketing channels, such as online ads, email campaigns, and website copy, to effectively promote the new financial service offering.

With Bedrock's fine-tuning functionality, the marketing manager can optimize their marketing initiatives without the need for extensive data annotation. Creating a private copy of the model, exclusively accessible to the financial company, ensures that the generated content adheres to the company's brand guidelines and captures the interest of potential customers in a personalized and impactful manner.

Bedrock also ensures that the customer's data remains private and secure. The original base models are not trained using any of the customer's data. Customers have the option to configure **Virtual Private Cloud** (**VPC**) settings to access Bedrock APIs, allowing them to provide data for fine-tuning the model in a protected manner. Additionally, all data is encrypted to further enhance security.

Following the training process, Bedrock automatically generates effective copy for various channels, including social media, display ads, and web content. Bedrock's capabilities enable customers to achieve personalized results without compromising the confidentiality of their data.

Amazon Bedrock provides a platform to make it easy to build and manage GenAI applications using FMs. However, the other big pain point for organizations trying to adopt GenAI is cost. FMs are trained on huge volumes of data, which requires a lot of CPU/GPU power to train the FMs, as well as for fast inferences to be made from them. To assist with the topic of price/performance, AWS has built some purpose-built accelerators.

AWS also announced agents for Amazon Bedrock. Amazon Bedrock agents introduce a streamlined and automated approach to prompt engineering and task orchestration based on user requests. Once set up, these agents take charge of constructing prompts and securely enriching them with company-specific data, delivering natural language responses back to users. These intelligent agents possess the capability to decipher the necessary actions for processing user requests automatically. They break down tasks into multiple steps, efficiently coordinate a sequence of API calls and data lookups, and retain context to fulfill users' actions effectively.

Let's get to the infrastructure side of things from AWS that specifically assists in GenAI.

Amazon EC2's Trn1n, Inf1/Inf2, and P5 instances

Amazon provides a few EC2 instances specifically for ML accelerations. Customers who are trying to build, run, and customize FMs need the most performant and cost-effective infrastructure. AWS Trainium instances are the most cost-effective and high-performant instances for training LLMs and diffusion models. **AWS Inferentia (Inf1)** provides the lowest cost per inference for running deep learning models in the cloud, whereas **AWS Inferentia2 (Inf2)** provides superior price/performance per inference for running LLMs.

Also recently announced were Amazon EC2 P5 instances, cutting-edge GPU instances designed to cater to the demands of high performance and scalability in AI/ML and HPC workloads. Powered by the latest NVIDIA H100 Tensor Core GPUs, P5 instances offer a remarkable reduction of up to six times in training time, significantly decreasing it from days to mere hours compared to previous-generation GPU-based instances. This enhanced performance empowers users to achieve accelerated and efficient processing, enabling faster and more impactful results in their AI/ML and HPC tasks.

AWS also powers GenAI-based applications that provide productivity for software engineers. Amazon CodeWhisperer is one great example of this.

Amazon CodeWhisperer

Amazon CodeWhisper allows customers to build applications faster by providing an AI-based coding companion. CodeWhisper can generate code suggestions in real time. It also allows users to scan the code for issues and vulnerabilities. By using CodeWhisper as a GenAI tool for coding, organizations can improve the productivity of their development teams, which allows for faster completion of projects.

CodeWhisperer is tailored to align seamlessly with your work preferences. You can choose from a diverse selection of 15 programming languages, such as Python, Java, and JavaScript, to cater to your specific coding needs. Additionally, you can work comfortably with your preferred **integrated development environments (IDEs)**, such as VS Code, IntelliJ IDEA, AWS Cloud9, AWS Lambda console, JupyterLab, and Amazon SageMaker Studio, ensuring a familiar and efficient coding experience. CodeWhisper can now also power AWS Glue Studio Notebooks, improving the data engineering experience along with boosting development productivity.

FMs using SageMaker JumpStart

Finally, one of the most important considerations for using GenAI on AWS is the flexibility it offers for organizations to either run open source FMs or help build ones on AWS. Using SageMaker JumpStart, organizations can find, explore, and deploy from many of the FMs available in the market.

The following screenshot shows many of the GenAI FMs that can be deployed using SageMaker JumpStart:

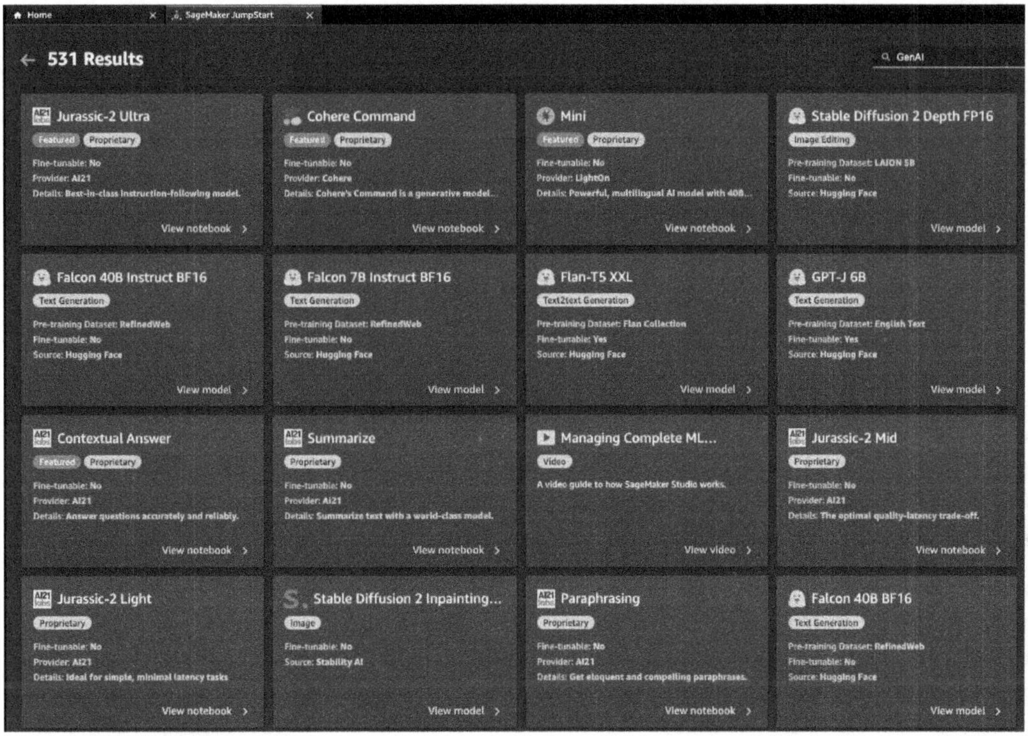

Figure 11.2 – Some of the many FMs made available in SageMaker JumpStart

You can choose the FM you want to deploy in your environment, and after trying it out, you can fine-tune it for your business and automate the ML workflow. The whole SageMaker platform makes it very flexible to leverage FMs for your domain.

Now, let's look at a use case of GenAI that can help in the field of data analytics.

Analytics use case with GenAI

It's just a matter of time before GenAI makes its way into most of the services used to build a modern data platform. In this section, we will just provide a glimpse of how GenAI can make analytics on AWS even easier. As always, here is a use case from GreatFin.

Use case for GenAI for data analytics

GreatFin has built a modern data platform on AWS and uses multiple purpose-built stores such as Amazon Redshift as a data warehouse, Amazon RDS as a transactional database, and a data lake on S3. To get data from these systems, complex SQL queries need to be written. Recently, there has been a steady request from non-technical users to provide them with a mechanism by which they can just converse in natural language and get the results from these data systems.

GreatFin has been asked to invest in mechanisms that allow anyone in the organization to request data using plain English questions. Under the covers, this is translated into the necessary queries understood by the systems. This will significantly save time as all personas can seek dynamic answers instead of requesting SQL-based reports to be built for them.

The goal of this implementation is to boost the efficiency of all business personas in the organization, including product owners and business domain experts. This can be accomplished by leveraging the power of GenAI. We aim to provide enterprise users with a user-friendly way to ask fact-based questions, without requiring in-depth knowledge of the underlying data structures. By providing this solution, we can simplify the process of writing SQL queries, making it easier to handle both simple as well as complex queries.

In this solution, the data source can be any of the ones described in the use case, or it can also be another third-party SaaS-based data store such as Snowflake. The main challenge in solving this use case is to provide the FM we will train the ability to understand the metadata of the data structures, and then auto-generate the desired SQL statement based on the input natural language question asked by the end user. The data that's returned from the source system is then translated back into plain language format so that the user can understand it easily.

The following figure explains this process of converting a natural language into SQL and the results from the database back into natural language by leveraging the power of an FM. The FM gets the metadata of all data sources from Glue Data Catalog, which is populated by crawling the data sources:

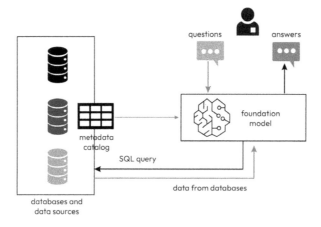

Figure 11.3 – Architecture for using FMs to simplify analytical queries

On the surface, this looks trivial, but the implementation requires some key complex steps to function with a high degree of accuracy. Let's understand the steps that we have to take to get this architecture pattern working.

The following figure highlights the inner working of the architecture:

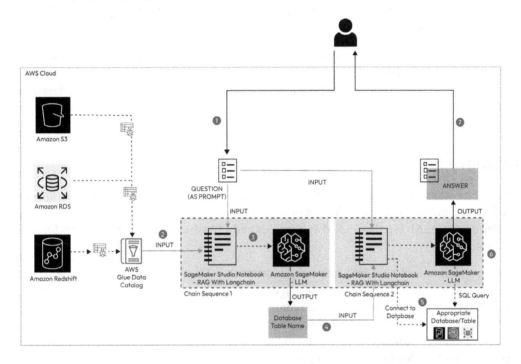

Figure 11.4 – Steps for using FMs to simplify analytical queries

Let's go through the steps:

1. A business user submits an English question as a prompt. For example, "What was the total revenue of product X in the state of Florida in May 2023?"

2. The AWS Glue crawler extracts metadata from databases and creates table definitions in AWS Glue Data Catalog. This catalog is then used as input for chain sequence 1.

3. LangChain, a tool designed for working with LLMs and prompts, is used within SageMaker Studio notebooks. In chain sequence 1, the prompt and Data Catalog metadata are provided to an LLM hosted on a SageMaker endpoint. LangChain utilizes this information to identify the relevant database and table.

4. The prompt, along with the identified database and table, is passed to chain sequence 2.

5. LangChain establishes a connection to the database and executes the SQL query to retrieve the desired results.

6. The obtained results are then passed to the LLM, which generates an English answer incorporating the data.

7. The user receives an English answer to their initial prompt, which involves querying data from multiple databases.

This example is just one of the many possible solutions that can significantly simplify how users interact with the data platform. Just by using a text-to-text FM, natural-language-to-SQL conversion was achieved and the results were output back in natural language form. By adding additional features to this solution, organizations can create applications that can work as technical chatbots for personas that are internal as well as external to the business.

Summary

In this chapter, we explored the latest trend around GenAI and how it is changing the ways businesses think about solving their use cases. We went through a range of possible use cases that each industry can solve using GenAI. We also looked at how FMs and LLMs are the core drivers for achieving GenAI outcomes.

We then pivoted toward how AWS helps organizations use GenAI for their use cases. Amazon Bedrock is a service that simplifies building and deploying GenAI applications using FMs in AWS. Purpose-built accelerators, such as AWS Trainium, are used for cost-effectively training LLMs, and AWS Inferentia and Inferentia2 are used to achieve best-in-class price performance to draw inferences from the FM models. Dedicated GenAI applications such as Amazon CodeWhisperer can help boost the productivity of the development team by auto-generating code. AWS also provides the flexibility to search for and choose from many of the FMs available in the market by using SageMaker JumpStart.

Finally, we looked at an analytics use case that helps all non-technical personas in the organization get relevant insights from the data just by asking questions in natural language instead of writing complex SQL code.

In the next chapter, we will look at operational analytics and how it helps solve specific business use cases. In the meantime, feel free to try out some of the GenAI workshops on AWS that are mentioned in the *References* section.

References

- Building GenAI applications workshop with SageMaker: `https://catalog.workshops.aws/building-gen-ai-apps-with-found-models/en-US`

- GenAI workshop on SageMaker: `https://catalog.us-east-1.prod.workshops.aws/workshops/972fd252-36e5-4eed-8608-743e84957f8e/en-US`

12
Operational Analytics

Every business performs certain operations to generate revenue. All these operations eventually generate lots of data, across multiple systems. Many organizations perform operations via the digital space by providing a variety of software applications. All these applications perform a ton of operational logs on the systems they are hosted on. There is a wealth of information in these log files – system errors, performance statistics, security aspects, network traffic patterns, customer information, and so forth. Across all these applications on multiple systems, the amount of daily log data that's generated can be overwhelming to store, manage, and analyze to get insights from it. Finding relevant pieces of information across all these logs is like finding a needle in a haystack.

To solve this problem of analyzing log data, there needs to be a suitable technology and supporting toolset that can help index all this data and make it easy to search from all the semi-structured log data. Log analytics plays a huge role across multiple use cases in many industries. Some of them are as follows:

- **Application monitoring**: Application latency issues, application errors, and infrastructure issues
- **Security monitoring**: Suspicious logins, IP tracing, and fraud investigation
- **Business insights**: Most/least frequently visited products and services and user activities
- **Observability**: Pinpoint faults in applications and narrows down latency issues

Log data is just one category of information that needs to be searched to derive insights from it. There might be other semi-structured data that needs to be searched. Traditional relational databases don't help much in these kinds of use cases since they typically store structured data in tables and to retrieve data elements, you need to provide SQL statements with specific column names.

To help with these challenges around operational analytics, we can leverage OpenSearch, and AWS makes it easy to implement operational analytics projects using Amazon OpenSearch Service. Let's get into the details of this service and go through a few use cases.

In this chapter, we will look at the following key topics:

- Amazon OpenSearch Service
- Amazon OpenSearch Service use cases

Amazon OpenSearch Service

OpenSearch (`https://opensearch.org/`) is an open source search engine forked from Elasticsearch 7.10.2. It also contains a visualization dashboard component that is forked from Kibana 7.10.2. OpenSearch has a distributed architecture where documents are collected in an index; these indices are divided into shards. Multiple nodes are present in an OpenSearch domain, where shards are replicated across nodes for high availability. In that sense, a lot of configuration, setup, and operational overhead is needed to set up a self-managed OpenSearch platform.

To alleviate the infrastructure setup pain, AWS provides a managed service that makes it easy to deploy, operate, and scale OpenSearch clusters. Amazon OpenSearch Service can either be created in provisioned mode, where users get to select the type and number of nodes to leverage in a cluster, or it can be in serverless mode, where there is no sizing to be done. Provisioned mode is suitable for steady and consistent workloads, whereas serverless mode is more suitable for intermittent or spiky workloads.

Amazon OpenSearch Service's architecture has many components to it. A leader node is responsible for all the coordination in the cluster, as well as maintaining the operating status of the cluster. The data nodes are where the actual index data is stored and managed. A low-cost storage tier called UltraWarm helps reduce the cost of storing the data in an S3-backed storage layer. This way, the hot data that is required for regular business needs is kept inside the OpenSearch-attached storage and as the data gets older and loses its value, it can be automatically transferred over to the UltraWarm tier. Ultimately, the data will move over to cold storage in S3. This smart way of moving data between tiers makes Amazon OpenSearch Service a very cost-effective solution for operational analytics.

The following figure shows a high-level architecture of how OpenSearch Service works:

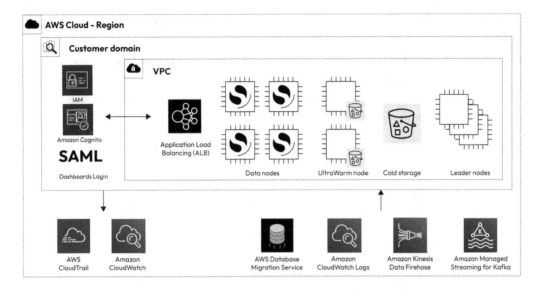

Figure 12.1 – Amazon OpenSearch Service architecture

There are a lot of things the service manages under the covers that make it even more worthwhile to use Amazon OpenSearch Service over a self-managed OpenSearch cluster. Some of the features of OpenSearch Service are as follows:

- AWS-managed scaling of clusters
- AWS-managed software installation and patching
- AWS handles Cross-Region replication with high availability
- No downtime for system updates and upgrades
- Tiered storage for cost optimization
- Auto-monitoring and repair of nodes
- Security features such as fine-grained control access, authentication, authorization, encryption, auditing, monitoring, and compliance

Before we get into some OpenSearch use cases, let's quickly look at how OpenSearch works at a high level:

1. Data from application servers, networking logs, system logs, and all other logs is first normalized and converted into JSON file format, which is then ingested into the OpenSearch domain. A continuous ingestion data pipeline is created.

2. Data is indexed in the OpenSearch domain, where all the fields are made searchable.

3. Application users, analysts, and security users can then access the OpenSearch data via REST APIs or via the OpenSearch dashboards, where they can create visualizations based on the type of analysis they want to perform.

The following figure highlights this high-level working model of OpenSearch:

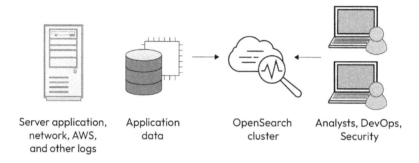

Server application,   Application   OpenSearch   Analysts, DevOps,
network, AWS,   data   cluster   Security
and other logs

Figure 12.2 – OpenSearch functionality

Amazon OpenSearch Service use cases

Let's dive straight into how Amazon OpenSearch Service can help solve many of the operational analytics use cases that organizations may have.

Application and security monitoring

Use case for application and security monitoring using Amazon OpenSearch Service

GreatFin, being a large financial conglomerate, has many applications, services, systems, and infrastructure setups across all LOBs. The security team wants to leverage a cost-effective solution to provide them with search capabilities in a centralized logging account. This will ensure that security can proactively monitor all threats and look for certain patterns in the log data. At the same time, each LOB also wants to monitor the logs for application issues and latency. The teams are looking for options to ingest data into this operational analytics platform and use dashboards with monitoring and alerting capabilities to look out for specific patterns in the data.

What the security team is requesting is the most common use case for OpenSearch. **Security Information and Event Management (SIEM)** is a system that can monitor and identify patterns in data and send alerts on certain events. However, getting all the log data into this system is the first piece of this puzzle.

Since all the different systems that produce log data are so diverse, it's always a challenge to gather the logs from all these systems, prepare them in a common pattern, and effectively store them in the OpenSearch domain. One great thing about log data analytics is that there is a big ecosystem of tools and services that helps you acquire, process, and provide mechanisms to stream the logs to an operational analytics platform. Logs from across all systems can be collected by many tools that act as log collectors. Once the logs have been picked up from the sources where they are produced, they need to be standardized and aggregated by tools called aggregators, before they can be efficiently stored in the OpenSearch domain.

The following figure highlights the data ingestion architecture using collector and aggregator tools:

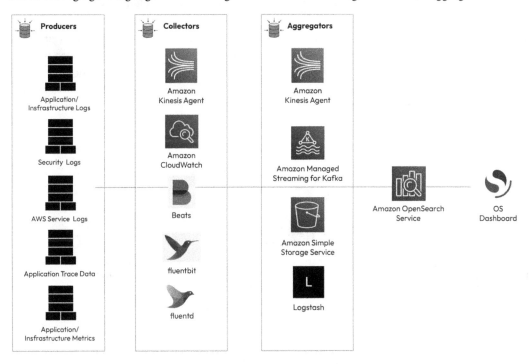

Figure 12.3 – Amazon OpenSearch Service – data ingestion

Some AWS services also act as collectors and aggregators. For example, all applications running on AWS can funnel their logs to AWS CloudWatch as a collector; from there, you can have a Lambda function that can normalize and aggregate the log data before it can be pushed into OpenSearch using bulk APIs.

The following figure shows the CloudWatch pattern with a Lambda function to ingest data into the OpenSearch domain:

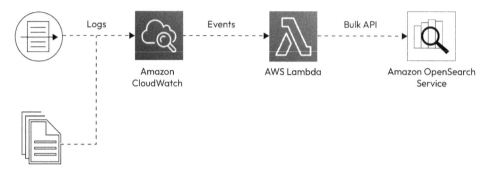

Figure 12.4 – Amazon OpenSearch Service – data ingestion with CloudWatch

The other common pattern to use to collect, normalize, and stream the logs into OpenSearch is to use Amazon Kinesis Firehose. Firehose can transform and aggregate the data and push it into OpenSearch. The following figure shows an ingestion pattern using Firehose. The Firehose agent is a handy tool that can collect logs from the logging systems and push them into Kinesis Firehose for further processing and aggregation:

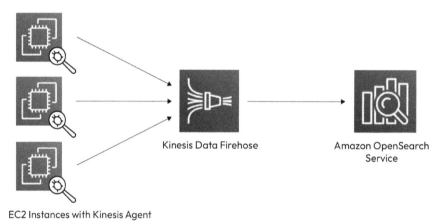

Figure 12.5 – Amazon OpenSearch Service – data ingestion using Kinesis Firehose

You can also leverage other third-party logging tools to collect, transform, aggregate, and finally push the normalized logging data into the OpenSearch domain.

The following figure shows an architecture pattern that uses fluentd, Logstash, and Kinesis to collect the log data and push it into Kinesis data streams before it's aggregated by Logstash and pushed into the OpenSearch domain:

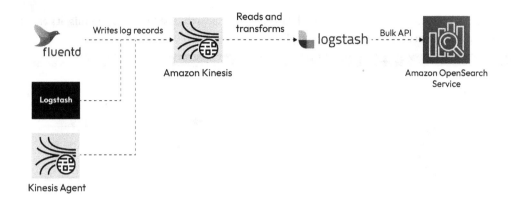

Figure 12.6 – Amazon OpenSearch Service – data ingestion using other logging tools

Once the data has been ingested in the Amazon OpenSearch Service domain, application owners can use the OpenSearch dashboards to monitor their apps for errors or latency issues. At the same time, the security team should be able to have a centralized dashboard for their SIEM system.

The following architecture is one way of solving this by using Kinesis Firehose as a streaming service to ingest the logs data from the AWS account in which the applications are running. Firehose can transform and normalize the data using a Lambda function. The application log data can be pushed into an Amazon OpenSearch Service domain in the same account for the application team to monitor. At the same time, this data is ingested in a centralized S3 bucket in the SIEM account so that it can be ingested into the security OpenSearch domain for monitoring and alerting specific to security purposes:

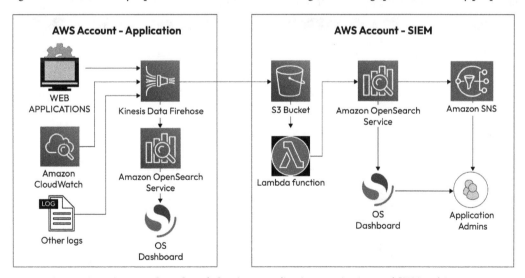

Figure 12.7 – Amazon OpenSearch Service – application monitoring and SIEM architecture

The following screenshot shows a configured Amazon OpenSearch dashboard. Using this, it's easy to visualize and summarize the findings in one place:

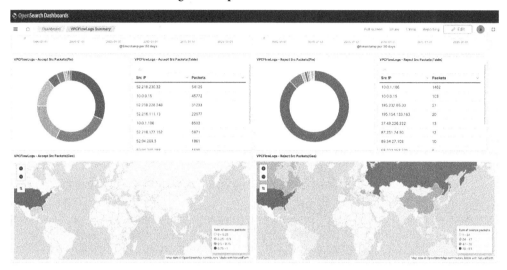

Figure 12.8 – Amazon OpenSearch Service Dashboards

OpenSearch Dashboards also allows the SIEM admin to search any data points within the log for further analysis. For example, the following screenshot shows all the rejected requests from the log data. This will allow the security admin to search for and understand particular patterns in the data after the notification has been sent out for too many rejections in a particular time window:

Figure 12.9 – Amazon OpenSearch Service Dashboards search

Let's look at one more important use case of OpenSearch before we close this chapter.

Observability

Application deployments have become more complex with microservices architectures. Critical applications are deployed with resiliency and high availability in mind. Distributed deployment patterns are used to ensure the applications are always up and running. However, with such deployment patterns, troubleshooting and debugging issues in an application becomes difficult. The logs are generated in multiple servers, which makes it difficult to correlate log data to pinpoint the issues in the application. This leads us to the topic of observability, where you need to co-relate logs, metrics, and traces across all systems to gather insights from the issues and gauge the health of these applications.

Let's get into the details of this topic by introducing a use case from GreatFin.

> **Use case for observability regarding Amazon OpenSearch Service**
>
> GreatFin, being a large financial corporation, has many critical customer-facing applications. These applications are architected based on microservices and have been deployed on a large auto-scalable farm of servers. Any issues, errors, or slowness in the applications directly affect the customer's experience and immediately need to be looked at. After this, continuous fixes and enhancements for the application need to be rolled out. The technical owners of all such applications are looking for a cost-effective platform that can help them troubleshoot issues in the application by understanding and correlating data from logs and traces.

Log data consists of events that applications generate at regular intervals. These get stored on the application servers as files. Traces are chains of related events that provide a complete request flow in any distributed system. To troubleshoot specific issues quickly, an operational analytics system needs to be in place that can ingest large volumes of logs and traces from such distributed applications, and help correlate them, so that it is easy to navigate to the actual issue. It's worth noting that there are many third-party prebuilt observability tools out there, but in this use case, for extremely large volumes of logs, a cost-effective and customizable solution is desired.

OpenSearch Dashboards has an observability plugin that helps with analyzing and correlating traces. The following screenshot highlights this option in OpenSearch Dashboards:

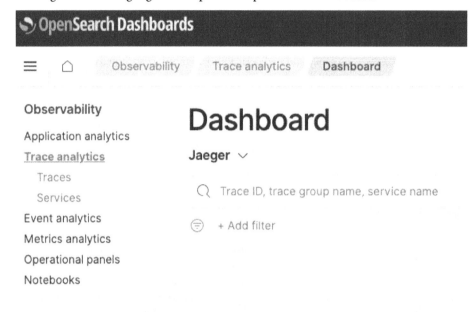

Figure 12.10 – Amazon OpenSearch Service – the Observability plugin

In our solution, we need to collect and process all the logs and traces that are generated from the microservices-based application and store them in indexes inside the OpenSearch domain.

Since logs, traces, and metrics can vary across different systems, an effort has been made to provide a unified set of standards to capture and export telemetry data to the observability backend. Collectively, this collection of tools, SDKs, and APIs is called OpenTelemetry (https://opentelemetry.io/). AWS provides a secure and production-ready version called AWS Distro for OpenTelemetry. Using this service, we can capture all the traces from the application and send correlated metrics and traces to the OpenSearch domain.

For the logs, you can use any of the ingestion tools we discussed earlier, including Amazon Kinesis, fluentd, and Logstash. For this use case, we will use FluentBit as an open source processor that collects, transforms, and sends the log data to the OpenSearch domain.

All traces and logs are also passed through the open source utility called Data Prepper, which makes it easy to enrich, normalize, and aggregate the data before it's stored in the OpenSearch indexes.

The following figure demonstrates an architecture pattern for solving this observability use case:

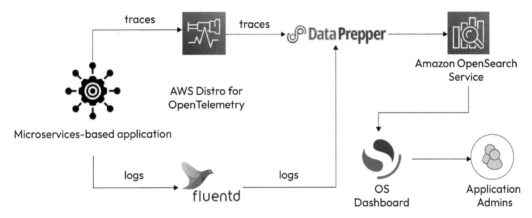

Figure 12.11 – Amazon OpenSearch Service – observability architecture

Once the solution has been deployed and the data pipeline is seamlessly pushing logs, metrics, and traces in the OpenSearch domain, you can set up observability analytics, along with visualization, inside OpenSearch Dashboards.

Using OpenSearch Dashboards, you can also query the data stored in the OpenSearch domain. This makes it easy to create customized search applications driven by OpenSearch APIs and SDKs.

The following screenshot shows a sample search query where all the "REJECT" event actions are searched for from a particular index. You can test sophisticated search patterns in the **Dev Tools** section of Dashboards and then deploy them as API calls from your calling applications:

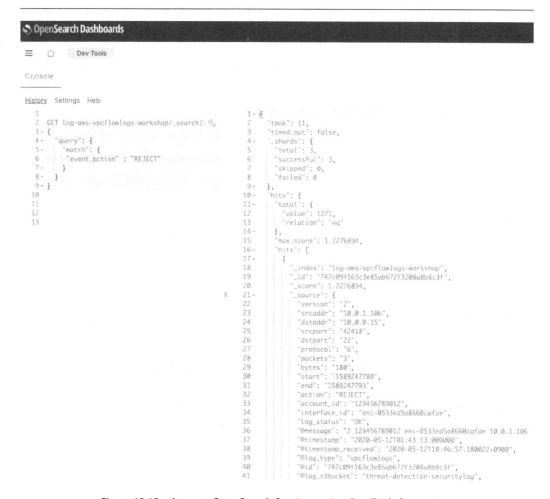

Figure 12.12 – Amazon OpenSearch Service – using Dev Tools for queries

We will keep this chapter short, but you now have an idea of what operational analytics is and how you can use Amazon OpenSearch Service to solve all use cases regarding log analytics. But before we wind down, let's look at a new capability around vector databases in which data is represented as *n*-dimensional vectors of numeric values instead of traditional rows/columns. A vector database offers an effective method for conducting similarity searches among vectors by utilizing specialized indexes, such as **k-nearest neighbors** (**k-NN**) indexes. Leveraging the vector database capabilities of OpenSearch Service enables you to integrate semantic search, **retrieval augmented generation** (**RAG**) with **language model-based logic** (**LML**), and recommendation engines, and conduct searches within rich media content.

I've added a link to a blog in the *References* section that explores the vector capabilities of OpenSearch Service in detail. Also, feel free to try the workshop to get some hands-on practice.

Summary

In this chapter, we looked at what operational analytics is and how organizations want a mechanism to gather insights from all their operational activities. All the system and application log data forms a major component of operational analytics.

We identified OpenSearch as the correct purpose-built tool for storing operational data. OpenSearch has a dashboard component that makes it easy to search for relevant information flexibly and cost-effectively. Along with specific plugins, OpenSearch Dashboards makes it easy to gain insights into log data.

We then looked into how Amazon OpenSearch Service makes the task of managing the OpenSearch cluster easy. Customers can focus on the operational insights part without having to manage the underlying infrastructure alongside the software configurations.

After, we walked through typical use cases that OS helps solve. We looked at a few options to ingest data into the OpenSearch domain. Once the data had been ingested, we looked at how application monitoring as well as a SIEM system is created using OpenSearch as the backbone service.

Finally, we looked at the latest trend around observability, where co-relations between different logs and traces need to be derived so that it's easy to troubleshoot distributed applications that follow the microservices architecture.

In the next chapter, we will look at business intelligence and how AWS can help in that area.

References

- Amazon OpenSearch Service workshop: `https://catalog.us-east-1.prod.workshops.aws/workshops/60a6ee4e-e32d-42f5-bd9b-4a2f7c135a72/en-US`
- Amazon OpenSearch Service vector database capabilities: `https://aws.amazon.com/blogs/big-data/amazon-opensearch-services-vector-database-capabilities-explained/`

13
Business Intelligence

From a business point of view, all the investments made to create a modern analytics platform is to get timely insights from the data. In many of the previous chapters of this book, we discussed topics ranging from data ingestion, data curation, data transformation and data storage. All the investment made in the analytics platform is only worth the time, effort and cost if valuable insights can be drawn from the data. Data consumption patterns dictate what an analytics platform should look like. One of the key data consumption patterns is around presenting the data to different personas in a way so that it can easily be understood. The whole point of doing data analytics is so that business decisions can be taken, to steer the organization towards rapid growth, based on the insights derived from the data. The process of deriving actionable insights from the data is termed as business intelligence (BI). To make it easy to gather insights, many organizations rely on BI tools.

Let's look at why BI tools are must for every organization building a data and analytics platform:

- **Data visualization**: The ability to visualize the data using easy to understand graphics is probably the single most important benefit of having a BI tool.

- **Business reporting**: Personas such as business leaders track performance of their businesses using BI tools that help them easily visualize data using charts and reports that can easily highlight key performance indicators (KPIs) and other metrics & measures of their business over a period of time. This helps them make key decisions depending on what they discover.

- **Operational excellence**: Using BI tools, businesses can track their product usage, remaining inventory, sales and demand tracking, operational bottlenecks, process inefficiencies and so forth. The BI tool interface makes it easy to analyze all the operational data.

- **Security and risk management**: Instead of trying to find needle in a haystack, the BI tools make it easy to bubble up all the important issues, risks and threats. The visualization component makes it easy to track the type and occurrences of such non-compliant issues.

- **Intuitive predictive analysis**: BI tools make it easy to forecast future trends, understand patterns from the data, detect anomalies using charts.

- **Embedded analytics**: Provide external customers the capabilities to analyze their own data in a visual manner.

- **Gain competitive advantages**: Ultimately every business strives to gain enough valuable insight, in the fastest possible way, to stay clear of competitors and stay ahead of the curve. BI tools fulfill a key role towards this goal.

In the ever-changing technology landscape, where the velocity, volume, variety of data collected is rapidly expanding; a lot of the legacy BI tools struggle to meet all the newer use-cases, in a performant and cost-effective manner. Legacy BI tools, especially the on-prem ones were all built to cater to specific types of data platforms. Organizations would end up using multiple BI tools, which in turn added additional operational complexity and extra licensing costs. Also, different teams with different skillsets had to be in charge of maintaining all these BI tools. Not to mention the infrastructure scaling challenges, as datasets grew bigger over time.

In this chapter we will look at the following key topics:

- Amazon QuickSight

- Amazon QuickSight use-cases

Amazon QuickSight

Keeping all the challenges of other BI tools in mind, Amazon QuickSight (QS) came about as a cloud based, unified and modern business intelligence tool for visualization and reporting purposes. QuickSight focuses on four key areas.

1. Enterprise BI capabilities allows businesses to use variety of visual options to interactively analyze all the data in a governed manner

2. Natural language processing with ML allows faster insights from data without explicitly creating rules of visualization

3. Enterprise ready reporting makes it easy to create paginated and scheduled reports in the cloud

4. Embedded analytics makes it easy to incorporate dashboards and visualization on to any custom web application

Let's look at some of the features of QuickSight that makes it a very appealing BI service for many businesses building their modern data platforms.

- Fully managed and serverless service with pay-for-usage model. Unified authoring and consumption features.

- Prebuilt connectors to data sources on-prem, in the cloud databases and also to other SaaS applications make it easy to quickly gather source data.

- Super-fast parallel in-memory calculation engine (SPICE) provides fast performance by importing up to 1 billion rows from source datasets.

- Integration synergies with other AWS data sources and services makes the whole BI experience cohesive with governance mechanisms around it.

- Paginated enterprise reporting allows high degree of formatting and printing.

- ML powered natural language query (NLQ) feature called QuickSight Q that enables users to ask questions in plain English and get back answers in BI formatted visuals and reports.

- Provides the ability to create embedded analytics. QuickSight can be embedded into any web application to get a seamless data experience to internal as well as external customers.

The following figure sums up Amazon QuickSight features and business outcomes for organizations that leverage it as a BI service, for its modern data platform.

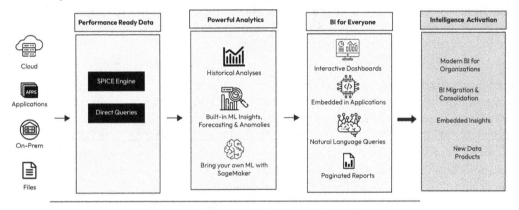

Figure 13.1 – Amazon QuickSight – capabilities and possibilities

Let's go over some of these features of Amazon QuickSight by looking at typical use-cases that customers have to solve.

Amazon QuickSight use-cases

Let's dive straight to how Amazon QuickSight can help solve many of the business intelligence and reporting use-cases that organizations may have.

Interactive dashboards

> **Use-case for interactive dashboards using Amazon QuickSight**
>
> Many LOBs of GreatFin have setup a combination of data lake on Amazon S3 along with data warehouse on Amazon Redshift. The data in the data lake is standardized in the data lake and multiple personas are able to query different datasets using Amazon Athena. Similarly, the data that's being stored in Amazon Redshift is all ready for consumption in the final base tables. Business also uses other data stores such as Amazon OpenSearch for operational analytics, Amazon Timestream for storing time series data.
>
> One of the key consumption patterns for this data is for business leaders to get an aggregated view of how the company is doing on a daily, weekly and monthly basis. The business also wants the ability to drill down on specific aspects of the dashboard to understand the underlying data that contributes to the dashboard.
>
> The business wants to setup dashboards that can visualize the data in an easy to setup tool - that is scalable, integrated with other AWS services, provides cost-effective pay as you go model of billing, and most importantly performs well.

A flexible, performant, easy to configure, easy to operationalize, cost-effective and user-friendly business intelligence tool that can help business leaders gather insights from all their data and make business decisions is the fundamental ask from all organizations. All this time and effort spent on standing up a modern data platform is of no use if it cannot guide the business on what it's going right, to double down on the efforts; and what it's doing wrong, in order to adjust and realign strategies. Business leaders don't have the time to write their own reports or find relevant pieces of information from a deluge of data. They need easy to digest dashboards that can summarize the findings in charts and graphs so that they can click on specific concerning areas to get better insights into.

There are so many BI tools out there. The decision to go with QuickSight hinges on the simple advantages we listed earlier. It's easy to configure and operationalize QuickSight, for it to work with all of the other AWS analytics services, in order to create a cohesive data platform. A hallmark of a modern data architecture is that different tools and services should seamlessly fit the different pieces of the puzzle. One of the overarching pieces of the puzzle being data governance and security. QuickSight seamlessly integrates with AWS Lake Formation to help provide a complete data governance mechanism required for business intelligence.

The following figure shows QuickSight being able to create dashboards from data stored in a data lake in S3 and also from data stored in a data warehouse in Amazon Redshift. AWS Lake Formation acts as a layer of data governance. We will discuss move about Lake Formation in our next chapter around data governance.

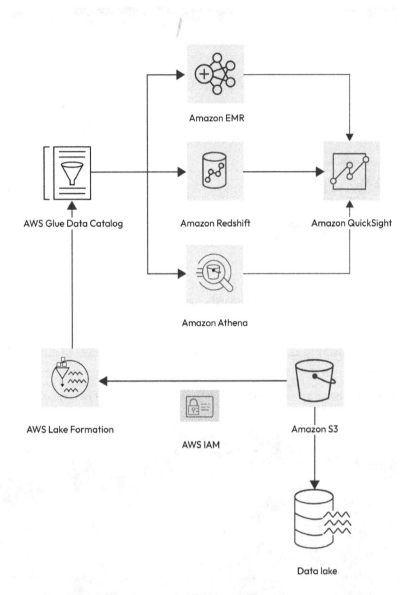

Figure 13.2 – Amazon QuickSight – AWS ecosystem synergies

Data dashboards are a collection of different charts and graphs. The publishers are users who setup the dashboards for the business leaders to use. Those setting up QS dashboards are the authors who can quickly add datasets and setup different kinds of charts.

The following screen shot shows how authors are able to quickly connect to any of the data sources and create charts by using easy to use, drag & drop UI.

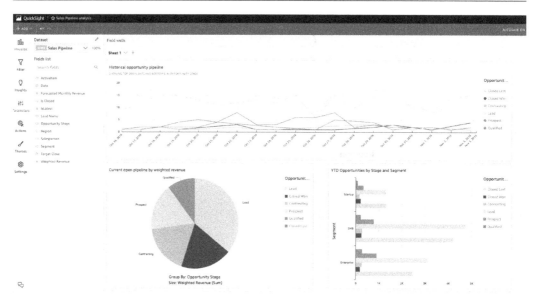

Figure 13.3 –Amazon QuickSight – authoring dashboards

Once the dashboards are authored, they can be published as links which can be setup with authentication and authorization mechanisms to allows different business leaders get access to different levels of insights from the data.

The following screen shot shows a dashboard from a business leaders' point of view, once they log in to their dashboard portal.

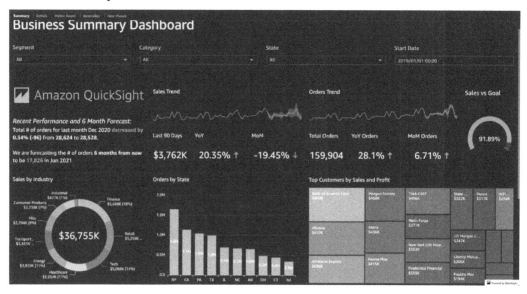

Figure 13.4 –Amazon QuickSight – business dashboard

The best thing about QS is that it has a good collection of connectors that can easily connect to other data sources as well and pull the necessary data for creating dashboards. The following figure highlights an architecture where QS dashboards can easily be created using operational data from Amazon OpenSearch Service and time-series data from Amazon Timestream database.

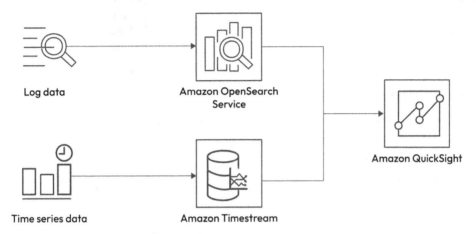

Log data

Amazon OpenSearch
Service

Amazon QuickSight

Time series data

Amazon Timestream

Figure 13.5 –Amazon QuickSight – other AWS data stores

QS can also connect to many third-party data sources, such as Snowflake and Salesforce, to fetch the data required for BI analytics.

Creating intelligent dashboards is the basic tenant of a BI tool and we saw in the above use-case how QS makes it easy to setup dashboards. However, the latest trend in the BI world is to have the ability to easily embed dashboards in any web portals for external customers to make use of it. Let's see how QS can be used for embedded analytics.

Embedded Insights

Let's get into the details of this topic by introducing a use-case from GreatFin.

> **Use-case for embedded analytics and insights**
>
> GreatFin market and securities LOB uses a web portal where customers can log in and look at their historical financial transactions and see how they performed over a period of time. The customers like to get insights of their transactions by categories, segment, industries, time ranges and other KPIs. GreatFin stores all this historical data about the customer in Amazon Redshift and would like to provide flexible capabilities where they can embed graphs and charts in the customer portal itself without having to custom build them. A cost-effective, scalable and easy to build and deploy solution is needed.

Embedded analytics generated a lot of interest lately simply because it takes a lot of time and effort to custom build graphs and charts in the web portal itself and every time a new chart with new dimensions need to be built, it takes a whole new project lifecycle to get it to production.

QuickSight provides 1-Click embedding that allows you to easily embed dashboards and any other supported visualizations into external customer facing web portals. This gives customers the ability to see and interact with their own dashboards and drill down onto details. From an organization point of view, this saves them from endless cycles of code changes to update existing setup or incorporate new logic in these visualizations.

To use the QuickSight 1-click embedding feature, typically these simple steps need to be followed:

1. **Build your dashboard or visualization in QuickSight**: Using the QuickSight service, create the dashboard or visualization you want to embed. Customize it with the desired data sources, filters, charts, and other interactive elements.

2. **Enable embedding**: In the QuickSight console, navigate to the dashboard you want to embed and select the "Embedding" option. Enable embedding for the dashboard and specify the desired embedding settings.

3. **Generate embedding code**: QuickSight generates the necessary code snippets that you can use to embed the dashboard in your application. The code includes an URL or JavaScript code that you can integrate into your application code or web page.

4. **Integrate the code into your application**: Take the generated embedding code and incorporate it into your application or web page. This typically involves adding the code to the appropriate section of your application code or HTML markup.

5. **Test and deploy**: Once you've integrated the embedding code, test your application to ensure that the embedded dashboard functions correctly within your application's context. Make any necessary adjustments or customizations as required.

The following screenshot shows a QS powered embedded visualization in a custom web site.

Figure 13.6 –Amazon QuickSight – embedded BI

Using embedded analytics in QS, organizations can easily create multi-tenant architecture patterns that can either use the same databases or different data sources. The following figure highlights a multi-tenant architecture pattern using Amazon QuickSight.

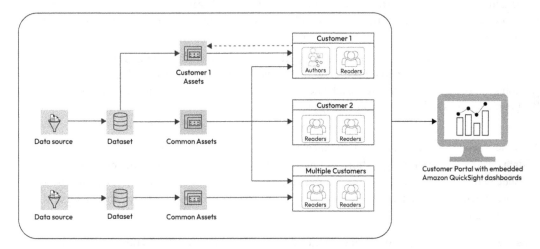

Figure 13.7 –Amazon QuickSight – multi-tenant external BI analytics

Let's look at another use-case that demonstrates QuickSight's ability to provide ML powered capabilities.

BI using ML powered NLQ

In the era of generative AI, where everyone needs answers by simply asking questions, executives want dynamic responses even from their BI tools. Amazon QuickSight Q is a ML powered feature of QuickSight that uses natural language query (NLQ) to understand intent behind the question asked to it and dynamically and immediately generates BI visualization and reports. This is going to be the future of BI tools where executives and company leaders get refined and diverse responses based on how they frame the question to the tool, so that they don't have to constantly revert back to the technical publishing team for new kinds of reports.

Let's understand QuickSight Q capability by introducing a use-case from GreatFin that specially requires ML powered capabilities to meet the requirements.

Use-case for ML powered dynamic BI visualization

GreatFin LOB leaders want to have access to dashboards that allow them provide inputs in simple English language and the tool presents them with visualization based on the context and intent behind the question. The reason they want this is because the nature of the business is such that they constantly need to seek KPIs that have different dimensions to it with respect to the business.

This capability will allow them to seek analytical insights from the data in seconds, instead of waiting for BI authors to publish new charts that would take days to build and deploy. The ability to see dynamic analytics results helps the executives to make decisions faster and take precise business adjustments on a daily basis.

Imagine an environment where non-technical users are able to seek any information from a vast sea of data, just by asking simple questions in English. It's like having a ChatGPT kind of response about the state of their business, but with dashboards and charts to make it easy to understand. This use-case is basically telling us that business leaders want insights right away, where they can self-serve their own requirements.

This is what QuickSight Q feature brings to the table. It's a ML powered NLQ feature that's baked inside the service. It empowers the users to ask questions about their business and the tool will translate it into reports & visualizations with the intended results. The knowledge layer of Q adds semantics and relationships to the underlying data and the intent is eventually represented as visuals in QS dashboards. The following figure shows how QuickSight Q works.

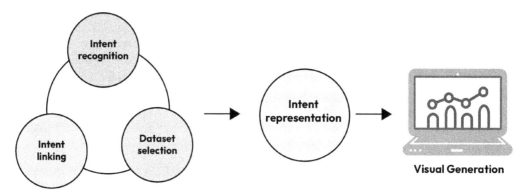

Figure 13.8 –Amazon QuickSight Q – service architecture

Once Q is setup, the users can simply type in their questions in QuickSight to generate the visualization corresponding to the context behind the question. The following screenshot shows a sample bar chart when it was asked to show total transactions by merchant type.

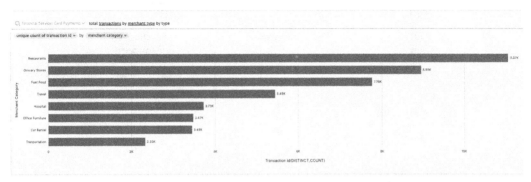

Figure 13.9 –Amazon QuickSight Q – sample visualization

With generative AI rapidly getting engrained into many services, business intelligence landscape will look completely different in the next few years. AWS also has taken the first step towards incorporating GenAI capabilities into QuickSight Q. These set of capabilities are called as 'Generative BI'. Key features include:

- **Instant visual creation**: Utilize the QuickSight Q-powered visual authoring experience to create visuals within seconds, reducing complexity and boosting productivity.

- **Intuitive visual fine-tuning**: Easily fine-tune and format visuals using natural language commands, simplifying the process and eliminating the need for specific syntax knowledge.

- **Seamless calculation creation**: Perform calculations using natural language, removing the requirement to master intricate syntax, and enabling more efficient data analysis.

For business users who consume and interact with dashboards, a new content type called Stories will be introduced. With Stories, business users can harness the power of generative BI to effortlessly generate, customize, and share captivating visual narratives through natural language prompts, delivering impactful insights and enhancing communication. Keep an eye on this topic as it will quickly become the future of BI.

Q is not the only ML driven feature in QuickSight. Many other features are also baked in the service, which provides mechanisms to leverage the full scale of the AWS platform. You can create predictive dashboards too using QuickSight. Under the covers QS uses Amazon SageMaker for ML, this removes all the undifferentiated heavy lifting required in making a BI tool work for predictive analytics. The following figure highlights this architecture feature of QS.

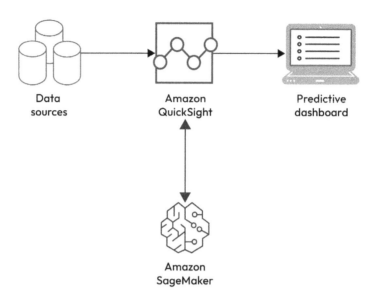

Figure 13.10 –Amazon QuickSight – predictive BI

You can also use QuickSight to build anomaly detection, forecasting and auto-narrative dashboards; which under the cover uses ML.

QuickSight is easy to get started with so we will keep this chapter short and you are always encouraged to try out the workshop from the reference section. I have also provided a link to different demos on QuickSight which will help understand the rich capabilities of the service better.

Summary

In this chapter we looked at how organizations leverage business intelligence tools. However, many of the legacy BI tools are either not able to cope with the new use-cases or struggle to keep the costs down.

Amazon QuickSight is a serverless BI service from AWS that's scalable, flexible, easy to use and operationalize; at the same time helps keep the costs down. QuickSight provides intuitive UI for authoring visualizations, dashboards and reports. The dashboards can also be embedded into other web portals to enable all customers to leverage the full power of a modern BI tool. QuickSight Q provides a ML powered NLQ feature that allows end users to ask questions in plain English and the service generates the necessary visualizations by interpreting the intent behind the question. QuickSight seamlessly integrates with other AWS services, especially with AWS Lake Formation to enable data governance with ease. A variety of BI use-cases can be easily solved using QS as it provides connectors to many of the data sources including third part SaaS data sources.

With that, we have wrapped up this chapter and also part two of this book. The core of the data platform is now set. However, the platform won't make it to production if all the components of the platform are not secured and the data cannot be governed easily and/or the platform doesn't perform well and is expensive to set up and operate in the long run to justify the return on investment.

In the last part of this book, we will cover each of these aspects in their respective chapters and provide solutions to them. The true definition of modern data architecture can only be achieved if these areas are addressed strategically.

References

- Amazon QuickSight workshop: `https://catalog.workshops.aws/quicksight/en-US`

- Amazon QuickSight Demo Central: `https://democentral.learnquicksight.online/`

Part 3: Govern, Scale, Optimize And Operationalize

In this part we cover a very important topic around governing the modern data platform, in order to make it more secure and compliant. We will also cover design aspects for scaling and optimizing the data platform. Finally, we will put this all together and show how the overall platform is operationalized and automated to run on a day-to-day basis in your production environment.

This part has the following chapters:

- *Chapter 14, Data Governance*
- *Chapter 15, Data Mesh*
- *Chapter 16, Performant and Cost-Effective Data Platform*
- *Chapter 17, Automate, Operationalize and Monetize*

14

Data Governance

A compass provides a clear sense of direction, guiding travelers through unfamiliar terrain. Similarly, data governance establishes a clear direction for an organization's data management efforts. It sets goals, defines strategies, and outlines the path toward effective data utilization, ensuring that data initiatives align with the organization's overall objectives. However, the term data governance can also get nebulous and cause friction in many organizations. Sometimes, data leaders throw the kitchen sink at it without really breaking down the individual components of data governance and understanding its relevance to the organization. A clear data strategy needs to be in place and the strategy needs to align with the business goals.

As we will uncover in this chapter, data governance is a very broad topic; trying to implement every component of governance at once, without clearly mapping value to the business, will lead to a data platform that is difficult to manage. Eventually, the return on investment in such an initiative will be negative. First, let's get clarity on what data governance means.

In this chapter, we will look at the following key topics:

- What is data governance?
- Data governance on AWS
- Data governance using Amazon DataZone
- Fine-grained access control using AWS Lake Formation
- Improving data quality using Glue Data Quality
- Sensitive data discovery with Amazon Macie
- Data collaborations with partners using AWS Clean Rooms
- Data resolution with AWS Entity Resolution

What is data governance?

Data governance refers to the overall management and implementation of policies, procedures, and standards for ensuring the high quality, integrity, and security of data in an organization.

Data is a business asset and is owned by specific LOBs in an organization. The process of improving data is continuous as new data is constantly generated and utilized by businesses for their daily operations. The improvement of data is quantified by data owners and its impact is linked directly to business outcomes.

Along with the data improvement process, the privacy and security portion of the data is also a key responsibility of the data owners. As soon as the data is compromised or misused, it can lead to severe consequences for an organization, impacting its operations, reputation, and financial well-being.

The following figure highlights the high-level components of data governance. We will dive into more details as we unfold this topic in this chapter:

Figure 14.1 – High-level components of data governance

Data strategy, data organization, and data compliance are at the very core of any data governance framework:

- **Data strategy**: Everything starts with a data strategy. A data strategy is all about how to generate value from the data and this strategy should align with the objectives of the business. For example, if you have a retail business and your goal is to provide the lowest price to your customers all the time, then your data strategy should align with that business goal. So, for this example, your data strategy would revolve around sourcing and analyzing competitors' data, continuously calculating the lowest possible prices, modernizing the price match system, performing predictive analytics on how the prices in the market will move in the future, creating a discount offer system based on customer purchase history, and so forth. All project activities revolve around the data strategy, which, in turn, pushes the business goals forward.

- **Data organization**: This involves multiple dimensions such as creating a cloud center of excellence to plan, monitor, execute, and enforce the best practices around creating and managing a data platform that aligns with the business goals. Data organization also enables you to create an operation model for the platform based on how the enterprise operates as a whole. The operation model could be a centralized, decentralized, or federated data platform, depending on your business alignment. We discussed centralized data lakes and federated analytics previously in this book. We will discuss the decentralized operating model in the next chapter, in which we'll cover data meshes.

- **Data compliance**: Data compliance could be industry-specific, such as HIPAA for the healthcare industry, or region-specific, such as GDPR for the European region.

The remaining components of data governance are implementation-specific. We will cover them in the next few sections as we unveil different AWS services to solve specific governance use cases.

Why the need for data governance?

To put it differently, data governance is the process of exercising authority and control – planning, monitoring, and enforcement – over how we manage data assets. The following figure highlights how data from input sources gets managed and governed using different mechanisms to create value for organizations based on the output generated from the data platform:

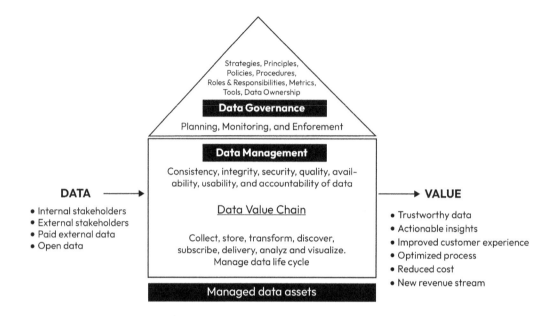

Figure 14.2 – Data governance's role in value creation

So, in short, data governance makes it easier and faster to create value from all the data while at the same time maintaining its security and integrity. A good data governance framework leads to a data-driven organization. However, being data-driven is often a challenging process due to many factors such as the exponential growth of data, the addition of new and diverse source systems, different technologies, tools, and services, strict security, regulatory and compliance requirements, and so forth. Without a sound data governance framework, businesses spend significant time creating inefficient patchwork mechanisms, which in the long run become inhibitors of a data-driven organization.

Data governance on AWS

AWS recognizes data governance as a combination of people, processes, and tools that all work in tandem to ensure that a modern data platform continuously maintains high-quality data securely. Data governance mechanisms are applied throughout the life cycle of the data – right from ingestion until consumption.

The following figure demonstrates the approach of having a governed data platform using a combination of people, processes, and technology:

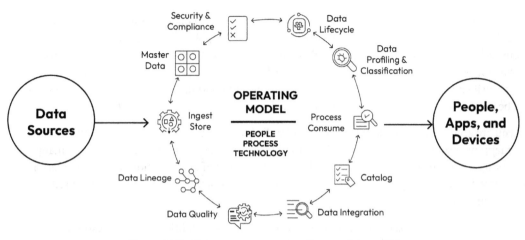

Figure 14.3 – Data governance operating model on AWS

When the rubber meets the road and you try to put technology into every type of process you want to govern, it often makes it challenging to use just a few tools or services. This is because the governance process is broad and diverse, even in terms of technology. Every tool, service, or vendor product focuses on certain components of governance. For example, some tools/vendors focus on data quality, some focus on data lineage, some focus on security and compliance, and some focus on the data life cycle.

The best thing about creating a modern data architecture on AWS is the ease with which you can leverage many of the partner solutions for specific purposes. AWS provides many services that help and assist in data governance and data security. However, there are always use cases that require niche capabilities from other technology vendors. Many vendor products work seamlessly in the AWS ecosystem.

The following figure highlights many of the AWS services that help support the creation of a data governance framework. For many other use cases, partner tools also can be leveraged to ensure business goals are met:

Figure 14.4 – AWS and partner ecosystems of services and tools to implement data governance

Once the data strategy has been defined and you have created a data platform, the next step is to identify areas across the whole platform where you need to apply a governed process. The process should add value to the business goals and enable the business to operate in an automated manner. During the project life cycle, where each area of the data platform is designed and built, the governance and security pieces should also be part of the planning and building phase. Data governance should not be an afterthought. It's an integral part of the data platform.

As you are architecting the platform, clearly map the business goals to the data strategy. When you are mapping specific AWS services as building blocks to this strategy, there should be a mapping that assigns data governance capabilities that should be part of every section of the data platform, including during data ingestion, data transformation, data storage, data curation, data enrichment, data sharing, and data consumption.

The following figure maps out some of the data governance capabilities of the corresponding AWS services and partner tools that can be leveraged to meet areas of governance:

Capability area	Capabilities	AWS tools	Partner tools
Data discovery, cataloging, and classification	Data discovery Business/technical catalog Sensitive data classification	AWS Glue Data Catalog Amazon DataZone Amazon Macie	
Data lifecycle management	Lifecycle management Data lineage Data quality Data protection Data compliance/sovereignty	Amazon CloudWatch AWS Backup AWS Glue	**Business catalog:** Collibra Alation Others
Entitlements management	Identity management Fine-grained access controls Access federation	AWS Lake Formation IAM	**Unified data access:** Privacera Okera Others
Data operations	Monitoring Reporting Auditing	Amazon CloudWatch AWS CloudTrail Amazon QuickSight	
Data integrations	Workflow management Automation/alerting Data collaboration	AWS Lambda AWS Step Functions AWS Clean Rooms	

Figure 14.5 – Data governance capabilities to AWS/partner tools mapping

Before mapping out the tools with the necessary capabilities, it is important that organizations first map out all the personas that will be interacting with the data platform at every step of the process. This helps us understand who will be interacting with the data platform and in what role. Identifying who needs what access is a critical part of a well-defined governance framework. This will make it easy to map out the tools needed to support all such interactions with the platform.

The following figure shows a sample role mapping matrix that clearly shows which personas own what portion of the data platform. Based on that, you can start building a map of all critical governance pieces that need to be in place to support business outcomes:

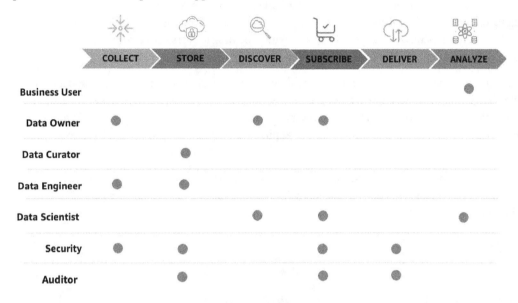

Figure 14.6 – Role mapping matrix with different stages of the data platform

As this book is all about defining use cases and architecting them, let's jump straight into some areas of data governance and the corresponding AWS services we should use to implement the solution.

Data governance using Amazon DataZone

When it comes to making data-driven business decisions, adopting an agile and productive mindset is essential. Rather than relying on a centralized data management platform that provides generalized analytics, organizations are empowering their business units to deliver data products. This approach allows LOBs and organizational units to operate autonomously, taking ownership of their data products from end to end. Meanwhile, the organization as a whole benefits from centralized data discovery, governance, auditing, data privacy, and compliance.

By decentralizing data management and encouraging ownership, organizations can unlock the full potential of their data assets. This shift empowers business units to respond quickly to evolving market needs, drive innovation, and tailor their data products to specific requirements. Simultaneously, the organization maintains oversight through centralized mechanisms that ensure compliance, privacy, and effective data governance.

Amazon DataZone

Amazon DataZone is a fully managed governance service that helps unlock data across organizational boundaries. DataZone empowers customers to seamlessly explore and exchange data at a large scale, bridging organizational barriers with robust governance and access controls. The service eliminates the tedious and time-consuming tasks associated with providing universal access to data and analytics tools within an organization.

Amazon DataZone streamlines operations, enabling business and data teams to work with data more efficiently, accelerating insights and facilitating well-informed decision-making based on accurate and reliable data. With Amazon DataZone, every individual in your organization gains the ability to effortlessly navigate through a personalized web application to discover both new and existing realms of data, all without requiring expertise in the underlying AWS data services.

The following figure highlights DataZone's value proposition by bridging the gap between the data producers and the data consumers without them having to create tightly coupled data platforms across the LOBs of the organization:

Data producers   **Amazon DataZone**   **Data consumers**

Figure 14.7 – Amazon DataZone – overview

At the core of Amazon DataZone are data producers, including data engineers and data scientists, who securely share data along with relevant business context with other members of the organization. On the other hand, data consumers, such as analysts, utilize this data to find insights and answers to business questions, subsequently sharing their findings with colleagues. This collaborative workflow establishes a decentralized and federated ownership model for both data production and consumption, often referred to as data mesh. We will go into the details of data mesh in the next chapter.

Within this model, data producers have the autonomy to publish, own, and govern their data assets by establishing publishing agreements with data stewards. This approach promotes a distributed ownership structure where data is managed at its source, ensuring accountability and expertise within each respective domain. Consequently, data consumers can access the data they require, following an approval workflow that involves interaction with the data owners.

First, let's start with DataZone's components. The following figure shows the main components of DataZone:

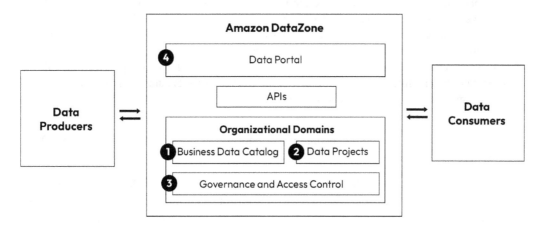

Figure 14.8 – Amazon DataZone – components

Amazon DataZone introduces four capabilities designed to enhance data management and analytics:

- **Organization-wide business data catalog**: With a business data catalog, users can efficiently organize their data and enrich it with valuable business context using comprehensive business metadata. This allows for a holistic view of data, combining technical metadata with relevant business insights.

- **Simplified access to analytics through projects**: DataZone introduces projects, enabling the creation of business-focused groups that encompass teams, tools, and data aligned with specific use cases. This approach provides a secure container for analytics work and reduces the effort required when transitioning between different services.

- **Governance and access control**: To ensure secure data sharing between producers and consumers, DataZone streamlines the process with an automated publish and subscribe workflow. This workflow guarantees that only authorized users have access to the right data for the intended purpose, enhancing governance and access control measures.

- **A data portal for enhanced exploration and collaboration**: DataZone offers a centralized data portal, providing users with an integrated and personalized data experience. Users can explore data, promote innovation, and collaborate across different functions effortlessly. The self-service nature of the data portal empowers users to work with data and tools seamlessly and efficiently.

Through these capabilities, Amazon DataZone empowers organizations to optimize their data management processes, improve collaboration, and drive innovation by providing a comprehensive and user-friendly environment for data exploration and analysis. Let's dive deep into DataZone by introducing a use case from GreatFin.

Use case for data governance using Amazon DataZone

GreatFin has multiple business units spread across different regions. The company aims to improve data collaboration and access across different LOBs while maintaining strong governance and control over data assets. They face challenges in efficiently discovering, sharing, and accessing data across organizational boundaries. The existing data infrastructure lacks centralized visibility and requires technical expertise in AWS data services, leading to delays and inefficiencies in data-driven decision-making. Many LOBs have built their data platform using AWS analytical services, and the organization as a whole is looking to streamline its data governance policies to gain insights faster across all business units.

Amazon DataZone maximizes your existing investments and seamlessly integrates with the AWS analytics stack, offering a comprehensive solution for the use case defined.

By utilizing DataZone, you can efficiently leverage your current infrastructure investments. Projects within DataZone enable you to organize source data from your Redshift warehouse or S3 data lake tables. This can be achieved by publishing the data to a dedicated Amazon DataZone domain. Once published, you can effortlessly consume the data through familiar tools such as Redshift Query Editor or Athena, ensuring a smooth transition and minimizing disruption.

Furthermore, DataZone empowers you to enhance your technical catalog by incorporating valuable business context. By adding business-specific metadata, you can enrich your existing data catalog, providing additional insights and context for improved data understanding and analysis.

To streamline permissions management and access control, Amazon DataZone seamlessly integrates with Lake Formation. This integration automates the process of granting and revoking permissions for users across your organization. By leveraging Lake Formation's robust permission enforcement capabilities, you can ensure that data access is properly governed and controlled and that it aligns with your organization's security and compliance requirements.

The following figure highlights the ease with which DataZone strategically fits into your existing analytics platform built using AWS services:

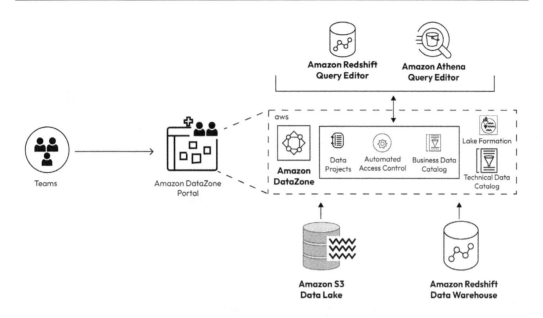

Figure 14.9 – Amazon DataZone extends the AWS analytics stack

In DataZone, everything starts with a domain where each LOB can create a domain for organizing all the metadata and and other organizational entities. Data can exist across any AWS account and in any region. The business data catalog provides a governed mechanism for teams who produce the data so that once they catalog the data, it can be published and subscribed to by others.

Domains provide the freedom to align your organization's structure by establishing hierarchical relationships between other domains. By appointing a team of skilled data experts as data stewards, you can ensure meticulous curation of metadata to uphold data quality. These experts have the authority to establish consistent terminology, specify publishing prerequisites, and enforce governance regulations for the continuous upkeep of data quality. The following figure enforces what we discussed about domains in this paragraph:

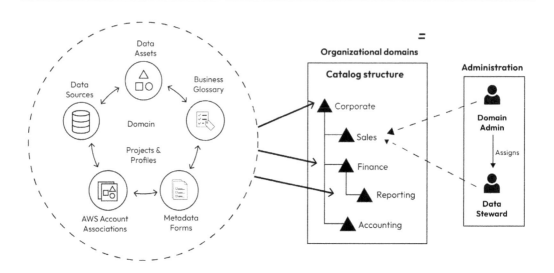

Figure 14.10 – Amazon DataZone domain

In the AWS console, when you open DataZone, it first asks you to create a domain for your organization. Once this domain has been created, a separate instance of your DataZone portal is created. The following screenshot shows the domain being created inside DataZone:

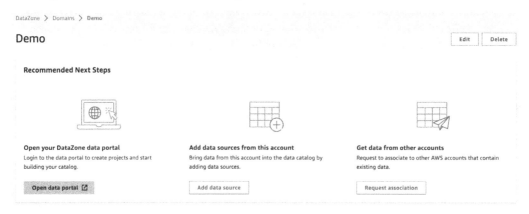

Figure 14.11 – Amazon DataZone domain creation

Once the domain has been created, it provides you with a link to a data portal and it also allows you to catalog data from all data sources.

With Amazon DataZone, you gain the capability to effortlessly publish data assets directly from Amazon Redshift or AWS Glue Data Catalog. This empowers you to harness the potential of these services to seamlessly import data from various sources, including the following:

- Your Amazon S3 data lake

- Many of the purpose-built databases on AWS through AWS Glue Crawler

- A vast selection of over 70 AWS Glue connectors

- More than 50 Amazon AppFlow connectors, enabling the acquisition of data from third-party applications such as Snowflake, Salesforce, and Google Analytics

The following figure highlights DataZone's capability to catalog all the data. This makes discovering data assets easier:

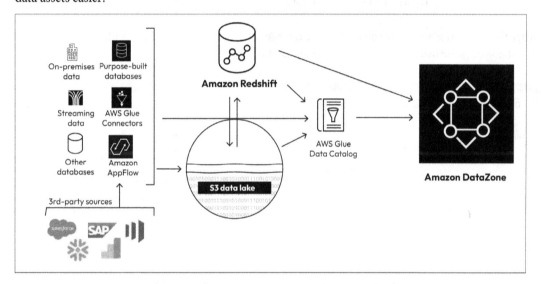

Figure 14.12 – Amazon DataZone – cataloging all the data

When you click on the Data Portal link from the domain, it opens a window outside of the AWS console, which makes it easy to integrate with your corporate identity provider. This will also enable it to be an independent application going forward.

The following figure shows the logging mechanism for the DataZone data portal, where authentication is typically done by external identity providers and authorization is done inside the AWS account:

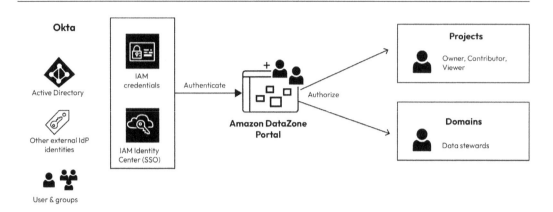

Figure 14.13 – Amazon DataZone – data portal landing page

After the authentication is complete, the user can see the landing page of the DataZone data portal. The following screenshot shows the data portal's first page once you log in:

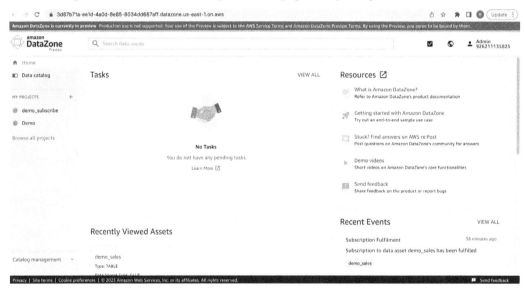

Figure 14.14 – Amazon DataZone – data portal landing page

When considering the entities responsible for publishing or subscribing to assets within a specific domain, Amazon DataZone provides the concept of data projects.

With DataZone, users can collaborate effectively by creating projects that group teams, tools, and data based on specific use cases. By leveraging projects, teams can conveniently access the necessary data assets and analytics tools required for their specific projects. They can also invite team members to collaborate on these data projects.

Projects offer managed data access for teams and groups, with their own access controls in place. This ensures that only authorized individuals, groups, and roles can access the projects and the data assets they have subscribed to. Additionally, only the tools configured within the project can be utilized. These tools or capabilities are defined during the creation of the project and can reference existing resources or policies, or in some cases, deploy new ones.

For instance, a data lake producer could create a project that deploys a Glue schema, S3 bucket, and Athena workgroup, with access provisions set up by Amazon DataZone. The following figure highlights a project inside DataZone and all its capabilities:

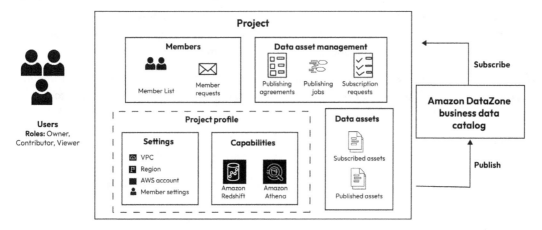

Figure 14.15 – Amazon DataZone – project

DataZone empowers projects to publish data assets to a designated DataZone domain. Furthermore, projects can discover assets from various domains and subscribe to them. Ultimately, subscriptions can be fulfilled by granting the project access to the subscribed data, enabling analysis using the project-authorized analytics services.

The following figure shows the publishing and subscribing mechanism using projects inside DataZone:

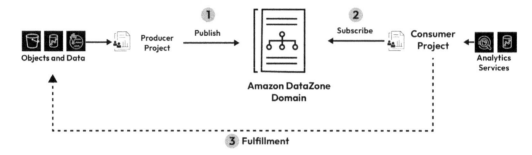

Figure 14.16 – Amazon DataZone – self-service analytics made easy

For a DataZone project to publish data, it is essential to establish a valid publishing agreement with a domain. This agreement functions as a contractual arrangement between the data producer and the catalog domain, outlining the terms and conditions of publishing and subscribing activities.

Here is a screenshot of how a publisher of the data would publish its data asset in DataZone through its project. A publishing job is created that would publish the assets that the publisher wants to make available for discovery:

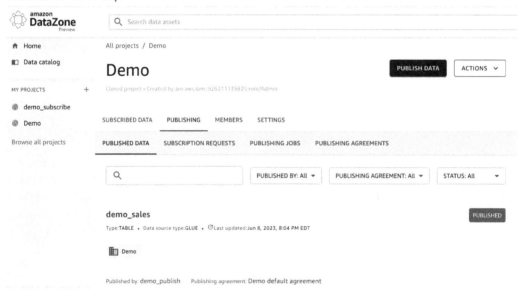

Figure 14.17 – Amazon DataZone – publisher project

Once data is published to a domain, data consumers have the opportunity to discover and request a subscription to the respective data asset.

The process starts when a data subscriber utilizes the DataZone data portal to search for and explore the catalog, aiming to find the desired data asset. Upon locating it, they can initiate the subscription request. This request includes relevant details and justification for their subscription.

The following screenshot shows the screen in DataZone for the subscriber to search for a published asset and request access to it:

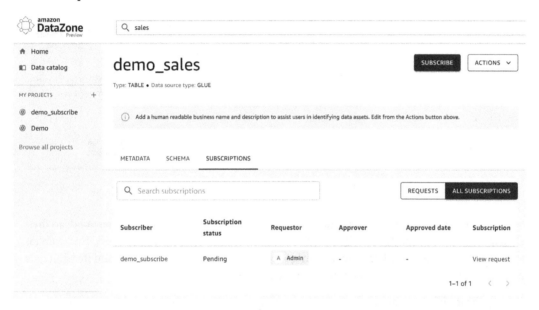

Figure 14.18 – Amazon DataZone – subscriber project

Next, the publisher of the data asset assesses the access request. They hold the authority to either approve or reject the request. Following the approval of a subscription, a fulfillment process is initiated, facilitating the subscriber's access to the data asset.

It's important to note that Amazon DataZone can automatically fulfill a subset of data assets. This depends on factors such as the type of data store and the permissions granted to the DataZone service.

The following screenshot shows the subscription request being approved by the publisher of the asset:

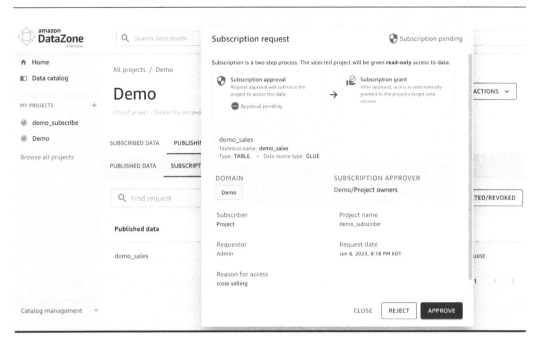

Figure 14.19 – Amazon DataZone – publisher approval

Within the Amazon DataZone data portal, users can simply click on a link that corresponds to their desired tool, be it Athena or Redshift Query Editor, within the context of a specific project. This seamless integration enables authorized users to directly query the S3 data lake using Athena and Redshift data using the Redshift Query Editor, thus streamlining the whole analytical process.

Following the initial setup, producers, consumers, and stewards gain the autonomy to independently perform tasks such as publishing, governing, discovering, requesting access to, and consuming data, all without relying on administrator cloud development teams. This approach effectively eliminates bottlenecks commonly encountered in centralized data lakes and/or data warehouses, while still upholding robust governance measures.

We will revisit DataZone and Lake Formation in the next chapter too, in which we'll discuss a hot trend around setting up a data mesh style of distributed data architecture pattern. Both these services assist in setting up a data mesh on AWS.

For now, let's visit another new service from AWS that plays a different role in the data governance process.

Fine-grained access control using AWS Lake Formation

One of the biggest challenges with setting up and operating data lakes on a large scale is to make sure all the data is secure. This challenge arises due to data being all over the place in a data lake, across multiple S3 buckets, and accessible via many cataloged tables. Setting up a unified permission model around who gets access to what portion of the data is not a trivial task. Imagine a very large data lake with thousands of databases and thousands of tables with 10,000 users continuously trying to access the data; to complicate things further, new users are getting onboarded every day and new datasets are constantly getting added to the data lake. Unless there is a robust mechanism to control fine-grained data access across all the datasets, the data lake would become a governance nightmare.

AWS Lake Formation

In a few of the previous chapters, we touched upon AWS Lake Formation as a service that helps in multiple aspects of a data lake on S3. In our batch ingestion chapter, we looked at how Lake Formation helps simplify the data ingestion process by providing blueprints. In our next chapter on data mesh, we will look at how Lake Formation helps share data in a distributed manner across multiple AWS accounts. However, the most important feature of Lake Formation is to provide a unified and comprehensive permissions model that allows fine-grained access control for the data inside the S3 data lake.

The data in the S3 data lake is cataloged using Glue Data Catalog. Direct access to files inside S3 buckets can be given using IAM policies. However, it's very difficult to govern the data in the lake with file-level access. The next logical step would be to put controls around the Glue Data Catalog tables so that certain users only get access to certain databases or tables inside the catalog. However, there are so many use cases where not all the content of the table needs to be accessed by certain users or roles.

AWS Lake Formation simplifies the process of granting and revoking fine-grained access by allowing the data stewards to have a unified permissions model that can restrict access at the row, column, and cell levels of the Glue Data Catalog table. The following figure highlights the key role Lake Formation plays in creating a governed data lake on S3:

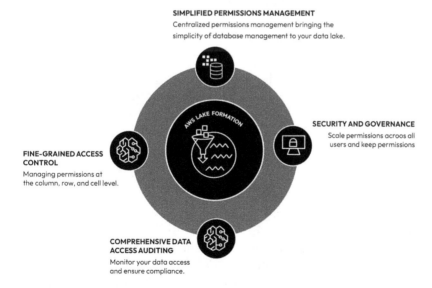

Figure 14.20 – AWS Lake Formation data lake governance capabilities

Let's get into the details of the Lake Formation permissions model by introducing a use case from GreatFin.

> **Use case for fine-grained access control using AWS Lake Formation**
>
> Many LOBs at GreatFin have started leveraging a data lake on S3 for their analytics reports. However, they now have new datasets being onboarded into the lake that contain sensitive data about their customers. These datasets are structured as rows and columns of certain dimension tables in Glue Data Catalog. The business wants to ensure that only the personas that need access to this sensitive data should get permission to view and/or change it across all data access patterns.
>
> The IT teams are looking for tool options that would help grant/revoke access at a granular level inside the table; at the same time, the tool should be easy to use and should have audit capabilities. The tool should also support other services that revolve around the data lake ecosystem.

Before Lake Formation, permissions could only be granted to the table level of Glue Data Catalog using IAM policies; to get to finer controls, complicated third-party or open source tools had to be configured. Lake Formation alleviates the operational complexity associated with administering fine-grained access control across the whole data lake. Just by using database-style grant/remove statements, Lake Formation can create a permission model on top of Glue Data Catalog.

The following figure shows the basic steps of how easy it is to create a unified governance framework for permission management on the entire S3 data lake using AWS Lake Formation:

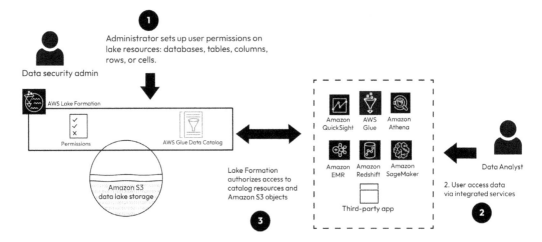

Figure 14.21 – AWS Lake Formation – data lake permissions model

Lake Formation shields the underlying S3 files and forces all access through Glue Data Catalog. Lake Formation augments the permissions already defined by IAM policies. When a user is authenticated, the first line of authorization into AWS is still defined by the IAM policies. Only after IAM authorization is complete is fine-grained access control enforced on Glue Data Catalog by Lake Formation.

Lake Formation makes it easy to govern the permissions model on the data lake by leveraging database-style Previously grant and remove permissions on resources. The permissions are then attached to principals, which could be users, groups, roles, and, in many cases, SAML-based identit. Just by granting permissions to the principal, an access hierarchy is created, where a principal gets a union of all the grants provided to it. The following table highlights this simplified permissions model using Lake Formation:

Principals	Resources	Capabilities
IAM users and roles	Catalog	CREATE_DATABASE
SAML users and groups	Databases	CREATE_TABLE, ALTER, DROP
	Table	ALTER, DROP, INSERT, DELETE, SELECT
	Columns, rows, and cells	SELECT

Figure 14.22 – AWS Lake Formation permissions model

Let's look at how the Lake Formation console helps apply these permissions. When you deploy in production, everything is automated using **Infrastructure as Code** (**IaC**), but to test in a lower environment, the UI is the best place to test the governance process.

The following screenshot shows selecting the principal who needs to be assigned with the permissions. A principal can be an IAM user or role, but it can also be a SAML-based user/group. A SAML user is typically configured in production as it will help integrate Lake Formation with the corporate identity provider. This allows easy authentication for any users that get onboarded in an organization.

The **External accounts** option is for providing cross-account access and it plays a big role in creating a data mesh design pattern. We will look at this pattern in detail in the next chapter:

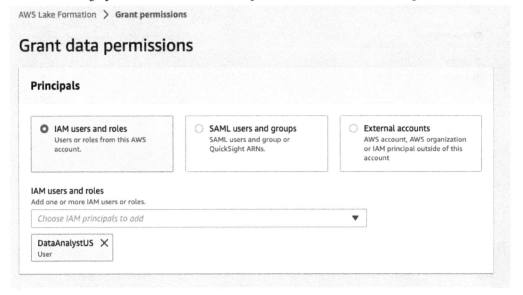

Figure 14.23 – AWS Lake Formation – selecting a principal

Once the principal has been selected, you must specify a resource that needs to be assigned to that principal. The following screenshot shows the resources from Glue Data Catalog that need to be assigned to the principal that was created earlier:

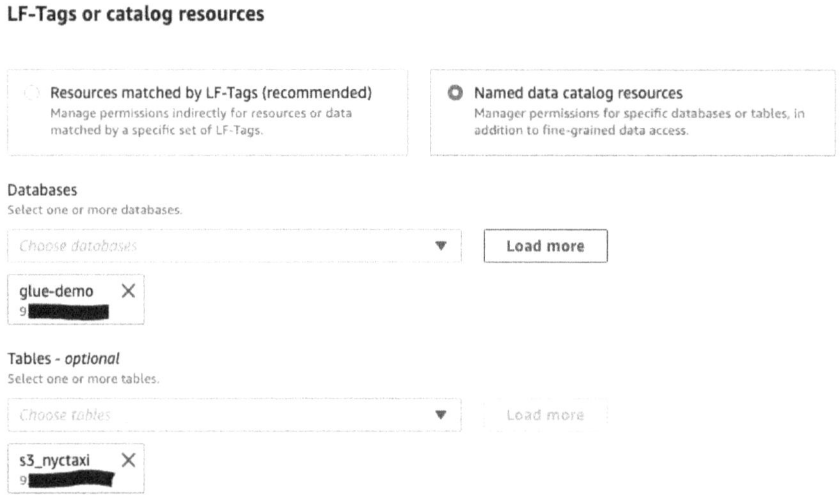

LF-Tags or catalog resources

Resources matched by LF-Tags (recommended)
Manage permissions indirectly for resources or data matched by a specific set of LF-Tags.

Named data catalog resources
Manager permissions for specific databases or tables, in addition to fine-grained data access.

Databases
Select one or more databases.

Choose databases ▼   Load more

glue-demo ✕
9▮▮▮▮▮▮▮

Tables - *optional*
Select one or more tables.

Choose tables ▼   Load more

s3_nyctaxi ✕
9▮▮▮▮▮▮

Figure 14.24 – AWS Lake Formation – selecting resources

Finally, the following screenshot shows the fine-grained access that needs to be assigned to the principal for the resources that were selected earlier:

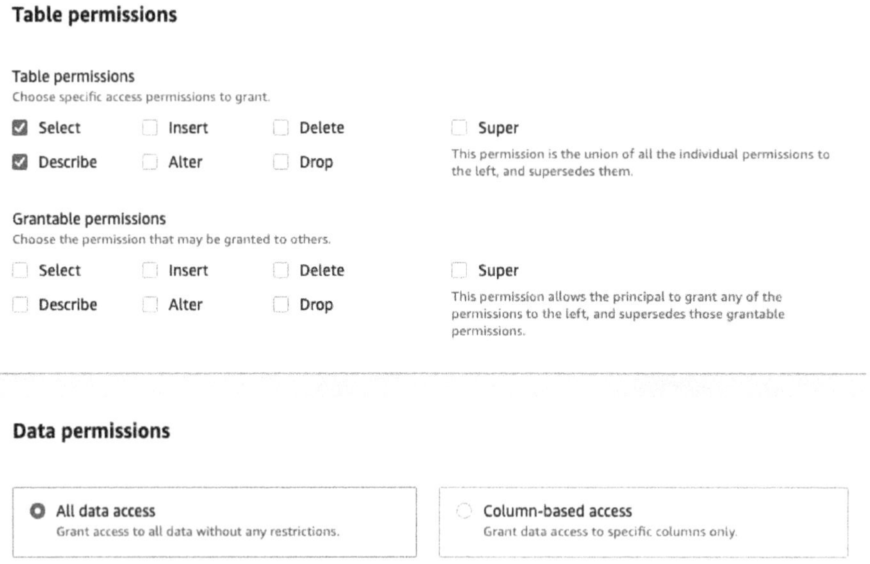

Table permissions

Table permissions
Choose specific access permissions to grant.

☑ Select   ☐ Insert   ☐ Delete   ☐ Super
☑ Describe   ☐ Alter   ☐ Drop

This permission is the union of all the individual permissions to the left, and supersedes them.

Grantable permissions
Choose the permission that may be granted to others.

☐ Select   ☐ Insert   ☐ Delete   ☐ Super
☐ Describe   ☐ Alter   ☐ Drop

This permission allows the principal to grant any of the permissions to the left, and supersedes those grantable permissions.

Data permissions

All data access
Grant access to all data without any restrictions.

Column-based access
Grant data access to specific columns only.

Figure 14.25 – AWS Lake Formation – Table permissions

If the permissions are to be assigned for specific columns, then you would need to select the necessary columns for which the grants need to be applied. You can either include or exclude columns from the permissions.

The following screenshot shows column-level permissions:

Data permissions

○ **All data access**
Grant access to all data without any restrictions.

◉ **Column-based access**
Grant data access to specific columns only.

Choose permission filter
Choose whether to include or exclude columns.

◉ **Include columns**
Grant permissions to access specific columns.

○ **Exclude columns**
Grant permissions to access all but specific columns.

Select columns

| Choose one or more columns   ▼ |

| trip_distance ✕ | tolls_amount ✕ | improvement_surcharge ✕ |
| double | double | double |

Figure 14.26 – AWS Lake Formation – column-level permissions

Row and cell-level filtering is also provided by Lake Formation, which uses PartiQL support in row filter expressions. It's easy to create data filters in Lake Formation and apply them as a model of permissions to different personas.

The Lake Formation permissions model gives row-level, column-level, and cell-level access to tables in the data lake on S3 and works well when you have a limited number of tables to deal with. However, in a large data lake implementation where a single database may contain thousands of tables, individually giving row and column-level grants to principals for so many tables may not always be feasible. To make the governance process easy for such cases, Lake Formation also allows **tag-based access control (TBAC)**.

In the TBAC model of permissions, the data admin creates specific tags and assigns values to it. For example, a class tag may be created for classifying data, and values such as `public`, `private`, and `confidential` may be assigned to the tag. These tags are then assigned to resources such as databases, tables, or columns. The policies are then created on these tags. This mechanism allows fine-grained access control at scale as you don't have to create thousands of policies for every principal.

The following figure highlights a tag-based permissions model using Lake Formation:

Figure 14.27 – AWS Lake Formation – tag-based permissions

In the Lake Formation console, you can create LF-Tags and then assign those LF-Tags to resources. The following screenshot shows how to assign LF-Tags to resources:

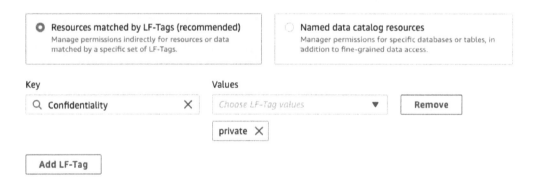

Figure 14.28 – AWS Lake Formation – tag-based assignment

Lake Formation also has an audit module, which easily allows admins to understand who tried to access what portions of the data. This makes it easy to create analytics reports to understand patterns of access and modify the permissions strategy accordingly.

But for now, let's move on to the next set of data governance challenges and find solutions to them using AWS services.

Improving data quality using Glue Data Quality

Data quality is one of the most important data governance components that no organization can ignore. To be a world-class data-driven organization, the data being used to derive insights needs to yield a high degree of accurate results. However, data analytics platforms collect, process, and consume data from many source systems, each with their own data formats and quality challenges. Therefore, data quality is a high-priority data governance measure that needs to be implemented judiciously.

Glue Data Quality

Recently, AWS introduced another feature in the Glue service that helps with data quality right inside the data pipelines. Let's discuss AWS Glue Data Quality by bringing up a use case from GreatFin.

> **Use case for data quality using AWS Glue Data Quality**
>
> One of the LOBs for GreatFin has architected a data lake on Amazon S3 and designed all the layers of the data lake. They will bring all the data from all the source systems into the raw layer of the lake. The raw layer will store the data as-is without any changes. However, when profiling the source data, the data analytics team discovered that many sources use different formats for their data, as well as that some data does not conform to the enterprise standard that is necessary for reporting.
>
> The team plans to use AWS Glue ETL with PySpark to transform the data from the raw layer and push it into the standardized layer of the S3 data lake. During this ETL process, certain data quality checks need to be put in place that will make the data in the standardized layer conform to technical data quality rules. The data engineering team is looking for the best options to bake data quality rules inside the data pipelines.

If you recall our discussions regarding our chapter on data lake on S3, when the data moves from the raw layer into the standardized layer, it undergoes technical data quality checks. These checks are necessary as the data from source systems may not always be ready for deriving accurate insights.

The data engineers can programmatically create their own rules using PySpark with Glue ETL. However, going down this path may not be a flexible and reusable effort as they will have to manually create rules for every data pipeline, and any time there is any change to the rule, the whole pipeline needs to be rebuilt, retested, and redeployed.

With that complexity in mind, AWS added a data quality module inside the Glue service that also makes the Data Quality tool a serverless, scalable, and highly performant part of the data platform. Glue Data Quality comes with built-in data quality rules and actions that make it easy to incorporate Data Quality logic by leveraging **Data Quality Definition Language** (**DQDL**), which is a declarative open language that allows users to easily create data quality rules and promote them as reusable assets to any environment.

Glue Data Quality is powered by Deequ (`https://github.com/awslabs/deequ`), which is an open source data quality library built on top of Apache Spark. This makes it a seamless fit with Spark-based Glue ETL jobs. Using the rules recommendation feature, the need to manually profile the data is eliminated. The engine will auto-recommend rules and you can then tweak the out-of-the-box rules so that they better align with your data quality objectives.

The following figure highlights the actions taken by the data engineer to incorporate Glue Data Quality into the Glue ETL pipelines:

Figure 14.29 – Glue Data Quality inside Glue ETL pipelines

The data engineer does not have to use another service for data quality. They can simply leverage the same Glue Studio experience to create data quality rules using drag-and-drop features and also reuse the rules for multiple data pipelines.

The following figure depicts the architecture for this use case:

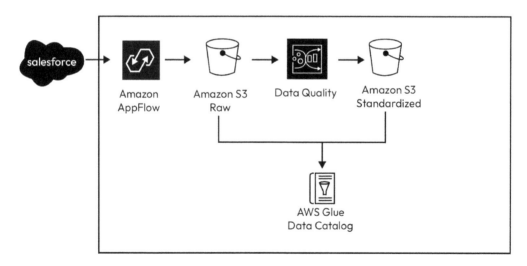

Figure 14.30 – Glue Data Quality for data quality inside an S3 data lake

In this architecture, Amazon AppFlow pulls the data from the Salesforce application and puts it into the raw layer of the data lake on S3. Using Glue Data Quality inside the Glue ETL process provides a cleansed and formatted set of data that is then put in the standardized layer of the data lake.

Glue Data Quality provides many types of built-in rules so that the data engineer can easily select the ones that apply to each column of the table and apply them within the ETL data pipeline. The following figure shows many such pre-built rules inside Glue Data Quality:

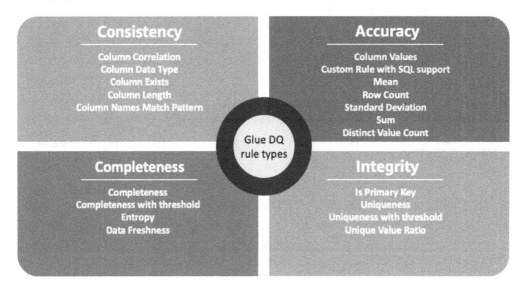

Figure 14.31 – Glue Data Quality built-in rule types

Glue Data Quality now shows up inside Glue Studio as a tab of its own and you can embed data quality transformations inside your ETL job using the Glue Studio UI itself. The following screenshot shows the **Data quality** tab and the data quality transformations that were added as part of the ETL job:

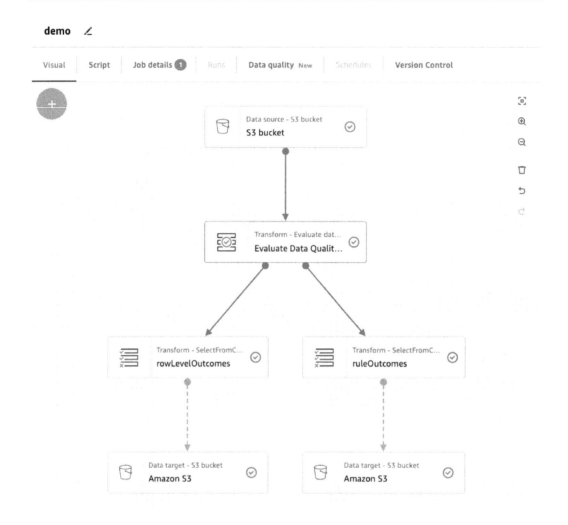

Figure 14.32 – The Data quality feature built inside Glue Studio

You can click on the data quality transformation and add whatever rules you want on your columns by selecting from many of the built-in rules. You can also add a custom rule if you want to. The following screenshot shows the details page of a data quality transform inside Glue Studio:

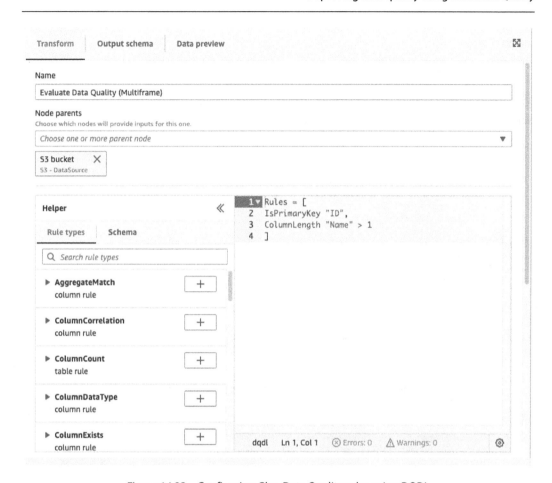

Figure 14.33 – Configuring Glue Data Quality rules using DQDL

And to make the whole development experience even more appealing, the data engineer can see all the boilerplate code in the **Script** tab and even customize and change it if required. This makes the whole ETL/Data Quality experience seamless and flexible. The following screenshot shows the PySpark script inside Glue Studio for all the logic that was generated behind the scenes:

demo ✎

| Visual | Script | Job details ❶ | Runs | Data quality New | Schedules | Version Control |

Script (Locked) Info

```
 1  import sys
 2  from awsglue.transforms import *
 3  from awsglue.utils import getResolvedOptions
 4  from pyspark.context import SparkContext
 5  from awsglue.context import GlueContext
 6  from awsglue.job import Job
 7  from awsgluedq.transforms import EvaluateDataQuality
 8
 9  args = getResolvedOptions(sys.argv, ["JOB_NAME"])
10  sc = SparkContext()
11  glueContext = GlueContext(sc)
12  spark = glueContext.spark_session
13  job = Job(glueContext)
14  job.init(args["JOB_NAME"], args)
15
16  # Script generated for node S3 bucket
17  S3bucket_node1 = glueContext.create_dynamic_frame.from_options(
18      format_options={},
19      connection_type="s3",
20      format="parquet",
21      connection_options={"paths": ["s3://█████████████████"], "recurse": True},
22      transformation_ctx="S3bucket_node1",
23  )
24
25  # Script generated for node Evaluate Data Quality (Multiframe)
26  EvaluateDataQualityMultiframe_node1686111957324_ruleset = """
27 ▾    Rules = [
28      IsPrimaryKey "ID",
29      ColumnLength "Name" > 1
30      ]
31  """
32
33  EvaluateDataQualityMultiframe_node1686111957324 = EvaluateDataQuality().process_rows(
34      frame=S3bucket_node1,
35      ruleset=EvaluateDataQualityMultiframe_node1686111957324_ruleset,
36 ▾    publishing_options={
37          "dataQualityEvaluationContext": "EvaluateDataQualityMultiframe_node1686111957324"
```

Figure 14.34 – Glue Data Quality PySpark script

Our use case was just for cleaning the data inside the data lake in S3. However, with the versatility of Glue ETL, you can add Glue Data Quality rules in any data pipeline with many other source and target data stores. The addition of Glue Data Quality has enabled a big component of the data governance process that directly feeds into the business outcomes. Let's move on to another component of the data governance process and see how AWS can help with that.

Sensitive data discovery with Amazon Macie

In the previous section, we saw how AWS Lake Formation helps with access control mechanisms, which is a vital piece of data governance. When certain datasets contain confidential data or sensitive data, you can use Lake Formation to selectively grant access to only certain columns by tagging them accordingly and granting access via those tags.

The big assumption we made was that data stewards of the data lake are already aware of all the confidential data in the data lake, along with its S3 bucket and filename. In a large implementation of a data lake with lots of contributing source systems, finding sensitive data and classifying it accordingly is like finding a needle in a haystack.

So many use cases require that data assets be classified and tagged accordingly so that accurate permissions can be granted to only the personas who should have access to the data. Doing this also ensures that such sensitive data is tracked as it migrates from one place to another. This allows for maintaining regulatory compliance too, which is a big part of the business outcome.

Amazon Macie

To help discover sensitive data inside the data lake on S3, AWS has a service called Amazon Macie. Let's dive into it by bringing up a use case.

Use case for sensitive data discovery using Amazon Macie

With so many data sources populating the data lake on S3, GreatFin is worried that sensitive customer data might get exposed to personas who should not have access to such datasets. The data team is planning to use Lake Formation's fine-grained access control mechanism to restrict access to sensitive data in the standardized, curated, and enriched layers of the data lake on S3.

However, the team is worried about correctly identifying all such data that lands in the raw layer. They are looking for an automated way to tag all such raw buckets where sensitive data is found so that restrictions can be placed on the raw data immediately. The team also wants a mechanism by which they can understand all the findings in detail so that they can create a governance strategy around access patterns for all such data discovered in the data lake. All findings eventually need to be presented in reports that can be visualized.

This use case definitely cannot be achieved in a manual, error-prone manner. This is where Amazon Macie steps in. Macie helps organizations discover, classify, and protect sensitive data stored in AWS. Macie uses ML and natural language processing techniques to automate data classification and identify sensitive data such as **personally identifiable information** (**PII**), financial information, intellectual property, and more.

Here are some of the key features of Amazon Macie:

- **Data discovery and classification**: Macie automatically scans data stored in AWS services such as Amazon S3 buckets and Amazon RDS databases to discover and classify sensitive data. It provides visibility into where sensitive data is located, helps identify data access patterns, and assigns risk scores to different data assets.

- **Sensitive data protection**: Macie helps protect sensitive data by providing alerts and notifications for unauthorized access, data leaks, and other security risks. It can integrate with AWS CloudTrail to monitor API activity and generate alerts based on policy violations or suspicious behavior.

- **Data access control**: Macie offers integration with **AWS Identity and Access Management (IAM)** to manage and enforce access control policies for sensitive data. It allows organizations to define granular permissions and restrict data access based on user roles and policies.

- **Data loss prevention (DLP)**: Macie includes built-in DLP capabilities to identify and prevent data loss. It supports predefined DLP rules and allows organizations to create custom rules to detect and block sensitive data from being shared or accessed inappropriately.

- **Compliance and reporting**: Macie assists with compliance requirements by continuously monitoring data access, usage, and sharing activities. It provides detailed reports and audit logs to demonstrate adherence to regulatory standards such as GDPR, HIPAA, PCI DSS, and others.

Amazon Macie is primarily used by organizations that handle sensitive data and need to comply with data privacy regulations. It helps enhance data security, reduces the risk of data breaches, and enables organizations to take proactive measures to protect their sensitive information.

To help with our use case, first, Macie can scan S3 buckets and send all the findings to Amazon EventBridge, a serverless event bus service, which can then trigger a rule for an AWS Lambda function to apply the necessary tags to the S3 buckets in which sensitive data was discovered. The following figure highlights the architecture pattern for solving the first part of the use case:

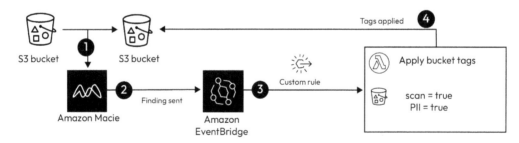

Figure 14.35 – Using Amazon Macie to tag sensitive data in S3 buckets

The findings from Macie can also be put in another S3 bucket, where data analysts can use Glue DataBrew to understand the findings and create jobs that can transform the findings into formats ready for reporting. Using Glue Crawlers, the standardized datasets are crawled so that metadata can be auto-created in Glue Data Catalog.

Once the tables have been created, Amazon Athena can be used to generate reports from the standardized data findings and, eventually, Amazon QuickSight can create visuals so that the different patterns can easily be understood by the data steward team. All this is done so that an appropriate governance strategy can be devised around access controls.

The following figure depicts the architecture for solving this use case. Amazon Macie plays a big role in generating all the data findings; these are then processed and curated, and reports are generated:

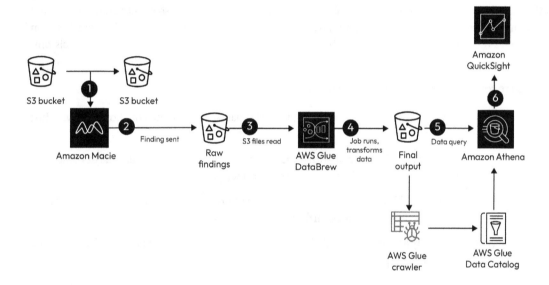

Figure 14.36 – Amazon Macie – visualizing the findings for the governance strategy

Let's look at the next big service that was recently accounted for by AWS that helps organizations achieve federated and distributed data governance.

Data collaborations with partners using AWS Clean Rooms

Collaborating on shared datasets while safeguarding the underlying raw data poses a common challenge for companies and their partners. Organizations often encounter data fragmentation across various applications, channels, departments, and partner networks, leading to interoperability and scalability issues. Numerous organizations seek improved methods for managing the collection, storage, and utilization of sensitive raw data while ensuring data privacy.

However, the methods that are traditionally used to utilize data in collaboration with partners can conflict with the objective of data protection. In certain cases, these methods have necessitated companies to share copies of their data with partners and rely on contractual agreements to prevent misuse. However, customers prefer to minimize data movement to safeguard their information, prevent misuse, and mitigate the risks of data leaks. Consequently, they often opt against collaboration, missing out on opportunities to enhance crucial business outcomes.

AWS Clean Rooms

Keeping in mind all the collaborative challenges of sharing data with partners, AWS recently came up with a new service called AWS Clean Rooms. It offers a solution that enables companies and their partners to analyze and collaborate on collective datasets securely and efficiently, all while safeguarding the underlying data. By utilizing AWS Clean Rooms, customers can establish a secure data clean room within minutes and engage in collaboration with other companies on the AWS cloud. This collaboration facilitates the generation of unique insights regarding advertising campaigns, investment decisions, and research and development.

Here are some of the key features and benefits of AWS Clean Rooms:

- **Easy setup**: Create a clean room swiftly, add participants, and initiate collaboration with just a few clicks

- **Secure collaboration**: Collaborate with a vast network of hundreds of thousands of companies on AWS without the need to share or expose the underlying data

- **Privacy protection**: Utilize a comprehensive range of privacy-enhancing controls specifically designed for Clean Rooms to safeguard the underlying data

- **Customized analysis**: Leverage built-in and flexible analysis rules to tailor queries according to your organization's specific business requirements.

With AWS Clean Rooms, companies and their partners can seamlessly collaborate, analyze data, and derive valuable insights while maintaining the highest level of data security and privacy.

Let's understand the details of AWS Clean Rooms with a use case.

Use case for partner collaboration using AWS Clean Rooms

GreatFin aims to gain a comprehensive understanding of its customers by leveraging data from various engagement channels and partner datasets. The goal is to create a unified and enriched 360-degree view of their customers to enhance personalized experiences and improve customer satisfaction.

At the same time, GreatFin wants to enhance its marketing and advertising strategies by collaborating with advertising and marketing partners. The goal is to improve campaign planning, activation, and measurement, and ultimately, provide better and more relevant consumer experiences.

This use case is precisely why the AWS Clean Rooms service was created. Clean Rooms helps with the following:

- **Multi-party collaborations**: A collaboration refers to a secure and isolated environment where members can perform SQL queries on data. These collaborations are created by the collaboration creator, who can invite up to five members to join. Before joining, all members can view the list of invited participants in the collaboration.

- **No data movement**: Within a collaboration, all members can contribute data directly from Amazon S3, provided it is in the form of a table in Glue Data Catalog. This eliminates the need to transfer or move data, ensuring efficient and secure data analysis.

- **Query controls and enforcement**: Each member of a collaboration can configure data access controls, allowing them to define specific analysis permissions for their tables within the collaboration. This ensures that data access is restricted to authorized analysis only, maintaining data security and privacy.

- **Cryptographic computing**: For added security, customers have the option to pre-encrypt their data before using it in an AWS Clean Rooms collaboration. This cryptographic computing step provides an additional layer of protection for sensitive data.

- **Programmatic access**: AWS Clean Rooms offers programmatic access, allowing customers to automate and integrate its functionality into their existing workflows and products. This flexibility enables the creation of custom, white-labeled Clean Rooms offerings, tailored to specific business requirements.

The following figure highlights the key areas of focus for Clean Rooms:

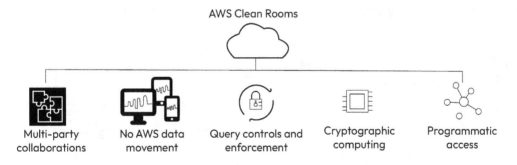

Figure 14.37 – AWS Clean Rooms focus areas

Let's look at how Clean Rooms works:

1. **Collaboration creation**: The collaboration creator initiates the process by creating a collaboration and inviting one or more members to join. During collaboration creation, specific member roles are assigned, such as the member who can perform queries and the member who can receive results.

2. **Joining and table configuration**: The invited member(s) joins the collaboration by creating a membership resource. They then configure an existing AWS Glue table for use within AWS Clean Rooms. This step can be performed either before or after joining the collaboration. Optionally, members can choose to pre-encrypt their data before configuring the tables.

3. **Analysis rule configuration**: After configuring the table, the invited member(s) add an analysis rule to the table. The analysis rule specifies the type of analysis that can be performed on the table, such as aggregation or listing.

4. **Granting access**: The invited member(s) provides AWS Clean Rooms with a service role that grants access to their AWS Glue tables. It is important to note that this role only allows AWS Clean Rooms to access the tables and execute permitted queries on behalf of the member who can query and receive results. Other collaboration members do not have access to the underlying tables.

5. **Query execution and enforcement**: The member who has permission to query and receive results can now run SQL queries on the configured tables. AWS Clean Rooms automatically enforces the analysis rules and output constraints defined for the collaboration. Only the results that comply with these rules are returned by AWS Clean Rooms.

The following figure highlights how AWS Clean Rooms enables secure and controlled data analysis with collaborators, ensuring that analysis rules are adhered to and only authorized results are obtained:

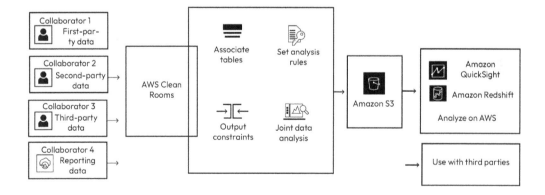

Figure 14.38 – AWS Clean Rooms working

The following screenshot shows the AWS Clean Rooms console, where you can create a new collaboration and add partner members to it:

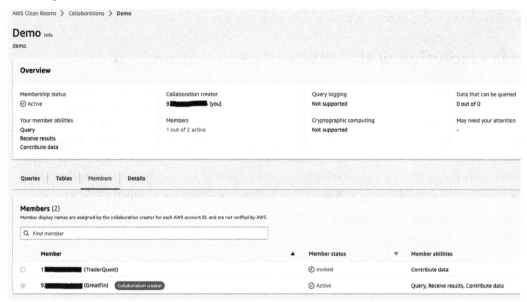

Figure 14.39 – AWS Clean Rooms collaborations

Once the collaboration has been created with members associated with it, you can then add tables that you want to collaborate on. The following screenshot highlights a table associated with the collaborator:

Figure 14.40 – AWS Clean Rooms associated tables

You can also select the types of analytics others may be able to perform on such tables by creating and listing analytics rules on them.

Now, let's cover another important topic of data governance around entity resolution.

Data resolution with AWS Entity Resolution

The best way to explain this topic would be to take the example of data at GreatFin, the example company we have been using in this book for use cases. GreatFin has data coming in from multiple LOBs. All LOBs have overlapping customer information. Sometimes, customers update details with one LOB but other LOBs don't always see that update. This eventually creates a web of conflicting information across the enterprise where a golden version of truth for a customer or any other entity doesn't exist. This is where inaccuracies arise in the operational systems as well as in the analytical environments. All organizations strive to create a golden or a master copy of their entities.

The following figure highlights the efforts of organizations to create a golden copy of the entity from across multiple sources of data:

Figure 14.41 – Entity resolution process

Let's introduce the service that AWS provides for entity resolution by bringing up a use case from GreatFin.

Use case for entity resolution

GreatFin serves millions of customers worldwide and manages a vast amount of customer data. However, due to various factors such as data entry errors, inconsistent data sources, and mergers with other financial institutions, the bank's database contains duplicate and fragmented customer records. This creates challenges in providing seamless customer experiences, hampers regulatory compliance efforts, and reduces overall operational efficiency.

GreatFin aims to implement an entity resolution system to identify and merge duplicate customer records across its various systems and databases. The primary goal is to achieve a single, accurate, and comprehensive view of each customer, which will enable the bank to streamline its operations, enhance customer service, and meet regulatory requirements more effectively.

Recently, AWS came out with a new service to help resolve entities. Let's dive deep into it and see how we can solve this use case.

AWS Entity Resolution

AWS Entity Resolution is an ML-powered service designed to facilitate seamless matching and linking of related records across various applications, channels, and data stores. With its user-friendly interface and highly adaptable workflows, companies can swiftly configure the service in just minutes. This innovative solution enables effortless data consolidation and retrieval, streamlining operations and maximizing efficiency.

Some of the key benefits of using AWS Entity Resolution are as follows:

- **Accelerate entity resolution workflows**: In a matter of minutes, you can set up entity resolution workflows, saving significant time compared to traditional months-long processes. You can effortlessly match, link, and analyze related records without the need for complex custom solutions.

- **Tailor matching techniques with ease**: You can enhance data accuracy according to your specific business requirements by easily configuring advanced matching techniques. You can leverage the power of flexible ML and rule-based methods to optimize record-matching for your unique needs.

- **Data protection and minimal movement**: With AWS Entity Resolution, you can safeguard your data and reduce unnecessary movement. The service reads records right where they reside, helping companies maintain data privacy and security while streamlining the resolution process.

These key benefits are possible due to the many features of the service, including a flexible and customizable data preparation process, configurable entity matching workflows, data protection and regionalization capabilities, ready-to-use rule-based matching, preconfigured ML matching, manual bulk processing, and automatic incremental processing and near real-time lookup of entity match IDs.

The following figure demonstrates how organizations can leverage the AWS Entity Resolution service to get to the end goal of getting a unified view of an entity:

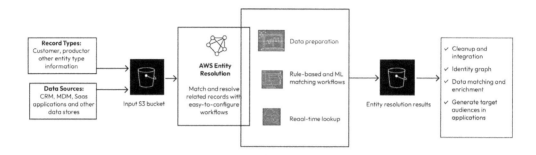

Figure 14.42 – High-level working solution using AWS Entity Resolution

When you get into the service, you will see that the user interface is very intuitive and will guide you through the steps. You have the option to create one or multiple matching workflows, allowing you to specify data inputs and normalization steps, as well as select your preferred matching techniques. These techniques include rule-based matching and ML matching. The following screenshot shows the matching workflow creation steps:

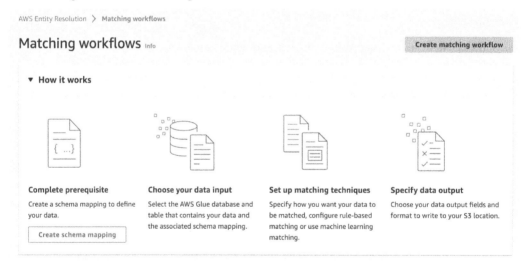

Figure 14.43 – Matching workflow process in AWS Entity Resolution

The first step in this process is to create a schema mapping. This process will walk you through a series of steps where you specify the data you wish to resolve. This involves defining input fields and attribute types, as well as establishing and organizing your match keys into groups. The following screenshot shows the schema mapping process:

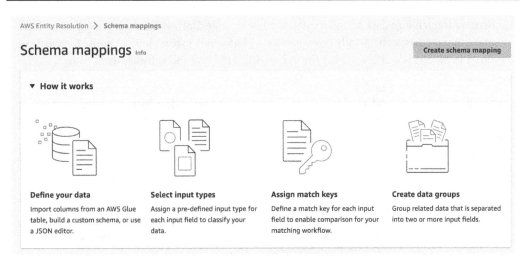

Figure 14.44 – Schema mapping process in AWS Entity Resolution

AWS Entity Resolution effectively addresses several common use cases, including the following:

- **De-duplicating records**: You can seamlessly de-duplicate related records, which allows for better data analysis, the ability to prepare data for AI model training, and ultimately, enhance overall business outcomes

- **Creating customer profiles**: You can establish comprehensive customer profiles by connecting various consumer interactions, enabling valuable insights and the identification of potential new customers

- **Personalizing experiences**: You can improve customer experiences by leveraging unified insights across advertising and marketing campaigns, customer support cases, loyalty programs, and e-commerce, leading to more relevant and tailored interactions

- **Linking product codes**: You can unify product codes such as SKUs, UPCs, or proprietary product IDs, optimize tracking capabilities across stores and supply chains, streamline inventory management, and enhance efficiency in product-related operations

This brings us to the end of this chapter. The topic of data governance is so vast that we could write a book by itself, but we have covered most of the major themes here. The one thing we did not cover is partner-driven governance architectures. There are so many AWS partners that provide niche solutions to data governance problems such as data lineage, data obfuscations, and more. So, if you feel like you have a governance use case that's not covered by an AWS service, many **independent software vendor (ISV)** products are available for use via the AWS Marketplace.

Also, often, we interchange data security with data governance. Both are distinct concepts but have many interconnected aspects. A fully governed data platform is incomplete without all aspects of data security in place, including securing the underlying hardware and software that's being used for processing the data.

Even though security on AWS could be a book by itself, the following figure highlights many of the security-related services provided by AWS around the fields of security, identity, encryption, and compliance:

Security	Identity	Encryption	Compliance
Amazon GuardDuty	AWS Identity and Access Management (IAM)	AWS Certificate Manager	AWS Artifact
AWS Shield		AWS Key Management Service (AWS KMS)	Amazon Inspector
AWS WAF	AWS Single Sign-On		AWS CloudHSM
Amazon Macie	Amazon Cloud Directory	Encryption at rest	Amazon Cognito
Amazon Virtual Private Cloud (Amazon VPC)	AWS Directory Service	Encryption in transit	AWS CloudTrail
	AWS Organizations	Bring your own keys, HSM support	Amazon Textract

Figure 14.45 – AWS services that supplement the data governance process

This space around data governance will continue to evolve rapidly and new tools and services will always come out in rapid succession to make the whole process easy. In the meantime, don't let the topic of data governance in our organization cause "analysis paralysis," where everyone overthinks on this subject and nothing gets done. Focus on aspects of governance that have a direct impact on the business outcomes and start early. A fully matured governed data platform doesn't come overnight – it's an iterative process that slowly adds to all the best practices accumulated over many years of managing the business objectives.

Summary

In this chapter, we looked at a whole range of data governance aspects. First, we laid out what data governance means and why organizations need it to create a world-class modern data platform. We also looked at how AWS views data governance, as defined by a combination of people, processes, and technology. All three aspects need to be aligned for data governance to be effective at an enterprise level.

We also spent quite a bit of effort explaining how a new service, Amazon DataZone, helps refine data governance and helps simplify the whole process across many of the individual analytics services of AWS. DataZone provides a comprehensive way of allowing publishers and subscribers to discover, publish, and subscribe to enterprise-wide data in a distributed manner. This alleviates the burden of creating cumbersome automations and setting up expensive tools to create a self-service analytics platform. In short, Amazon DataZone helps democratize data faster.

Afterthat, we looked at the next challenge in the data governance space around how to define a framework that allows fine-grained access controls on the data that's stored in the data lake on S3. By using AWS Lake Formation, businesses can create a mechanism by which column-level, row-level, and cell-level permissions can be granted to any principal that wants to access the data from the data lake, by forcing an additional layer of governance via Glue Data Catalog.

We also looked at data quality as one of the most important aspects of the data governance process and, by using a use case, we evaluated AWS Glue Data Quality as a feature to solve the data quality puzzle. Glue Data Quality makes it easy for data engineers to bake in reusable Data Quality rules inside their ETL pipelines. This ensures that data consumers get quality data during and after the data transformation process.

We also looked at how Amazon Macie helps us discover sensitive data in all the buckets in S3, hence eliminating the need to place expensive and complicated solutions to detect and restrict access to sensitive data.

Then, we introduced another new service, called AWS Clean Rooms, which makes it easier for organizations to collaborate with many of the partners of their datasets without the need to expose the underlying data assets. Clean Rooms takes over the operational overhead associated with sharing datasets outside with other organizations using their own AWS accounts.

With data stored and managed across so many data sources, the need to accurately get details about an entity has become a key part of the data governance process. To assist with this activity, AWS recently came up with the AWS Entity Resolution service, which is an ML-powered service that helps you match and link related records stored across multiple applications and data stores.

Data governance also leads to the creation of data mesh. In the next chapter, we will look at what data mesh architecture is, how organizations benefit from it, and how AWS Lake Formation and Amazon DataZone play a critical role in setting up data mesh.

As always, if you are curious to do some hands-on workshops, don't forget to try out the links in the following *References* section.

References

- Amazon Lake Formation workshop: `https://catalog.us-east-1.prod.workshops.aws/workshops/78572df7-d2ee-4f78-b698-7cafdb55135d/en-US`

- AWS Glue Data Quality blog series: `https://aws.amazon.com/blogs/big-data/aws-glue-data-quality-is-generally-available/`

- Amazon Macie workshop: `https://catalog.us-east-1.prod.workshops.aws/workshops/9982e0dc-0ccf-4116-ad12-c053b0ab31c6/en-US`

- AWS Entity Resolution blog: `https://aws.amazon.com/blogs/aws/aws-entity-resolution-match-and-link-related-records-from-multiple-applications-and-data-stores/`

15
Data Mesh

In this chapter, we will look at the following key topics:

- Data mesh concepts
- Data mesh on AWS
- Data mesh on an Amazon S3-based data lake
- Data mesh on Amazon Redshift

Data mesh concepts

If you recall from *Chapter 8, Data Sharing*, we kept the important topic of a distributed data lake that spans multiple AWS accounts open-ended. Now is a good time to complete that story. Even today, the vast majority of use cases that require a data lake can be solved by building a centralized data lake. However, as organizations become bigger, new **lines of businesses (LOBs)** that work as autonomous units become a reality. All these LOBs add more data sources to grow their business units, resulting in the exponential growth of data at the enterprise level.

Sharing data within an enterprise presents its fair share of challenges. Different LOBs have invested in cloud-based data lakes, along with customized analytics solutions, tailored to address their specific business needs. However, these systems are often designed to cater to particular types of data and may not seamlessly translate to other problem domains.

For many large organizations with many LOBs, a centralized data lake on S3 may possess some challenges:

- **Bottlenecks regarding the central data team**: The central data team often struggles to scale effectively as they need to cater to various business domains without possessing expertise in those specific areas.
- **Limited scalability for data consumers**: Due to security restrictions, only a few individuals within the organization possess the necessary access credentials to utilize and analyze the data. This limitation hampers the implementation of a data-driven culture throughout the organization as data should be accessible to more than just data experts.

- **Difficulty in data discovery and consumption**: Data is stored in multiple locations across the organization, creating data silos. There is no centralized repository to easily discover the available data and facilitate access to it.

- **Absence of central data governance**: Lack of comprehensive data governance at scale increases the risk of data security issues, particularly when dealing with **personally identifiable information (PII)**.

- **Insufficient data auditability**: There is a lack of visibility into how data is being utilized or shared, making it challenging to track and monitor data usage effectively.

All these challenges brought about a concept in the data and analytics space called data mesh. Let's dive straight into it.

What is data mesh?

Data mesh is a decentralized approach to managing and organizing data within an organization. It aims to address the challenges associated with centralized data platforms by promoting a more distributed and domain-oriented data architecture. In a data mesh model, data is treated as a product, and the ownership of data is decentralized to individual domain teams. Each team is responsible for the data within their domain, including its quality, availability, and governance.

To understand the concept better, let's look at the four core principles of a data mesh architecture pattern:

1. **Decentralized data ownership**: In a data mesh framework, data domains serve as nodes within data lake accounts, emphasizing the decentralization and distribution of data responsibility to individuals closely involved with the data. The following figure highlights the data ownership principle, where the accountability for the data domain and its consumption patterns lies with the data owner:

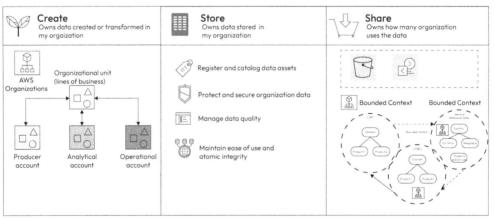

Figure 15.1 – Data mesh principle #1 – data domain ownership

2. **Data product mindset**: Data is treated as a product within data mesh, where data producers contribute one or more data products to a central catalog housed within a data mesh account. Individual teams take ownership of their data and structure it as data products. Each data product offers interfaces such as APIs, SQL, or reports to facilitate interaction with other teams or stakeholders. The aim is to eliminate usability friction and meet users where they are, ensuring a seamless experience. Additionally, comprehensive supporting metadata and lineage information is provided for all data products. These data products hold intrinsic value and serve as valuable assets in their own right, contributing to the overall data ecosystem.

The following figure highlights this principle, where domain-driven design techniques are created, establishing a bounded context for data products:

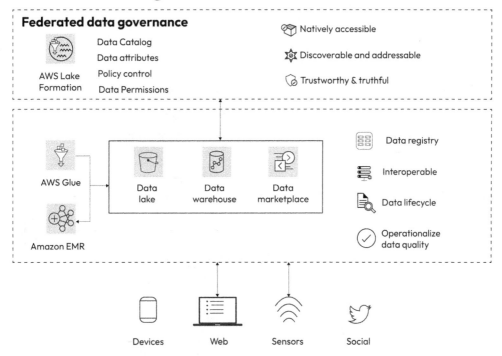

Figure 15.2 – Data mesh principle #2 – data as a product

3. **Self-service collaboration**: The data mesh platform enhances the user experience by enabling data users to easily discover, access, and utilize data products. Simultaneously, it streamlines the experience for data providers, enabling them to efficiently build, deploy, and maintain data products.

The self-service principle of data mesh focuses on designing data solutions that are easily accessible and adoptable for a non-specialist majority. It enables personas to actively engage with data products by facilitating discovery, learning, understanding, consumption, and maintenance. By fostering a collection of interoperable data products, data mesh empowers cross-functional domains to produce and consume data effortlessly, fostering autonomy and scalability.

The following figure highlights the self-service principle of data mesh:

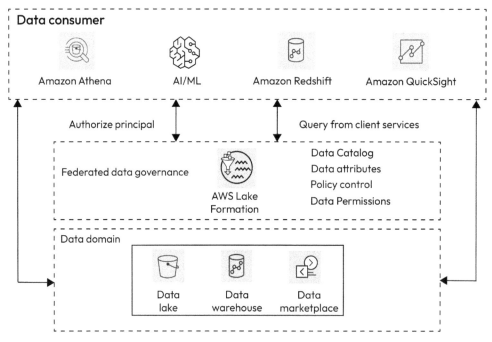

Figure 15.3 – Data mesh principle #3 – self-service collaboration

4. **Federated governance:** The governance of data products within data mesh is based on a federated computational model. This governance team, represented by members from all participating teams in the data mesh, collaboratively establishes global policies and standardization to ensure interoperability across the system. This approach ensures that data sharing incorporates discoverable metadata and auditability, with decisions made through a federated decision-making process.

The following figure highlights the federated data governance principle of the data mesh pattern:

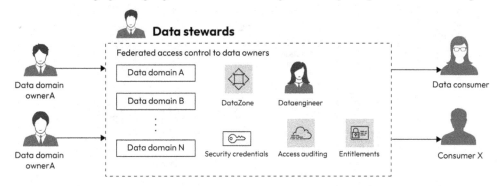

Figure 15.4 – Data mesh principle #4 – federated data governance

Data mesh on AWS

To translate the concepts of data mesh to a data platform built using AWS services, we need to look at how the data is ingested, proceeded, and shared for consumption. The core purpose-built AWS analytics services remain the same, each performing specific tasks in the data platform. However, instead of placing all such services inside a single AWS account, they are all spread into different AWS accounts, owned and managed by different teams or business units. These accounts are constantly producing and/or consuming data, with the eventual goal of deriving value for the whole organization.

All the analytics services and architectures we've discussed in this book remain the same – it's just the design philosophy around data production, data sharing, and data governance all become distributed and completely decoupled in nature. Instead of point-to-point data sharing across AWS accounts using bucket and IAM policies, a completely different mechanism of sharing data in a governed manner can be introduced using AWS Lake Formation and Amazon DataZone, with the data still inside S3 as the data lake and Amazon Redshift as the data warehouse. We will learn more about this in the next section.

The following figure highlights the data mesh design principle as implemented using AWS services:

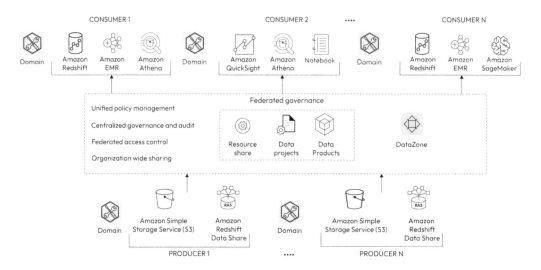

Figure 15.5 – Data mesh architecture on AWS

Data mesh on an Amazon S3-based data lake

If you recall from our previous chapter on data governance, we used AWS **Lake Formation** (**LF**) as a tool to provide fine-grained access control to data that resides in the S3 data lake via the Glue Data Catalog. The same LF permissions mechanism can be leveraged to share data but in a cross-AWS account manner, which opens the doors to implementing a true data mesh architecture, where the data lake doesn't have to be a central repository for the whole enterprise. Each LOB can establish its own data lake on S3 inside its own AWS account. Some LOB accounts will be data owners, meaning they will produce, store, and consume their data for analytics purposes, from their own data lake on S3. However, if another LOB needs access to some datasets that belong to a different LOB, instead of copying data around, both the producer and consumer LOBs can leverage LF's cross-account sharing mechanism.

Let's introduce the use case for implementing a data mesh on an S3 data lake using LF cross-account sharing.

Use case for data mesh on an S3 data lake

GreatFin, being a leading financial services company, deals with a wide range of financial products, including banking, investments, insurance, and asset management. With a vast amount of data generated from various sources, they aim to improve data accessibility, enable data-driven decision-making, and enhance collaboration across different business units.

Here are the current challenges that are faced at GreatFin:

1. **Data silos**: The company's data is currently fragmented across multiple systems and platforms, resulting in data silos that hinder efficient data sharing and collaboration. Each LOB has set up a data lake to break down its application data silo, but at an enterprise level, since all the LOBs operate independently, the silos still exist.

2. **Limited data governance**: Inconsistent data governance practices make it difficult to ensure data quality, privacy, and compliance across the organization.

3. **Slow time-to-insights**: Data consumers in many LOBs face challenges in discovering and accessing relevant data, leading to delays in generating valuable insights. The current process to discover and access other LOB data assets is not efficient.

GreatFin is looking for a way to make data sharing across all LOBs easier and more of a self-driven process instead of them having to rely on IT teams. GreatFin wants all the data lakes across all LOBs to find a way to create a more scalable and automated mechanism to allow each LOB to have governed access to other LOBs' data. This will accelerate deriving insights from enterprise-wide data, leading to value creation for the organization as a whole.

Setting up a data mesh pattern is not a trivial task. Hence, it may not always be advantageous in all situations. In this use case, since GreatFin has so many independent LOBs, each with its data sources, and there is a strong desire to share data assets from one LOB to another, it makes a strong case to enable a data mesh pattern. Let's look at how AWS LF cross-account sharing helps with an easy way to enable controlled sharing of data from the S3 data lake.

The following figure shows the sequence of steps that need to occur for data producers in one AWS account to share data with data consumers who are in a different AWS account. A third AWS account acts as a centralized governance account, responsible for the federated governance layer:

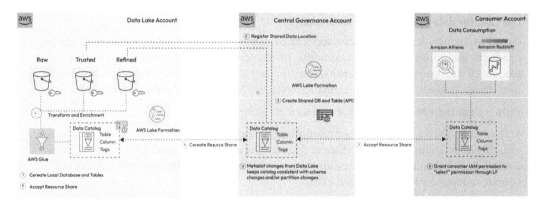

Figure 15.6 – Data mesh pattern on an S3 data lake using AWS Lake Formation

The workflow from producer to consumer within the data mesh pattern follows these steps:

1. Producers create and register their data source locations in their AWS Glue Data Catalog within their respective accounts.

2. When a dataset is presented as a product, producers create corresponding entities (database, table, columns, and attributes) in the central governance account's Glue Data Catalog. This facilitates easy discovery of catalogs by consumers, but access permissions are managed by the producer.

3. The central Glue Data Catalog shares the catalog resources back to the producer account, granting the necessary permissions through LF resource links for metadata databases and tables.

4. Producers with specific roles, such as data engineers, receive LF permissions in the central account to manage schema changes and perform data transformations on the central data catalog.

5. Producers accept the resource share from the central governance account, enabling them to make future schema changes as needed.

6. Any modifications to data within the producer account are automatically synchronized with the central governance copy of the catalog.

7. When a consumer requests access and needs to make the data visible in their AWS Glue Data Catalog, the owner of the central account grants LF permissions to the consumer account. This can be done through direct entity sharing or tag-based access controls by leveraging data classification, a cost center, or an environment.

8. Within the consumer account, LF defines access permissions on the datasets, allowing local users such as data analysts and data scientists to consume the data using their preferred tools, such as Athena and Amazon Redshift.

By following this workflow, data can flow seamlessly from producers to consumers in the data mesh, with controlled access and effective governance facilitated by AWS LF.

To help with cross-account sharing, LF provides an option to register the external account with which the data assets need to be shared. All the remaining steps to control permissions stay the same. The following screenshot shows the external account option when you get into the LF console to grant permissions:

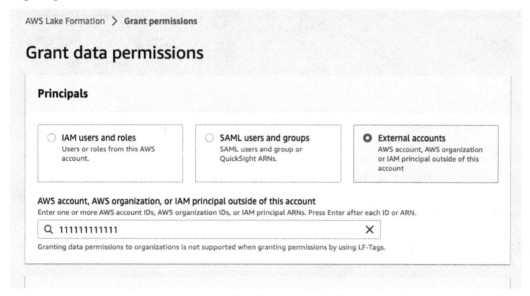

Figure 15.7 – AWS Lake Formation cross-account permissions

The preceding steps become difficult to execute and manage when there are a large number of producer/consumer accounts and new LOB accounts continue to be added regularly. To make decentralized data ownership with a federated governance process easy to implement and manage, Amazon DataZone can fully automate the process by seamlessly integrating with S3 data lakes, the Glue Data Catalog, and AWS Lake Formation. DataZone becomes a one-stop shop for creating and managing data mesh architecture on S3 data lakes.

From an analytics data store point of view, typically, the data mesh is either around a data lake or a data warehouse. DataZone supports Glue Data Catalog-based S3 data lakes, as well as Amazon Redshift-based data warehouses, to easily configure a data mesh.

The following figure shows the key role Amazon DataZone plays in achieving a data mesh. In our next section on data mesh in Redshift, I will provide many screenshots from DataZone that will help you digest this process better:

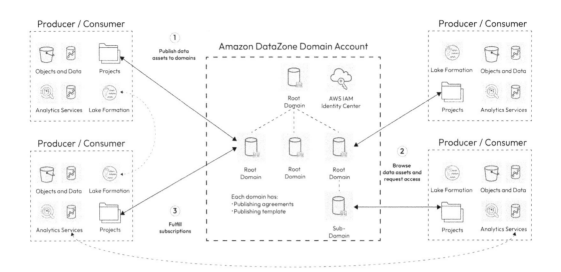

Figure 15.8 – Data mesh simplification using Amazon DataZone

Many times, data is stored inside an Amazon Redshift data warehouse instead of a data lake on S3. In *Chapter 13, Data Sharing*, we looked at how, using the Redshift datashare feature, you can easily help share data across multiple clusters in any AWS account. Let's dive into how organizations also create a data mesh with Amazon Redshift.

Data mesh on Amazon Redshift

A data mesh is an architecture pattern that's not just limited to a single kind of analytics setup. A data lake is a prominent architecture that benefits from a data mesh in a large organization setup, with many independent analytics environments. However, data warehouses are also a foundational data store for analytics operations, and many times, data warehouses are the primary driving force of a data platform. Let's look at how to establish a data mesh architecture using Amazon Redshift and Amazon DataZone.

The Redshift datashare feature plays a huge role in creating a data mesh using just Redshift. Any number of Redshift clusters, in any AWS account and region, can share datasets with other such clusters. This allows data producers to share data just by using SQL statements inside Redshift. Also, the consumers in other Redshift clusters use SQL statements to gain access to such shared assets.

However, distributed federated governance is the big architecture piece that is missing with the Redshift datashare feature. Amazon DataZone makes it easy for publishers and subscribers to participate in a data mesh with Amazon Redshift. The DataZone service takes charge of coordinating and orchestrating Redshift datashares, ensuring smooth data exchange between the producer and consumer cluster. This process is entirely self-service.

The following figure highlights the data share operations in Redshift that DataZone helps simplify:

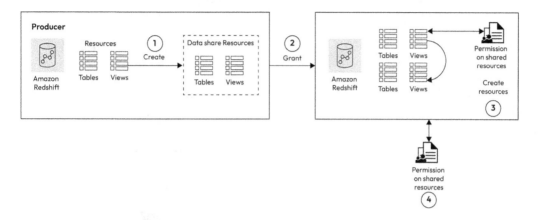

Figure 15.9 – Data mesh with Amazon Redshift using Amazon DataZone

The four steps shown in the preceding figure are as follows:

1. Establish a Redshift datashare and incorporate tables or views from the producer data warehouse.

2. Provide the consumer data warehouse with usage privileges for the data share.

3. Generate views within the consumer data warehouse based on the data share.

4. Allocate permissions to the relevant principals.

Let's look at some screenshots from DataZone that will help you walk through these steps and demonstrate how easy it is to create a data mesh on Redshift using DataZone.

We are assuming that you have already set up DataZone, which involves creating a data domain. One AWS account can have just one data domain that acts as a federated governance layer for the data mesh and contains all the publishing templates and contracts. Each publisher or subscriber AWS account can then create projects within that domain. Projects act as containers for all the resources a particular data team has permission to operate.

The publisher will create its own project that will allow them to access their Redshift cluster resources. Inside the project, the publisher will create a publishing job that can be run either manually or scheduled to run periodically. This publishing job, under the covers, is just running a Glue crawler that will crawl the Redshift tables the publisher has configured in the publishing job template. The underlying crawler creates the necessary catalog inside the DataZone-managed catalog so that these assets can be easily discovered by any other subscriber, from any other AWS project configured under that data domain.

The following screenshot shows the publisher project and the publishing job that was created so that Redshift tables can be cataloged in the DataZone-governed catalog:

Figure 15.10 – Publishing job in the publisher project in DataZone

When the publishing job runs, all the necessary Redshift tables that the publisher wanted to share with the enterprise get added to the DataZone catalog. These assets can be searched from the search bar of DataZone or can be browsed using the **Data Catalog** tab. The following screenshot shows the published tables from the Redshift producer cluster in the DataZone catalog:

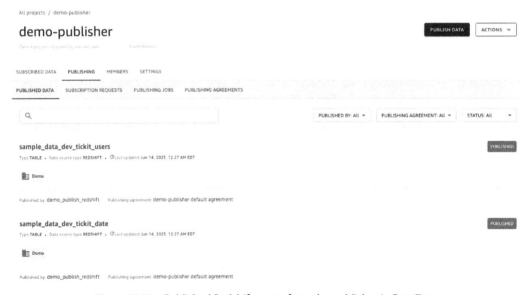

Figure 15.11 – Published Redshift assets from the publisher in DataZone

Once the necessary Redshift tables have been published, the data subscriber searches for these tables from inside its subscriber project. This easy-to-search mechanism for data assets inside DataZone plays a huge part in self-service analytics, by allowing anyone in the enterprise who is part of this data domain to search for and discover datasets that they would like to leverage for reporting purposes.

The subscriber will then select the table and request access to that asset by providing proper reasoning. This will trigger a workflow that will go back to the publisher for approval. The following screenshot shows a subscriber requesting access to one of the Redshift tables:

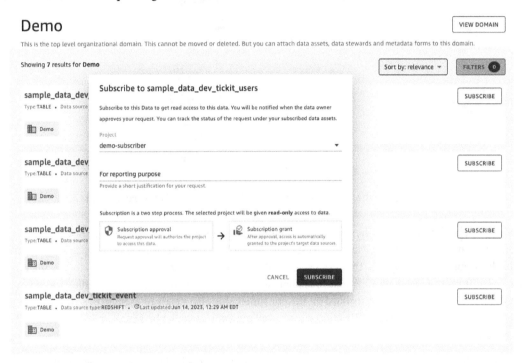

Figure 15.12 – Subscribing to Redshift tables from the subscriber project in DataZone

The approval request comes back in the **Subscription request** tab of the publisher. The publisher then approves or rejects the request by providing a reason. The following screenshot shows the subscription request in the publisher's project, seeking access to a particular Redshift table the publisher owns:

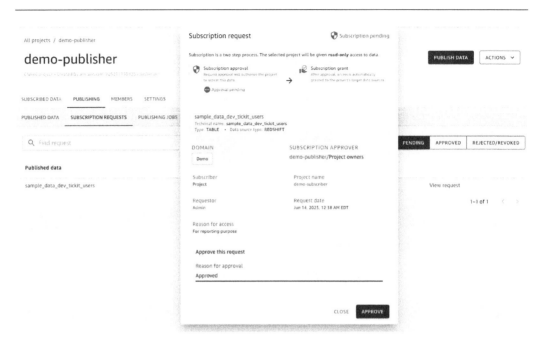

Figure 15.13 – The publisher approves the request from the publisher project in DataZone

Once the publisher approves the request, the subscriber is notified of this inside their subscriber project in DataZone so that they can access specific Redshift tables. The real magic happens when the publisher approves the request. The series of SQL statements that a data steward needs to execute on the Redshift producer cluster to enable data sharing to a particular consumer, followed by the series of SQL statements that the data steward on the consumer side also needs to execute to see the shared data assets inside their consumer Redshift cluster – all are auto-executed by DataZone inside Redshift on behalf of the publisher and the subscriber.

The Redshift datashare grants were executed as part of this process by DataZone and you can see the linking done by DataZone between the producer and consumer Redshift cluster. Under the covers, it's still the Redshift datashare mechanism that's sharing data assets, but the whole governance process has been simplified. This alleviates a huge pain point when large organizations have many such Redshift clusters, across different LOBs. All LOBs can publish their data assets with DataZone, where they can easily be discovered and subscribed to by other LOBs across the whole organization.

The following screenshot shows the **Subscription grant** page, which shows the Redshift link between the producer and the consumer cluster using the Redshift datashare mechanism:

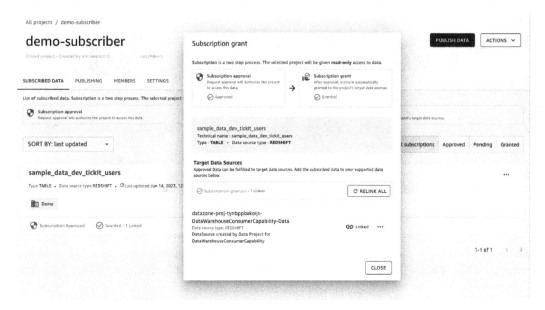

Figure 15.14 – Granted subscription to a Redshift table in DataZone

DataZone also provides a deep link to Redshift query editor, which allows subscribers to launch the editor from DataZone itself and start querying the data that was shared with them. The shared assets in Redshift are always in read-only mode, hence all shared objects show up in the **Views** section of the consumer Redshift database.

The following screenshot shows the shared table from the producer, seen as a read-only view inside the consumer Redshift database:

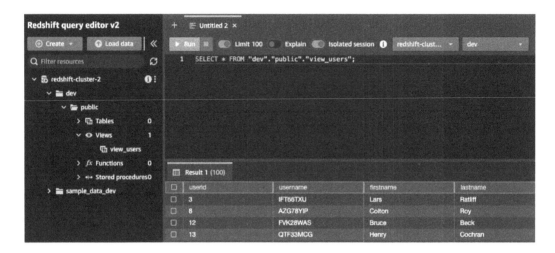

Figure 15.15 – Consumer view of the shared table inside Redshift query editor

Amazon DataZone has simplified the process of creating and maintaining the data mesh design pattern by making it easy for the data producers, data consumers, and data stewards to publish, discover, govern, and consume data in a self-service manner, without any heavy involvement from the IT teams.

The following figure shows a holistic view of data mesh's operation using Amazon DataZone:

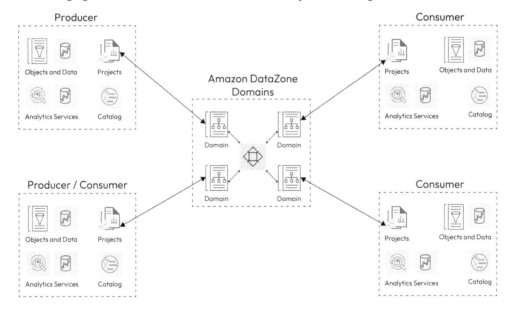

Figure 15.16 – Data mesh pattern using Amazon DataZone

We have come to the end of this chapter. Like any architectural approach, it's important to understand when to use it and when not to use it. Here are some considerations for when to use a data mesh architecture:

- **Large and complex data ecosystems**: Data mesh is most beneficial in organizations dealing with a high volume of diverse data sources and data consumers. It helps manage the complexity and diversity of data by breaking it down into manageable domains.

- **Scalability challenges**: If your organization's data infrastructure is struggling to handle the increasing volume and variety of data, data mesh can provide a scalable way to distribute data responsibilities across teams.

- **Cross-functional collaboration**: Data mesh promotes collaboration between different teams, such as data engineers, data scientists, analysts, and domain experts. It allows each team to own and manage their domain's data, improving agility and autonomy.

- **Flexibility and agility**: Data mesh enables data domains to operate independently, making it easier to iterate and innovate within specific areas without causing disruptions across the entire data ecosystem.

Similarly, not every implementation may benefit from a data mesh pattern. Here are some considerations where a data mesh architecture may not be suitable:

- **Small and simple data environments**: If your organization has a relatively small and straightforward data ecosystem with limited data sources and consumers, implementing a full-blown data mesh might introduce unnecessary complexity.

- **Lack of clear domain boundaries**: Data mesh relies on defining clear and meaningful data domains. If your organization's data doesn't naturally align with distinct domains, implementing a data mesh pattern might not be as effective.

- **Strong existing centralization**: If your organization has already established a centralized data architecture that is working well, transitioning to a data mesh pattern might lead to disruption and additional overhead without clear benefits.

- **Limited cross-team collaboration**: Data mesh emphasizes collaboration between different teams. If your organization's culture and structure don't support this kind of collaboration, implementing a data mesh pattern might face resistance and challenges.

- **Significant upfront investment**: Implementing a data mesh pattern requires significant changes to existing processes, tools, and culture. If your organization is not ready to commit to this transformation, it might be better to explore other data management approaches.

The decision to adopt a data mesh architecture pattern should be based on a thorough assessment of your organization's data ecosystem, its complexity, scalability needs, culture, and willingness to undergo significant changes. It's not a one-size-fits-all solution and should be carefully considered in the context of your organization's unique challenges and goals.

Summary

In this chapter, we looked at what data mesh is and how the four principles of data mesh help create a highly distributed, scalable, and governed data platform. AWS analytics services such as Amazon Redshift, S3 data lakes, AWS Lake Formation, and Amazon Athena contribute toward building a data mesh architecture; many features of these services assist in enabling a data mesh pattern.

We then looked at how, using AWS Lake Formation, organizations can create a cross-account permissions model that helps create a data mesh on an S3 data lake. Using Amazon DataZone, the process of publishing and subscribing to data assets become even easier to manage.

Finally, we looked at how you can use the Amazon Redshift datashare feature to create a data mesh pattern by allowing Redshift clusters in different AWS accounts and regions to share data assets. DataZone helps here too by simplifying the process of federated governance and fostering a self-service analytics culture.

In the next chapter, we will get into the details of cost optimizations and performance best practices. Both are critical components to get the best return on investment for building and operating this data platform.

References

To learn more about the topics that were covered in this chapter, take a look at the following resources:

- Amazon Lake Formation cross-account workshop: `https://catalog.us-east-1.prod.workshops.aws/workshops/78572df7-d2ee-4f78-b698-7cafdb55135d/en-US/configure-lakeformation/default-catalog-settings`

- Data mesh on AWS blog: `https://aws.amazon.com/blogs/big-data/design-a-data-mesh-architecture-using-aws-lake-formation-and-aws-glue/`.

16

Performant and Cost-Effective Data Platform

In this chapter, we will look at the following key topics:

- Why does a performant and cost-effective data platform matter?
- Data storage optimizations
- Compute resource optimizations
- Cost optimization tools
- Tool-specific performance tuning

Why does a performant and cost-effective data platform matter?

One of the key pillars of a modern data architecture on AWS is around the performance and cost of the data platform being built. Users of the platform are not going to wait 5 minutes for a report to load. Also, if an organization were to measure the return on investment from the data platform, getting a dollar's worth of benefit is not sustainable if it costs them two dollars to get the result.

The performant and cost-effective pillar of modern data architecture on AWS matters for several reasons:

- **Cost-efficiency**: Optimizing costs is crucial for any organization. By implementing a cost-optimized data architecture, you can minimize unnecessary expenses and achieve a better return on investment. AWS provides a wide range of services and tools to help you control and optimize your data-related costs.

- **Scalability**: AWS offers highly scalable services that allow you to scale your data infrastructure based on demand. By designing a performant and cost-optimized architecture, you can ensure that your data processing and storage can scale efficiently without incurring excessive costs. This scalability is especially important for handling large volumes of data and fluctuating workloads.

- **Performance**: The performant aspect of the architecture ensures that your data processing and analysis tasks can be completed efficiently and within acceptable timeframes. By leveraging the right AWS services and optimizations, you can achieve high performance in data processing, enabling faster insights and decision-making.

- **Resource utilization**: Optimizing costs involves making the most efficient use of available resources. With a cost-optimized data architecture, you can ensure that resources are allocated effectively, avoiding overprovisioning or underutilization of compute and storage resources. This leads to improved resource utilization and cost savings.

- **Competitiveness**: In today's data-driven business landscape, organizations that can process and analyze data quickly and cost-effectively have a competitive advantage. By adopting a performant and cost-optimized data architecture on AWS, you can gain insights faster, make data-driven decisions more efficiently, and stay ahead of the competition.

- **Flexibility and agility**: AWS provides a wide range of services and features that enable flexibility and agility in data processing and analysis. A well-designed data architecture allows you to adapt to changing business requirements and integrate new technologies seamlessly. This flexibility enables you to respond quickly to market demands and innovate more effectively.

- **Data governance and compliance**: Implementing a cost-optimized data architecture also ensures proper data governance and compliance. AWS offers various security and compliance features that help protect data and meet regulatory requirements. By following best practices and leveraging AWS services, you can ensure data integrity, privacy, and compliance while optimizing costs.

Overall, this pillar of modern data architecture on AWS is essential for organizations aiming to efficiently process and analyze data while effectively managing costs. It allows businesses to maximize the value of their data assets, improve decision-making, and maintain a competitive edge in the market.

Here are some key considerations and components of the performant and cost-optimized pillar:

- **Data storage optimizations**: AWS provides a range of storage and processing services suitable for different data workloads. To optimize costs, it is important to choose the right storage options based on data access patterns and frequency. Also, implementing data life cycle management strategies helps optimize costs by moving data to appropriate storage tiers based on its age and access patterns. Services such as Amazon S3 Intelligent-Tiering automatically move objects between different storage tiers, optimizing costs without sacrificing performance.

    Additionally, compressing data before storing it in AWS services can help reduce storage costs. AWS services such as Amazon S3 provide built-in compression options.

- **Compute resource optimizations**: AWS offers various compute services that can be used to process and analyze data. Choosing the right compute resources is crucial for performance and cost optimization. Services such as Amazon **Elastic Compute Cloud (EC2)** provide customizable virtual servers for running applications, while serverless services such as AWS Lambda allow you to execute functions without you having to provision or manage servers, thus optimizing costs by paying only for actual usage.

  Also, many of the compute resources can be auto-scaled, reserved, or used from the Spot Instance category to bring down the compute costs. A vast majority of the cost of your data platform comes from compute resources.

- **Cost optimization tools**: AWS provides various tools and services to help you monitor and optimize costs. Services such as AWS Cost Explorer and AWS Budgets provide insights into your usage and spending, allowing you to identify cost optimization opportunities and set budget limits.

- **Tool-specific tuning**: Many services in AWS provide options to improve performance. By experimenting with different configurations, organizations can find the right balance between price and performance.

By considering all these aspects and leveraging the appropriate AWS services and tools, you can build a performant and cost-optimized data architecture on AWS, ensuring efficient data processing and analysis while minimizing operational expenses.

Let's get into the details of each of these topics.

Data storage optimizations

In any data platform, the storage layer is the foundation since all the data across different systems inside the platform is stored in different types of storage. Even though the data storage cost is often not the most dominant part of the overall expenditure on the data platform, it can start to creep up if the best practices are not followed.

Let's bring up a scenario that requires a deep dive into storage optimization.

Use case for storage optimization

GreatFin has established a data platform on AWS and uses many of the data and analytics services provided by AWS to operate different areas of the platform. After onboarding data from a variety of sources, the combined platform storage across all LOBs has grown to a petabyte scale. GreatFin's storage infrastructure on AWS lacks optimization, leading to potential challenges such as high storage costs, performance bottlenecks, limited scalability, and inadequate data protection.

The company requires a **Well-Architected Review (WAR)** of its storage infrastructure to identify areas for optimization, enhance performance, improve cost-efficiency, ensure compliance, and strengthen data security.

A use case for reviewing storage infrastructure for the data platform typically arises due to rising storage costs, along with scalability and performance bottlenecks. Let's dive deep into how we would approach the review process and look at some of the storage optimization techniques.

Let's start with the most common and heavily used storage type, Amazon S3, and see how we can optimize the S3 storage layer.

Amazon S3 optimizations

Amazon S3 is an object store and is used to store all kinds of file-based data. In the world of analytics, almost all data lakes on AWS are built with S3 as the default storage layer. Even though S3 storage is cost-effective, over a certain period with vast amounts of data, the storage costs can creep up and add to the platform's costs.

S3 storage optimization typically has three key steps, as highlighted by the following figure:

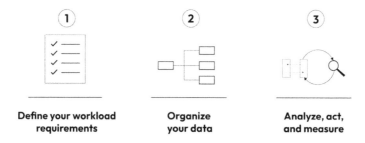

Figure 16.1 – Amazon S3 storage optimization steps

Defining the workload is always step one, simply because the workload dictates what the most important requirements are from the storage layer. Criteria such as redundancy, availability, performance, access patterns, and so forth are often defined by the type of workload. For example, in an ML workload, historical datasets are no longer accessed immediately. In the case of analytics, different use cases can define what is more important.

Once the workloads have been defined, it's important to organize the data in S3 accordingly. This step is one of the most important ones as it directly impacts performance and cost. Since we want to focus on analytics workloads in this book, we will highlight two key dimensions for organizing the data so that the analytics platform is performant, as well as cost-effective, from a storage point of view.

Data partitioning

In Amazon S3, data partitioning refers to the practice of organizing your data into logical partitions based on specific criteria. It involves structuring your data in a way that allows you to efficiently query and access subsets of the data without you having to process the entire dataset. Partitioning can be done by creating a hierarchical structure within your S3 bucket, where each level represents a different partition.

Typically, partitioning in S3 involves using prefixes or folders to define the partitions. For example, if you have a dataset that contains sales data, you might partition it based on the date. In this case, you could create a folder structure where each folder represents a specific date, such as `sales/year=2023/month=06/day=20/`. Within each date folder, you would store the corresponding data files.

By partitioning your data, you gain several benefits. The ones specific to performance and cost are as follows:

- **Improved query performance**: Services such as Amazon Athena and Redshift Spectrum can benefit from a correct partition strategy. Partitioning allows you to selectively access only the relevant partitions during data analysis or querying. Instead of scanning the entire dataset, you can focus on the specific partitions that contain the data of interest. This improves query performance as it reduces the amount of data that needs to be processed.

- **Cost optimization**: Partitioning enables partition pruning, where query engines such as AWS Glue or Athena can skip irrelevant partitions when executing queries. This reduces the amount of data that's scanned and processed, leading to cost savings by minimizing the resources required for query execution.

By leveraging data partitioning in S3, you can optimize data processing, improve query performance, reduce costs, and enhance the overall efficiency of your data workflows.

Data compression

Data compression refers to the practice of compressing data files before storing them in S3. Compression reduces the size of data by encoding it in a more compact representation, resulting in reduced storage requirements and potential performance improvements during data transfer and processing.

The following table shows different types of compression algorithms and their corresponding characteristics:

Algorithm	Splittable	Compression Ratio	Algorithm Speed	Good For
Gzip	No	High	Medium	Raw Storage
bzip2	Yes	Very High	Slow	Very Large Files
LZO	Yes	Low	Fast	Slow Analytics
Snappy	Depends on source format	Low	Very Fast	Slow & Fast Analytics

Figure 16.2 – Data compression techniques

If you recall from our data lake on S3 chapter, Apache Parquet is a preferred file format choice for analytics when you're storing structured data in S3. Parquet, being a columnar file format, when coupled with the Snappy compression technique, provides a good compression ratio while maintaining a high data retrieval speed.

Here are some ways in which data compression in S3 helps with analytics:

- **Reduced storage costs**: Compressing data before storing it in S3 can significantly reduce storage costs. Compressed data occupies less space, allowing you to store more data within the same amount of storage. This becomes especially advantageous when you're dealing with large datasets as the cost savings can be substantial.

- **Improved data transfer**: Compressed data takes less time to transfer over the network. When you retrieve the compressed data from S3 for analytics purposes, it requires less bandwidth and reduces the time required to download or transfer the data to your analytics environment. This results in faster data access and reduced latency.

- **Faster data processing**: Compressed data can lead to faster data processing in analytics workflows. When you perform analytics operations on compressed data, such as querying or running analytical jobs, the smaller data size allows for quicker data processing. The reduced I/O time and disk access contribute to improved query performance and faster analytics results.

- **Optimized performance**: Data compression in S3 can help optimize the performance of query engines and analytical tools. Many query engines, such as AWS Athena and Apache Spark, have built-in support for reading and processing compressed file formats, such as Parquet and ORC. These formats are designed to be highly compressed and optimized for analytical workloads. By storing your data in compressed formats, you can leverage these optimized file formats and gain better query performance and data processing efficiency.

- **Data transfer cost savings**: Compressed data requires less bandwidth during data transfer between different services or regions within AWS. This reduction in data transfer size can result in cost savings, particularly if you are transferring data across different AWS services, such as S3 to EC2 or S3 to Redshift. By compressing data, you can minimize the data transfer costs associated with these operations.

The third step in optimizing storage on S3 revolves around analyzing the storage, acting on the analysis, and measuring it. To assist in this third step, AWS provides three tools, as shown in the following figure:

S3 Storage Lens   **Storage Class Analysis**   **S3 Inventory**

Figure 16.3 – Data compression techniques

Let's look at these in more detail:

- **S3 Storage Lens**: Utilize S3 Storage Lens to gain insights and analyze your storage utilization and activity across multiple accounts and buckets. This powerful tool enables you to visualize and understand how your storage is being utilized.

- **Storage Class Analysis**: Employ Storage Class Analysis to monitor the access patterns of your objects. By tracking the frequency of object access, you can identify opportunities to transition infrequently accessed data to more cost-effective storage classes. This helps optimize costs while ensuring data availability.

- **S3 Inventory**: Leverage S3 Inventory to efficiently organize your objects based on their size. By batching objects according to their sizes, you can effectively manage and optimize storage costs. This feature provides valuable information that aids in cost optimization strategies.

Now, let's look at some other ways you can optimize storage costs.

S3 storage classes

To further optimize S3 storage for cost as well as performance, different classes of storage are provided. It is the data architect's responsibility to design the platform in such a manner that it selects the correct storage class in S3 for specific scenarios.

The following figure highlights different storage classes in S3:

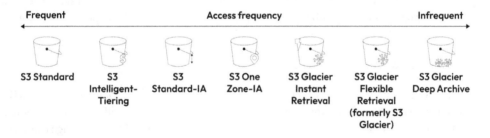

Figure 16.4 – Amazon S3 storage classes

Let's briefly describe them all, along with their characteristics and usage patterns:

- **S3 Standard**: This is the default storage class for Amazon S3. It provides high durability, availability, and low latency. This class is ideal for frequently accessed data and real-time applications. It offers high performance and immediate access to data.

- **S3 Intelligent-Tiering**: This automatically moves objects between two access tiers based on usage patterns. It analyzes access patterns to determine which data is frequently and infrequently accessed. It also optimizes costs by automatically moving objects to the most cost-effective access tier. This is suitable for workloads with changing or unpredictable access patterns.

- **S3 Standard-IA (Infrequent Access)**: This is designed for data that is accessed less frequently but requires rapid access when needed. It offers lower storage costs compared to the S3 Standard class. It is suitable for backups, disaster recovery, or long-term storage of infrequently accessed data.

- **S3 One Zone-IA**: Similar to S3 Standard-IA but stores data in a single availability zone instead of multiple zones. It provides a lower-cost option for infrequently accessed data with reduced availability compared to S3 Standard-IA. This is ideal for scenarios where data redundancy is not a critical requirement.

- **S3 Glacier Instant Retrieval**: This is the newest class in long-term archival storage. It offers immediate data-accessible capabilities but is suitable for low-rate access patterns, where data is accessed in rare cases; for example, during an audit, where the entire historical trail of a record needs to be accessed.

- **S3 Glacier Flexible Retrieval**: This provides long-term archival storage at significantly lower costs. It offers high durability but with slower access times (retrieval times in minutes to hours). This is suitable for archiving data, compliance records, and regulatory requirements.

- **S3 Glacier Deep Archive**: This is the most cost-effective storage class in Amazon S3. It is designed for long-term retention and archiving with retrieval times in hours. This is suitable for data that is rarely accessed and stored for compliance or regulatory purposes.

Each storage class provides different durability, availability, performance, and pricing characteristics. Choosing the appropriate storage class depends on factors such as data access patterns, latency requirements, cost considerations, and regulatory compliance requirements. By leveraging the right storage class, organizations can optimize costs and performance based on their specific data storage and retrieval needs.

Patterns of cost optimization on S3

For data with known or predictable access patterns, the S3 life cycle feature should be leveraged. The S3 life cycle refers to managing data stored in S3 based on predefined rules. S3 life cycle management allows you to define rules that automate the transition of objects between different storage classes or take specific actions on objects based on their age or usage patterns.

The following figure highlights an S3 life cycle policy that moves data between S3 storage classes based on the age of the objects inside the S3 bucket:

S3 Standard   100 days   **S3 Glacier Instant Retrieval**   365 days   **S3 Glacier Deep Archive**

Figure 16.5 – Amazon S3 life cycle policies

For data with unknown or changing access patterns, you should use the Intelligent-Tiering option in S3, which automatically moves objects between different storage classes. With S3 Intelligent-Tiering, you don't need to manually manage the transition of objects between storage classes. Instead, S3 monitors the access patterns of your data and automatically moves objects to the most cost-effective tier based on their access frequency. This helps you achieve cost savings without sacrificing performance or availability.

The following figure shows the automatic data movement within S3 storage classes when using Intelligent-Tiering:

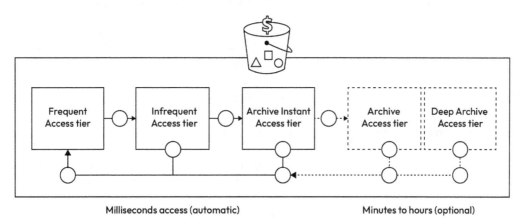

Figure 16.6 – Amazon S3 Intelligent-Tiering

Other storage optimizations

We discussed S3 optimizations in detail since it's the predominant type of storage used for setting up a data lake for analytical purposes. However, other types of storage are also used when the data platform is created.

Many other analytics services, including Amazon EMR, use **Elastic Block Storage** (**EBS**) volumes, which get attached to the different EMR nodes in provisioned mode. Choosing the right set of EBS volumes can help with the best price/performance, depending on the workload's characteristics and outcome expectations:

- **General Purpose SSD (gp2/gp3)**: Suitable for a wide range of workloads with balanced performance and cost
- **Provisioned IOPS SSD (io1/io2)**: Provides high-performance storage for applications that require low latency and high IOPS

- **Throughput Optimized HDD (st1)**: Designed for big data and data analytics workloads that require high throughput, but can tolerate higher latency

- **Cold HDD (sc1)**: Ideal for infrequently accessed data that doesn't require high performance, such as data archiving or log storage

As services become fully managed, including providing a serverless option, the underlying storage is typically optimized for use; for example, on Amazon Redshift using autonomics, the best compression algorithm is applied to each type of column on all tables, allowing the data to auto-optimize in the storage layer.

On the analytics platform, the majority of the storage optimization effort goes into S3. The remaining storage options can be selected in the service itself or they can be changed to switch to a different storage tier; for example, in Amazon OpenSearch Service, you can switch the storage tier depending on the age of the data and save overall costs while still meeting the use case.

Compute resource optimizations

In any typical data modern data platform that's been built using AWS data and analytics services, the platform infrastructure expenses will be dominated by the compute expenses provided by many of the services. Take any service we discussed in this book, be it DMS for data ingestion, Glue and EMR for data processing, Kinesis and MSK for streaming data, Redshift for data warehouses, Athena for ad hoc analytics on the data lake, different SageMaker tools for ML, OpenSearch Service for operational analytics, QuickSight for business intelligence and many other supporting services – if you look at the overall cost of each of these services, you will find that the vast majority of the expense comes from the compute resources supporting these services. The reason is simple – CPUs/GPUs are significantly more expensive than storage, memory, and networking.

Compute resources are also one of the most important dimensions regarding the optimal performance of the service. The more compute power you add, the faster the service works – provided there are no other bottlenecks in the infrastructure. Every organization wants to use a fast but less expensive service to get a specific job done. While building a data platform, the goal is always to leverage the best practices and optimize whatever resources that are being used to justify the return on investment.

Let's use this section to go over some ways by which you can optimize the compute resources of many of the services we have used in building a modern data platform on AWS. As always, here's a typical problem statement that leads to a compute optimization review of the data platform.

Use case for compute resources optimization

GreatFin is leveraging AWS analytics services to power its modern data platform and perform various data analytics tasks on a day-to-day basis. However, the company is facing challenges related to compute resource optimization.

The specific pain points faced by GreatFin include the following:

1. **Inefficient resource allocation**: The company cannot accurately allocate compute resources based on workload demands. As a result, they experience underutilization of resources during periods of low demand and encounter performance bottlenecks during peak workloads.

2. **Rising costs**: The current approach to provisioning compute resources leads to unnecessary costs. The company is spending more on compute resources than required due to suboptimal allocation and utilization practices.

3. **Scalability challenges**: The company struggles to effectively scale compute resources to accommodate fluctuating workloads. This hinders their ability to handle sudden spikes in data processing requirements, leading to delays in critical analytics tasks.

4. **Performance degradation**: The inefficient allocation and utilization of compute resources adversely impact the performance of data processing and analysis tasks. This hampers the overall efficiency and timeliness of critical financial analytics processes.

GreatFin recognizes the need for an optimized compute resource allocation strategy that aligns with their workload demands. They are seeking an AWS analytics solution that can provide automated resource scaling, accurate capacity planning, and improved cost efficiency. The desired outcome is a data platform that can dynamically allocate compute resources based on workload fluctuations, optimize costs by eliminating resource wastage, and ensure consistent performance even during peak periods.

By optimizing compute resources, organizations can cost-optimize their data platform. Different services follow different mechanisms to utilize compute and by leveraging simple best practices, organizations can streamline their platform. Let's look at each area of compute instance optimization in detail and relate them to some of the data and analytics services we've discussed in this book that helped us build a modern data platform on AWS.

Compute instance families

AWS offers different compute instance families, each optimized for specific workloads – such as compute-intensive, memory-intensive, or storage-intensive workloads. Let's look at how you can choose the appropriate instance family that aligns with your analytics requirements.

Amazon EMR-supported instances

EMR provisioned clusters allow you to select the compute instance family for the cluster. It is important to select the correct type of instance for the appropriate type of workload. The following figure highlights some of the prominent instance family types used for certain known types of workloads:

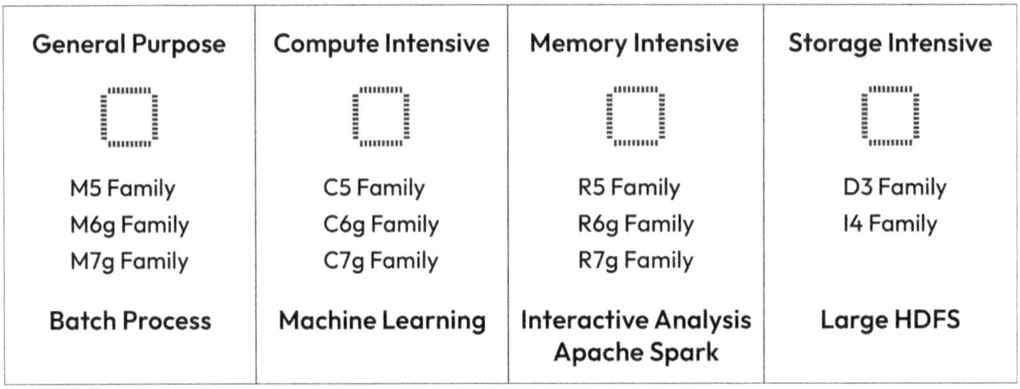

General Purpose	Compute Intensive	Memory Intensive	Storage Intensive
M5 Family	C5 Family	R5 Family	D3 Family
M6g Family	C6g Family	R6g Family	I4 Family
M7g Family	C7g Family	R7g Family	
Batch Process	**Machine Learning**	**Interactive Analysis Apache Spark**	**Large HDFS**

Figure 16.7 – Amazon EMR instance family

A lot of big data workloads on EMR run the Apache Spark framework for data processing. Graviton instances are a type of Amazon EC2 instance that are powered by the AWS Graviton2/3 processors, which are based on the ARM architecture. These instances offer several benefits when it comes to running Apache Spark workloads:

- **Cost-efficiency**: Graviton instances can provide cost savings compared to traditional x86-based instances. The ARM architecture is known for its energy efficiency, which translates into lower operational costs for Spark workloads, especially for long-running and compute-intensive jobs.

- **Performance**: AWS Graviton2/3 processors offer strong performance for a wide range of workloads, including Spark. They feature multiple cores and high clock speeds, enabling efficient execution of Spark tasks and computations.

- **Scale-out capabilities**: Graviton instances are available in various instance types, allowing you to scale your Spark clusters both vertically and horizontally. You can choose instance types based on your specific requirements for CPU, memory, and storage resources, enabling efficient scaling for Spark workloads.

When you select provisioned deployment mode for EMR, always experiment with different workloads with different instance family types and benchmark them all. The final selection should be made in favor of the one that gives the best price/performance at scale. EMR also provides the option of creating instance fleets, where you can mix and match different instance families together to get the best performance from each type of compute resource, for mixed types of workloads.

AWS Glue worker types

When it comes to Glue ETL, for data ingestion as well as for data processing, selecting the correct worker type for the specific type of workload can help optimize price/performance. AWS Glue provides different **data processing unit (DPU)** types to choose from, based on your data processing requirements. DPUs are units of processing capacity that Glue uses to run ETL jobs and other data processing tasks.

The choice of DPU type depends on the size and complexity of your data processing tasks. Smaller Spark jobs with less demanding requirements can be executed effectively using G.1X DPUs, while larger and more resource-intensive jobs may require G.2X, G.4X, or G.8X DPUs to achieve optimal performance.

The following screenshot shows the different worker type selections you can make when creating a Glue ETL Spark job:

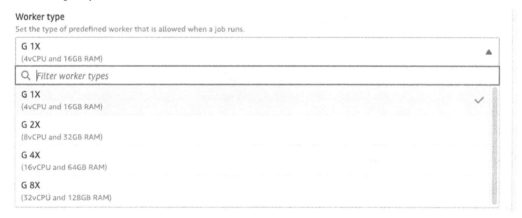

Figure 16.8 – AWS Glue Spark ETL worker types

Also, not all data processing jobs require the distributed computing power of Spark. Many jobs can be completed easily by using pure Python-based shell jobs that require significantly less DPU power to execute. The following screenshot shows a Python-based shell job setup in Glue where you can select as little as 1/16 DPU to execute the workload – provided the jobs can be completed in a reasonable time, as defined by the SLA:

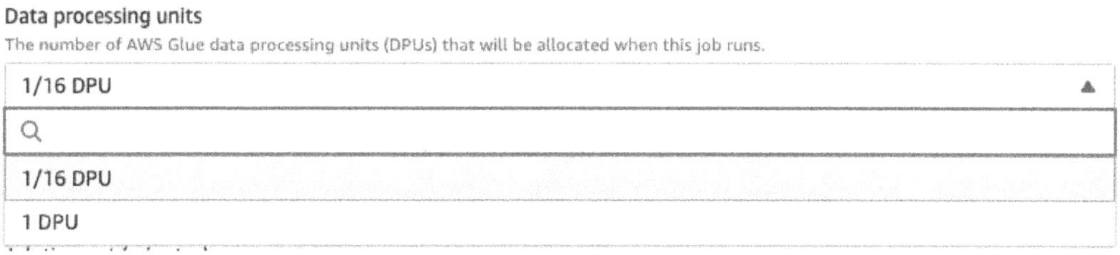

Figure 16.9 – AWS Glue Python ETL DPU selection

Amazon Redshift node types

When it comes to provisioning a Redshift cluster, many projects benefit from the RA3 instance type due to its separation of storage and compute. They provide a good balance between compute and storage capacity and are suitable for mixed workloads that require both high performance and storage capacity.

Dense Compute (**DC**) instances are designed for demanding workloads that require high computational power and query performance. They have a smaller ratio of storage to CPU and memory, making them suitable for scenarios where processing speed is a priority. However, since storage and compute come together, they are more appropriate for clusters with smaller data footprints, typically under a terabyte.

Other services

Many other AWS analytics services, specifically the ones that offer a provisioned mode of deployment, offer the option to select the correct type of instance family. Services such as Amazon MSK and Amazon OpenSearch Service offer this option to select appropriate family types depending on the workload.

By selecting the appropriate instance family for your analytics platform, you can ensure that you have the right balance of compute, memory, storage, and specialized resources required to optimize performance, cost-efficiency, and scalability. It's essential to analyze your workload characteristics and match them with the strengths of different instance families to achieve the desired optimizations.

Right-sizing compute instances

Selecting the correct instance family for compute is the first challenge that needs to be solved, followed by determining the number of instances that are required to optimally process the workload. Many services provide the concept of auto-scaling, where compute is automatically added when needed by a workload and taken away when not needed. However, we have certain services that still have to be right-sized for specific analytics workloads.

Right-sizing Amazon Redshift nodes

To better understand the optimal number of instances needed for an Amazon Redshift provisioned cluster, the Redshift console provides a sizing tool that guides the users through the process of selecting a specific number of instances from a particular instance family. Users can proceed with the recommendations from the sizing tool as a starting cluster configuration to load-test the Redshift cluster and then adjust accordingly. Using the Redshift elastic resize feature, it is easy to add and remove instances from an existing Redshift cluster.

The best way to right-size a Redshift provisioned cluster would be to find the minimum number of nodes required so that the cluster can be utilized 75% of the time for day-to-day normal workloads. A buffer will help during peak loads and anything above it should be planned to be executed using the concurrency scaling feature of Redshift, which we will discuss later in this chapter.

The following screenshot shows the Redshift sizing estimator inside the Redshift UI when you first try to create a new cluster but don't know the number of nodes that will be needed:

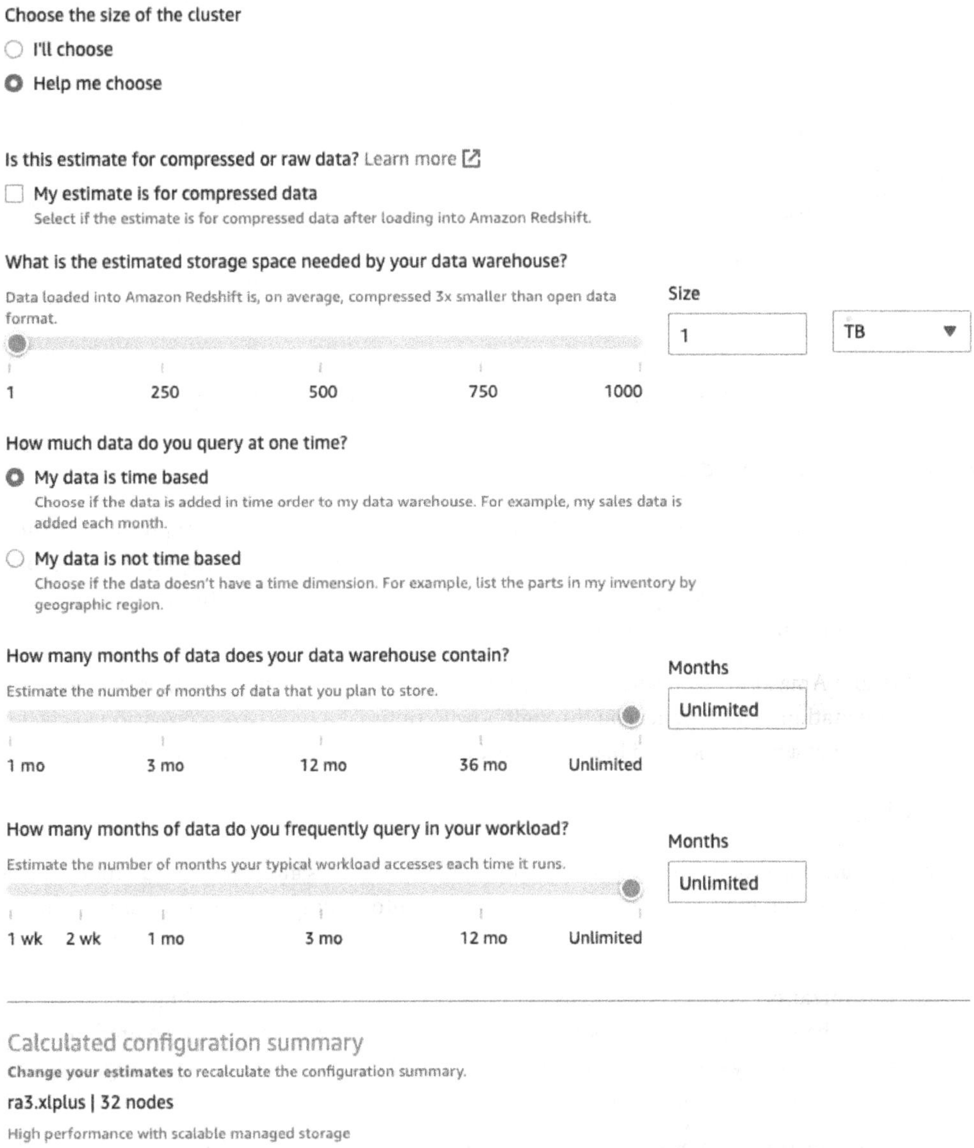

Choose the size of the cluster

◯ I'll choose

⦿ Help me choose

Is this estimate for compressed or raw data? Learn more ☑

☐ My estimate is for compressed data
    Select if the estimate is for compressed data after loading into Amazon Redshift.

What is the estimated storage space needed by your data warehouse?

Data loaded into Amazon Redshift is, on average, compressed 3x smaller than open data format.

| 1 | 250 | 500 | 750 | 1000 |

Size

| 1 | TB ▼ |

How much data do you query at one time?

⦿ My data is time based
    Choose if the data is added in time order to my data warehouse. For example, my sales data is added each month.

◯ My data is not time based
    Choose if the data doesn't have a time dimension. For example, list the parts in my inventory by geographic region.

How many months of data does your data warehouse contain?

Estimate the number of months of data that you plan to store.

| 1 mo | 3 mo | 12 mo | 36 mo | Unlimited |

Months

| Unlimited |

How many months of data do you frequently query in your workload?

Estimate the number of months your typical workload accesses each time it runs.

| 1 wk | 2 wk | 1 mo | 3 mo | 12 mo | Unlimited |

Months

| Unlimited |

Calculated configuration summary

Change your estimates to recalculate the configuration summary.

ra3.xlplus | 32 nodes

High performance with scalable managed storage

Figure 16.10 – Amazon Redshift cluster sizing estimate tool

Once the cluster is working and you have loaded data, stress test it to understand how the CPU and other infrastructure are getting utilized; then, use elastic resize to fine-tune the exact number of nodes needed for optimal day-to-day operations.

The following screenshot from the monitoring section of an existing Redshift cluster shows the CPU utilization over a certain period:

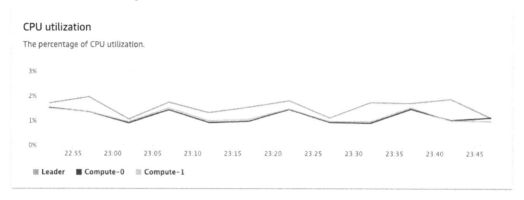

Figure 16.11 – Amazon Redshift cluster CPU utilization monitoring

Right-sizing other services

It is difficult to right-size data processing AWS services such as Glue and EMR, simply because there are way too many variables regarding how Spark uses resources to optimally complete the workload. For the same reason, both services provide auto-scaling so that you don't have to carry out extensive tests to find the optimal size of the execution environment per workload.

Amazon MSK and Amazon OpenSearch Service provide sizing guidelines in the best practices section of their documentation, which walks you through how to optimally right-size a provisioned cluster. Kinesis is a fully managed service and has inbuilt features that help manage compute resources.

Auto-scaling

Auto-scaling is an important feature provided by AWS that allows automatic adjustments to be made to compute resources based on workload demands. Auto-scaling is particularly important for several reasons:

- **Cost optimization**: Auto-scaling helps optimize costs by automatically scaling your resources up or down based on demand. It ensures that you have just enough resources required to handle your workload at any given time, avoiding overprovisioning or underprovisioning. This way, you only pay for the resources you need, leading to cost savings.

- **Performance and availability**: Auto-scaling helps maintain the desired performance and availability of your application or service. During periods of high demand, auto-scaling adds more resources to handle the increased load, ensuring that your application remains responsive and available. Conversely, during periods of low demand, auto-scaling reduces the resources to save costs while still maintaining adequate performance.

- **Scalability**: Auto-scaling enables your application to scale automatically based on demand. It allows you to handle sudden traffic spikes without manual intervention, ensuring that your application can seamlessly accommodate a large number of users or requests. Auto-scaling also provides elasticity, allowing you to scale resources up or down quickly to match the changing workload patterns.

- **Fault tolerance**: Auto-scaling enhances the fault tolerance of your application by distributing the workload across multiple instances. If any instance fails or becomes unavailable, auto-scaling replaces it with a new one, ensuring that your application continues to function without interruption. This helps in building resilient and highly available architectures.

- **Operational efficiency**: Auto-scaling simplifies the management and operation of your infrastructure. It eliminates the need for manual scaling adjustments, allowing you to focus on other critical aspects of your application. Auto-scaling integrates with other AWS services such as Elastic Load Balancing and CloudWatch, enabling you to set up dynamic and automated scaling rules based on various metrics, such as CPU utilization or network traffic.

Auto-scaling is particularly helpful for Spark-based workloads on AWS Glue and Amazon EMR. The nature of big data processing is such that at any given point in time, different jobs may be getting executed in Spark, and the resources required by each workload are variable and unpredictable. To optimize compute resources, data engineering teams would want to leverage the auto-scaling feature provided by Glue and EMR.

In EMR, for jobs that run only during a particular time of the day, it's optimal to have a transient cluster spun up, complete the workloads, and shut the cluster down. For long-running workloads or workloads that need persistent clusters, auto-scaling is particularly helpful as variations in workloads would allow the cluster to add/remove nodes from a running cluster.

When you create an EMR cluster, you can enable the EMR-managed scaling option by providing the min-max cluster size, along with how you want those nodes to be distributed inside the cluster. Under the hood, EMR will monitor and scale the cluster based on a wide range of observations, including CPU, memory, and storage. The following screenshot shows the EMR-managed scaling creation option inside the EMR console:

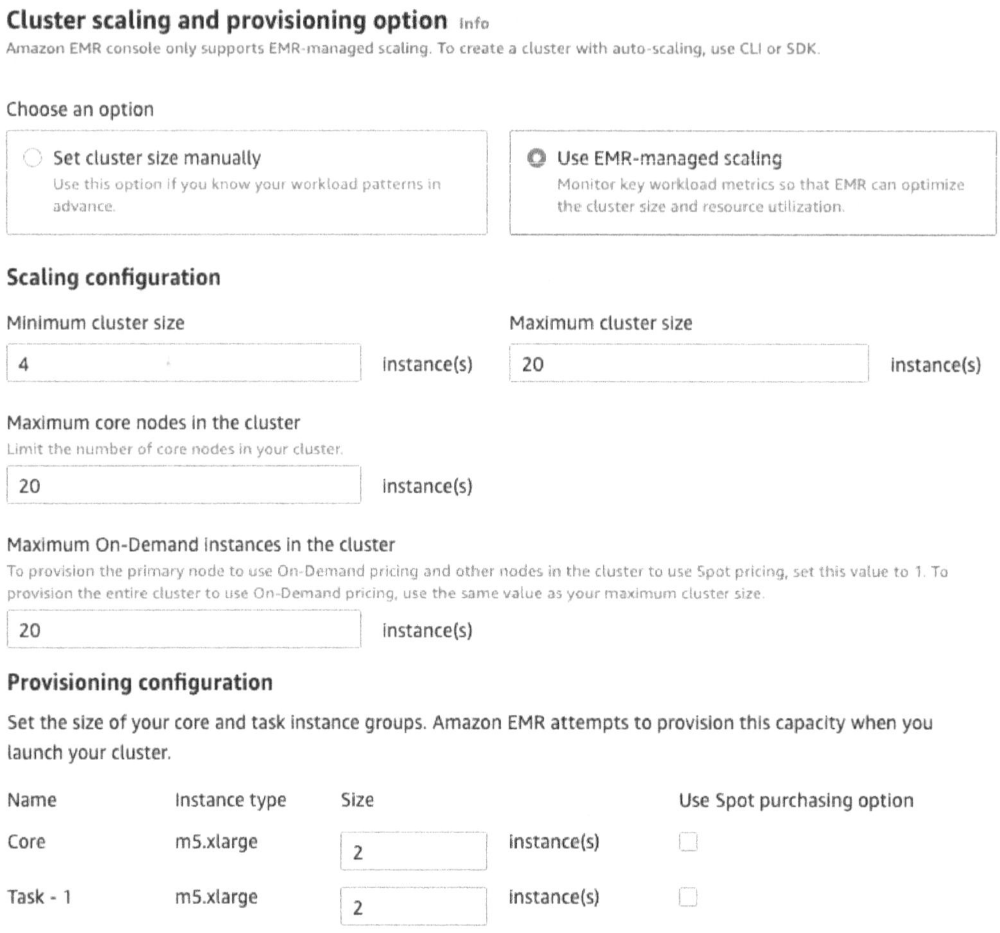

Cluster scaling and provisioning option Info

Amazon EMR console only supports EMR-managed scaling. To create a cluster with auto-scaling, use CLI or SDK.

Choose an option

○ Set cluster size manually	● Use EMR-managed scaling
Use this option if you know your workload patterns in advance.	Monitor key workload metrics so that EMR can optimize the cluster size and resource utilization.

Scaling configuration

Minimum cluster size

| 4 | instance(s) |

Maximum cluster size

| 20 | instance(s) |

Maximum core nodes in the cluster
Limit the number of core nodes in your cluster.

| 20 | instance(s) |

Maximum On-Demand instances in the cluster

To provision the primary node to use On-Demand pricing and other nodes in the cluster to use Spot pricing, set this value to 1. To provision the entire cluster to use On-Demand pricing, use the same value as your maximum cluster size.

| 20 | instance(s) |

Provisioning configuration

Set the size of your core and task instance groups. Amazon EMR attempts to provision this capacity when you launch your cluster.

Name	Instance type	Size		Use Spot purchasing option
Core	m5.xlarge	2	instance(s)	☐
Task - 1	m5.xlarge	2	instance(s)	☐

Figure 16.12 – Amazon EMR managed scaling

For workloads that use AWS Glue ETL, auto-scaling DPU is also an option when you configure the Glue job. The following screenshot shows a Glue auto-scaling flag being set while creating a job. Depending on the demands of the workload, it will allow this particular Glue job to scale the DPUs up and down to a max of 10 workers:

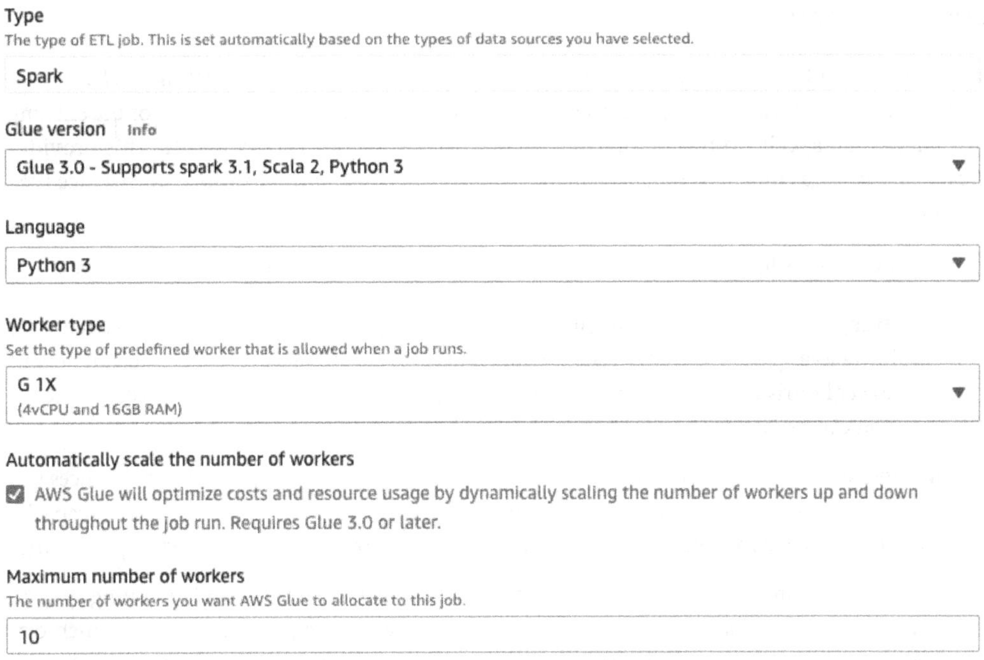

Type

The type of ETL job. This is set automatically based on the types of data sources you have selected.

Spark

Glue version   Info

Glue 3.0 - Supports spark 3.1, Scala 2, Python 3	▼

Language

Python 3	▼

Worker type

Set the type of predefined worker that is allowed when a job runs.

G 1X (4vCPU and 16GB RAM)	▼

Automatically scale the number of workers

☑ AWS Glue will optimize costs and resource usage by dynamically scaling the number of workers up and down throughout the job run. Requires Glue 3.0 or later.

Maximum number of workers

The number of workers you want AWS Glue to allocate to this job.

10

Figure 16.13 – AWS Glue job auto-scaling

Auto-scaling is typically provided for services that require server-based configurations, where the data platform architect can design the optimal usage of a particular service by enabling auto-scaling. Some other AWS analytics services provide auto-scaling features, while for others, you can design your own scaling architecture by creating rules for adding/removing extra compute resources.

The bottom line is that due diligence must be made to ensure that compute capabilities are optimally used. Having extra compute lying idle can be compared to paying rent for a house you don't live in. At the same time, not allocating enough compute resources would impact performance negatively.

Capacity reservations and discounted compute instances

AWS provides many mechanisms by which you can reduce the cost of compute required in your data platform operations. Some mechanisms also allow you to reserve compute capacity upfront to lower the overall operational costs. Let's look at some of these mechanisms.

Reserved instances

If you have predictable and steady workloads, consider purchasing **reserved instances** (**RIs**) from AWS. RIs are not a new type of compute instance, it's just a term used to reserve many of the existing EC2 instances for a specific duration of time to lower the overall costs of compute. This provides significant cost savings compared to On-Demand instances as you commit to a specific instance type and duration.

RIs offer several benefits for analytics workloads on AWS. Here are some of the key advantages:

- **Cost savings**: RIs provide significant cost savings compared to On-Demand instances. By committing to a specific instance type, region, and term length (1 or 3 years), you can benefit from a lower hourly rate. This is particularly advantageous for long-running analytics workloads where you can predict instance usage.

- **Capacity assurance**: With RIs, you have reserved capacity, which guarantees that the instances you need for your analytics workloads will always be available, even during peak demand. This capacity assurance helps ensure consistent performance and availability for your analytics processing.

- **Flexibility**: RIs offer flexibility in terms of instance size, instance family, and operating system. You can choose the RI attributes that best match your analytics requirements, such as memory, CPU, and storage capacity. This flexibility allows you to optimize your infrastructure for the specific demands of your analytics workloads.

- **Instance utilization**: RIs encourage higher instance utilization. Since you have committed to a specific instance type, you are motivated to utilize the instances effectively. This can help maximize the return on your investment and reduce idle or underutilized resources.

- **Billing benefits**: RIs provide consolidated billing benefits. If you have multiple AWS accounts under the same payer account, the cost savings from RIs can be aggregated and applied to the overall bill. This simplifies billing and allows for better cost management across your organization.

- **Enterprise commitments**: For larger enterprises, RIs provide you with an opportunity to commit to a specific infrastructure capacity and predict costs in advance. This can align well with budgeting and financial planning processes, allowing for better resource allocation.

It's important to note that RIs require upfront payment or a significant portion of the term commitment, and they are recommended for stable or predictable workloads. For highly dynamic or fluctuating workloads, AWS also offers options such as Spot Instances and On-Demand Instances, which provide greater flexibility but may have a higher cost per hour of usage.

If you are using Redshift, EMR, or OpenSearch Service provisioned capacity deployment for your workloads, always plan to get RIs for workloads that are steady and utilize the underlying resources well. By leveraging RIs, you can achieve substantial cost savings, ensure capacity availability, optimize utilization, and gain flexibility for your analytics workloads on AWS.

On-Demand Capacity Reservations

AWS **On-Demand Capacity Reservations (ODCRs)** allow you to reserve capacity for your Amazon EC2 instances in a specific Availability Zone for any duration. Here are some key aspects:

- It ensures you always have access to EC2 capacity when you need it, without having to pre-provision instances

- It gives you the ability to instantly provision capacity if your application requirements change

- You only pay for what you use with no long-term commitments or upfront payments

- It provides a significant discount compared to On-Demand instance pricing (up to 72% for some instance types)

- Reservation discounts apply automatically to the matching instances as they are launched

- Available for Linux, Windows, and other platforms across a wide range of instance types and sizes

- Reservations are flexible and can be shared across multiple accounts within an organization

- Unused reservations can be canceled and refunded hourly to free up the reserved capacity

- Supported instance attributes such as instance type, OS, tenancy, and more can be modified on the reservations as needed

ODCRs offer flexible, discounted, and instantly available EC2 capacity to meet your fluctuating workload needs while eliminating the need to pre-provision instances. EMR supports the use of ODCRs while creating a provisioned cluster.

Spot Instances

AWS Spot Instances allow you to use spare EC2 capacity in the AWS cloud, which can significantly reduce costs. Spot Instances are ideal for fault-tolerant workloads and can be used with services such as Amazon EMR and AWS Glue ETL for data processing. Often, you can use Spot Instances and save up to 90% in terms of compute costs.

During EMR cluster setup, it's recommended to add Spot Instances to task nodes so that your workloads can continue to run even if the extra spot capacity from the task group is taken away. Similarly, in Glue, while setting up Spark jobs, you can select flex execution to allow Glue to tap into Spot Instances for running the jobs, thus providing you with cost savings.

AWS Savings Plans also help save costs on compute. We will look at this in the next section. For now, let's move on to another compute topic around containers.

Containerization

For certain workloads, use containerization technologies such as Docker and Amazon **Elastic Container Service** (**ECS**) or **Elastic Kubernetes Service** (**EKS**) to package and deploy your analytics applications. Containers provide isolation, portability, and scalability, enabling efficient resource utilization.

EMR on EKS provides a container-based approach that separates the analytics job from the underlying services and infrastructure responsible for processing it. This approach allows you to focus more on application development while reducing the operational burden. With EMR on EKS, the infrastructure is dynamically configured based on the specific requirements of the job, including compute, memory, and application dependencies. This eliminates the need for manual infrastructure management and allows infrastructure teams to centrally oversee a common compute platform, consolidating EMR workloads with other container-based applications.

Serverless computing

Many teams prefer to use serverless architecture patterns while building their data platform. This approach is suitable for event-driven analytics workloads with sporadic or unpredictable processing demands. Many of the core AWS services also offer a serverless mode of deployment. AWS analytics such as Redshift, EMR, MSK, and OpenSearch Service all have a serverless mode of deployment. Serverless is preferred in many cases simply because it provides a better price/performance for workloads that don't need the infrastructure resources up and running all the time. This helps save costs in the long run. Also, serverless services allow organizations to focus on solving business problems instead of spending time managing the infrastructure used by the analytics service.

In the next section, we will discuss some tools that help identify and assist in cost optimization, but the rule of thumb for using the serverless option, for many of the AWS services that offer more than one mode of deployment, would be for scenarios where computing requirements are challenging to predict, such as variable workloads, periodic workloads with idle time, and steady-state workloads with spikes. Additionally, it serves as an excellent solution for addressing ad hoc analytics requirements and for setting up test and development environments efficiently.

Cost optimization tools

AWS provides several cost optimization tools that can help you manage and optimize your AWS spending. The following sections show some key cost optimization tools offered by AWS.

AWS Cost Explorer

AWS Cost Explorer is a built-in cost management tool that provides visibility into your AWS costs and usage. It allows you to analyze your costs, view historical spending patterns, and forecast future costs. You can drill down into specific cost categories, services, or regions to identify areas where cost optimizations can be made.

Cost Explorer allows you to look at different service spends for each month, as shown in the following screenshot. This gives you a good understanding of rising costs that might require optimization reviews:

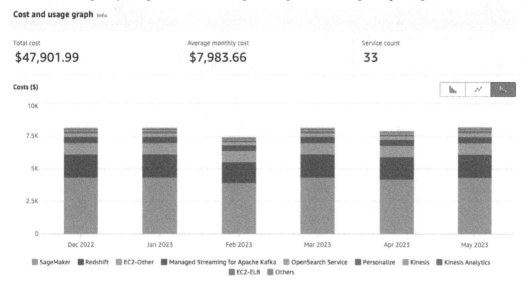

Figure 16.14 – AWS Cost Explorer

AWS Budgets

AWS Budgets enables you to set cost and usage budgets for your AWS resources. You can define spending thresholds and receive alerts when your costs or usage exceed the specified limits. AWS Budgets helps you stay informed about your spending and take proactive actions to control costs.

The following screenshot shows a sample budget dashboard where you can also track budget versus actuals and trigger alerts if thresholds are crossed:

Figure 16.15 – AWS Budgets

AWS Cost Anomaly Detection

Cost Anomaly Detection is a feature within AWS Cost Explorer that uses ML algorithms to identify unusual spending patterns and anomalies in your AWS costs. It automatically detects potential cost-saving opportunities and alerts you to investigate and take appropriate actions.

The following screenshot shows the dashboard for Cost Anomaly Detection:

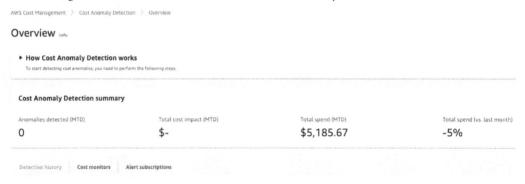

Figure 16.16 – AWS Cost Anomaly Detection

AWS Cost and Usage Reports

AWS Cost and Usage Reports provides detailed insights into your AWS costs and usage patterns. These reports can be exported to Amazon S3 or Amazon Redshift, allowing you to perform custom analysis or integrate the data with third-party cost management tools.

The following screenshot shows different reports that the billing admin team can create to help track down costs:

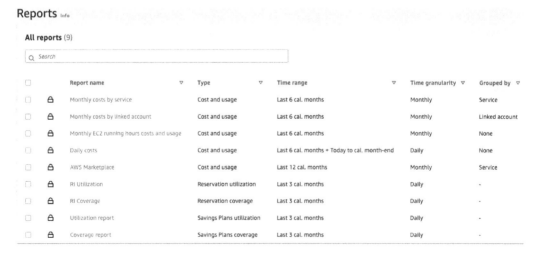

Figure 16.17 – AWS Cost Explorer reports

AWS Trusted Advisor

Trusted Advisor is an automated tool that helps optimize your AWS infrastructure across various areas, including cost optimization. It provides recommendations to improve cost efficiency, such as identifying idle or underutilized resources, right-sizing instances, and leveraging RIs for cost savings.

The following screenshot shows the dashboard for Trusted Advisor recommendations:

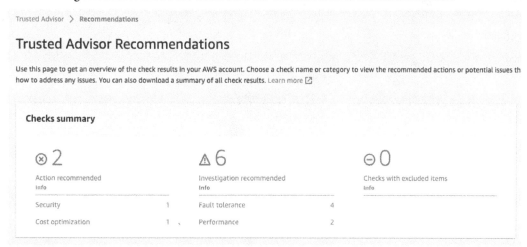

Figure 16.18 – AWS Trusted Advisor

AWS Savings Plans

Savings Plans offers flexible pricing options for Amazon EC2 instances and also for Amazon SageMaker. They provide significant cost savings compared to On-Demand instances by offering lower, consistent hourly rates in exchange for a commitment to usage over a 1 or 3-year term.

You can also select a payment option, such as all upfront, partial upfront, or no upfront. Once you have a savings plan, you can track the utilization and coverage using reports that are provided as part of the savings plan tool. Unlike RIs, Savings Plans don't guarantee capacity reservations. They offer cost savings by reducing the hourly rate but don't guarantee availability during peak times. Savings Plans offer greater flexibility to match changing needs and workloads, making them suitable for variable or unpredictable workloads.

The following screenshot shows the Savings Plan UI from where you can purchase Savings Plans:

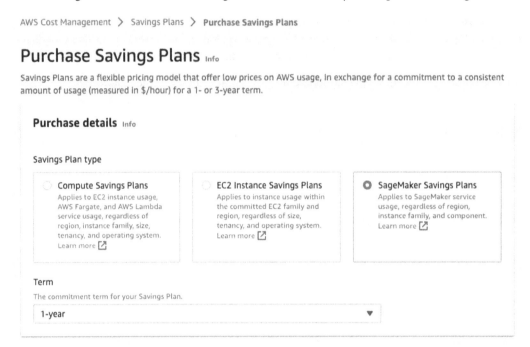

Figure 16.19 – Savings Plans

AWS Compute Optimizer

Compute Optimizer analyzes your EC2 instances utilization patterns and provides recommendations on instance types, sizes, and families that can optimize performance and reduce costs. It helps you identify opportunities for right-sizing your instances based on actual utilization.

The following screenshot shows the dashboard for the AWS Compute Optimizer tool, where you can track savings opportunities due to some of the optimization recommendations that are provided as part of the tool:

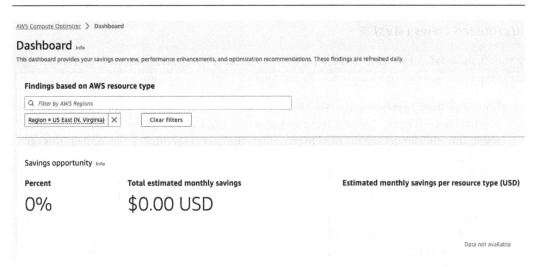

Figure 16.20 – AWS Compute Optimizer

These are just a few examples of the cost optimization tools provided by AWS. By utilizing these tools and implementing best practices, you can effectively manage and optimize your AWS spending, ensuring cost efficiency and maximizing the value of your AWS resources.

Tool-specific performance tuning

We covered a lot about optimizing the service infrastructure in this chapter. However, often, optimizations happen at the service or tool level. This is caused by changing the configurations of the service or fine-tuning the logic that runs on these services. Typically, tuning is done to improve performance, which also helps save costs. It will not be possible to cover every aspect of performance tuning in this section, but we will try to cover some of the obvious ones from some of the key services that help build a data platform on AWS.

Performance tuning measures on Amazon Redshift

Many aspects of performance tuning depend on root cause analysis; hence, we may not be able to cover every tunable in Redshift. Also, recent Redshift autonomics advancements have made a lot of tunable settings automatic now; things such as data distribution, sorting, and analyze and vacuum operations can all be made automatic by the service. However, some common tunable approaches apply to almost all Redshift implementations. Let's go over some of them.

Materialized views (MVs)

In Redshift, **materialized views** (**MVs**) can significantly improve query performance by precomputing and storing the results of complex queries. Here's how MVs help in Redshift:

- **Improved query performance**: MVs store the results of expensive and complex queries as physical tables. When queries are executed against the MV, Redshift retrieves the pre-computed results directly, eliminating the need to recompute the query every time it is executed. This can greatly reduce query execution time, especially for queries that involve aggregations, joins, or complex calculations.

- **Reduction in query complexity**: MVs simplify query complexity by transforming complex queries into simple SELECT statements. Instead of joining multiple tables and performing extensive calculations each time the query is executed, the query is executed against the pre-computed results stored in the MV. This can significantly reduce the computational resources required for query execution.

- **Accelerated aggregations**: MVs are particularly useful for accelerating aggregations, such as sum, count, average, or any other type of group-by operation. By pre-computing these aggregations and storing them in an MV, subsequent queries can retrieve the aggregated results directly, without the need for expensive computations to be performed on the underlying data.

- **Query optimization**: Redshift's query optimizer can leverage MVs to optimize query execution plans. When a query involves tables that have associated MVs, the optimizer can choose to use the MV instead of scanning the underlying tables, leading to faster query performance.

- **Incremental maintenance**: Redshift allows you to define refresh policies for MVs, specifying how often the MV needs to be updated. You can set up incremental refreshes, where only the changed or updated data is processed, reducing the overhead of refreshing the entire MV. This ensures that the MV stays up to date with the underlying data.

In the following example, we are creating an MV named mv_total_order_amount. The SELECT statement inside the CREATE MATERIALIZED VIEW statement performs the calculation to get the total order amount for each customer. It joins the orders and customers tables based on the customer_id column and groups the result by customer_id and customer_name. The SUM function calculates the total order amount.

After executing this query, the MV is created, and it contains the pre-computed results of the total order amount for each customer. You can also put the MV in auto-refresh mode, which will automatically update the MV with the latest changes from the tables regularly, as determined by multiple factors, including system load and frequency of updates:

```
CREATE MATERIALIZED VIEW mv_total_order_amount
AUTO REFRESH YES
AS
SELECT
```

```
    customers.customer_id,
    customers.customer_name,
    SUM(orders.order_amount) AS total_order_amount
FROM
    orders
JOIN
    customers ON orders.customer_id = customers.customer_id
GROUP BY
    customers.customer_id, customers.customer_name;
```

If you prefer to refresh the MV after a particular data load job, you can manually do so by executing the following command:

```
REFRESH MATERIALIZED VIEW mv_total_order_amount;
```

Once the MV has been created, you can query it like any other table in Redshift. This way, the results are directly fetched from the MV itself, making the report perform well. Here's an example of how to do this:

```
SELECT * FROM mv_total_order_amount;
```

In Amazon Redshift, you can also benefit from automatic query rewriting to accelerate query workloads by letting the system automatically rewrite queries to utilize MVs. This feature enables performance optimization, even for queries that do not explicitly reference an MV. Under the covers, Redshift will analyze repeated query submissions and create a temporary MV to make that operation run faster and will automatically drop that temporary MV once the same query pattern stops.

Concurrency scaling

With concurrency scaling, your Amazon Redshift cluster gains the ability to dynamically increase its capacity in response to incoming workloads. By default, concurrency scaling is deactivated, but you can enable it for any **workload management** (**WLM**) queue. Once enabled, it empowers your cluster to effortlessly scale to handle a virtually unlimited number of concurrent queries while maintaining consistently fast query performance.

Concurrency scaling allows certain sets of queries to not get stuck in the queue. This helps keep critical queries performing well on provisioned clusters, which, in turn, helps you right-size the cluster and not overprovision it.

Enable autonomics

Autonomics refers to letting the system make many adjustments to improve performance. Wherever possible, it's always advisable to start with the AUTO option turned on. This allows the system to analyze different patterns and take appropriate actions, without the admins having to explicitly do them. The following figure shows some of the autonomic options available from Redshift:

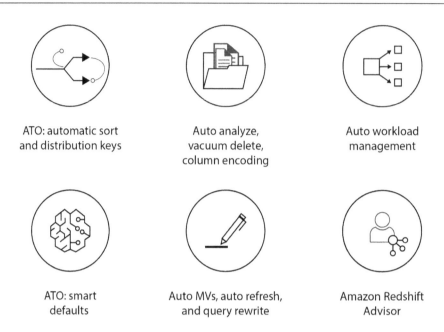

ATO: automatic sort
and distribution keys

Auto analyze,
vacuum delete,
column encoding

Auto workload
management

ATO: smart
defaults

Auto MVs, auto refresh,
and query rewrite

Amazon Redshift
Advisor

Figure 16.21 – Amazon Redshift autonomics

Data loading best practices

Redshift uses columnar storage; hence, bulk load is always preferred using the COPY command. The COPY command is executed on all slices on all the nodes directly, thus parallelizing the load process. Redshift now offers an auto-copy option, where as soon as data lands in an S3 bucket, the copy job will automatically load the data into the tables. Similarly, to push the data back into the S3 data lake, the UNLOAD command will improve performance.

Also, the **Redshift streaming ingestion (RSI)** feature is the preferred way to load streaming data into Redshift tables. RSI uses Amazon Kinesis Data Streams or Amazon MSK to simplify the process of ingesting large volumes of real-time data inside Redshift.

Query optimizations

A lot of performance improvement can be made by making sure the queries behind all the complex reports are written optimally. Redshift provides many system tables that store valuable information regarding how your query is performing.

The SVL_QUERY_METRICS_SUMMARY system view in Amazon Redshift provides the maximum metric values for completed queries, while the STL_QUERY_METRICS and STV_QUERY_METRICS views offer information at 1-second intervals for completed and running queries, respectively. You can also analyze the plan of the query and see where the query is spending most of its time/resources by using the EXPLAIN command in front of the query.

Performance tuning measures on Amazon EMR

The vast majority of workloads on EMR are Spark workloads. Data engineering teams that are used to fine-tune the Spark parameters can continue to do so even in EMR when they set up a Spark environment. With the EMR-managed scaling option, the need to customize a Spark environment should not arise that frequently. Every team wants to focus on getting the data engineering piece solved by Spark on EMR while keeping the job execution environment as simple as possible.

One of the Spark defaults is `spark.dynamicAllocation.enabled`, which is set to `true` by EMR so that you don't have to explicitly set all other Spark executor-related parameters for Spark while running the job.

To optimize resource allocation for your executors in an Amazon EMR cluster, you can enable the `maximizeResourceAllocation` setting in the Spark classification configuration. By setting `maximizeResourceAllocation` to `true`, Amazon EMR determines the maximum available compute and memory resources for an executor on each instance in the core instance group. Subsequently, it configures the corresponding spark-defaults settings based on these calculated maximum values.

The following screenshot shows `maximizeResourceAllocation` set to `true` while creating an EMR cluster. All other configurations can also be passed to the cluster via the **Software settings** tab in EMR:

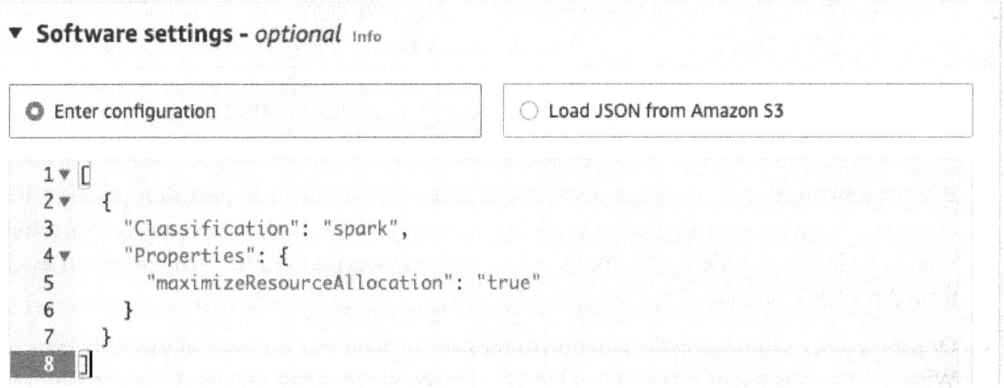

Figure 16.22 – Amazon EMR – configuration settings

There are many best practices for optimizing the Spark code itself, specifically around shuffle partitions, dynamic partition pruning, joins conditions, and so forth. We won't get into the details of those optimizations. However, if you need to understand details regarding how your Spark job is doing, EMR provides access to the Spark UI console, where you can troubleshoot how the job is performing and what steps are taking the most time. Based on that, you can tune your jobs so that they perform optimally.

Performance tuning measures on Amazon Athena

We emphasized how important it is to organize your data in S3 into partitions that allow queries to skip scanning all the content in S3 so that they can find the relevant datasets. Also, storing files in Parquet format with Snappy compression cuts down the amount of data scanned by Athena, which boosts performance and cuts costs.

Let's look at some other best practices with Athena that will make queries run faster and cost-effectively:

- **Optimal file sizes**: File sizes matter a lot when it comes to Athena's performance. In scenarios where your files are relatively small, be it a few MBs or even in KBs, the execution engine may incur additional overhead due to tasks such as opening S3 files, listing directories, retrieving object metadata, setting up a data transfer, reading file headers, and reading compression dictionaries. Conversely, if your files are non-splittable and too large, over a GB, query processing can be impacted as it waits for a single reader to finish reading the entire file. This situation can potentially limit parallelism and affect performance.

- **Limit scans**: Since Athena's cost and performance is dependent on the amount of data scanned, limit the number of columns you scan by explicitly providing the required columns instead of using the * operator. Also, use filters in the query at all times and wherever possible, add a LIMIT clause to the query to limit the number of rows returned.

- **Query operators**: Optimize the usage of memory-intensive operations such as JOIN, GROUP BY, ORDER BY, and UNION since they all require large amounts of data to be loaded into memory, which may slow down the query's execution. Find workarounds to replace some of the intensive operators; for example, use UNION ALL instead of UNION and use CTAS to store intermediate results from subqueries.

- **Partition projection**: For highly partitioned tables with predictable partition patterns, it's better to use partition projection instead. In partition projection, the calculation of partition values and locations is derived from the table configuration itself, rather than being retrieved from AWS Glue Data Catalog.

- **Optimize joins**: Optimizing the join order is crucial for achieving optimal query performance. When performing a join between two tables, it is recommended to specify the larger table on the left-hand side of the join and the smaller table on the right-hand side. This approach allows Athena to efficiently distribute the smaller table to worker nodes and stream the larger table for the join operation. By utilizing less memory when dealing with the smaller table, the query can execute faster and result in improved performance.

Performance tuning measures on other AWS services

Before we close this chapter, it's important to recognize that every AWS service has its best practices and fine-tuning options that would lead to better performance and lower costs. This chapter would never end if we went into details of all such measures. However, the theme is common across the data platform: always build the data platform by ensuring the best practices and limitations of the service being used are looked into first. This will help you avoid all the headaches that would come later when you have to troubleshoot pain points.

Also, another important thing to keep in mind is that just before any major component of the data platform is ready for production deployment, it is always helpful to do a WAR exercise. For analytics, AWS provides a Well-Architected framework called Data Analytics Lens. Understand all the pillars of WAR and ensure that all of them are adhered to before you roll out anything major in production. The link to WAR for Data Analytics Lens can be found in the *References* section.

Summary

This chapter was all about ensuring that the data platform that's built is performant as well as cost-effective. We started by understanding the need for a data platform that operates optimally. If any part of the data platform is either not performing well or is very expensive, it often creates a snowball effect and affects the business negatively.

A lot of cost optimization can be achieved by optimizing the infrastructure used by the AWS services under the covers. By optimizing storage and compute resources, we can save significant costs. We also looked at some of the tools AWS provides that help in the cost optimization process.

Finally, we looked at some of the service-specific tuning settings that can help with performance improvements. The list of such improvements can be quite long for each service, but the key message was to leverage the best practices for each service and always perform a WAR before deploying workloads in production.

In the next and last chapter of this book, we will put the whole platform together by looking at some automation techniques so that the whole platform operates without a lot of manual intervention in production.

References

Amazon Well-Architected Framework – Data Analytics Lens: `https://docs.aws.amazon.com/wellarchitected/latest/analytics-lens/analytics-lens.html`.

17

Automate, Operationalize, and Monetize

In this chapter, we will look at the following key topics:

- The need for automation
- The DevOps process
- The DataOps process
- The MLOps process
- Data monetization
- Wrap-up

The need for automation

Even though we have come to the last chapter of the book, a data platform cannot be sustainable in the long run if a large number of teams manually manage all the day-to-day operations. In a mature organization, personas who help build and operate the data platform do not get access to the AWS console in production. So, the main question arises: *how do they manage and operate a modern data platform?* The answer is simple – *each and every aspect of the data platform is managed and operated through automation scripts and pipelines.*

Before we dive into what automation entails, let's quickly highlight why automation is needed in the first place.

Automation plays a crucial role in an analytics platform on AWS for several reasons:

- **Efficiency**: Automation eliminates manual, repetitive tasks, allowing analytics processes to run more efficiently. It reduces the time and effort required to perform data ingestion, transformation, modeling, and visualization, enabling analysts to focus on higher-value tasks such as data interpretation and decision-making.

- **Scalability**: Analytics platforms often deal with vast amounts of data that can grow rapidly. Automation enables the platform to scale seamlessly by automatically handling data ingestion from multiple sources, processing large volumes of data, and scaling compute resources up or down based on demand. This ensures the platform can handle increasing workloads without manual intervention.

- **Data integrity**: Automation helps ensure data integrity by enforcing standardized processes and reducing the risk of human error. By automating data quality checks, data validation, and data cleansing procedures, the analytics platform can maintain consistent and reliable data across different stages of the analytics pipeline. It enhances the accuracy and reliability of insights derived from the data.

- **Timeliness**: Real-time or near-real-time analytics is becoming increasingly important in many industries. Automation enables the analytics platform to continuously process incoming data, trigger alerts or notifications based on predefined conditions, and generate timely insights. This empowers organizations to make data-driven decisions promptly, leading to improved operational efficiency and competitiveness.

- **Cost optimization**: Automation helps optimize costs in several ways. By automating resource provisioning and de-provisioning, the platform can dynamically allocate compute resources based on demand, thereby avoiding underutilization or overprovisioning. Automation also reduces the need for manual intervention, which saves time and reduces operational costs. Moreover, automation enables organizations to leverage serverless computing services on AWS, where they only pay for the actual usage of resources, further optimizing costs.

- **Reproducibility**: In an analytics platform, it is crucial to ensure that data pipelines, transformations, and analyses can be reproduced consistently. Automation allows for the creation of repeatable and reusable workflows and processes. By defining and automating the steps required to generate insights, organizations can ensure that analyses can be replicated consistently, making it easier to validate and audit results.

- **Flexibility and customization**: Automation provides the flexibility to customize and tailor the analytics platform to specific business needs. Workflows and processes can be easily modified, extended, or integrated with other systems through automation frameworks and tools. This enables organizations to adapt quickly to changing requirements and business objectives, empowering them to derive maximum value from their analytics platform.

Automation allows organizations to leverage the full potential of their data by streamlining processes, reducing errors, and enabling timely and reliable insights, ultimately leading to improved decision-making and business outcomes.

Let's jump straight to the process itself. To fully operationalize a data platform in production, all stages of the platform need to be automated. To further complicate the situation, automation can be related to the underlying infrastructure of the AWS services and its infrastructure, to the different data pipelines that need to run on a daily basis, or to the **machine learning** (**ML**) operations that it is required to run for predictive analytics. Automating the whole platform can be a daunting task; however, AWS provides many tools and services to simplify managing all the operations of the platform.

Let's first start by asking the most obvious question – *how do we provision, configure, build, test, deploy, and monitor the AWS service itself in a continuous and automated manner?* This is where the field of DevOps comes into the picture.

The DevOps process

DevOps, short for development and operations, is an approach to software development and deployment that aims to bridge the gap between development teams, which are responsible for creating the data platform, and operations teams, which are responsible for deploying and managing the service in production environments. DevOps emphasizes collaboration, communication, and automation to streamline the software development life cycle and improve the speed, efficiency, and quality of software delivery.

DevOps aims to stabilize the priorities of two competing forces in the business. The following figure highlights this friction between the development and operations teams.

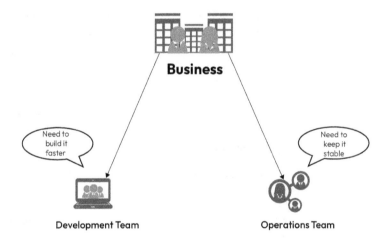

Figure 17.1 – Competing forces between the development and operations teams

Before we get to the use cases and the tools and services used for DevOps, let's first understand the key principles of DevOps:

- **Collaboration and communication**: DevOps process encourages close collaboration and effective communication between developers, operations teams, and other stakeholders. By breaking down silos and fostering a shared responsibility mindset, DevOps promotes a culture of collaboration, where teams work together to achieve common goals.

- **Continuous Integration and Continuous Delivery (CI/CD)**: CI/CD is a set of practices that emphasizes frequent and automated integration, testing, and delivery of software. It involves automating the build, test, and deployment processes to ensure that software changes can be rapidly and reliably delivered to production environments.

- **Infrastructure as Code (IaC)**: IaC is an approach to managing and provisioning infrastructure resources using machine-readable configuration files or scripts. By treating IaC, DevOps teams can automate the provisioning and configuration of infrastructure, making it more consistent, repeatable, and version-controlled.

- **Automation**: Automation plays a critical role in DevOps. By automating repetitive and manual tasks, such as code builds, testing, deployment, and infrastructure provisioning, DevOps teams can reduce the number of errors, improve efficiency, and free up time for more value-adding activities. Automation tools and frameworks enable the rapid and consistent delivery of software.

- **Monitoring and feedback**: The DevOps process emphasizes the importance of monitoring the performance and health of software systems in production environments. By collecting and analyzing data on application metrics, logs, and user feedback, DevOps teams can identify issues, gain insights into system behavior, and continuously improve the software and infrastructure.

- **Continuous learning and improvement**: The DevOps process promotes a culture of continuous learning and improvement. Teams actively seek feedback, conduct post-implementation reviews, and use metrics and data to identify areas for optimization. DevOps teams embrace a mindset of experimentation, learning from failures, and iterating on processes and systems to drive continuous improvement.

DevOps practices are often supported by a range of tools and technologies, such as version control systems, build and deployment automation tools, configuration management tools, containerization platforms, and monitoring and logging solutions.

To put DevOps into perspective, the following figure summarizes the challenges faced by organizations and how DevOps is able to solve them.

Figure 17.2 – Challenges along with solutions provided by the DevOps process

Let's kickstart DevOps on AWS with a use case from **GreatFin**.

> **Use case for DevOps**
>
> **GreatFin** has finished building and testing a data platform with AWS services and it is ready to deploy in a production environment. It aims to improve decision-making, optimize operations, and enhance customer experiences. To ensure efficient, scalable, and reliable data-driven insights, the company wants to adopt a DevOps approach for its analytics platform.
>
> Many LOB teams are used to the traditional deployment process in the monolith development life cycle. The **cloud center of excellence (CCoE)** team at GreatFin has realized that it needs to adopt a CI/CD process. The CCoE has put forward some key guiding principles on how the platform should be managed and operationalized. These include continuous and automated delivery of analytics solutions, infrastructure scalability and elasticity, data integrity and security, continuous monitoring and optimization, collaboration between development and operations teams; and a faster insight-gathering process.

Key DevOps components

DevOps is not just a singular process/tool for automation. It involves multiple practices put together and each practice involves multiple tools/services. The following figure highlights the key components of the DevOps process. Together, they all work in tandem to create a unified process that helps organizations with full automation and management of all data services, along with the code that runs inside these services.

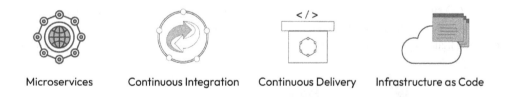

Figure 17.3 – Key DevOps components

Typically, the traditional software deployment life cycle would apply a monolithic approach to building, testing, releasing, and monitoring the software/service. The following figure highlights this approach.

Figure 17.4 – Monolithic software deployment life cycle

In a traditional application, multiple teams often share a single release pipeline, which can lead to bottlenecks and delays. However, when teams have the autonomy to operate at a rapid pace, they can continuously release new features, sometimes multiple times per day.

In the microservices world, where small changes are spread across multiple services and tools, they all need to be built, tested, released, and monitored in parallel and independent of each other. The following figure highlights the microservices DevOps process for individual units of development, spread across multiple LOBs in the organization.

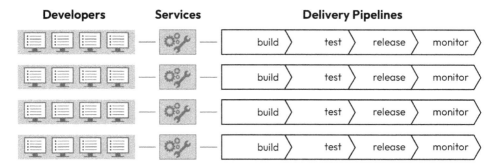

Figure 17.5 – Microservices-based software deployment life cycle

CI/CD

A critical part of the DevOps process is CI/CD, which emphasizes the automation of build, test, and deployment processes to ensure that software changes are rapidly and reliably integrated, tested, and released. CI/CD enables development teams to deliver new features, bug fixes, and improvements more efficiently, with shorter release cycles, reduced manual errors, and increased overall software quality. The following figure represents the continuous cycle of the deployment process using a CI/CD process.

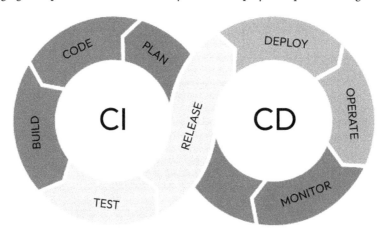

Figure 17.6 – CI/CD process

AWS provides a few services to assist in the CI/CD process and some of the key services are as follows:

- **AWS CodePipeline: CodePipeline** is a fully managed CI/CD service that orchestrates the end-to-end software release process. It enables the creation of automated pipelines for building, testing, and deploying applications. CodePipeline integrates with various AWS and third-party tools, allowing developers to design flexible and customizable release workflows.

- **AWS CodeBuild: CodeBuild** is a fully managed build service that compiles source code, runs tests, and produces software artifacts. It integrates with CodePipeline and supports a wide range of programming languages, build tools, and frameworks. CodeBuild enables the automated building and testing of applications in a scalable and controlled environment.

- **AWS CodeDeploy: CodeDeploy** is a deployment service that automates application deployment to EC2 instances, on-premises servers, Lambda functions, and other AWS services. It allows developers to define deployment configurations, rollbacks, and canary deployments. CodeDeploy ensures consistent and reliable application deployments across different environments.

- **AWS CodeCommit: CodeCommit** is a fully managed source code control service that hosts Git repositories. It provides secure and scalable version control and collaboration capabilities for teams working on code repositories. CodeCommit integrates with other AWS services, including CodePipeline and CodeBuild, to enable seamless integration within the CI/CD workflow.

IaC

Before we get into how we can use CI/CD pipelines to automate and operationalize our data platform, we also need to look at another very important part of the DevOps process, which is **IaC**. IaC refers to the process of defining and provisioning cloud resources using code-based templates or scripts. Instead of manually configuring and managing infrastructure components such as Amazon EC2 instances, networking, storage, and other resources, IaC allows you to define and manage them through code.

AWS provides a service called AWS CloudFormation, which is a popular choice for implementing IaC. With CloudFormation, you can define your infrastructure using a declarative template written in JSON or YAML format. The template describes the desired state of your infrastructure, including the resources, their configurations, and the relationships between them.

By using IaC with CloudFormation, you can version-control your infrastructure, apply source code management practices, and easily reproduce or update your infrastructure in a consistent and automated manner. It also enables you to create, modify, and delete AWS resources in a predictable and repeatable way, reducing manual errors and providing greater agility in managing your infrastructure.

In addition to CloudFormation, there are other tools and frameworks available for implementing IaC on AWS, such as AWS CDK and AWS SAM, along with third-party tools such as Terraform and Ansible. These tools provide a higher level of abstraction and flexibility in defining and managing your infrastructure, allowing you to use programming languages and reusable components to describe your AWS resources and configurations.

The following figure highlights IaC components in the AWS ecosystem that assist in the DevOps process.

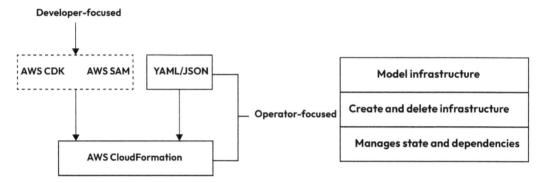

Figure 17.7 – AWS IaC process

Many partners have niche solutions that complement AWS DevOps services. Many organizations promote the idea of managing infrastructure and deployments through version-controlled Git repositories. A Git repo acts as the single source of truth for both application code as well as infrastructure configuration. This process of DevOps where the source code is versioned-controlled in Git repos is also called **GitOps**.

The following figure highlights AWS services as well as partner solutions for managing all the components of the GitOps process.

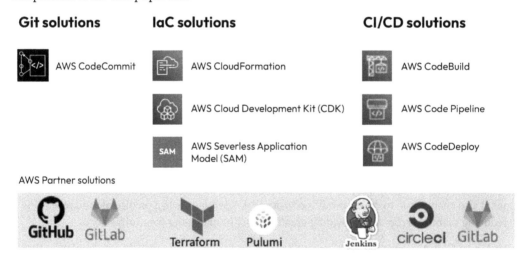

Figure 17.8 – The AWS GitOps stack

Let's quickly take an example of how the DevOps process will actually work for automating our data platform. Suppose you have spun up a persistent EMR cluster for Spark jobs that run throughout the day. The initial cluster provisioning was done through the CloudFormation stack. The data engineering team now has a need to change one of the configuration defaults in Spark inside EMR. It's easy to do it from the AWS console; however, as a best practice in production, everything is updated and managed through the DevOps process.

The following figure explains the process of managing changes to an existing EMR cluster in the data platform, using all the steps of the DevOps process.

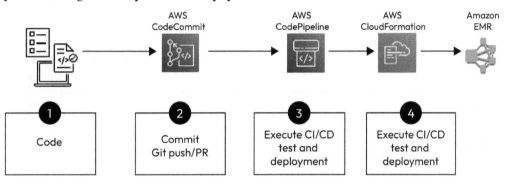

Figure 17.9 – Managing deployment changes through DevOps

The CloudFormation code to change the Spark configuration on EMR is first pulled from the Git repo on AWS CodeCommit:

1. The YAML-based code for the EMR configuration change is within the `Classification` section of the configuration as shown in the following sample code:

```
Configurations:
      - Classification: spark-defaults
      Properties:
            spark.executor.memory: "4g"
#Set executor memory
```

2. The changed code is pushed back to the Git repo.

3. Each commit to the repository undergoes a merge request process and flows through CI/CD automation via AWS CodePipeline.

4. Infrastructure changes to the EMR cluster are made through the AWS CloudFormation stack. If there are any errors during this process, an automated rollback takes the stack back to the previous state.

This was just an easy example, but almost all infrastructure changes, including complex code submissions, are accomplished by the DevOps process. The underlying tools/services can differ, but the common theme of achieving automated operations is the same across all such implementations.

Data engineers like to use AWS Glue to create ETL jobs in Spark. Glue also has direct support for pushing the code to a Git repository, which makes it easy to version-control and also makes the CI/CD process with Glue a lot easier to achieve. The following is a screenshot from Glue where the version control process has direct integration with AWS CodeCommit and GitHub.

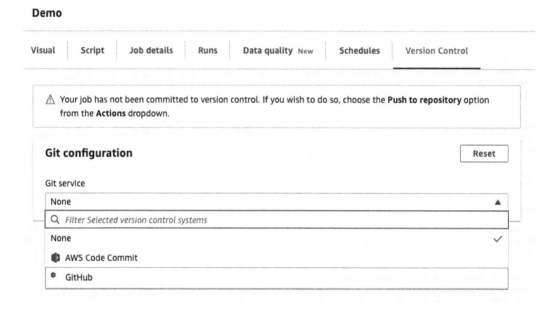

Figure 17.10 – Git integration with Glue ETL

There are many other tools and services that aid and assist in the DevOps process, including some that use ML to make the process easier. We would not be able to cover all services in this chapter; in fact, the topic of DevOps could be a separate book by itself. The following figure highlights many such tools that assist in different stages of the DevOps process.

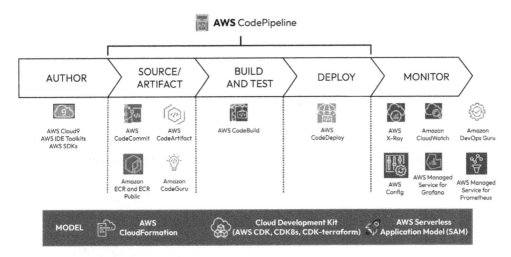

Figure 17.11 – End-to-end DevOps process with many AWS services

So far, we have looked at managing the AWS services and the underlying infrastructure through the DevOps process. But what about managing all the day-to-day data jobs that run on the platform along, with their operations and automation?

Let's venture into the closely related topic of DataOps.

The DataOps process

DataOps in AWS refers to the application of DevOps principles and practices to data-related workflows and processes. It focuses on optimizing the development, deployment, and management of data pipelines, data integration, and data analytics solutions.

DataOps aims to improve the speed, quality, and reliability of data operations by fostering collaboration, automation, and repeatability across the data life cycle. It combines data engineering, data integration, data governance, and data analytics with the principles of CI/CD, version control, and IaC.

On AWS, several services and tools can be leveraged to implement DataOps practices:

- **AWS Glue**: The AWS Glue ETL service simplifies data preparation and integration. It allows you to create and manage data pipelines using workflows, perform data transformations, and automate ETL jobs.

- **AWS Lake Formation**: AWS Lake Formation is a service that simplifies the process of building, securing, and managing data lakes on AWS. It provides capabilities for data ingestion, metadata management, and access control, allowing organizations to establish a secure and governed data lake environment.

- **AWS Lambda**: AWS Lambda is a serverless compute service that allows you to run code without provisioning or managing servers. It can be used for event-driven data processing and serverless ETL operations, where Lambda functions are triggered by events such as file uploads or changes in data sources.

- **AWS Step Functions**: AWS Step Functions is a serverless workflow service that enables you to coordinate and orchestrate multiple AWS services into business-critical workflows. It can be used to build and manage complex data pipelines with different stages and dependencies.

- **Amazon Managed Workflows for Apache Airflow (MWAA)**: MWAA is a managed service provided by AWS that can be leveraged for DataOps workflows. MWAA allows you to run Apache Airflow, an open source platform for orchestrating and managing workflows, in a fully managed environment on AWS.

- **AWS EventBridge**: This is a fully managed event bus service that enables you to build event-driven architectures by simplifying the process of ingesting, routing, and processing events from various sources and sending them to different targets. EventBridge can help facilitate the automation and orchestration of data-related events, making it a valuable tool in a DataOps workflow.

By adopting DataOps practices in AWS, organizations can achieve faster and more reliable data pipelines, improved data quality, easier collaboration between teams, and better overall management and governance of data workflows and analytics processes.

The following figure highlights the DataOps structure for analytics.

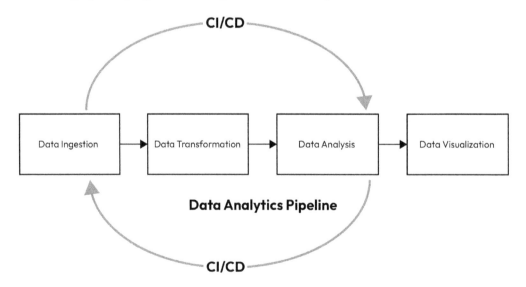

Figure 17.12 – The DataOps process for analytics

DataOps can be a very broad topic too with lots of tools and services to orchestrate and automate the data pipelines in the data platform. However, let's look at two key AWS services that help orchestrate the DataOps process.

Amazon MWAA

MWAA is the AWS-managed version of Apache Airflow.

Here's how MWAA can support DataOps on AWS:

- **Workflow orchestration**: MWAA enables you to define and manage complex data workflows using Apache Airflow. You can create **Directed Acyclic Graphs** (**DAGs**) to define tasks and dependencies, schedule workflows, and monitor their execution.

- **Data pipelines**: MWAA can be used to orchestrate and automate data pipelines, including data ETL processes. You can schedule and coordinate tasks, such as data ingestion, data transformation, and data export, within the MWAA environment.

- **Scalability and resilience**: MWAA automatically handles the infrastructure provisioning, scaling, and maintenance of the Apache Airflow environment. It ensures that your workflows can scale to handle large datasets and process workloads efficiently. MWAA also provides built-in monitoring and logging capabilities for troubleshooting and performance optimization.

- **Integration with AWS services**: MWAA seamlessly integrates with various AWS services, allowing you to incorporate them into your DataOps workflows. You can leverage AWS Glue for data cataloging and metadata management, Amazon S3 for data storage, AWS Lambda for serverless data processing, and other services to build end-to-end data solutions.

- **Security and governance**: MWAA provides security features, including encryption at rest and in transit, AWS **Identity and Access Management** (**IAM**) integration, and fine-grained access control for your workflows and data pipelines. This helps ensure compliance and data governance requirements are met.

- **IaC**: MWAA can be provisioned and managed using AWS CloudFormation or other IaC tools. This allows you to define your MWAA environment as code, enabling automation, version control, and repeatability in your DataOps processes.

By using MWAA for DataOps, you can benefit from a fully managed Apache Airflow environment that simplifies the orchestration and management of data workflows. MWAA handles the infrastructure aspects, allowing you to focus on designing and executing your data pipelines effectively.

Let's bring up a use case that will help you understand how MWAA helps with the DataOps process.

> **Use case for DataOps using Amazon MWAA**
>
> Many LOBs at GreatFin use Amazon Redshift as their data warehouse. Every day, data is ingested, processed, and consumed from Redshift. The data comes from various source systems and some even through third-party **Application Programming Interfaces (APIs)**. Once the data is loaded into the staging tables of Redshift, various data processing scripts need to run inside Redshift to transform the data, before being loaded into the core base tables for reporting purposes. There are a lot of dependencies among these jobs, where some tables need to be loaded in parallel, and for some tables, the order of data load needs to be maintained. Also, many error-handling scenarios occur, which need to be monitored and appropriate actions need to be taken. Alert and notification mechanisms also need to be incorporated into the flow.
>
> Overall, all LOBs are looking for a robust DataOps tool that can orchestrate, schedule, and execute all the jobs in Redshift in a workflow with dependency management, error handling, monitoring, and notifications.

This is the kind of use case that fits really well with Apache Airflow, and, with Amazon MWAA, managing the whole DataOps process becomes even more easier. Let's look at each stage of the use case and how MWAA can help provide a comprehensive solution:

- **Data ingestion**: Apache Airflow can be configured to schedule and automate data ingestion from various sources, such as S3 buckets, relational databases, or third-party APIs. It can use Airflow's operators or custom operators to fetch data from these sources and load it into staging tables in Amazon Redshift.

- **Data transformation**: After the data is ingested into Amazon Redshift, Apache Airflow can orchestrate data transformation tasks. It can execute SQL scripts or run Python scripts that perform data cleansing, aggregation, or enrichment operations within Amazon Redshift. These tasks can be scheduled at specific intervals or triggered by specific events.

- **Workflow orchestration**: Apache Airflow allows you to define complex workflows using DAGs. Each task in the DAG represents a step in the data integration and analytics process. For example, the workflow can include tasks such as data extraction, data loading, data transformation, and data quality checks. Dependencies between tasks can be defined to ensure sequential execution or parallel processing as needed.

- **Dependency management**: With Airflow, you can define dependencies between tasks, ensuring that tasks are executed in the correct order. For example, data transformation tasks can depend on the completion of data ingestion tasks. This ensures that data is available and up to date for subsequent processing steps.

- **Scheduling and monitoring**: Apache Airflow provides a visual interface for scheduling tasks and monitoring their execution. You can define task schedules using cron expressions or interval-based triggers. Airflow's user interface allows you to monitor the progress of tasks, view logs, and identify any failures or issues in the workflows. This facilitates better visibility and debugging of the DataOps processes.

- **Alerting and notifications**: Airflow can be configured to send alerts or notifications if workflow failures or exceptions happen. This allows the operations team to be promptly notified and take necessary actions to address any issues.

- **Integration with Redshift**: Apache Airflow integrates seamlessly with Amazon Redshift through the use of SQL scripts or custom Python operators. It can execute SQL queries against Redshift, interact with Redshift's **Data Definition Language (DDL)** and **Data Manipulation Language (DML)** statements, and perform data loading and unloading operations.

The following figure represents an architecture flow for using MWAA for DataOps on Amazon Redshift.

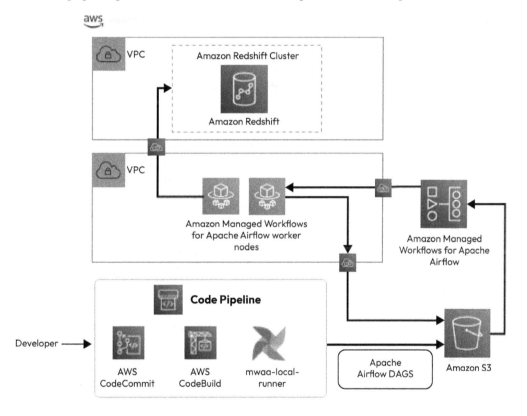

Figure 17.13 – MWAA for DataOps with Amazon Redshift

Let's look at another orchestration service, **AWS Step Functions**.

AWS Step Functions

AWS Step Functions is a fully managed service that enables you to coordinate and orchestrate workflows involving multiple AWS services and custom applications. It allows you to build serverless workflows using a visual interface or JSON-based language, known as **Amazon States Language**. Let's bring up a use case to understand how it can help with the DataOps process.

> **Use case for DataOps using AWS Step Functions**
>
> **GreatFin** uses **Amazon EMR** for many of its big data processing tasks. It has migrated many Spark jobs from the on-premises Hadoop platform into **EMR**. However, many teams are facing challenges in orchestrating all the jobs. The key emphasis is on the orchestration tool being fully managed, serverless, and easy to manage.
>
> It wants to ensure that its Spark jobs can be orchestrated via easy-to-create and manage workflows, where it can create dependencies among all the jobs. Error handling and retry logic should be robust as many jobs often fail due to data issues. Many jobs need to be conditionally triggered based on the status of the previous jobs. The workflow process should also support parallel execution of jobs. Monitoring, notifications, and seamless integration with other AWS services are highly desired.

AWS Step Functions is a fully managed serverless service that provides robust integration with all AWS services. Using Step Functions Workflow Studio, you can quickly drag and drop workflow steps to build the complete orchestration process required as part of the DataOps process.

Here's how AWS Step Functions can help with DataOps on EMR:

- **Workflow orchestration**: Step Functions allows you to define and manage complex workflows for data processing on EMR. You can design state machines that define the sequence of steps involved in your DataOps processes, such as data ingestion, transformation, analysis, and reporting. Step Functions enables you to define the dependencies between these steps and control the flow of data processing.

- **Task coordination**: With Step Functions, you can coordinate and manage the execution of tasks on EMR clusters. Each task can represent a specific data operation, such as data ingestion from external sources, running Spark or Hadoop jobs for data transformation, executing ML algorithms, or generating reports. Step Functions ensures that these tasks are executed in the desired order and that their inputs and outputs are properly connected.

- **Dynamic scaling**: EMR clusters can be dynamically scaled based on the workload requirements. AWS Step Functions allows you to incorporate dynamic scaling capabilities into your DataOps workflows. You can define steps that monitor the workload or data volume and automatically scale the EMR cluster up or down based on predefined thresholds or rules. This ensures optimal resource utilization and improves the efficiency of data processing.

- **Error handling and retry logic**: DataOps processes may encounter errors or transient issues during data processing on EMR. AWS Step Functions provides built-in error handling capabilities, allowing you to define error handling paths and retry strategies. For example, if a task fails on EMR due to an error or timeout, Step Functions can trigger a retry or take corrective actions based on predefined rules.

- **Conditional branching and decision making**: Step Functions allows you to incorporate conditional branching and decision-making logic into your DataOps workflows on EMR. You can define decision points based on specific conditions or business rules. This enables you to branch the workflow based on the output of a task or the evaluation of certain conditions. Conditional branching helps in dynamically adapting the workflow based on varying data conditions or business requirements.

- **Monitoring and logging**: AWS Step Functions provides monitoring and logging capabilities, allowing you to track the execution of your DataOps workflows on EMR. You can monitor the progress of individual tasks, capture logs, and gain insights into the overall workflow performance. Step Functions integrates with CloudWatch Logs and CloudWatch Events, enabling you to monitor the workflow execution, troubleshoot issues, and optimize your DataOps processes on EMR.

- **Integration with other AWS services**: Step Functions seamlessly integrates with various AWS services, enabling you to incorporate them into your DataOps workflows on EMR. For example, you can integrate with Amazon S3 for data storage, AWS Glue for data cataloging and metadata management, AWS Lambda for serverless data processing, and more. This integration allows you to build end-to-end data solutions on EMR and leverage the full capabilities of the AWS ecosystem.

Let's look at how Step Functions makes it easy to orchestrate AWS services; for our use case, we want to create an automated workflow for Spark jobs on EMR. Using Step Functions Workflow Studio, you can quickly create the whole sequence of your workflow by dragging/dropping icons related to EMR actions, which are nothing but APIs in EMR pertaining to specific actions. The designer tool creates JSON-based code for the whole flow. The following snapshot shows Step Functions Workflow Studio, where we are adding EMR actions.

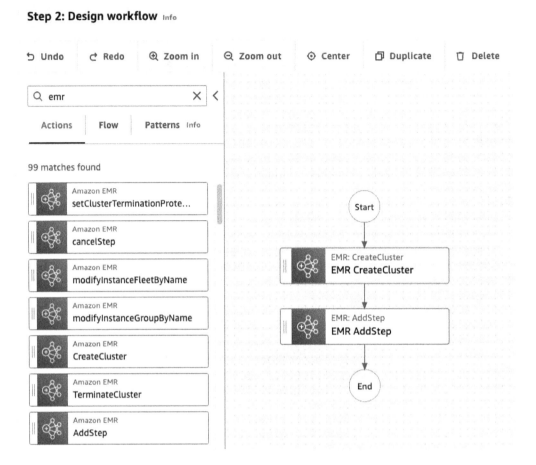

Figure 17.14 – Step Functions Workflow Studio

Once the complete workflow is ready, you can schedule the Step Functions state machine to run periodically or based on certain events. The following figure shows a sample EMR state machine, which creates a cluster, completes all the Spark jobs, and then terminates it.

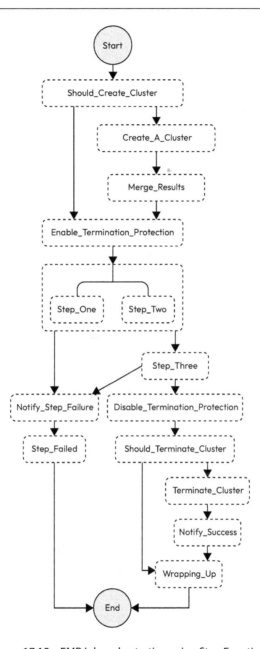

Figure 17.15 – EMR job orchestration using Step Functions

By leveraging AWS Step Functions for DataOps on EMR, you can achieve orchestration, coordination, and monitoring of your data processing workflows. AWS Step Functions enables efficient task execution, error handling, dynamic scaling, and integration with other AWS services, empowering you to build robust and scalable DataOps solutions on the entire data platform.

Using AWS Step Functions and Amazon MWAA, you can design and orchestrate all the DataOps use cases for the modern data platform. We won't be able to cover all such use cases in this section, but now you get a good idea of how to operationalize your data flow in a flexible, repeatable, and automated manner.

The MLOps process

Machine Learning Operations (**MLOps**) in AWS refers to the practices and tools employed to manage and operationalize ML workflows and models on the AWS platform. MLOps aims to streamline and automate the deployment, monitoring, and management of ML models, ensuring their reliability, scalability, and reproducibility.

MLOps has a direct impact in the following ways:

- It boosts data scientists' productivity by simplifying the ML process
- It helps maintain high model accuracy
- It helps enhance the security and compliance of the ML platform

ML is an iterative process and without MLOps, creating an end-to-end ML process would be a challenge. Every stage in the ML life cycle has its own set of activities, and specific tools in Amazon SageMaker assist at every stage.

The following figure highlights all the different stages the whole ML process goes through.

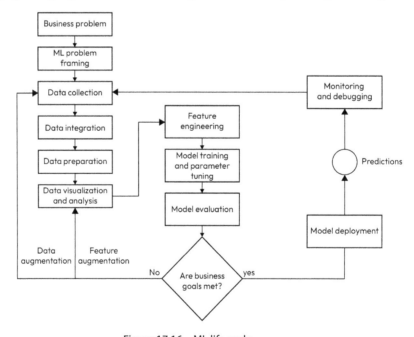

Figure 17.16 – ML life cycle

Using DevOps tools, you can build your own MLOps system; however, to make it easier, SageMaker provides a few tools, as shown in the following figure:

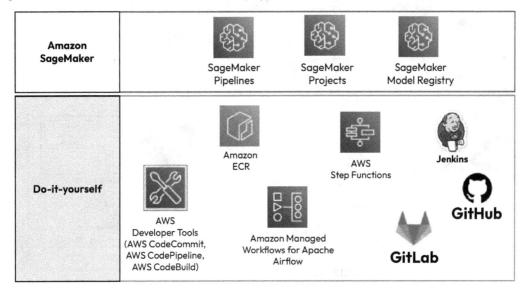

Figure 17.17 – Amazon SageMaker MLOps tools

Let's go through some of the features of Amazon SageMaker:

- **Amazon SageMaker Pipelines**: This is a feature of Amazon SageMaker that helps you build, automate, and manage end-to-end ML workflows. It provides a purpose-built, CI/CD service for ML pipelines. SageMaker Pipelines allows you to define and execute workflows that encompass data preprocessing, model training, hyperparameter tuning, model deployment, and monitoring.

- **Amazon SageMaker Projects**: This is a feature of Amazon SageMaker that provides a collaborative environment for managing end-to-end ML workflows. It helps teams organize, track, and share resources related to ML projects, including code, data, experiments, and models.

- **Amazon SageMaker Model Registry**: This is a feature of Amazon SageMaker that provides a central repository for managing and versioning ML models. It enables teams to organize, track, and govern the life cycle of their ML models, making it easier to deploy and manage models in production environments.

The SageMaker-provided MLOps tools, instead of creating your own operations pipelines, help speed up the ML process as these tools work seamlessly with other SageMaker components. The following figure summarizes the role of the MLOps tools provided by SageMaker in automating and simplifying the entire ML pipeline.

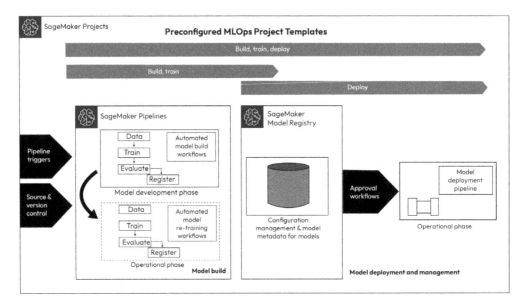

Figure 17.18 – Amazon SageMaker MLOps tools

Since we did not cover the MLOps portion in the *predictive analytics* chapter, we did not paint a full picture of all SageMaker's features and capabilities in establishing an end-to-end ML platform. Now that we have the MLOps tools established, the following figure highlights how the end-to-end ML platform looks when using SageMaker.

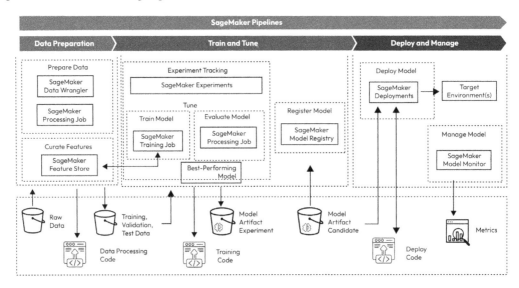

Figure 17.19 – Amazon SageMaker-driven end-to-end ML process

Now that the whole data platform on AWS is built and operationalized, how should organizations monetize the data, to justify the investment made into the platform? Let's quickly look at it.

Data monetization

All the time and effort spent by organizations to build a modern data platform on AWS is for a reason; to get the best **return on investment (ROI)**. Typically, ROI can be measured in monetary terms and, most of the time, we think of external monetization, where we get profit from the data sold outside the organization. However, data monetization has many other forms including direct, indirect, and internal monetization.

All organizations want to treat *data as a product*, which refers to the concept of treating data as a valuable asset that can be packaged, managed, and monetized. AWS provides various services and tools that enable organizations to leverage their data and create data-driven products for internal as well as external use.

There are several ways to monetize data using the data platform built on AWS. Here are some common data monetization types:

- **Selling data products on AWS Marketplace**: AWS Marketplace allows you to package and sell data products to other organizations or customers. You can create datasets, data models, APIs, or pre-built ML models and list them on the marketplace for others to purchase and use.

- **Data analytics and insights services**: AWS provides various analytics services such as Amazon QuickSight, Amazon Redshift, and AWS Data Pipeline that can help you derive insights from your data. You can offer analytics and insights as a service to clients by performing data analysis, generating reports, and providing valuable insights based on their data.

- **Data APIs**: You can expose APIs that allow others to access and use your data programmatically. This can be done using AWS API Gateway and AWS Lambda, where you can create APIs that provide specific data sets or functionalities to clients who subscribe to your API services.

- **Data streaming and real-time data services**: AWS provides services such as Amazon Kinesis, AWS IoT, and Amazon EventBridge to handle real-time data ingestion, processing, and analysis. By offering real-time data streaming services, you can monetize data by enabling clients to process and analyze streaming data in real time.

- **Data as a Service (DaaS)**: With AWS, you can build data platforms and provide DaaS to customers. This involves offering access to specific datasets, data catalogs, or data lakes that clients can use for their own analysis, research, or development purposes.

- **Data partnerships and collaborations**: AWS offers opportunities for collaboration and partnerships with other organizations. By sharing and combining data assets with partners, you can create new insights or value-added data products that can be monetized jointly.

It's important to note that when monetizing data, organizations need to consider data privacy, security, and compliance requirements. It is crucial to ensure that appropriate data usage agreements and legal frameworks are in place to protect the interests of all parties involved and adhere to relevant regulations and policies.

The following figure highlights some strategies for data monetization.

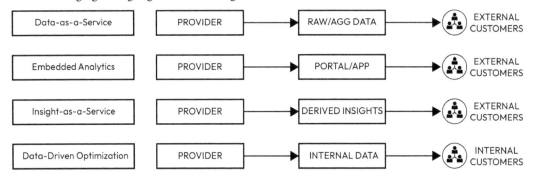

Figure 17.20 – Data monetization strategies

Let's go through some solution architectures for data monetization strategies.

DaaS

With AWS, you can build data platforms and provide DaaS to customers. This involves offering access to specific datasets, data catalogs, or data lakes that clients can use for their own analysis, research, or development purposes.

The following figure highlights an architecture pattern for a DaaS monetization technique, using the data platform built on AWS.

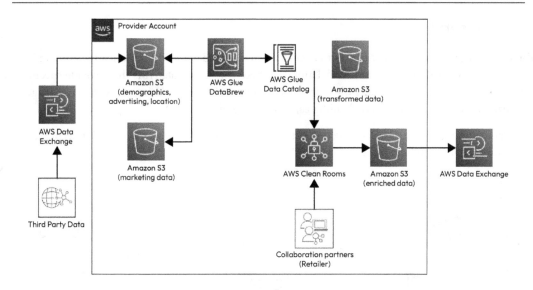

Figure 17.21 – DaaS

Insights-as-a-service

AWS provides various analytics services such as **Amazon QuickSight**, **Amazon Redshift**, and **AWS Data Exchange** that help you derive insights from your data. You can offer analytics and insights as a service to clients by performing data analysis, generating reports, and providing valuable insights based on their data.

The following figure provides an architecture pattern for an insights-as-a-service monetization technique, using the data platform built on AWS.

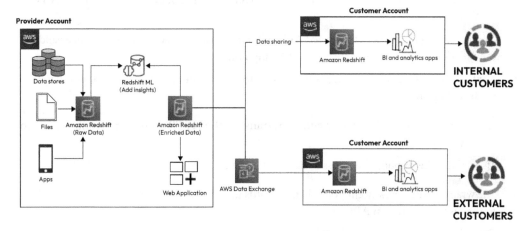

Figure 17.22 – Insights-as-a-service

API-as-a-service

You can expose APIs that allow others to access and use your data programmatically. This can be done using AWS API Gateway and AWS Lambda, where you can create APIs that provide specific datasets or functionalities to clients who subscribe to your API services. Using AWS Data Exchange, organizations can make usage-based billing easy to set up and manage.

The following figure provides an architecture pattern for an API-as-a-service monetization technique, using the data platform built on AWS.

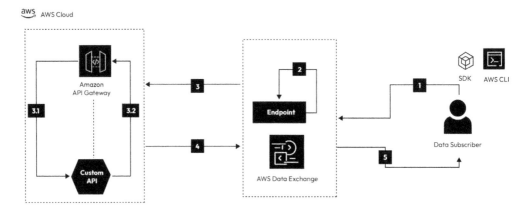

Figure 17.23 – API-as-a-service

The following are the high-level steps on how API-as-a-service can work:

1. The process begins with the data subscriber subscribing to the product and initiating an HTTP request to an endpoint hosted by AWS Data Exchange. This can be done using the AWS CLI or AWS SDK.

2. Upon receiving the request, the hosted API endpoint provided by AWS Data Exchange validates the caller's authorization to access the API endpoint.

3. Next, AWS Data Exchange forwards the request to the wrapper API Gateway endpoint created by the data providers:

    I.   The wrapper API Gateway endpoint transfers the HTTP request from subscribers to your custom API.

    II. Once the response becomes available, it is then sent back to the wrapper API endpoint.

4. The wrapper API Gateway endpoint then forwards the received HTTP request from subscribers to the respective custom API.

5. Once the response is generated by the custom API, it is sent back to the wrapper API endpoint.

We have focused on direct monetization techniques. However, indirect data monetization techniques also exist, which involve leveraging data to create value-adding products or services that can be sold or used to generate revenue without directly selling the raw data itself. These techniques focus on extracting insights, building applications, or enhancing processes using data. Here are some examples:

- **Data-driven insights**: Analyze your data to uncover valuable insights and trends that can inform business decisions. Offer reports, dashboards, or consultancy services to clients who need actionable insights derived from their data.

- **Personalization services**: Use customer data to create personalized experiences, recommendations, or content. Offer this personalization capability to businesses aiming to enhance customer engagement and satisfaction.

- **Behavioral analysis**: Analyze user behavior and interactions to help businesses understand customer preferences. Offer behavioral insights that can drive targeted marketing campaigns or product improvements.

- **Recommendation systems**: Build recommendation engines that suggest products, services, or content to users based on their preferences and behavior. Offer this capability to e-commerce platforms or content providers.

- **Supply chain optimization**: Analyze supply chain data to identify inefficiency and optimize logistics processes. Offer supply chain optimization services to manufacturers and distributors.

- **Energy efficiency solutions**: Use data from sensors and devices to optimize energy usage in buildings. Offer energy management solutions that help organizations reduce costs and improve sustainability.

- **Healthcare analytics**: Analyze medical and patient data to identify treatment patterns, disease trends, and patient outcomes. Offer healthcare analytics solutions to hospitals, clinics, and pharmaceutical companies.

- **Real-time monitoring**: Develop real-time monitoring solutions that track assets, equipment, or systems and provide alerts for anomalies or maintenance needs. Offer these solutions to industries such as manufacturing, transportation, and utilities.

- **Risk assessment**: Use data analysis to assess risks in various domains such as finance, insurance, or cybersecurity. Offer risk assessment services to clients seeking to mitigate potential threats.

- **Location-based services**: Utilize location data to develop location-based applications, such as navigation, geofencing, and targeted advertising. Offer these services to businesses aiming to engage with customers based on their location.

- **Employee productivity solutions**: Analyze employee data to optimize workforce productivity and engagement. Offer employee productivity solutions to companies looking to enhance their HR practices.

In these indirect monetization techniques, the data itself isn't sold but is used to create value-adding services or insights that customers are willing to pay for. It's important to ensure that you have the necessary data rights, privacy protections, and compliance measures in place when using customer data for such purposes.

Let's wrap up this chapter and the book with the final reference architecture diagram for building a modern data architecture on AWS.

Wrap-up

Finally, we will wrap up this book with a final reference architecture for a data platform on AWS. Not all the services are represented here, but the most common ones used are shown in their own section. The **Data Consumption** section represents a variety of purpose-built stores, ML platforms, as well as query and visualization services. You can add many more services depending on the use case being solved and can also leverage third-party partner solutions.

The following figure represents the data and analytics reference architecture built on AWS.

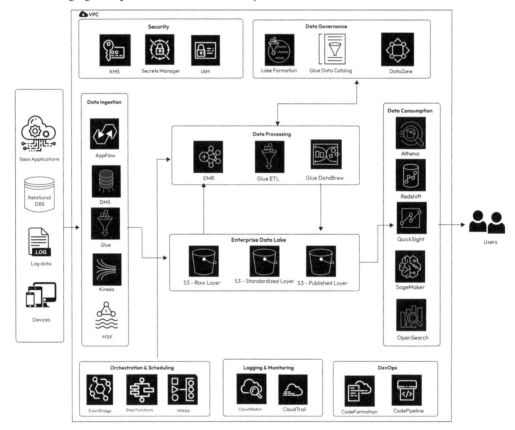

Figure 17.24 – Reference architecture of the data platform on AWS

Finally, I want to leave you with the following thoughts. The future evolution of data and analytics platforms is expected to be driven by several key trends. These include the following:

- **Increased adoption of cloud**: Cloud-based data and analytics platforms will continue to gain prominence, offering scalability, agility, and cost-effectiveness. Organizations will increasingly leverage cloud services, such as AWS, to build robust data infrastructure and perform advanced analytics.

- **Emphasis on data governance and privacy**: As data regulations become more stringent, data governance and privacy will take center stage. Organizations will focus on ensuring compliance, implementing robust data governance frameworks, and adopting technologies that enable secure data management and responsible data usage.

- **Augmented analytics and AI/ML**: Augmented analytics, powered by **artificial intelligence** (**AI**) and ML, will become more prevalent. These technologies will automate data preparation, uncover hidden patterns, and generate actionable insights, empowering organizations to make data-driven decisions more efficiently.

- **Democratization of analytics**: The democratization of analytics will continue, with organizations providing self-service analytics tools and capabilities to a wider audience. Business users, with minimal technical expertise, will be empowered to access and analyze data independently, fostering a data-driven culture throughout organizations.

- **Integration of real-time analytics**: Real-time analytics will play a crucial role as organizations strive to gain actionable insights from streaming data. Platforms will need to support real-time data ingestion, processing, and analysis to enable instant decision-making and proactive responses to changing conditions.

- **Collaboration and data sharing**: Collaborative analytics and data sharing will become more prevalent as organizations seek to leverage external data sources and work together to gain comprehensive insights. Data marketplaces and secure data exchange platforms will facilitate this collaboration while maintaining data privacy and security.

- **Focus on explainable AI and ethical data usage**: With the increasing use of AI and ML, there will be a growing emphasis on explainability and ethical data usage. Organizations will seek to understand and interpret AI models' decisions, ensuring transparency and avoiding biased or discriminatory outcomes.

Last but not least, we are just in the infancy stages of leveraging generative AI to completely transform business outcomes. Many more use cases will be solved with GenAI in the near future and all data and analytics tools and services will incorporate GenAI-driven features. Organizations will evolve their data strategies along the way and this will force all the personas in the organization to start thinking differently. Do not be afraid to try out new ways of solving problems, and don't be scared to challenge the conventional way of architecting.

I hope you had a good experience progressing through the different chapters of this book. In the world of technology, a problem can be solved in many ways, so feel free to try out different solutions in your AWS account. Doing things hands-on is the best way to learn and retain knowledge. And of course, keep learning; the more you learn, the more you will realize how much you don't know.

Summary

In this chapter, we concluded the book by providing you with options for automating your data platform. We looked at DevOps, DataOps, and MLOps as the three ways to completely automate and operationalize your data platform.

In the DevOps process, we looked at how CI/CD and Iac help organizations with an automated, repeatable, and organized way to operationalize their AWS infrastructure, services, and the features inside those services. DataOps focuses on simplifying the data pipelines by leveraging orchestration services such as Amazon MWAA and AWS Step functions. MLOps on the other hand helps to manage the entire life cycle of the ML process and Amazon SageMaker provides capabilities to make MLOps a seamless process.

Finally, we looked at how organizations can monetize their data by either using DaaS, insights-as-a-service, or API-as-a-service. All organizations have the common goal of deriving value from their data platform, either directly by monetizing the data or indirectly by making key business decisions based on the insights gained from the data.

As always, I'm providing a few links to automation workshops in the *References* section, as doing hands-on will make these concepts clear and open doors for all kinds of creative solutions to common use cases.

References

- *CI/CD on AWS workshop*: `https://catalog.workshops.aws/cicdonaws/en-US`
- *AWS CloudFormation workshop*: `https://catalog.workshops.aws/cfn101/en-US`
- *AWS CDK workshop*: `https://catalog.us-east-1.prod.workshops.aws/workshops/10141411-0192-4021-afa8-2436f3c66bd8/en-US`
- *AWS Step Functions workshop*: `https://catalog.workshops.aws/stepfunctions/en-US`
- *Amazon Managed Workflows for Apache Airflow workshop*: `https://catalog.workshops.aws/amazon-mwaa-for-analytics/en-US`
- *Modern data architecture workshop*: `https://catalog.workshops.aws/modern-data-architecture/en-US`

Index

A

`Packtpub.com`

Subscribe to our online digital library for full access to over 7,000 books and videos, as well as industry leading tools to help you plan your personal development and advance your career. For more information, please visit our website.

Why subscribe?

- Spend less time learning and more time coding with practical eBooks and Videos from over 4,000 industry professionals

- Improve your learning with Skill Plans built especially for you

- Get a free eBook or video every month

- Fully searchable for easy access to vital information

- Copy and paste, print, and bookmark content

Did you know that Packt offers eBook versions of every book published, with PDF and ePub files available? You can upgrade to the eBook version at `packtpub.com` and as a print book customer, you are entitled to a discount on the eBook copy. Get in touch with us at `customercare@packtpub.com` for more details.

At `www.packtpub.com`, you can also read a collection of free technical articles, sign up for a range of free newsletters, and receive exclusive discounts and offers on Packt books and eBooks.

Other Books You May Enjoy

If you enjoyed this book, you may be interested in these other books by Packt:

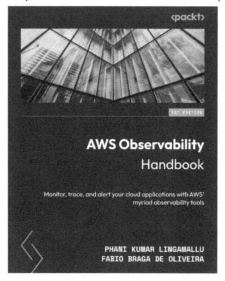

AWS Observability Handbook

Phani Kumar Lingamallu, Fabio Braga de Oliveira

ISBN: 978-1-80461-671-0

- Capture metrics from an EC2 instance and visualize them on a dashboard
- Conduct distributed tracing using AWS X-Ray
- Derive operational metrics and set up alerting using CloudWatch
- Achieve observability of containerized applications in ECS and EKS
- Explore the practical implementation of observability for AWS Lambda
- Observe your applications using Amazon managed Prometheus, Grafana, and OpenSearch services
- Gain insights into operational data using ML services on AWS
- Understand the role of observability in the cloud adoption framework

AWS FinOps Simplified

Peter Chung

ISBN: 978-1-80324-723-6

- Use AWS services to monitor and govern your cost, usage, and spend

- Implement automation to streamline cost optimization operations

- Design the best architecture that fits your workload and optimizes on data transfer

- Optimize costs by maximizing efficiency with elasticity strategies

- Implement cost optimization levers to save on compute and storage costs

- Bring value to your organization by identifying strategies to create and govern cost metrics

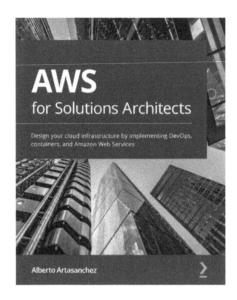

AWS for Solutions Architects

Alberto Artasanchez

ISBN: 978-1-78953-923-3

- Rationalize the selection of AWS as the right cloud provider for your organization
- Choose the most appropriate service from AWS for a particular use case or project
- Implement change and operations management
- Find out the right resource type and size to balance performance and efficiency
- Discover how to mitigate risk and enforce security, authentication, and authorization
- Identify common business scenarios and select the right reference architectures for them

Packt is searching for authors like you

If you're interested in becoming an author for Packt, please visit `authors.packtpub.com` and apply today. We have worked with thousands of developers and tech professionals, just like you, to help them share their insight with the global tech community. You can make a general application, apply for a specific hot topic that we are recruiting an author for, or submit your own idea.

Share Your Thoughts

Now you've finished *Modern Data Architecture on AWS*, we'd love to hear your thoughts! Scan the QR code below to go straight to the Amazon review page for this book and share your feedback or leave a review on the site that you purchased it from.

`https://packt.link/r/1-801-81339-6`

Your review is important to us and the tech community and will help us make sure we're delivering excellent quality content.

Download a free PDF copy of this book

Thanks for purchasing this book!

Do you like to read on the go but are unable to carry your print books everywhere?

Is your eBook purchase not compatible with the device of your choice?

Don't worry, now with every Packt book you get a DRM-free PDF version of that book at no cost.

Read anywhere, any place, on any device. Search, copy, and paste code from your favorite technical books directly into your application.

The perks don't stop there, you can get exclusive access to discounts, newsletters, and great free content in your inbox daily

Follow these simple steps to get the benefits:

1. Scan the QR code or visit the link below

https://packt.link/free-ebook/9781801813396

2. Submit your proof of purchase
3. That's it! We'll send your free PDF and other benefits to your email directly